Revolutionizing Data Science and Analytics for Industry Transformation

Paul Devasahayam Manuel
Kuwait University, Kuwait

Kalim Uddin Qureshi
Kuwait University, Kuwait

Thamilarasi Venkatachalam
Sri Sarada College for Women, India

IGI Global
Scientific Publishing
Publishing Tomorrow's Research Today

Vice President of Editorial	Melissa Wagner
Managing Editor of Acquisitions	Mikaela Felty
Managing Editor of Book Development	Jocelynn Hessler
Production Manager	Mike Brehm
Cover Design	Phillip Shickler

Published in the United States of America by
IGI Global Scientific Publishing
701 East Chocolate Avenue
Hershey, PA, 17033, USA
Tel: 717-533-8845
Fax: 717-533-8661
Website: https://www.igi-global.com E-mail: cust@igi-global.com

Library of Congress Cataloging-in-Publication Data

Names: Manuel, Paul, 1957- editor. | Qureshi, Kalim Uddin, 1960- editor. | Thamilarasi, V., 1979- editor.
Title: Revolutionizing data science and analytics for industry transformation / edited by: Paul Manuel, Kalim Uddin Qureshi, Thamilarasi V.
Description: Hershey PA : IGI Global Scientific Publishing, [2025] | Includes bibliographical references. | Summary: "This book delivers key understanding of data analytics and data science concepts. It describes the role of data science in industry transformation and illustrates the role of data science in industry development and decision making"-- Provided by publisher.
Identifiers: LCCN 2024058283 (print) | LCCN 2024058284 (ebook) | ISBN 9798369378687 (hardcover) | ISBN 9798369378694 (paperback) | ISBN 9798369378700 (ebook)
Subjects: LCSH: Data mining--Industrial applications.
Classification: LCC QA76.9.D343 R48 2025 (print) | LCC QA76.9.D343 (ebook) | DDC 006.3/12--dc23/eng/20250124
LC record available at https://lccn.loc.gov/2024058283
LC ebook record available at https://lccn.loc.gov/2024058284

British Cataloguing in Publication Data
A Cataloguing in Publication record for this book is available from the British Library.

Table of Contents

Preface xv

Chapter 1
Introduction to Data Science and Analytics 1
Gourav Arora, PCTE Institute of Engineering and Technology, India
Shairy Kalra, PCTE Institute of Engineering and Technology, India
Gurpreet Kaur, The University of Melbourne, Australia

Chapter 2
The Role of Data Visualization in Industry Development: Data Visualization in Industry 29
Kriushanth Mariadoss, St. Joseph's College, India
Ashok Kumar, Skyline University, Nigeria

Chapter 3
An Effective Data Visualization Overview and Impact 55
Vijayalakshmi P. S., Dr. N.G.P. Arts and Science College, India
Poorana Senthilkumar S., Dr. N.G.P. Arts and Science College, India
Rajan John, College of Engineering and Computer Science, Jazan University, Saudi Arabia

Chapter 4
Analysis of Crime Against Women Data Using Machine Learning and Statistical Methods 93
P. Tamilarasi, Sri Sarada College for Women, India
R. UmaRani, Sri Sarada College for Women, India
T. JayaSudha, Sri Sarada College for Women, India
Yusliza Yusoff, Universiti Teknologi Malaysia, Malaysia
C. KumuThini, Dr. N.G.P. Arts and Science College, India

Chapter 5
Intelligent Decision Model Based on Deep Reinforcement Learning for Soccer Games Outcome Prediction Using Optimal Feature Extraction and Optimization 119
V. Thamilarasi, Sri Sarada College for Women, India
R. Roselin, Sri Sarada College for Women, India
Kirti H. Wanjale, Vishwakarma Institute of Technology, India
P. Pushpa, East China University of Technology, China

Chapter 6
Foundations and Obstacles of Deep Learning in Healthcare 153
Lakshmi Devi S., Sri Krishna Adithya College of Arts and Science, India
Vijaya Lakshmi P. S., Dr. N.G.P. Arts and Science College, India
Satheesh Kumar Nataraj, University of Technology Bahrain, Bahrain

Chapter 7
Data Science In Healthcare 175
T. Jayasudha, Sri Sarada College for Women, India
R. Uma Rani, Sri Sarada College for Women, India
P. Tamilarasi, Sri Sarada College for Women, India

Chapter 8
Survey on Data Science Application on Healthcare Analysis 207
S. Hemalatha, Panimalar Engineering College, India
Krithick Ajay S., Panimalar Engineering College, India

Chapter 9
Data Analytics and Visualization Tools and Applications 225
Harishchander Anandaram, Amrita School of Artificial Intelligence, India
Rakheeba Taseen, Presidency University, India
Haseeba Yaseen, Vasavi College of Engineering, India
Anup Bhange, KDK College of Engineering, India
Nidhya M. S., Dayananda Sagar University, India

Chapter 10
A Sentimental Analysis of Legal Documents Using Mask Attention BERT Networks 243
D. Thamarai Selvi, Department of Computer Science and Engineering, National Engineering College, India
S. Kalaiselvi, Department of Computer Science and Engineering, National Engineering College, India
V. Anitha, Department of Information Technology, National Engineering College, India
S. Santhi, Department of Information Technology, National Engineering College, India
V. Gomathi, Department of Computer Science and Engineering, National Engineering College, India
Sathish Kumar Sekar, East China University of Technology, China

Chapter 11
AI Implementation for Smart Wearable 265
P. Mohammed Shameem, University of West London, UK
A. Sampath Dakshina Murthy, Vignan's Institute of Information Technology, India
Judy Flavia B., SRM Institute of Science and Technology, India
Nidhya M. S., Dayananda Sagar University, India
Mohit Tiwari, Bharati Vidyapeeth's College of Engineering, India
Balajee Maram, SR University, India

Chapter 12
Analysis on Implantable IoT Sensors 283
C. H. Gangadhar, Prasad V. Potluri Siddhartha Institute of Technology, India
Ramakrishna Kolikipogu, Chaitanya Bharathi Institute of Technology, India
K. Santarao, GMR Institute of Technology, India
Benita Christopher, Westford University, UAE
Nidhya M. S., Dayananda Sagar University, India

Chapter 13
Attacks in IoT Healthcare Wearable Sensors 309
A. Sampath Dakshina Murthy, Vignan's Institute of Information Technology, India
Nidhya M. S., Dayananda Sagar University, India
E. Gurumoorthi, CMR College of Engineering and Technology, India
Mohit Tiwari, Bharati Vidyapeeth's College of Engineering, India

Chapter 14
IoT Technologies 5G and 6G 325
Charanjeet Singh, Deenbandhu Chhotu Ram University of Science and Technology, India
M. Prasad, Vellore Institute of Technology, Chennai, India
B. Aarthi, SRM Institute of Science and Technology, India
Ranjeet Yadav, Government Polytechnic Daman, India
Nidhya M. S., Dayananda Sagar University, India
Balajee Maram, SR University, India

Compilation of References 341

About the Contributors 377

Index 385

Detailed Table of Contents

Preface.. xv

Chapter 1
Introduction to Data Science and Analytics 1
Gourav Arora, PCTE Institute of Engineering and Technology, India
Shairy Kalra, PCTE Institute of Engineering and Technology, India
Gurpreet Kaur, The University of Melbourne, Australia

This chapter provides an in-depth introduction to the fundamental principles, methodologies, and applications that define these fields and delves into the historical evolution of data science and analytics, tracing their roots from traditional statistics and computer science to the modern era characterized by big data and advanced computing technologies. It introduces key concepts such as big data, machine learning, data mining, and data visualization, elucidating how these elements converge to extract valuable insights from complex datasets. A detailed overview of the data science process is presented, outlining each critical stage from data collection and cleaning to exploratory data analysis, modeling, and deployment. This orderly approach guarantees that peruses get a handle on the whole lifecycle of data-driven projects. Additionally, the chapter highlights the essential tools and technologies used in the field.

Chapter 2
The Role of Data Visualization in Industry Development: Data Visualization in Industry 29
Kriushanth Mariadoss, St. Joseph's College, India
Ashok Kumar, Skyline University, Nigeria

The digital age has ushered in a period of extraordinary data growth, reshaping industries and enabling unprecedented opportunities for innovation and business development. Sectors such as manufacturing, healthcare, finance, and retail stand at the forefront of this transformation, generating and analyzing vast volumes of data. As organizations strive to capitalize on the wealth of information available, data-driven decision-making has emerged as an essential strategy for driving growth, streamlining operations, and fostering innovation. However, the sheer scale and complexity of modern data landscapes often present significant challenges that hinder organizations from fully leveraging their data resources. These challenges range from managing diverse datasets to extracting actionable insights efficiently. In this context, data visualization has become a cornerstone of effective data utilization.

It serves not merely as a means of making data visually appealing but as a critical tool for simplifying complex information and enabling stakeholders to interpret and act on data insights.

Chapter 3
An Effective Data Visualization Overview and Impact 55
Vijayalakshmi P. S., Dr. N.G.P. Arts and Science College, India
Poorana Senthilkumar S., Dr. N.G.P. Arts and Science College, India
Rajan John, College of Engineering and Computer Science, Jazan University, Saudi Arabia

The modern world generates a tremendous amount of data every day. Additionally, when evaluating data for specific trends, it can occasionally be challenging to spot patterns of the data left in the raw format. This is avoided by the use of data visualization. This data visualization identifies it easier to understand, view, and interpret the data by providing a clean, organized graphical visualization of the data. When working in data, it might be difficult to completely explain the information it is only provided in tabular format. When compared to a table and a CSV file holding the data, this makes correlations, patterns, and trends simpler to observe. In this chapter, the authors show how to visualize data using Python and several modules. The primary aim is to access high data and interpret it to show emerging areas and patterns more quickly. This is mainly important because it comes in massive amounts of information and data analysis, as the big amount of data can be debilitating in the absence of efficient visualization methods.

Chapter 4
Analysis of Crime Against Women Data Using Machine Learning and Statistical Methods 93
P. Tamilarasi, Sri Sarada College for Women, India
R. UmaRani, Sri Sarada College for Women, India
T. JayaSudha, Sri Sarada College for Women, India
Yusliza Yusoff, Universiti Teknologi Malaysia, Malaysia
C. KumuThini, Dr. N.G.P. Arts and Science College, India

Analyzing, cleaning, manipulating, and modelling datasets to conclude the data they include is the process known as data analytics. Qualitative and quantitative data analysis are two more categories into which data analytics may be separated. The scientific and mathematical study of algorithms is known as machine learning (ML). Crime against women has grown to be a major issue. Numerous nations are always working to avoid this offence, which is something that must be done. Crimes against women have increased dramatically in recent years. Every year, a massive dataset is created based on the reporting of crimes. To a certain extent, this data can help us prevent crime by analyzing and forecasting it. The crime rate against women is predicted in this chapter using a variety of statistical techniques, including the correlation coefficient ANOVA, and hypothesis testing with ML models in Python, including linear regression. The results are finally presented based on the performance of the ML algorithms using evolution metrics, such as MAE, MSE, and R2.

Chapter 5
Intelligent Decision Model Based on Deep Reinforcement Learning for Soccer Games Outcome Prediction Using Optimal Feature Extraction and Optimization 119
V. Thamilarasi, Sri Sarada College for Women, India
R. Roselin, Sri Sarada College for Women, India
Kirti H. Wanjale, Vishwakarma Institute of Technology, India
P. Pushpa, East China University of Technology, China

In this study, the authors propose an intelligent decision model, the deep reinforcement learning for soccer games outcome prediction (DRL-SGO), using optimal feature extraction and optimization. Initially, they design a feature extraction model based on DenseNet to extract soccer games domain knowledge, including recency and rating features, from the given dataset. Subsequently, they use the artificial rabbit optimization (ARO) algorithm to optimize features, selecting the best among a multitude of options. Additionally, they employ deep reinforcement learning (DRL) techniques to enhance the accuracy of predicting soccer game outcomes. Finally, they validate the performance of the proposed DRL-SGO model using the 2017 soccer prediction challenge dataset. Remarkably, the DRL-SGO model achieved an accuracy of 93.991%, precision of 89.169%, recall of 90.537%, and F-measure of 89.843%, showcasing its impressive predictive in the realm of soccer game outcome forecasting.

Chapter 6
Foundations and Obstacles of Deep Learning in Healthcare 153
Lakshmi Devi S., Sri Krishna Adithya College of Arts and Science, India
Vijaya Lakshmi P. S., Dr. N.G.P. Arts and Science College, India
Satheesh Kumar Nataraj, University of Technology Bahrain, Bahrain

Proven results show that deep learning (DL) plays a key role in smart manufacturing and logistic supply chain management. DL was effective in the healthcare sector because of its capacity to manage vast amounts of complex data with little assistance from humans. To improve the quality of care and health for patients, physicians, and other healthcare workers, deep learning (DL) is being implemented in the current healthcare system. It was discovered that DL was useful for diagnosing illnesses, detecting acute diseases, analyzing images, finding new drugs, delivering drugs, and monitoring smart health. This chapter offers a cutting-edge analysis of the

DL foundations, challenges, and applications in healthcare systems to meet multi-objective aims.

Chapter 7
Data Science In Healthcare 175

T. Jayasudha, Sri Sarada College for Women, India
R. Uma Rani, Sri Sarada College for Women, India
P. Tamilarasi, Sri Sarada College for Women, India

Cardiovascular disease (CVD) has been the leading reason of death up to this point. Cardiovascular illness must be diagnosed as soon as possible to save patients' lives. The intention of this research is identifying the most important features to predict CVD by using feature selection method, and find out the most effective classification model to forecast cardiovascular diseases. This study makes use of patient datasets from the UCI repository for prediction. For data scaling, Min-Max Scaler is employed. Data transformation is accomplished using the label encoding technique. The Z-score method is applied to handle the outlier. The most essential features were picked using the chi square approach. For classification, logistic regression, support vector machine, naive bayes, decision tree, and boosted random forest were employed. The achievement was assessed by applying confusion matrix, accuracy, recall, F1 score, and precision, and ROC. Among five classifiers, boosted random forest classifier achieved the highest accuracy (87.3%).

Chapter 8
Survey on Data Science Application on Healthcare Analysis 207

S. Hemalatha, Panimalar Engineering College, India
Krithick Ajay S., Panimalar Engineering College, India

The application of data science is revolutionizing healthcare, spurring advances in tailored care, diagnosis, and treatment. This survey offers a thorough review of data science's role in healthcare, with a particular emphasis on its applications in drug development, genomics, predictive analytics, medical imaging, and patient care management. The ability of key data science approaches, such as big data analytics, machine learning, deep learning, and natural language processing, to handle large amounts of complicated healthcare data is examined. In addition to highlighting new developments like precision medicine and AI-driven health monitoring, the study also addresses difficulties, such as data privacy, model interpretability, and integration of disparate data sources. In the end, this research highlights how data science has the capacity to revolutionize patient outcomes, streamline healthcare processes, and promote innovation in the medical industry.

Chapter 9
Data Analytics and Visualization Tools and Applications 225
Harishchander Anandaram, Amrita School of Artificial Intelligence, India
Rakheeba Taseen, Presidency University, India
Haseeba Yaseen, Vasavi College of Engineering, India
Anup Bhange, KDK College of Engineering, India
Nidhya M. S., Dayananda Sagar University, India

Data visualisation allows for the visual representation of data and information. Trends and changes in data may be seen with the use of data visualisation tools and visual data analysis using visual elements. The basic goal of data visualisation is to help people better comprehend and examine data—that is, to comprehend the outcomes of their processing—by transforming it into a visual environment. Humans have the quickest cognitive pathway in the visual canal. This is why visual data is more appealing than text or audio data. It is common for quick data processing, analysis, and presentation to become more important in daily life in this era of digital data overproduction. Processing tools and visual data analysis undergo continual upgrading as a result of the two-way communication between developers, managers, and users. With that in mind, this chapter will examine and contrast the efficiency of the various visual data analysis and visualisation techniques available today.

Chapter 10
A Sentimental Analysis of Legal Documents Using Mask Attention BERT Networks 243
D. Thamarai Selvi, Department of Computer Science and Engineering, National Engineering College, India
S. Kalaiselvi, Department of Computer Science and Engineering, National Engineering College, India
V. Anitha, Department of Information Technology, National Engineering College, India
S. Santhi, Department of Information Technology, National Engineering College, India
V. Gomathi, Department of Computer Science and Engineering, National Engineering College, India
Sathish Kumar Sekar, East China University of Technology, China

Legal systems can function more efficiently by processing cases faster and having a higher case clearance rate when complex legal texts are automatically analysed for logical patterns. The most crucial task in doing this is classifying sentences in legal documents automatically based on their content. This chapter suggests a deep learning model for sentiment analysis-based legal text analysis and judgment generation. The transformer model is an innovative encoder-decoder that uses self-awareness to analyse speech patterns which runs noticeably quicker and allows for parallel processing. In this work, the glove embedding and the BERT algorithm—bidirectional encoder representation for transformer model—are utilised to construct sentiment analysis for text categorization. Prior to extracting valuable data from textual input, a preprocessor is used to enhance the quality of the data. Next, pre-trained glove word embedding methods and term frequency-inverse document frequency (TF-IDF) feature weighting are used.

Chapter 11
AI Implementation for Smart Wearable 265
P. Mohammed Shameem, University of West London, UK
A. Sampath Dakshina Murthy, Vignan's Institute of Information Technology, India
Judy Flavia B., SRM Institute of Science and Technology, India
Nidhya M. S., Dayananda Sagar University, India
Mohit Tiwari, Bharati Vidyapeeth's College of Engineering, India
Balajee Maram, SR University, India

Evolution of AI in the medical field is the biggest challenge. Research organisations are committed to continuing the in-depth quest for intelligence because of specific long-term demands and challenges in medicine. Because of developments in areas like the internet of things, cloud computing, and 5G mobile networks, artificial intelligence (AI) technology is being used in healthcare. Additionally, improved public services are made possible by the extensive integration of IoT technology and artificial intelligence, which gradually enhances diagnostic and therapeutic capabilities. The authors join the thoughts behind unambiguous calculations like to portray situation-based applications like distant conclusion and clinical coordination, pediatric escalated care units, cardiovascular concentrated care units, trauma centers, venous thromboembolism, patient consideration, and imaging utilizing the web of things (IoT), the cloud, huge information examination, and AI in medical services.

Chapter 12
Analysis on Implantable IoT Sensors 283
C. H. Gangadhar, Prasad V. Potluri Siddhartha Institute of Technology, India
Ramakrishna Kolikipogu, Chaitanya Bharathi Institute of Technology, India
K. Santarao, GMR Institute of Technology, India
Benita Christopher, Westford University, UAE
Nidhya M. S., Dayananda Sagar University, India

Miniaturization has allowed for greater efficiency and increased power in implantable electronic devices. Glucose levels, blood pressure, and cerebral activity are just few of the many physiological characteristics that may be tracked with the use of biomedical sensors. A body area network, also known as a wireless sensor network, is primarily comprised of a set of sensors operating in tandem inside a human body. The present status of the workmanship in remote biomedical sensor correspondence and controlling frameworks are talked about in this chapter, alongside their expected applications. Additionally, up-to-date integration techniques are outlined for making the sensors smaller and well suited for implantation. For a collection of sensors to function as a BAN, they must first join forces to establish a network. At long last, versatility approaches for embedded sensors are provided, along with details on the challenges that must be overcome throughout the development of such networks.

Chapter 13
Attacks in IoT Healthcare Wearable Sensors 309
A. Sampath Dakshina Murthy, Vignan's Institute of Information Technology, India
Nidhya M. S., Dayananda Sagar University, India
E. Gurumoorthi, CMR College of Engineering and Technology, India
Mohit Tiwari, Bharati Vidyapeeth's College of Engineering, India

The internet of things (IoT) concept has recently received a lot of attention in the IT industry. It makes it easier to share data and connect to the internet. Smart surveillance, environmental monitoring, smartphones, and body sensors all make use of the internet of things (IoT). However, serious new threats to consumers' safety and privacy have emerged as a result of the internet of things' rapid growth. Due to the millions of IoT devices that are at risk, an attacker could quickly hack into an application, render it unreliable, and steal valuable user data and information. Both the architecture of the internet of things and the many forms of cyberattacks on these devices are examined in this chapter. It aims to advance IoT research by shedding light on the numerous security issues IoT is currently facing and the available security solutions we can use to make IoT devices safer. To uncover appropriate security solutions for securing IoT devices, the authors analyse them in this research across three categories: secure authentication, secure communications, and application security.

Chapter 14
IoT Technologies 5G and 6G 325
Charanjeet Singh, Deenbandhu Chhotu Ram University of Science and Technology, India
M. Prasad, Vellore Institute of Technology, Chennai, India
B. Aarthi, SRM Institute of Science and Technology, India
Ranjeet Yadav, Government Polytechnic Daman, India
Nidhya M. S., Dayananda Sagar University, India
Balajee Maram, SR University, India

Optical wireless technologies have garnered significant attention in recent years due to their potential to address the growing demands of 5G and 6G networks. These technologies promise to revolutionize physical-world applications by providing enhanced energy efficiency, higher speeds, and cost-effective solutions. However, their implementation faces numerous challenges, particularly in the context of sensors deployed in the internet of things (IoT). This chapter examines critical issues such as the limitations of wireless optical communication, frequent handovers, inter-cell interference losses caused by atmospheric variations, and the need to mitigate flickering effects. By analyzing these challenges, the authors aim to contribute to the development of robust and sustainable optical wireless communication systems, paving the way for their seamless integration into next-generation IoT ecosystems.

Compilation of References 341

About the Contributors 377

Index 385

Preface

In the rapidly evolving world of data science and analytics, industries across the globe are undergoing transformation as they harness the power of data to drive innovation, improve decision-making, and streamline operations. This book, *Revolutionizing Data Science and Analytics for Industry Transformation*, offers a comprehensive exploration of how data science, machine learning, and advanced analytics are reshaping diverse sectors such as healthcare, sports, manufacturing, and more. By bringing together leading experts from academia and industry, this volume delves into the cutting-edge applications, challenges, and technologies at the forefront of the data revolution.

CHAPTER OVERVIEW

Chapter 1: Introduction to Data Science and Analytics

This foundational chapter lays the groundwork by providing a thorough introduction to the key principles, methodologies, and applications that define data science and analytics. The chapter traces the historical evolution of these fields, from traditional statistics and computer science to the current era of big data and machine learning. It also offers an overview of the data science process, highlighting the critical stages from data collection to model deployment, ensuring readers understand the lifecycle of data-driven projects.

Chapter 2: The Role of Data Visualization in Industry Development: Data Visualization in Industry

As industries generate vast amounts of data, the importance of effective visualization becomes paramount. This chapter explores how data visualization is integral to interpreting complex datasets and making data-driven decisions across sectors like manufacturing, healthcare, and finance. By simplifying intricate data patterns, visualization empowers stakeholders to act swiftly and confidently, driving innovation and operational efficiency.

Chapter 3: An Effective Data Visualization Overview and Impact

Building on the previous chapter, this section provides a deeper dive into the tools and techniques used in data visualization. It focuses on how visualizing data through platforms such as Python enhances the process of identifying patterns, correlations, and trends, particularly in the context of large datasets. The chapter underscores the significance of visualization in transforming raw data into actionable insights.

Chapter 4: Analysis of Crime Against Women Data Using Machine Learning and Statistical Methods

This chapter highlights the use of data science techniques to address critical social issues. It demonstrates how machine learning and statistical methods can be applied to analyze and predict crimes against women, with the goal of using data to prevent and mitigate such crimes. Through the use of various models and metrics, this chapter showcases how data analytics can have a direct, positive impact on societal challenges.

Chapter 5: Intelligent Decision Model Based on Deep Reinforcement Learning for Soccer Games Outcome Prediction

In the realm of sports analytics, this chapter introduces a novel deep reinforcement learning (DRL) model for predicting soccer game outcomes. By optimizing feature extraction and using advanced machine learning techniques, the authors present a model that achieves impressive prediction accuracy, offering insights into the growing field of AI-driven sports analytics.

Chapter 6: Foundations and Obstacles of Deep Learning in Healthcare

Deep learning has revolutionized healthcare by enabling better diagnostic accuracy and treatment outcomes. This chapter explores the applications of deep learning in healthcare systems, highlighting its potential to transform patient care while addressing challenges such as data complexity and model interpretability.

Chapter 7: Data Science in Healthcare

Focusing specifically on healthcare, this chapter delves into the use of data science in diagnosing and predicting cardiovascular diseases. By applying feature selection methods and classification models, the authors demonstrate how data-driven approaches can improve healthcare outcomes and contribute to life-saving decisions.

Chapter 8: Survey on Data Science Application in Healthcare Analysis

Expanding on the healthcare theme, this survey offers a comprehensive review of how data science is transforming various aspects of healthcare, including drug development, genomics, predictive analytics, and patient care. The chapter emphasizes the role of machine learning, big data analytics, and AI in addressing healthcare challenges.

Chapter 9: Data Analytics and Visualization Tools and Applications

This chapter shifts focus to the essential tools and applications in data analytics and visualization. It provides an overview of the latest tools, methods, and technologies that enable efficient data analysis and decision-making in today's digital age, particularly in industries inundated with vast amounts of data.

Chapter 10: A Sentimental Analysis of Legal Documents Using Mask Attention BERT Networks

Exploring the intersection of data science and law, this chapter proposes an innovative approach to sentiment analysis using deep learning models for the analysis of legal documents. By leveraging BERT networks and attention mechanisms, the authors demonstrate how AI can enhance legal systems by streamlining case processing and judgment generation.

Chapter 11: AI Implementation for Smart Wearables

Artificial intelligence is making its mark in the field of smart wearables, particularly in healthcare applications. This chapter highlights the integration of IoT, AI, and cloud computing in the development of wearables that monitor various health parameters, offering real-time insights that improve patient care and treatment.

Chapter 12: Analysis on Implantable IoT Sensors

Focusing on the future of medical devices, this chapter explores the development and applications of implantable IoT sensors. These miniaturized sensors, capable of monitoring a range of physiological characteristics, are transforming healthcare by enabling continuous monitoring and improving patient outcomes.

Chapter 13: Attacks in IoT Healthcare Wearable Sensors

As IoT devices proliferate, so do the risks associated with their use. This chapter examines the security challenges faced by IoT healthcare devices, including potential cyberattacks, and provides insights into solutions to secure these devices and safeguard sensitive patient data.

Chapter 14: IoT Technologies 5G and 6G

In the final chapter, the authors explore the potential of 5G and 6G technologies in revolutionizing IoT applications. These advanced networks promise to enhance connectivity, speed, and efficiency, enabling smarter and more integrated systems across industries, especially healthcare.

Together, these chapters highlight the transformative potential of data science, machine learning, and artificial intelligence in diverse sectors. They provide not only technical insights but also practical solutions that organizations can leverage to stay ahead in an increasingly data-driven world.

Chapter 1
Introduction to Data Science and Analytics

Gourav Arora
https://orcid.org/0009-0009-7227-088X
PCTE Institute of Engineering and Technology, India

Shairy Kalra
https://orcid.org/0009-0005-2138-5901
PCTE Institute of Engineering and Technology, India

Gurpreet Kaur
The University of Melbourne, Australia

ABSTRACT

This chapter provides an in-depth introduction to the fundamental principles, methodologies, and applications that define these fields and delves into the historical evolution of data science and analytics, tracing their roots from traditional statistics and computer science to the modern era characterized by big data and advanced computing technologies. It introduces key concepts such as big data, machine learning, data mining, and data visualization, elucidating how these elements converge to extract valuable insights from complex datasets. A detailed overview of the data science process is presented, outlining each critical stage from data collection and cleaning to exploratory data analysis, modeling, and deployment. This orderly approach guarantees that peruses get a handle on the whole lifecycle of data-driven projects. Additionally, the chapter highlights the essential tools and technologies used in the field.

DOI: 10.4018/979-8-3693-7868-7.ch001

WORKING AND APPLICATIONS OF DATA SCIENCE

The Author had previously been presented by a software developer friend at one of Europe's largest conferences on information technology. He showed authentic enthusiasm and inquired whether we could join. The Author replied positively, saying let's broaden our understanding together. The Author eager to discuss technology with the reader. A few days later, the authors found ourselves at a big gathering. The initial presenter took the stage and shared some of his expert insights for succeeding in record-breaking contests. As the following speaker delved into tensor algebra, The authors noticed a weary expression on my friend's face. What took place?

The Authors asked. – The Authors wonder when company will show us the robots? (Mitchell, 1997)

The Authors must educate ourselves to avoid false expectations. Before the reader can build a house, the reader need to know more about how a hammer works. It is important for all types of managers to have knowledge of the environment they are managing. Software development managers must understand computer programming. Factory inspectors must understand the manufacturing process. The role of Data Intelligence Director is certainly no exception. The initial section of the book offers a clear overview of the fundamental ideas surrounding information technology. The Authors will dissect it and explore it further. Data mining has gained immense popularity, and numerous business professionals are eager to enhance their knowledge about data mining and apply it to address challenges.

Most people form their first impressions of information intelligence from background news, interviews, etc. Unfortunately, most of these sources are fraudulent, and instead of giving the true picture of information technology and information technology, the media is talking about the end of the tools that will solve all our problems. Technological oddities are coming. General income frugality is coming. Unless machines learn like humans and let them. In fact, the authors are still far from creating a universal algorithm for voice recognition and voice enhancement. This section examines the current capabilities and routines in the basic implements for data intelligence, deep learning as well as machine learning. In this section, the authors shall discuss the areas of focus below:

- Introduction to AI
- Introduction to Machine learning
- Introduction to Data Science
- Introduction to Analytics
- All the concepts that are the basic part of Data Science

1.1 Introduction to AI

News and media platforms utilize artificial intelligence as a cover varied innovation relevant to information investigation. Reality, artificial intelligence may be a domain within computer studies wisdom as well as arithmetic. All of it begun with in the 1950s, at the time a few experimenters begun inquiring the ability of computers to learn, assume, as well as logic. 70 times latterly, we remain uncertain the reply. Still, we have created critical advance within a particular form of artificial intelligence that tackles totally indicated contract assignments frail AI. Science manufacture books conversation around devices that can analyze and assume such as people. Logical dialect, they are portrayed like solid artificial intelligence. Solid artificial intelligence is able to assume such a mortal, as well as its mental capacities can be vastly more progressed. The development of solid artificial intelligence persists as the most lasting aspiration of the logical society. Still, viable operations act as each around frail artificial intelligence. Whereas solid artificial intelligence strives to break the issue from common insights, frail artificial intelligence is concentrated upon working single limit perception errand, comparable as insight, discourse, or else harkening. exemplifications of powerless artificial intelligence errands as well as varied discourse acknowledgment, picture bracket, and client churn vaticination. Powerless artificial intelligence serves a critical portion in our existence, revolutionizing how we work, assume, as well as live. Ready to discover effective operations of powerless artificial intelligence in each range of our realities. Craftsmanship, showcasing, robotics, medicine, coordinations and music in every aspect advantage based on later propels in powerless artificial intelligence.

1.2 Introduction to ML

Machine proficiency is achieved through distant that foremost imperative apparatus information researcher. This permits to deliver calculations which find designs in information with more than thousands of factors. We will presently investigate distinctive sorts and capabilities of machine proficiency calculations.

Machine proficiency may be a logical field that considers calculations that perform assignments without enlightening, checking designs in information. For illustration, able to utilize calculations to forecast the obligation of having a complaint or evaluate the danger of disappointment in difficult fabricating equip. Each machine learning calculation takes after a basic equation. Within the taking after illustration, you'll be able see a tall- position choice handle that's grounded on a machine learning calculation. Each machine education demonstrates devours information to deliver data that can bolster mortal suppositions or totally robotize them.

We'll presently investigate the meaning of each piece in advance detail within the coming segment.

1.2.1 Choices and Understandings Offered by an ML Algorithm

upon tackling a problem through ML, you typically aim to streamline

Process of making decisions or acquire perspectives on bolster their reasoning.

An instance, their might seek an algorithm to output a list of possible diseases, given a patient's medical history and current condition. If machine learning solves your task completely, or end to end, this means that the algorithm's output can be used to make a final decision without further thinking; in our example, determining the disease the patient is suffering from and prescribing suitable medication automatically. The execution of this decision can be manual or automatic. We say that machine learning applications like these are end to end. They provide a complete solution to the task. Let's look at digital advertising as an example. An algorithm can predict whether you will click on an ad. If our goal is to maximize clicks, we can make automated and personalized decisions about which specific advertisement to show to each user, solving the click-through rate maximization problem end to end.

1.2.2 Anatomy of Machine Learning

Let's look at the common use cases for machine learning. Arguably the most common one is 'prediction. Predictive algorithms tell us when something will happen, but not necessarily why it will happen. Some examples of prediction tasks are: Will this user churn in the next month? Does this person have a high risk of developing Alzheimer's disease? Will there be a traffic jam in the next hour? Often, we want to have explanations instead of predictions. Solving an inference task means to find supporting evidence for some claim in the data by asking Why? questions. Why did this person win the election? Why does this medicine work and the other doesn't? Statistical inference helps us to find an explanation or to prove the efficiency of our actions. When we do inference, we seek answers for the present or the past. When we try to look into the future, prediction comes into play. Sometimes, we are not interested in predicting the future or finding evidence. We want machines to recognize complex patterns in data, such as objects in an image, or to analyze the sentiment of a text message. This group of tasks is called recognition. Machine learning covers many types and flavors of models. But why do we need such variety of different algorithms? The reason lies in a theorem called the no free lunch principle. It states that there exists no best model that will consistently give you the best results on each task for every dataset. Each algorithm has its own benefits and pitfalls. It may work flawlessly on one task, but fail miserably at another. A part of the most important aims of a data researcher is to find the best model to solve the problem at hand.

1.3 Understanding the Essence of Data Science

To understand the connection between AI & machine proficiency, let's take a deep dive into the concept of articulate data wisdom and effectively addressed through visual representation

Artificial intelligence is a broad empirical topic which encompasses all aspects relevant to limited and advanced artificial intelligence. We will not spend vastly time on artificial intelligence because the majority of practical operations are performed by its domains, that we describe as well as explain in remainder from Section 1"What is Data Science?" machine competence an area of artificial intelligence which examines systems which regulate gestures and may modify in response to incoming input without explicit programmer instructions.

Deep competence is an area of machine competence that investigates a particular form of machine competence model known as DNN.Data intelligence is an interdisciplinary area which uses a variety of techniques to retrieve information based on data as well as enhance decision process. Machinery skills as well as deep understanding exist as one of the most crucial instruments for data intelligence.

The most important thing in data intelligence seeks to resolve challenges by gaining Insights derived from data as well as drawing complicated conclusions from it. A most important thing in problem solving is to have a good understanding of the environment. You want to succeed in the insurance industry by using data intelligence to analyze risks. You want to develop an automated quality assurance chain to know more about the product manufacturing chain. First of all, you go full circle. Next, you identify the challenge. However, if you neglect this segment, you are most likely working on the wrong problem. Once you have written a good problem statement, it is time to look for results. Imagine you established a show which explores an activity. A show about ML in isolation is not going to appeal to anyone. So it has no value. To be valuable, the model needs to be packaged with materials that can be seen and manipulated. In other words, a computer program needs to be developed around the model. Information literacy has always gone hand in hand with the development of computer program systems. A machine learning demonstration requires a computer program. Without computer programs, models would only exist in the computer's memory, no matter who they are.

Data intelligence is not just about intelligence. Industry information and software development are equally important. Without them, the results will not be complete.

1.3.1 Impact of Data Science

There's a awesome certainty in information insights. It impacts our day by day existence. Healthcare providers understand how to analyze as well as foresee genuine wellbeing challenges. Organizations utilize this to discover inventive ways to draw in undiscovered guests and materialize their administrations. We utilize huge information analytics for hereditary qualities and fly control drugs. Sound-controlled buses are getting to be a reality much appreciated to progresses in data insights. Much appreciated to the Web and worldwide robotization, we create incalculable sums of information each day. Progressively expansive sums of information make it conceivable to robotize human assignments. Shockingly, for each utilizes case that changes our lives, there are continuously two that make the situation even more awful. To supply a confounding outline, let us see within China. The government of China is testing advanced community rating framework. Reconnaissance cameras are utilized to track citizens' day by day lives at a expansive size. Computer vision technologies can capture as well as record each movement you are doing whereas traveling to work, holding up line inside a public office, or strolling domestic following a party. An extraordinary community score is additionally computed using security behaviors. This grade has real-life suggestions for people's lives. In specific, open transport admissions may alter depending on your score. Moo Scores allows you to charge a expense to apply for different government employments. Confinements of Information Science Like every toolset, information science has its restrictions. Some time recently setting out on a plan with a driven thought, it is vital to consider the limits of current conceivable outcomes. An assignment that appears simple to illuminate may not be achievable in hone. A poor understanding of the specialized aspects of information science can cause genuine issues in your framework. You will begin with a plan and after that realize simply cannot solve the errand at all. Indeed more regrettable, you might as it were realize after arrangement that nothing is working as arranged - possibly affecting genuine individuals, depending on the utilize case. Understanding the key standards behind information shrewdness can assist you dodge numerous of the particular pitfalls that will decide the destiny of your plan some time recently it indeed starts.

1.3.2 Data Science

Data is available everywhere and in abundance. The question is what do we do with the data? How do we make sense of that data? How is it applied that information for make better decisions? The answers to all these questions lie in data science. Data science focuses on understanding data through processes, tools, and techniques that aid in decision making. It involves techniques for identifying, collecting, and exploring the data using colorful plots and graphs. Let us take the example of data regarding rainfall in our city and the application of data science in this situation. The first step would be to collect the data. Next step would be to create some diagrams to clarify the data. It process of creating graphs and plots is called data visualization. It helps in identifying trends in the data, like which month receives maximum rainfall, which part of the day receives rainfall, etc. The next step would be to derive more information from the data, like average rainfall across different time periods, whether it follows any pattern, any particular season gets more rainfall compared to the other? This process of probing more deeply to understand the data better is called data mining. And finally using the past data, we can predict whether it will rain tomorrow or not. This is called model building in data science. Data science techniques and methods have a wide range of applications cutting across all domains and sectors. The growing awareness related to the application of this concept has strongly established the significance of decision data-driven decision-making instead of relying on intuition.

1.4 Analytics

Analytics involves the organized computational evaluation involving data. It makes use of data, statistical evaluation, and quantitative methods to identify trends, uncover insights, and support decision process. Analytics can take on a predictive, diagnostic, descriptive or prescriptive Based on the goals and context the analysis.

This process involves using a combination of data, statistical methods, and mathematical techniques to discover trends, draw insights, and guide choices *(James, Witten, Hastie, & Tibshirani, 2013).* Essentially, analytics turns raw data into actionable information by applying various computational approaches. It is used across many fields to help understand past events, predict future outcomes, and recommend actions. For instance, businesses use analytics to track their sales performance, identify customer preferences, and optimize marketing strategies. By analyzing data in a structured way, organizations can make informed decisions that improve their operations and outcomes.

Analytics exists in four key types: predictive, descriptive, prescriptive as well as diagnostic, each fulfilling a specific role based on the goals of the analysis. Descriptive analytics looks at historical data to summarize what has happened. For example, a retail store might use descriptive analytics to review sales figures from the past year to understand which products were popular. Diagnostic analytics digs deeper into the data to understand why certain outcomes occurred. For instance, if the same store noticed a rapid downturn in sales, analytical diagnostics would aid explore possible reasons, like shifts in customer preferences or increased competition. Predictive analytics leverages past data to predict upcoming trends. In our example, store might use predictive analytics to anticipate future sales patterns and prepare for peak shopping seasons. Finally, Prescriptive analytics offers advice regarding the best actions to adopt. Based on the insights from the previous types of analytics, it might suggest strategies to boost sales or improve customer engagement. A real-life example of analytics in action is Netflix's recommendation system. Netflix uses a blend of all four types of analytics to enhance user experience. Descriptive analytics helps Netflix understand which shows are currently popular. Diagnostic analytics can reveal why certain shows gained or lost viewers. Predictive analytics forecasts what new shows users might like based on their viewing history, and prescriptive analytics helps Netflix recommend shows that align with users' preferences, keeping them engaged and satisfied with the service.

2. BRIEF HISTORY OF DATA SCIENCE

From the early 19th century, since when information technology was invented, generating, capturing, and processing data have become more complex and extremely powerful. More than 50 years ago, the foundation of data science was laid by John W. Tukey,a mathematician, in his article "The Future of Data Analysis." The other prominent names in this domain are as follows:

John Chambers, Consulting Professor, Stanford University. He was presented the Software System Award for the design of the S system in 1999. The S system is the basis for all the future statistical programming languages, including the R language, which will be discussed in this book.
Jeff Wu, Coco Cola chair in Engineering Statistics and Professor at Georgia Tech, coined the term "Data Science" in 1997.
William Cleveland, Distinguished Professor of Statistics and Professor of Computer Science at Purdue University, authored many books on data visualization.
Leo Breiman, distinguished statistician at the University of California, Berkeley, was one of the pioneers in "machine learning," which is one of the advanced data science techniques. *(Schutt & O'Neil, 2013)*

Each of them played a vital part in the emergence regarding datas science. Over the last five decades, this field has evolved into an undisputable domain. However, the 20th century has witnessed drastic advancements particularly due to certain developments explained in detail in Section 1.3.

3. A GROWING FOCUS ON DATA SCIENCE

Though data science as a concept has been around for more than 50 years, it has recently attracted a lot of attention from the industry, government, and academia. The reasons for the gradual but steady gain in momentum could be attributed to the following points:

- Availability and the increasing usage of the Internet, which has generated more data.
- Growing usage of smart phones, tablets, and digital devices capturing huge volume of data through various applications.
- Increasing usage of social media behind digital footprints, which are easily and increasingly tracked.
- Increasing computational capability with both hardware and software becoming powerful by the day.
- Programming languages to work with such data are freely available through open-source platforms.
- Programmers across the world are creating complex algorithms and contributing to the open-source developers' community.
- Easy and speedy access to such data for every individual or organization irrespective of their size.
- Storage of data is becoming cheaper.

Recently, Internet facilities have become available and accessible to a major part of the population across the globe. According to the latest 2024 report by the International Data Corporation (IDC), the global data landscape is evolving rapidly. IDC forecasts that the volume of data generated globally will persist in increasing significantly, reaching approximately 181 zettabytes by 2025, compared to the 59 zettabytes generated in 2020. This reflects a compound annual growth rate (CAGR) of around 26% between 2020 and 2024.

The proliferation of AI, the IoT, along with the increasing consumption of digital content is key drivers of this growth. The report also indicates a shift in the composition of data, with a growing emphasis on replicated data (data that is copied and consumed) over unique data (newly created and captured data). By 2024, replicated data is expected to constitute 90% of the total global data sphere.

This rapid increase in data volume poses significant challenges and opportunities for industries, as they must develop advanced data management, processing, and analysis capabilities to harness the potential of this vast amount of information. The shift towards AI-driven technologies and the expansion of IoT devices are also expected to further accelerate data generation in the coming years.Every minute on the Internet,

1. Surge in Daily Active Users (DAUs):
   Prominent social media networks such as TikTok, Facebook, Twitter (X) and Instagram, have seen massive user engagement, with Facebook leading at over 2.03 billion DAUs and TikTok surpassing 1.2 billion DAUs.
2. Explosion of Content Creation:
   Platforms like Facebook, Instagram, and TikTok witness the daily upload of hundreds of millions of photos and videos. YouTube users alone upload over 500 hours of video content every minute.
3. Massive Data Generation:
   Social media giants like Facebook generate around 4 petabytes of data per day, driven by vast amounts of content sharing, messaging, and media uploads.
4. Significant User Interaction:
   Communication apps like WhatsApp and Facebook Messenger see extensive usage, with WhatsApp users sending 100 billion messages daily, and Facebook Messenger starting 260 million new conversations every day.
5. Expansion of Meeting Apps:
   Meeting apps such as Zoom, Microsoft Teams, and Google Meet have become integral to remote work, with Zoom hosting over 300 million daily meeting participants and Teams exceeding 280 million monthly active users.
6. High Meeting Volume:
   Zoom, Microsoft Teams, and Google Meet collectively handle billions of meeting minutes daily, with Zoom alone facilitating over 3.3 trillion meeting minutes annually.
7. Extensive Data Usage in Meetings:
   Video conferencing on platforms like Zoom and Microsoft Teams consumes significant data, with Zoom using approximately 1 GB per hour in group meetings, and Google Meet consuming around 2.4 GB for an hour-long 1080p call.
8. Proliferation of Recorded Content:
   The demand for recording meetings has skyrocketed, with platforms like Zoom and Microsoft Teams saving millions of hours of recorded content monthly.
9. Remote Work's Impact on Data Generation:

The shift to remote work has significantly contributed to the increase in data generation, with more users relying on meeting apps for daily communication and collaboration, leading to higher data output.

10. Evolution of Digital Socialization:

    Social media and meeting apps have evolved into critical tools for personal and professional interactions, with users generating unprecedented amounts of data through everyday activities, reflecting broader digitalization trends in society.

4. FUNDAMENTALS FIELDS OF STUDY RELATED TO DATA SCIENCE

Data science has been drawn from many traditional fields of study like mathematics, computer science and statistics. All these fields provide the foundation for the data science domain.

Mathematics and statistics are the foundations of data science. Basic mathematical operations are applicable in data science also. A sound knowledge of basic mathematics and statistics will help data scientists comprehend the logic underlying the data science algorithms. The fundamental theories of mathematics and statistics, such as descriptive statistics, probability, inferential statistics, distribution of data, multivariate analysis,and hypothesis testing, are an integral part of data science. Mathematical modeling, which involves applications such as allocation of limited resources based on constraints to arrive at an optimal solution for decision making, is also applicable in the data science domain.

Computer science or information technology forms another key pillar of data science, which gives the structure of the programming language. This structure forms the basis for the algorithms. The creation of such algorithms requires basic programing skills. People without prior programming knowledge can also easily understand the programming languages R and Python, which are explained in detail in the forthcoming chapters. These languages are called high-level programming languages. They have commands in simple English, which even a non-programmer can easily learn and implement. Therefore, proficiency in data science can be developed by both programmers as well as non-programmers.

Finally, but most importantly, a strong knowledge in the concerned domain helps in clear articulation of the problem or objective in hand. The domain knowledge helps a data scientist understand the objective or the problem better. It is also essential for creating effective metrics to meaningfully interpret the data and fruitfully utilize it for better decision making. The algorithms give the output, but the interpretation of the output is easy and effective if there is knowledge of the concerned domain.

For example, to interpret the output regarding a model in the domain of medicine, some basic knowledge of the terms is very important. To understand an engineering problem better, domain knowledge of that particular branch will help to understand the problem as well as the output better. However, it is not possible for a single person to have domain knowledge in varied fields; therefore, the data scientist has to acquire some basic knowledge of the domain depending on the applications he or she is involved in.

5. DATA SCIENCE AND RELATED TERMINOLOGIES

Data science as a domain is closely interlinked with many concepts. A clear understanding of these concepts will help in comprehending their application in the real world. A brief description of these intertwining terminologies is as follows:

5.1 Big Data

Big data is any data which is too huge and complex to be processed using traditional processing systems (Marr, 2017). In other words, it is any data which is beyond the computational capability of traditional data-processing systems. It is characterized by the four Vs: volume, velocity, variety, and veracity.

Volume: Volume explains the amount of data being generated across different media daily. All industries are grappling with the dilemma of how to handle such vast data. Volume is quantified using gigabytes (1 billion bytes), terabytes (one million million (10^{12})), and sometimes petabytes (one thousand million million (10^{15})).

Velocity: Velocity indicates the rate with the data that gets produced, which could be by the hours and now even by milliseconds. We saw in Section 1.3 the kind of data getting generated by the minute throughout the globe.

Variety: Data might exist as tables, script, voice, or video and are classified into semi-structured, structured and un-structured data. Organized data are typically captured inspread sheets or Excel sheets represented by rows and columns. Semi-structured data, on the other hand, includes data generated in the form of emails, chats, phone conversations, image, files, graphics, etc. Data can also be in the form of pictures or images like genetic data, data from X-rays, computerized tomography (CT/CAT) scans, microarray expression images, from GPS location, RFID, smart meters, sensors, etc. Unstructured data would include data captured from the social media in the form of chats, videos, twitter feeds, etc. With more and more people using the social media to record their thoughts and expressions, this form of unstructured data is also increasingly becoming available. Algorithms are specifically created to deal with such data.

Veracity: Veracity deals with the authenticity of the data being captured, whether it is trustworthy and bias free. Because of the speed, amount and types of data generated, the authenticity of such data becomes a huge challenge.

5.2 Business Intelligence

Hans Peter Luhn, the computer scientist from IBM, published an article way back in 1958 titled "A Business Intelligence system." However, the term "business intelligence" was popularized by Howard Dressner, an analyst at the Gartner group in the early 1990s. Business intelligence (BI) involves gathering, preprocessing, and most importantly presenting such data using data visualization tools and techniques through charts, plots, tables, and dashboards. The objective of a BI system is to provide appropriate information in a timely manner to aid decision making. The BI system derives data from the different software systems like ERP mechanisms, OLAP, and data mining techniques.

5.3 Data Mining

It's no surprise that data mining, as a truly interdisciplinary subject, can be defined in numerous different ways. Indeed the term data mining does n't really present all the major factors in the picture. To relate to the mining of gold from jewels or beach, we say gold mining rather of gemstone or beach mining. Analogously, data mining should have been more meetly named " knowledge mining from data, " which is unfortunately kindly long. still, the shorter term, knowledge mining may not reflect the emphasis on mining from large quantities of data. nonetheless, mining is a pictorial term characterizing the process that finds a small set of precious nuggets from a great deal of raw material. therefore, such a misnomer carrying both " data " and " mining " came a popular choice. In addition, numerous other terms have a analogous meaning to data mining — for illustration, knowledge mining from data, knowledge birth, data pattern analysis, data archaeology, and data dredging *(Witten, Frank, Hall, & Pal, 2016)*.

Data mining is the technology used for recycling large volumes of data with a blend of traditional data analysis ways and complex machine learning algorithms. The ideal of data mining is to induce consequences from data similar as relating trends in stock prices, grading guests grounded on their preferences, catching on the purchasing patterns of guests, prognosticating pupil performance in an educational institution, lie discovery in dealing with culprits, etc. Data booby-trapping ways are told by propositions and models in other affiliated disciplines like information technology, optimization, database operation, and signal processing. operations of data mining can be seen in the field of husbandry, education, artificial engineering, marketing, healthcare, etc. numerous people treat data mining as a reverse for another popularly used term, knowledge discovery from data, or KDD, while others view data mining as simply an essential step in the process of knowledge discovery. *(Han, Pei, & Kamber, 2011)* The knowledge discovery process is an iterative sequence of the following way:

1. Data drawing Real- world data tend to be deficient, noisy, and inconsistent. Data drawing (or data sanctification) routines essay to fill in missing values, smooth out noise while relating outliers, and correct inconsistencies in the data. Dealing with Missing Values: How can we go concerning the missing data for this trait? These form the styles that we can opt for this:
2. We can neglect the tuples this represents generally performed when any of the section maker is missing (assume in which the missing activity involve in the bracket).This approach is not really efficient, he defines then the tuple has more than 1 properties with incomplete data. Impute the absent value manually: This indicates a generalized way of filling missing values but can be time consuming in case we have large dataset with many number of NA:.
3. Add the missing value with global constant Substitute all trait elements that are considered as missing by a single (global) constant similar to a marker like "Unknown" or -∞. yet, say " Jobient to fill the missing values by Unknown.
4. A central tendency measure for the attribute (e.g., average or standard) are used to fill in absent value measures of central tendency == center | (Across a data distribution. The mean applies well to normally distributed data (symmetric) but the standard should be employed with disposed data distribution.
5. Substitute the missing values based on trait mean or standard within each class (or order): for example, when kind guests by credit threat, fill in missing values with overall income value from visitors of same feature given that credit danger type as this requested tuple. But the median value should be a safer bet, If it is ranged disposition of data for any particular class.
6. Set the missing value to its most likely (e.g., by backfill, probabilistic tools based on Bayesian approach or decision tree methodology). For instance, the alternative client properties in your dataset may yield that you can build a decision tree to predict what income a given piece of demographic information will correspond for? StyleFromNumber is expected to give a value from 0-6, where anything >2 means biasing the data — this number needs to be filled in and it might not be right for options with styles of 3 through 6. Method 6, however,

is a constant favourite. Amongst the other styles, it takes more insights from current data to estimate missing values. (McKinney, 2017)

5.3.1 Inconsistent Data

"What is noise?" Noise is a random error in a measured variable. We have learned some basic statistical description in the last chapter and that plots like box-plots, scatter-plots or data-visualization can be helpful to spot outliers which means probably noise. How do we take any numeric attribute, like a price, and "smooth" the data to eliminate as much noise? *(Mitchell, 1997)*

5.3.2 Data Smoothing Techniques

1. Binning: Binned data has neighbours Sorted Values l Dis () Sorted data for price ($): 4,8,15,21, 24,25:28.34

   Bin (according to same-frequency):
   Bin 1: 4, 8, 15
   Bin 2: 21, 21, 24
   Bin 3: 25, 28, 34
   Smoothing by bin means:
   Bin 1: 9, 9, 9
   Bin 2: 22, 22, 22
   Bin 3: 29, 29, 29
   Smoothing along bin boundaries
   Bin 1: 4, 4, 15
   Bin 2: 21, 21, 24
   Bin 3: 25, 25, 34

For example, consider data grouping approaches for data smoothing techniques *(Aggarwal, 2015)*

tributed into several "buckets," or containers. Because binning approaches consider the values' vicinity, they conduct local smoothing. An example demonstrates several binning strategies. In this illustration, the price data is initially organized before being segmented into three uniform-frequency intervals. Applying bin means for smoothing replaces each value found in a bin with its corresponding average value. In this instance, the average pertaining to the numbers 4, 8, and 15 in Bin 1 amounts to 9. As a result, all original measurements in this bin gets changed with the result 9. In a similar fashion, bin median smoothing can be utilized, replacing each bin value with its corresponding median. Bin-wise smoothing borders identifies The minimal and maximal values in a specific interval. Every specific bin value is subsequently substituted with the nearest Extremum value. In general, the The impact of smoothing grows stronger as the breadth increases. Another approach involves using equal-width bins, maintaining a steady interval range of values across each bin. Interval grouping functions as a discretization strategy.

5.3.3 Regression Analysis

Sample smoothing may also remain accomplished via data modeling values toward a model, which is known predictive modeling. LR acts as process of determining "best" Connecting line for two qualities, allowing an approach to estimate another. Numerous LR a kind of LR that involves beyond double features as well as applies a multidimensional surface to the data.

5.3.4 Analysis of Outliers

Using clustering can help in identifying outliers, for instance A two-dimensional depiction of consumer data based on client at a city locations, displaying threefold sample bunch. The centre point of every bunch is indicated using a "+", which represents cluster's mean position in a spatial context. Values that fall outside the clusters can be classified as outliers.

5.4 The procedure of Data Cleaning

The two-step process of discrepancy detection and data transformation (to correct discrepancies) iterates. This process, however, is error-prone and time consuming.

The first step in data cleaning as a process is *discrepancy detection*. Discrepancies can be caused by several factors, including poorly designed data entry forms that have many optional fields, human error in data entry, deliberate errors (e.g., respondents not wanting to divulge information about themselves), and data decay (e.g., outdated addresses).

The information need to additionally be tested concerning precise policies, consecutive regulations, and null rules. a unique rule says that every cost of the given characteristic have to be one of a kind from all different values for that characteristic. A consecutive rule says that there may be no missing values between the lowest and highest values for the attribute, and that all values must also be specific (e.g., as in take a look at numbers). A null rule specifies the use of blanks, question marks, special characters, or different strings that could indicate the null situation (e.g., wherein a cost for a given attribute isn't to be had), and how such values need to be treated.

There are a number of unique industrial equipment which can resource inside the discrepancy detection step. facts scrubbing equipment use easy area know-how (e.g., know-how of postal addresses and spell-checking) to come across mistakes and make corrections in the records. that equipment depend upon parsing and fuzzy matching strategies while filtering inputs through a couple of reference. Statistics inspecting gear discover discrepancies by using reading the information to identify guidelines and standards as well as assessing inputs which breach similar circumstances.

Trade gear is able to provide inside facts changeover phase. statistics relocation equipment permit easy changes to be detailed inclusive in order to substitute a sequence "gender" via "intercourse." ETL techniques permit members leadind to outline converts by means of visual consumer gateway. these equipment usually aid most effective a constrained collection of transformations in order which, frequently, we might opt to write down unique scripts for this element of the facts cleaning procedure. *(Mitchell, 1997)*

The two-phase approach for identifying discrepancies as well as data conversion (to rectify discrepancies) repeats. These method, but, mistakes-inclined as well as duration ingesting. a few variations may introduce extra discrepancies. a few hierarchical discrepancies might additionally best be identified following others had taken place constant. As an instance, a typo together with "20010" in a yr subject may additionally best appear after all date values were standardized into a uniform format.

5.4.1 Data Aggregation

Integration from various data repositories. Careful consolidation can help cut down on and prevent duplication and deviations in the output data. These helps increase the precision and efficiency of the continuous information search procedure.

5.4.2 Entity Recognition Issue

Data aggregation merges data from various entities through one database, such as a statistical database. These sources may include a variety of files, index files, and else plain text files.

There exists a few things until keep in mind while the data aggregation process. Mixing as well as harmonizing elements is possible to be difficult. In what way do you keep the number of places in the world equal from different places? This is called an identity issue. To illustrate, in what way a statistical researcher or computational program ensure the referenced customer_id existing in a specific database has the same properties as customer_number in differrent database? Instances of descriptive data for each progress encompass the callback, statistic category, and value type taken by the attribute, as well as defaults for handling null, 0, alternatively empty entries. This data descriptive serves to mitigate errors in schema integration.

On comparing the properties while moving data from one database to another, it's important to be attentive to the structure of the data. That, ensuring everything is operational features as well as restrictions on relevant equipment affect the performance and usage restrictions on the target computer. For example, one machine may be scaled down once, while another machine may be scaled down sequentially for each product line. If this is not always the case before integration, the gadget on the target device will be scaled down.

5.4.3 Redundancy Along With Dependency Analysis

Unnecessary repetition acts as supplementary critical trouble in the consolidation of facts. A characteristic (such as yearly turnover) could exist as unnecessary in case it can be "inferred" from other properties or combinations of progress. Discrepancies in the naming of properties or measurements can also lead to redundancies within the resulting data set.

A few unnecessary repetitions may be found with the aid of data relationship evaluation. Considering the properties, these types of evaluation can degree how one attribute predicts the other, primarily derived at the accessible information. For categorical records, we utilize the $\chi 2$ take a look at. For quantitative attributes, those are able to utilize the correlation and covariance measures, each of which get admission to the way one attribute's values range based on the ones related to another.

3. Data extraction: diminishes the size of the data set through the elimination of irrelevant or duplicate attributes. The aim of selection of relevant features seeks to determine a reduced set of attributes resulting in a probability distribution that of the data classes is as near as feasible to the primary distribution derived from all attributes.

"How can we find a 'good' subset of the original attributes?" (Witten, Frank, Hall, & Pal, 2016) For n attributes, there are 2n possible subsets. An exhaustive search for the optimal subset of attributes can be prohibitively expensive, especially as n and the number of data classes increase. The "best" (and "worst") attributes are typically determined using tests of statistical significance, which assume that the attributes are independent of one another. Many other attribute evaluation measures can be used such as the *information gain* measure used in building decision trees for classification.

1. **Stepwise forward selection:** The procedure starts with an empty set of attributes as the reduced set. The best of the original attributes is determined and added to the reduced set. At each subsequent iteration or step, the best of the remaining original attributes is added to the set.
2. **Stepwise backward elimination:** The procedure starts with the full set of attributes. At each step, it removes the worst attribute remaining in the set.
3. **Combination of forward selection and backward elimination:** The stepwise forward selection and backward elimination methods can be combined so that, at each step, the procedure selects the best attribute and removes the worst from among the remaining attributes.

5.4.4 Decision Tree Induction

Decision tree algorithms (e.g., ID3, C4.5, and CART) were originally intended for classification. Decision tree induction constructs a flowchartlike structure where each internal (nonleaf) node denotes a test on an attribute, each branch corresponds to an outcome of the test, and each external (leaf) node denotes a class prediction. At each node, the algorithm chooses the "best" attribute to partition the data into individual classes.

5.5 Data Transformation

Occasionally, data transformation as well as integration is done prior to the data selection approach, especially during data warehousing. Data compression may also be done to produce a lesser representation from the primary data without compromising its reliability. In data conversiondata is converted or combined within a form suitable for data mining *(Provost & Fawcett, 2013)*. information migration strategies include the below:

1. Smoothing is used to remove noise from the data. The methods include grouping, regression and clustering.
2. Character construction (or custom construction), create and add new characters from the given character to help the mining process.
3. Aggregation, which uses content or aggregation for data. For example, monthly and annual figures can be calculated by aggregating daily sales data. This step is often used to create data metrics for data analysis at different levels of abstraction. 4. Normalization, which scales character data to a small range, such as -1.0 to 1.0 or 0.0 to 1.0.

5. Discretization, where the values of numerical attributes (such as age) are replaced with time symbols (such as 0-10, 11-20, etc.) or labels (such as young, old, elder). In contrast, the text will be recursively organized into higher contexts, thus creating a conceptual hierarchy of the number's properties. the conceptual hierarchy of the value chain. Multiple levels of thinking can be defined for the same behavior to suit the needs of different users.
6. A conceptual hierarchy of nominal data is created, where properties such as roads can be generalized to higher-level meanings such as towns or countries. Many hierarchies of nominal properties are implicit in the database schema and can be defined at the schema definition level.

5.6 Data Mining

After applying the all four (1-4) steps next part is the mining of the data and find the different patterns of the data there are some of the techniques in data mining are used for mine the information as follows:

5.6.1 Classification

Assigning items to predefined categories. For example, classifying emails as junk or legitimate
Example Technique: DT, Random Forests, SVM.

5.6.2 Clustering

Classifying similar data points by their attributes without predefined categories. Useful for market segmentation.
Example Algorithms: K-means, Hierarchical Clustering, DBSCAN.

5.6.3 Rule of Association Learning

Determining connections among variables in extensive datasetsFrequently utilized in market basket analysis
Example Algorithms: Apriori Algorithm, FP-Growth.

5.6.4 Anomaly Detection

Identifying unusual data points that do not conform to expected patterns, often used in fraud detection.

Example Algorithms: Isolation Forest, One-Class SVM.

5.6.5 Regression

Predicting a continuous value based on the input features. Used in sales forecasting and risk management.
Example Algorithms: Linear Regression, Polynomial Regression, Regression Trees.

5.6.6 Pattern Evaluation

The evaluation process generally involves the following steps:

- **Define Interestingness Criteria:** Establish the criteria for what constitutes an interesting pattern based on business needs (e.g., high confidence, support).
- **Select Evaluation Metrics:** Choose relevant measures (support, confidence, lift) to assess the discovered patterns.
- **Filter Patterns:** Use the chosen metrics to filter out uninteresting patterns based on predefined thresholds.
- **Validate Patterns:** Ensure that the patterns discovered are not just statistically significant but also make practical sense in the business context.

5.6.7 Knowledge Presentation

Knowledge presentation employs a variety of techniques to convey information effectively:

Data Visualization:
Visuals and Charts: Widely recognized types are pie charts, bar charts, histograms as well as line graphs. These tools help in illustrating trends, distributions, and comparisons.
Heatmaps: Used to represent the density of data points or the strength of relationships between variables.
Dashboards:
Interactive dashboards provide current insights into KPIs. They enable users to visualize data along with explore specific topics of interest.
Reports:

Structured reports summarize findings, methodologies, and implications. These reports can be tailored for different audiences, from technical teams to executive leadership.

Infographics:

Combining graphics with data, infographics provide a visually appealing way to present key insights and findings. They can be particularly effective for summarizing complex data in a concise manner.

Ways 1–4 are various techniques of data pretreatment that prepare data for extraction. The data mining process could interface alongside the stoner or an information repository. The noteworthy patterns represent given for the stoner as well as can saved as new insights in the data repository. An antedating approach presents data mining as a method stage in the process of knowledge discovery, however a critical bone.

since it reveals retired models for analysis. Still, assiduity, across media, and within the exploration terrain, the concept of data mining is frequently utilized to relate for the overall knowledge discovery procedure (maybe since it is less lengthy than knowledge discovery from data). Thus, borrow a general overview of data mining features Data mining involves the exploration of intriguing trends and insights from extensive quantities of information. Potential data sources include databases, information storages, the internet, further informatio depositories, or data that flow into the system stoutly.

5.7 Data Mining Processes a Large Repository of Data Into Insights

A search engine acquires numerous queries every single day. Every search can be regarded as a transaction “in which the user expresses their need for information. The innovative and practical insights Is it possible for a search engine to learn from such a vast dataset of user queries collected over time? Curiously, various patterns observed in User search queries can reveal priceless insights that cannot be acquired through reading isolated data points. To illustrate, Google's Flu Trends utilizes distinct search phrases as measures of flu activity. It established a tight link between the number of users looking for flu-related details and the quantity of people who truly display signs of flu. A consistent pattern is observed in the collective search queries pertaining to flu are compiled. Leveraging combined Google search data, Flu Trends can assess flu activity up to two weeks ahead of traditional systems. This example illustrates how data mining can transform “a vast dataset into insights that can assist in addressing a pressing global issue.

5.7.1 What Types of Data Can Be Extracted?

As a general technology, data mining can be applied to any kind of data as long as the data are meaningful for a target application. The most basic forms of data for mining applications are database data, data warehouse data, and transactional data. The concepts and techniques presented in this book focus on such data. Data mining can also be applied to other forms of data (e.g., data streams, ordered/sequence data, graph or networked data, spatial data, text data, multimedia data, and the WWW). Data mining will certainly continue to embrace new data types as they emerge.

5.8 Types of Analytics

5.8.1 Descriptive Analytics

Descriptive Analytics is the initial step in the Data Science process model. It basically refers to the description of the data and deriving meaningful inference from past data with pattern recognition and data visualization techniques. Basic mathematical and statistical operations are implemented on the past data to generate interpretations. The output is generally presented through customized dashboards for real-time tracking. It typically answers the question "What has happened?" There is a considerable amount of human intervention needed at this stage (Marr, 2017).

Advantages:

- Easily report on ROI by demonstrating how evaluation meets corporate or desired results.
- Early detection of lacks and evaluation difficulties can prevent problems from occurring.
- Identify seekers who need enhanced support, regardless of the number of pupils or employees.
- Detect proficient learners and provide positive feedback or resources.
- Evaluate the effectiveness of course design and learning resources.

Some of the examples of descriptive analytics are mentioned as:

5.8.2 Diagnostic Analytics

Diagnostic analytics is an extension of Descriptive Analytics that asks the problem "Why did it happen?" It probes into the reasons for occurrence, analyzes the underlying causes for such occurrences, and eventually helps increase the accuracy of predictive and prescriptive analytics. It comprises the technique of data discovery and data mining. There is a considerable amount of human intervention needed at this stage also, but slightly lesser than descriptive analytics. For example, if the descriptive analytics states that sales in a few months of the year are very less compared to the other months, diagnostic analytics tries to analyze why the sales have dipped during those few months *(Marr, 2017)*.

5.8.3 Predictive Analytics

Predictive Analytics is about forecasting the future. It comprises model building involving prediction of the future trends, behavior, etc. using forecasting and simulation. It replies to the problem "What will happen?" The output of Predictive Analytics is the probability of a future occurrence. Techniques like association rule mining, clustering, regression, Decision Tree, SVM, Artificial Neural Networks, etc. are most implemented predictive analytics techniques. All these techniques will be discussed in the forthcoming chapters. This type of analytics involves lesser human intervention than descriptive analytics. For example, predictive analytics will give us the probability of a customer defaulting a loan, the probability of a student passing or failing a course, probability of earthquake occurring during a particular period, etc.

Another example is that application for prophetic Analytics has advanced above the world of statisticians and is developing more affordable and available for various demands and diligence, including the area of training and enhancement. For online literacy, predictive analytics is commonly included into the Learning Management System, but it can also be obtained individually as technical application. For the observer, prophetic soothsaying may be as basic as a display panel placed on the main screen after logging in to pierce a class. Assaying information from the previous and present gain, visible markers on the display panel could be used to indicate if the hand was on track with the learning conditions or not.

Advantages:

Workers' training needs may be epitomized by discussing their weaknesses, strengths, and sins; specialized literacy sources and tutoring can be provided to meet particular requirements (Marr, 2017).

Predict what skills and literacy levels will best advance their career trajectories by monitoring and comprehending their professional development. The design of unborn training also benefits from knowing what skills employees require.

By providing intervention assistance before their performance puts them in danger, you may help workers who could be declining before or not achieving their objectives.

When prophetic soothsaying is required, simplified reporting and graphics keep everyone organized.

5.8.4 Prescriptive Analytics

Prescriptive analytics complements both predictive and descriptive analytics. While predictive analytics provides alternatives, it does not guide on the most appropriate alternative. On the other hand, prescriptive analytics involves prescribing some viable alternative action plan about the future and helps in prioritizing among the alternatives. It automates the decision-making process and answers the question "What shall we do?" The best part of prescriptive analytics is the fact that it not only presents the options, but also the consequences of choosing one of the options. Prescriptive Analytics concludes the problem "What will happen if option 1 is chosen compared to option 2?" Recommendation on the best options available is also presented in this form of analytics. Prescriptive analytics techniques are advanced compared to descriptive and predictive techniques and requirerelatively very minimal human intervention. Techniques used are optimization, game theory, and stochastic dynamic programming.

Example: A training director does predictive analysis to determine that the majority of students who lack a specific talent would fail to finish the freshly released course. What can be done? Conventional analytics may now provide support on the issue and assist in determining action plans. Perhaps an algorithm can identify learners who are enrolled in that new module but require specific competence and deliver a robotic suggestion that they seek out a new learning tool to obtain the expertise. The delicacy of a given judgment or suggestion is still limited by the standard of the data and analytical models used. What works for a company's training desires may be ambiguous when implemented in another's training department. Training models should be adapted to every specific scenario as well as demand.

Descriptive vs Predictive vs Prescriptive Analytics

Descriptive Analytics focuses entirely on actual data. Predictive Analytics may be thought of as employing this actual data to construct statistical techniques that read about potential outcomes.

Conventional or Prescriptive Analytics builds on Predictive Analytics by predicting the outcomes of potential read difficulties.

6. APPLICATIONS OF DATA SCIENCE

In recent times, applications of data science are enormous and cut across all domains. A few applications are discussed here. A more detailed description of the applications is presented in Chapter 16. Healthcare is a data-driven industry where the health data of individuals are captured in huge volumes. This gives immense scope for application of data science. Data in this domain are mostly unstructured or semi-structured in the form of clinical information. Analysis of genomic data helps to understand the structure and function of genes. Other typical applications of healthcare include analyzing data for personalized patient care, disease prediction, healthcare cost cutting, etc. In the domain of earth sciences, the earth orbiting satellites deployed by organizations such as NASA capture data, which will help apprehend the earth's weather, temperature, and related information. In the retail industry, data are collected from the point of sales (POS) systems, which will be in the form of bar codes, smart cards, and RFID. These data can beused for segmenting the customers, creating customized promotions, designing store layouts, and generating recommendation engines.

Natural Language Processing (NLP) is one of the founding branches of AI. Text analytics is a subcategory of NLP. It is an analytic technique applied on unstructured and semi-structured data existing in the form of mails, blogs, newspaper articles, data from chat bots, files, etc. Data thus captured are processed to identify the latest trends, pressing issues that the society faces, the latest trending topic in the social media, etc. The sentiment of the people is analyzed using text analytics. It also has many applications in the biomedical and legal domains. Data science applications on crime data began as early as 1829 when an Italian geographer and French statistician first visualized crime data. In this domain, the applications of analytics have taken shape much more dominantly in the second half of the 20th Century. Applications include crime mapping to identify criminal hot spots, predicting the likelihood of occurrence of a crime, and social network analysis to detect organized crime.

7. DATA SCIENCE PROCESS MODEL

The data science approach to any problem solving would involve the following steps as mentioned in,

The initial step is to identify the problem and define the problem statement.
The second step is to gather the data from the different resources. The data should be collected to address the problem in the organization.
The third step is exploratory data analysis. It involves the steps in data preprocessing.
The fourth step is to visualize the data.
The fifth step involves preparing the data for model building. It involves creating new variables or doing factor analysis to decrease the amount of variables.

The final step is model building. The modeling techniques involve supervised and unsupervised machine learning algorithms and advanced ensemble, deep learning, and AI techniques.

SUMMARY

Data Science is the field of understanding data with the help of processes, utilities, and methods that support decision making. The foundation of Data Science was laid by John W. Tukey more than 50 years ago in his article "The Future of Data Analysis." This field has evolved into an undisputable domain in the recent times. Data science has been drawn from many traditional fields of study such as statistics, mathematics, and computer science. Data science is also closely interlinked with many concepts. Big data is any data which is too huge and complex to be processed using traditional processing systems. Business intelligence involves gathering, preprocessing, and presenting such data using data visualization tools and techniques. Data mining is the technology used for processing vast amount of data with a mix of traditional techniques data analysis and complex machine learning algorithms. Artificial Intelligence is the design of smart machines or algorithms that can enact functions or project which commonly needs intelligence of human. Machine learning refers to the modeling techniques where the model learns on its own without human intervention. Deep learning aims at pattern recognition by imitating the human brain.

REFERENCES

Aggarwal, C. C. (2015). *Data Mining: The Textbook*. Springer. DOI: 10.1007/978-3-319-14142-8

Han, J., Pei, J., & Kamber, M. (2011). *Data Mining: Concepts and Techniques*. Morgan Kaufmann.

Hastie, T., Tibshirani, R., & Friedman, J. (2009). *The Elements of Statistical Learning: Data Mining, Inference, and Prediction*. Springer. DOI: 10.1007/978-0-387-84858-7

James, G., Witten, D., Hastie, T., & Tibshirani, R. (2013). *An Introduction to Statistical Learning: With Applications in R*. Springer. DOI: 10.1007/978-1-4614-7138-7

Marr, B. (2017). *Data Strategy: How to Profit from a World of Big Data, Analytics and the Internet of Things*. Kogan Page.

Mitchell, T. M. (1997). *Machine Learning*. McGraw-Hill.

Provost, F., & Fawcett, T. (2013). *Data Science for Business: What You Need to Know about Data Mining and Data-Analytic Thinking*. O'Reilly Media.

Schutt, R., & O'Neil, C. (2013). *Doing Data Science: Straight Talk from the Frontline*. O'Reilly Media.

Witten, I. H., Frank, E., Hall, M. A., & Pal, C. J. (2016). *Data Mining: Practical Machine Learning Tools and Techniques*. Morgan Kaufmann.

Chapter 2
The Role of Data Visualization in Industry Development:
Data Visualization in Industry

Kriushanth Mariadoss
https://orcid.org/0009-0002-0843-1086
St. Joseph's College, India

Ashok Kumar
Skyline University, Nigeria

ABSTRACT

The digital age has ushered in a period of extraordinary data growth, reshaping industries and enabling unprecedented opportunities for innovation and business development. Sectors such as manufacturing, healthcare, finance, and retail stand at the forefront of this transformation, generating and analyzing vast volumes of data. As organizations strive to capitalize on the wealth of information available, data-driven decision-making has emerged as an essential strategy for driving growth, streamlining operations, and fostering innovation. However, the sheer scale and complexity of modern data landscapes often present significant challenges that hinder organizations from fully leveraging their data resources. These challenges range from managing diverse datasets to extracting actionable insights efficiently. In this context, data visualization has become a cornerstone of effective data utilization. It serves not merely as a means of making data visually appealing but as a critical tool for simplifying complex information and enabling stakeholders to interpret and act on data insights.

DOI: 10.4018/979-8-3693-7868-7.ch002

1. INTRODUCTION

In today's rapidly evolving landscape of digital transformation, organizations across various sectors are generating vast quantities of data at an unprecedented pace. Industries such as manufacturing, healthcare, finance, and retail are at the forefront of this data revolution, where data-driven decision-making has emerged as a fundamental pillar for fostering business growth and innovation. However, the immense volume and intricate nature of this data often pose significant challenges, hindering companies from extracting meaningful insights that can drive strategic initiatives.

This is where the significance of data visualization becomes paramount. Data visualization transcends the mere aesthetic presentation of data; it serves as a robust tool that empowers stakeholders to comprehend complex datasets, identify trends, and make informed decisions. By transforming raw data into visual formats such as charts, graphs, and dashboards, organizations can facilitate a clearer understanding of their data landscape, enabling them to communicate insights effectively across teams and departments.

This chapter delves into the critical role of data visualization in business development, highlighting its importance in navigating the complexities of modern data environments. It will explore the myriad benefits that data visualization offers, including enhanced clarity, improved decision-making, and the ability to uncover hidden patterns within data. Additionally, the chapter will address the challenges organizations face in implementing effective data visualization strategies, such as data quality issues, the need for skilled personnel, and the integration of diverse data sources.

Furthermore, the chapter will examine the diverse applications of data visualization across various industries, showcasing real-world examples of how organizations leverage visual tools to drive performance, optimize operations, and enhance customer experiences. By understanding the multifaceted nature of data visualization, businesses can harness its power to not only overcome data-related challenges but also to unlock new opportunities for growth and innovation in an increasingly data-driven world.

2. LITERATURE REVIEW

Data visualization has emerged as a critical tool in both academia and industry, enabling stakeholders to interpret complex data sets efficiently. The role of data visualization in enhancing understanding and decision-making processes across various fields. Kelly et al. (2017) synthesizes research findings that relate to Kelly's work, emphasizing the significance of data visualization in different contexts, including supply chain management, pharmacology, and astronomy, while identifying gaps in current knowledge and suggesting future research directions.

Data Visualization Renarrated: Probing the Role of Renarrating in Data Visualization Reimagining explores the transformative role of renarrating in the context of data visualization. Zhao et al. (2024) review synthesizes existing research findings related to data visualization techniques, tools, and their implications on understanding complex data, while identifying knowledge gaps and suggesting future research directions.

The increasing complexity of financial data necessitates innovative approaches to data analysis and interpretation. Hasan Chy (2023) emphasized the critical role of data visualization in enhancing decision-making processes within the financial sector. This literature review synthesizes existing research findings related to data visualization's impact on financial analysis, uncovering knowledge gaps and suggesting future research directions.

Lande et al. (2024) review synthesizes current research and identifies key trends and gaps in the field of data visualization for strategic decision-making. It incorporates insights from academic sources, industry research, and case studies to provide a comprehensive overview of the topic while maintaining academic rigor and practical relevance.

Ejup et al. (2022) identified that this analysis integrates both established research and contemporary understanding of data visualization's role in modern analytics. I focused on providing a comprehensive yet accessible overview that would be valuable for both technical and non-technical readers. The structure progresses logically from basic concepts to more complex implications, maintaining engagement through varied sentence structures and concrete examples.

Bandi et al. (2017) found that the increasing complexity of data in various fields, particularly in the tech industry, necessitates effective data visualization skills. This research contributed to discourse by developing a course aimed at equipping professionals with the necessary competencies to create impactful data visualizations. This literature review synthesizes key research findings related to data visualization, highlighting the relevance of these insights to the course, identifying knowledge gaps, and suggesting directions for future research.

Ruhi et al. (2024) assessed the impact of digital data visualization tools on strategic decision-making in the Indian advertising industry. It highlights how these tools enhance content generation, audience engagement, and income optimization, as evidenced by case studies of Zomato, Brand Y, and Brand Z. While data visualization significantly improves business initiatives, challenges such as costs and the need for specialized expertise persist. The research offers valuable insights into local customer behavior, suggesting areas for further exploration in broader contexts.

Ravi et al. (2024) highlighted the transformative role of data visualization tools in enhancing business decision-making, including in the advertising industry. These tools have evolved from basic charts to advanced AI-powered platforms, enabling automated generation, pattern recognition, and predictive analytics. This evolution has significantly improved decision speed, accuracy, and user engagement, leading to better ROI and decision-making efficiency. The integration of these tools allows advertisers to analyze data effectively, facilitating informed strategies and optimizing campaign performance.

Data visualization tools play a crucial role in the advertising industry by transforming complex data into visually engaging formats, enabling marketers to uncover trends, correlations, and anomalies. These tools facilitate real-time performance monitoring through dashboards and interactive charts, allowing for prompt responses to market changes. Rewa et al. (2024) elaborated the leveraging data visualization, advertising professionals can make informed decisions that optimize campaigns, enhance customer targeting, and ultimately drive business growth, thereby gaining a competitive edge in a data-driven marketplace.

Abdulla et al. (2024) addred the role of digital data visualization tools in the advertising industry. However, it highlights the importance of data visualization in enhancing decision-making and operational efficiency in sales forecasting, marketing analytics, and financial reporting. Insights from industry professionals indicate that visualizing data can drive business growth, suggesting that similar benefits could be applicable in advertising, although the study does not directly explore this domain.

Groger et al. (2012) underscores the critical role of CityGML as an interoperable framework for semantic 3D city models, enabling their application across various domains. While significant progress has been made in the field, ongoing research is essential to address existing knowledge gaps, particularly concerning the integration of new technologies and the socio-economic implications of 3D city modeling. By focusing on these areas, future research can enhance the effectiveness and applicability of CityGML in urban planning and development.

The integration of AR into manufacturing processes presents significant opportunities for enhancing operational efficiency and supporting workers in complex environments. The research by Mourtzis et al. (2018) contributes to the growing body of literature that advocates for AR's role in the Industry 4.0 paradigm. However, addressing implementation challenges, understanding user dynamics, and exploring the synergies between AR and other emerging technologies are essential for realizing the full potential of AR in industrial applications. Future research should focus on these areas to bridge existing knowledge gaps and facilitate the successful integration of AR into smart manufacturing practices.

The intersection of IoT, GIS, and cybersecurity presents both challenges and opportunities. Elsisi et al. (2021) reviewed underscore the critical role of machine learning in enhancing the security of IoT-enabled GIS systems against cyber-attacks. However, significant knowledge gaps remain that must be addressed through targeted research efforts. By advancing our understanding of the unique vulnerabilities of GIS applications and leveraging emerging technologies, we can develop more resilient systems that safeguard the integrity of spatial data in an increasingly digital landscape.

The bibliometric analysis by Bahuguna et al. (2023) sheds light on the evolving landscape of GHRM research, identifying significant trends and practices that promote sustainability within organizations. As the field continues to grow, it is essential for future research to address the identified gaps, particularly in understanding the mechanisms of GHRM practices and their impact on employee behavior and organizational performance. The integration of stakeholder theory, leadership commitment, and innovative practices will be crucial in advancing GHRM research and its practical applications in promoting environmental sustainability.

The role of data visualization in strategic decision-making is multifaceted, encompassing technical, social, and emotional dimensions. Seyi-Lande et al. (2024) contribute significantly to this discourse, reinforcing the notion that effective visualization is essential for informed decision-making in the tech industry. As organizations continue to navigate complex data landscapes, the integration of tailored visualization approaches and advanced techniques will be crucial for enhancing decision quality and driving organizational success. Future research should aim to address existing knowledge gaps, particularly in the context of organizational culture and the emotional aspects of data interpretation, to fully leverage the potential of data visualization in strategic decision-making.

3. THE IMPORTANCE OF DATA VISUALIZATION

Data visualization plays a crucial role in transforming unstructured data into comprehensible graphical formats such as charts, graphs, maps, and dashboards. This transformation is essential for several reasons, each contributing to the overall effectiveness of data-driven decision-making in organizations.

3.1 Simplifying Complex Data

Big data often presents intricate structures and interdependencies that can be overwhelming. Data visualization simplifies these complexities, allowing decision-makers to extract key insights without sifting through vast amounts of raw data. For instance, heatmaps are commonly employed in web traffic analysis to visualize user behavior patterns. By representing data in a visual format, companies can quickly identify areas of interest or concern, enabling them to optimize website interactions and enhance user experience.

3.2 Enhancing Decision-Making

When data is presented visually, executives can swiftly analyze trends, compare metrics, and forecast future developments. A notable example is Toyota's implementation of real-time data dashboards in its manufacturing facilities. These dashboards provide immediate access to critical information, allowing managers to make prompt decisions that eliminate inefficiencies and enhance product quality. This capability to act quickly based on visualized data can significantly impact operational effectiveness.

3.3 Identifying Trends and Relationships

The ability to quickly identify trends, relationships, and anomalies can provide a competitive advantage, particularly in fast-paced industries like finance and retail. For example, Walmart utilizes data visualization tools to analyze customer shopping patterns. By visualizing this data, Walmart can adjust inventory levels and improve customer service in real time, ensuring that they meet consumer demands effectively and efficiently.

3.4 Improving Communication and Collaboration

Data visualization fosters better communication within organizations by presenting data in an accessible format. This accessibility facilitates collaboration among teams, as stakeholders can easily interpret and discuss the visualized data. A case in point is General Electric's use of Tableau, which allows cross-functional teams to analyze and share operational data seamlessly. This improved communication leads to enhanced efficiency and a more cohesive approach to problem-solving.

3.5 Increasing Data Accessibility

One of the most significant advantages of data visualization is its ability to democratize access to insights. By presenting data in a visual format, non-technical stakeholders can engage with the information without needing specialized technical expertise. For instance, dashboards created with Microsoft’s Power BI are widely used across various industries, enabling business teams to view performance metrics and make informed decisions. This increased accessibility empowers a broader range of employees to contribute to data-driven initiatives, fostering a culture of informed decision-making throughout the organization.

4. BENEFITS OF DATA VISUALIZATION FOR INDUSTRY DEVELOPMENT

Data visualization serves as a vital tool for businesses seeking to optimize performance, enhance customer experience, facilitate innovation, manage risk, and support strategic planning. Each of these areas benefits significantly from the ability to transform complex data into clear, actionable insights.

4.1 Optimizing Performance

Data visualization plays a crucial role in helping businesses manage and optimize their performance. For instance, real-time dashboards in manufacturing settings allow companies to monitor production metrics, machine performance, and equipment uptime. This proactive approach enables organizations to identify and address potential issues before they escalate into significant problems. A notable example is Tesla's Gigafactories, where data analytics are employed to streamline processes and reduce inefficiencies. By visualizing operational data, Tesla can enhance productivity and ensure that manufacturing processes run smoothly.

4.2 Enhancing Customer Experience

Analyzing customer behavior through data visualization allows companies to tailor their products and services to better meet customer needs. Amazon exemplifies this by utilizing advanced data visualization techniques to analyze customer interactions and predict purchasing behavior. By visualizing patterns in customer data, Amazon can enhance the user experience, optimize inventory levels, and ensure that the right products are available at the right time. This customer-centric approach not only improves satisfaction but also drives sales and loyalty.

4.3 Facilitating Innovation

In fields such as engineering and research and development (R&D), data visualization tools enable faster hypothesis testing and the adoption of new ideas. For example, Google's engineers leverage data visualization to accelerate the development of machine learning models. By interpreting complex datasets visually, they can quickly identify trends and insights that guide their innovations. This capability fosters a culture of experimentation and creativity, allowing organizations to stay ahead in competitive markets.

4.4 Risk Management

Data visualization is also essential for risk management, particularly in industries such as finance and insurance. Organizations use data models to assess and mitigate risks effectively. The London Stock Exchange, for instance, employs real-time monitoring tools to detect market anomalies. By visualizing market data, they can identify potential risks and take proactive measures to manage them, ultimately leading to better risk management practices and enhanced financial stability.

4.5 Supporting Strategic Planning

Companies increasingly rely on data visualizations for detailed and realistic strategic planning. Tools like Tableau and Power BI are commonly used to forecast business performance based on historical data, enabling organizations to allocate resources more efficiently. For example, Nike's strategic planning teams utilize data visualization to track sales performance across global markets. By visualizing this data, they can adjust marketing strategies and make informed decisions that align with market demands and consumer behavior.

5. APPLICATIONS OF DATA VISUALIZATION IN KEY INDUSTRIES

Data visualization is a powerful tool utilized across various industries to enhance operational efficiency, improve decision-making, and drive innovation. Here's a closer look at how different sectors leverage data visualization:

Figure 1. Data visualization in key industries

5.1 Manufacturing

In the manufacturing sector, data visualization is essential for tracking processes, analyzing supply chain efficiency, and predicting equipment failures. For instance, Ford Motor Company employs heatmaps and real-time dashboards to identify bottlenecks in its assembly lines. By visualizing production data, Ford can optimize product distribution and minimize downtime, ensuring that manufacturing operations run smoothly and efficiently. This proactive approach allows the company to address issues before they escalate, ultimately improving productivity and reducing costs.

5.2 Healthcare

In healthcare, data visualization plays a critical role in patient care management and disease tracking. During the COVID-19 pandemic, Johns Hopkins University developed an interactive dashboard that provided real-time tracking of global disease rates. This visualization tool enabled governments and health organizations to allocate resources more effectively, monitor the spread of the virus, and implement timely interventions. By presenting complex health data in an accessible format, healthcare professionals could make informed decisions that ultimately saved lives.

5.3 Finance

Financial analysts heavily rely on data visualization to analyze market trends, assess risks, and manage investments. Hedge funds, for example, utilize various visualization techniques such as candlestick charts, heatmaps, and trendlines to make quick investment decisions based on real-time stock market data. These visual tools allow analysts to identify patterns and trends that inform their strategies, enabling them to respond swiftly to market changes and optimize their investment portfolios.

5.4 Retail

Retailers like Target harness data visualization to analyze customer shopping behaviors and enhance inventory management. Real-time sales dashboards provide insights into product performance, allowing retailers to monitor sales trends and adjust inventory levels dynamically. By visualizing customer data, Target can ensure that high-demand products are always in stock, improving customer satisfaction and driving sales. This data-driven approach helps retailers stay competitive in a rapidly changing market.

5.5 Energy and Utilities

The energy sector utilizes data visualization tools to monitor consumption and improve grid efficiency. Companies like Siemens, particularly in the renewable energy industry, rely on data models to manage solar and wind generation. By visualizing energy production and consumption data, these companies can balance supply with real-time demand, optimizing energy distribution and reducing waste. This capability is crucial for enhancing sustainability and ensuring reliable energy delivery.

5.6 Freight and Logistics

In the freight and logistics industry, companies like FedEx and UPS use tracking tools to monitor shipments and optimize their processes. By analyzing data from GPS and inventory tracking systems, these companies can reduce delays and improve the efficiency of their supply chains. Data visualization allows logistics managers to visualize shipment routes, monitor delivery times, and identify potential bottlenecks, enabling them to make informed decisions that enhance operational efficiency and customer satisfaction.

6. APPLICATIONS OF DATA VISUALIZATION IN KEY INDUSTRIES

Data visualization has become an essential tool across various industries, significantly enhancing operations and decision-making processes. By transforming complex data into visual formats, organizations can gain insights that drive efficiency, improve performance, and foster informed decision-making. Here's a detailed look at how data visualization is applied in different sectors:

6.1 Manufacturing

In the manufacturing industry, data visualization is crucial for tracking production processes, analyzing supply chain efficiency, and predicting machine failures. Tools such as heat maps and real-time dashboards enable manufacturers to visualize key performance indicators (KPIs) and identify bottlenecks in the production line. For example, a heat map can highlight areas where production is lagging, allowing managers to allocate resources more effectively and optimize workflows. By predicting machine failures through data analysis, manufacturers can schedule maintenance proactively, reducing downtime and enhancing overall productivity.

6.2 Health Management

In healthcare, data visualization plays a vital role in patient care management, disease tracking, and operational productivity. By visualizing patient profiles and health data, healthcare providers can make more accurate diagnoses and develop tailored treatment plans. For instance, visual analytics can help identify trends in patient outcomes, enabling clinicians to adjust their approaches based on real-time data. Additionally, visualizing operational metrics can improve clinical management by highlighting areas for improvement, ultimately leading to better patient care and resource utilization.

6.3 Finance

The financial sector heavily relies on data visualization to analyze market trends, evaluate investment opportunities, and assess risk. Tools such as candlestick charts, heat maps, and trend lines provide traders and financial analysts with visual representations of market data, allowing them to make informed decisions quickly. For example, a candlestick chart can illustrate price movements over time, helping analysts identify patterns and potential entry or exit points for investments. By visualizing risk factors and market dynamics, financial professionals can enhance their strategies and respond effectively to market fluctuations.

6.4 Retail

Retailers utilize data visualization to gain insights into customer behavior, track inventory levels, and analyze sales trends. Dashboards that display sales data, product performance, and customer demographics enable retailers to make data-driven marketing and sales decisions. For instance, visualizing sales trends over time can help retailers identify peak shopping periods and adjust inventory accordingly. By understanding customer preferences through visual analytics, retailers can tailor their offerings and marketing strategies to enhance customer engagement and drive sales.

6.5 Energy and Resource Consumption

In the energy sector, data visualization is critical for monitoring energy consumption, determining maintenance needs, and improving grid efficiency. Visual analytics are particularly important for managing renewable energy sources such as solar and wind. By visualizing energy production data, companies can forecast output and balance supply with real-time demand. For example, a dashboard that displays energy generation from solar panels can help operators optimize energy distribution and reduce waste. This capability is essential for enhancing sustainability and ensuring reliable energy delivery.

6.6 Logistics and Supply Chain Management

Logistics companies leverage data visualization to optimize delivery routes, track shipments, and enhance overall service efficiency. Tools such as heat maps and flow charts can highlight areas of delay or inefficiency within the supply chain. For instance, a heat map can visualize shipment delays across different regions, allowing logistics managers to identify problem areas and implement corrective actions. By analyzing data visually, logistics companies can streamline operations, reduce costs, and improve customer satisfaction through timely deliveries.

7. TOOLS AND TECHNOLOGIES IN DATA VISUALIZATION

The evolution of data visualization in various industries is significantly influenced by a range of powerful tools and technologies. These tools enable organizations to transform complex data into meaningful visual representations, facilitating better insights and decision-making. Here's an in-depth look at some of the key tools driving this evolution:

7.1 Tableau

Tableau is a leading data visualization tool that provides users with the ability to create interactive dashboards and complex visualizations from various data sources. Its user-friendly interface allows individuals, regardless of their technical expertise, to explore and analyze data effectively. For instance, Tesla utilizes Tableau to track and optimize the design of its electric cars. By visualizing data related to design processes, performance metrics, and customer feedback, Tesla can make informed decisions that enhance product development and innovation. Tableau's capabilities in handling large datasets and providing real-time insights make it a valuable asset for organizations aiming to leverage data for strategic advantage.

7.2 Power BI

Microsoft Power BI is a widely recognized business analytics tool known for its seamless integration with other Microsoft products, such as Excel and Azure. This integration makes Power BI particularly popular among businesses that already use Microsoft solutions. Companies like Accenture rely on Power BI to track project performance and customer engagement metrics. The tool allows users to create interactive reports and dashboards that provide a comprehensive view of business operations. With its robust data modeling capabilities and user-friendly interface, Power BI empowers organizations to make data-driven decisions and monitor key performance indicators (KPIs) effectively.

7.3 D3.js

D3.js is a powerful JavaScript library specifically designed for creating custom data visualizations on web platforms. It allows developers to bind data to the Document Object Model (DOM) and apply data-driven transformations to the document. The New York Times, for example, has utilized D3.js to create unique graphics and interactive visualizations for its data journalism projects. By leveraging D3.js, the publication can present complex data in an engaging and accessible manner, enhancing reader understanding and interaction. D3.js is particularly valued for its flexibility and ability to create highly customized visualizations that can adapt to various data types and formats.

7.4 QlikView

QlikView is a dynamic data analysis and visualization platform optimized for speed and performance. It enables users to explore data in real time, making it an ideal choice for organizations that require quick insights for decision-making. ING Bank, for instance, uses QlikView to analyze financial data in real time, allowing for faster and more informed decisions. The platform's associative data model enables users to navigate through data intuitively, uncovering hidden insights and relationships. QlikView's focus on speed and interactivity makes it a valuable tool for businesses operating in fast-paced environments where timely information is critical.

7.5 Google Looker Studio

Google Looker Studio is a free tool that allows users to create interactive dashboards and reports from multiple data sources. Its accessibility and ease of use make it particularly appealing to startups and small businesses looking for cost-effective solutions to visualize their marketing and sales operations. By integrating with various Google services, such as Google Analytics and Google Sheets, Looker Studio enables users to consolidate data and create comprehensive visual reports. This capability helps organizations track performance metrics, analyze trends, and make data-driven decisions without the need for extensive technical expertise.

The tools and technologies driving the evolution of data visualization are transforming how organizations interact with data. By providing intuitive interfaces, powerful analytics capabilities, and customizable visualizations, these tools empower businesses to harness the full potential of their data. As industries continue to embrace data-driven decision-making, the importance of effective data visualization tools will only grow, enabling organizations to gain insights, improve performance, and stay competitive in an increasingly data-centric world.

8. CASE STUDIES OF DATA VISUALIZATION IMPACT

Data visualization has become a pivotal strategy for organizations across various sectors, enabling them to analyze data effectively and make informed decisions. Here are some detailed case studies that illustrate how different companies leverage data visualization to enhance their operations and customer experiences:

Case Study 1: Walmart – Enhancing the Customer Experience With Data Visualization

Walmart employs a variety of data visualization techniques to track customer behavior and improve inventory management. By utilizing real-time dashboards, Walmart can visualize sales data and identify trends in customer preferences. This allows the company to adjust inventory levels proactively, ensuring that popular products are always in stock while minimizing excess inventory. As a result, Walmart has achieved a more efficient supply chain, reduced costs, and significantly improved customer satisfaction. The ability to respond quickly to changing customer demands has solidified Walmart's position as a leader in the retail industry.

Case Study 2: Johns Hopkins University – COVID-19 Global Dashboard

During the COVID-19 pandemic, Johns Hopkins University developed one of the most widely recognized data visualization dashboards to track the spread of the virus. This tool provided real-time updates on global infection rates, mortality statistics, and recovery data, assisting public health officials and the general public in understanding the pandemic's impact. The dashboard's clear visualizations enabled users to grasp complex data quickly, facilitating informed decision-making regarding public health responses. The success of this dashboard highlighted the importance of data visualization in crisis management and public health communication.

Case Study 3: General Electric – Real-Time Industrial Analysis

General Electric (GE) utilizes data visualization tools through its Predix platform to monitor industrial equipment in real time. This platform visualizes machine performance metrics, predicts potential machine failures, and provides maintenance recommendations. By leveraging these insights, GE can reduce costly downtime across its global operations, enhance equipment reliability, and optimize maintenance schedules. The use of data visualization in this context not only improves operational efficiency but also contributes to significant cost savings for the company.

Case Study 4: Netflix – Content Recommendation System

Netflix employs advanced data visualization techniques to analyze viewer preferences and behavior. By visualizing data related to user interactions, such as viewing history and ratings, Netflix can develop personalized content recommendations for its subscribers. This data-driven approach has been instrumental in enhancing user engagement and satisfaction, leading to increased subscription retention rates. The ability to visualize complex data patterns allows Netflix to tailor its content offerings effectively, ensuring that users receive recommendations that align with their interests.

Case Study 5: Airbnb – Dynamic Pricing Strategy

Airbnb uses data visualization to optimize its dynamic pricing strategy. By analyzing market trends, local events, and competitor pricing, Airbnb visualizes data to determine optimal pricing for its listings. This approach allows hosts to adjust their rates in real time based on demand fluctuations, maximizing occupancy rates and revenue. The visual analytics provided by Airbnb's platform empower hosts to make informed pricing decisions, ultimately enhancing the overall user experience and increasing profitability for both hosts and the company.

Case Study 6: FedEx – Route Optimization

FedEx leverages data visualization tools to optimize its delivery routes and improve operational efficiency. By visualizing data related to traffic patterns, weather conditions, and package delivery times, FedEx can identify the most efficient routes for its delivery vehicles. This data-driven approach not only reduces delivery times but also minimizes fuel consumption and operational costs. The ability to visualize real-time data allows FedEx to respond quickly to changing conditions, ensuring timely deliveries and enhancing customer satisfaction.

9. CHALLENGES IN DATA VISUALIZATION

Data visualization is a powerful tool for interpreting complex datasets and facilitating informed decision-making. However, several challenges can arise in the process of creating and utilizing visualizations. Here's an elaboration on the existing challenges, along with additional ones that organizations may face:

9.1 Data Quality Problems

Poor data quality is one of the most significant challenges in data visualization. Inaccurate, incomplete, or outdated data can lead to misleading graphics, which in turn can result in erroneous decisions. For instance, in the healthcare sector, inaccurate health information can compromise patient safety if it leads to misdiagnoses or inappropriate treatments. Organizations must implement robust data governance practices to ensure data integrity, accuracy, and consistency before visualizing it. This includes regular data audits, validation processes, and the establishment of clear data entry protocols.

9.2 Oversimplification

While data visualization aims to simplify complex information, oversimplification can obscure critical insights. For example, in financial markets, reducing complex market data to basic charts may hide important nuances, such as volatility or underlying trends. This can lead to risky decisions based on an incomplete understanding of the data. To mitigate this challenge, it is essential to strike a balance between simplicity and detail, ensuring that visualizations convey the necessary context and complexity without overwhelming the audience.

9.3 Misinterpretation of Graphics

Complex or poorly structured graphics can lead to misinterpretation, as they may not effectively communicate the intended message. For instance, if financial forecasts are presented in a convoluted manner, stakeholders may perceive them as inaccurate, resulting in incorrect financial projections. To address this issue, organizations should prioritize clarity in their visualizations, using intuitive designs and clear labeling. Additionally, providing context and explanations alongside graphics can help guide interpretation and reduce the risk of misunderstanding.

9.4 Security and Privacy Issues

The visualization of sensitive information, such as personal health records or financial data, poses significant security and privacy risks. If such data is shared across departments without adequate safeguards, it can lead to unauthorized access and potential breaches of confidentiality. Organizations must implement strict data security measures, including encryption, access controls, and compliance with regulations such as HIPAA or GDPR. Additionally, training employees on data privacy best practices is crucial to mitigate risks associated with data visualization.

9.5 Technical Barriers

Advanced data visualization models often require specialized technical expertise, which can limit their adoption in organizations that lack such skills. This can create a gap between data scientists and decision-makers, hindering effective communication and collaboration. To overcome this challenge, organizations should invest in training programs to upskill employees in data visualization tools and techniques. Additionally, user-friendly visualization platforms can empower non-technical users to create and interpret visualizations without needing extensive technical knowledge.

9.6 Cognitive Overload

When too much information is presented in a single visualization, it can lead to cognitive overload for the viewer. This can make it difficult for individuals to extract meaningful insights from the data. For example, a dashboard filled with numerous charts and metrics may overwhelm users, causing them to miss critical trends or anomalies. To combat cognitive overload, it is essential to prioritize the most relevant information and design visualizations that guide the viewer's attention to key insights. Utilizing techniques such as progressive disclosure, where information is revealed gradually, can also help manage cognitive load.

9.7 Lack of Standardization

Inconsistent visualization practices across an organization can lead to confusion and miscommunication. Different teams may use varying formats, colors, and scales, making it challenging to compare data effectively. Establishing standardized guidelines for data visualization can help ensure consistency and clarity across all visual outputs. This includes defining color schemes, chart types, and labeling conventions, which can enhance understanding and facilitate collaboration among teams.

9.8 Resistance to Change

Organizations may face resistance to adopting data visualization tools and practices, particularly if employees are accustomed to traditional reporting methods. This resistance can stem from a lack of understanding of the benefits of data visualization or fear of new technology. To address this challenge, organizations should promote a data-driven culture by demonstrating the value of data visualization through training sessions, workshops, and success stories. Encouraging a mindset shift towards embracing data as a strategic asset can facilitate smoother adoption of visualization practices.

While data visualization offers significant benefits for decision-making and insight generation, it is essential to recognize and address the challenges that can arise. By implementing best practices in data quality, visualization design, security, and training, organizations can enhance the effectiveness of their data visualizations and ultimately drive better outcomes. As the reliance on data continues to grow, overcoming these challenges will be crucial for organizations seeking to leverage data visualization as a strategic advantage.

10. FUTURE TRENDS IN DATA VISUALIZATION

As technology continues to evolve at an unprecedented pace, data visualization is poised to become increasingly immersive, interactive, and seamlessly integrated into daily business processes. This evolution will not only enhance the way organizations interpret and utilize data but also empower users to make informed decisions with greater confidence and clarity. The upcoming features in data visualization promise to redefine the landscape, making it more intuitive and user-friendly. Here are some key advancements to look forward to:

10.1 Integration of AI and Machine Learning

The integration of artificial intelligence (AI) and machine learning (ML) with data visualization is a transformative development that will significantly enhance the analytical capabilities of organizations. By leveraging advanced algorithms, businesses can automate the generation of insights, enabling predictive analytics that forecast trends and outcomes based on historical data. This capability allows organizations to identify patterns and anomalies that may not be immediately apparent, thereby improving the decision-making process. For instance, in the retail sector, AI can analyze customer purchasing behaviors to suggest inventory adjustments, while in healthcare, it can predict patient outcomes based on treatment data. As AI and ML technologies continue to advance, the ability to visualize complex data relationships will become more sophisticated, allowing users to explore various scenarios and make informed decisions with greater accuracy. This integration will ultimately lead to more proactive strategies and a competitive edge in the marketplace.

10.2 Augmented and Virtual Reality

Augmented reality (AR) and virtual reality (VR) technologies are set to revolutionize data visualization by offering immersive, 3D visual experiences that engage users in unprecedented ways. These technologies allow users to interact with data in a spatial context, enabling them to explore complex datasets through dynamic visualizations that traditional 2D formats cannot achieve. For example, in urban planning, stakeholders can use VR to visualize city layouts and infrastructure projects, facilitating better collaboration and understanding of potential impacts. AR can overlay data visualizations onto real-world environments, providing context and enhancing decision-making in fields such as manufacturing and logistics. As AR and VR technologies become more accessible and affordable, they will transform how organizations present and interact with data, making it more engaging, intuitive, and impactful. This immersive experience will not only enhance user engagement but also foster deeper insights and understanding of the data being analyzed.

10.3 Real-time Data Visualization

The demand for real-time data analytics is growing exponentially, particularly in industries such as finance, logistics, and healthcare, where timely decision-making is critical. Improvements in real-time data streaming and imaging technologies will continue to drive the industry forward, enabling organizations to rely on dashboards that provide live updates and insights. This capability allows decision-makers to respond swiftly to changing conditions, ensuring that they remain agile in a fast-paced environment. For instance, in financial markets, traders can monitor live stock prices and market trends, enabling them to make quick investment decisions. In logistics, real-time tracking of shipments can optimize delivery routes and improve customer satisfaction. As the need for immediacy increases, real-time data visualization will become a standard expectation across various sectors, enhancing operational efficiency and responsiveness. This shift will empower organizations to make data-driven decisions that are timely and relevant, ultimately leading to improved outcomes and performance.

10.4 Natural Language Processing (NLP)

The integration of natural language processing (NLP) into data visualization tools will significantly enhance user interaction and accessibility. By allowing users to interact with visualizations through voice commands or natural language queries, data will become more approachable for non-technical users. This democratization of data access means that individuals without a background in data analysis can easily ask questions and receive insights in a format they understand. For example, a marketing manager could simply ask, “What were our top-performing campaigns last quarter?” and receive a visual representation of the data without needing to navigate complex software. This capability will empower more stakeholders within an organization to engage with data, fostering a culture of data-driven decision-making and collaboration. As NLP technology continues to improve, the ability to communicate with data in a conversational manner will further enhance user experience and satisfaction.

10.5 Increased Customization

As technology advances, data management tools are becoming more flexible and user-centered, leading to enhanced customization options. Future data visualization tools will allow users to modify and design visual representations according to their individual preferences and needs. This could include options such as changing color schemes, adjusting layouts, selecting specific data filters, or choosing from a variety of chart types. Users will also have the ability to integrate multiple data sources, create dynamic inferences, and leverage real-time updates. This level of customization ensures that visualizations are not just generic but are carefully designed to effectively communicate the specific insights that different users are looking for. By tailoring visualizations to meet the unique requirements of various audiences, organizations can enhance the relevance and impact of their data presentations, making them more appropriate, practical, and actionable. This personalized approach will not only improve user engagement but also facilitate better understanding and retention of information.

10.6 Collaborative Visualization

The future of data visualization will also see an increase in collaborative features that allow teams to work together in real-time. As remote work becomes more prevalent, tools that enable multiple users to interact with and edit visualizations simultaneously will be essential. This collaborative approach fosters teamwork and ensures that diverse perspectives are considered in the analysis process. For instance, marketing teams can collectively analyze campaign performance, while product development teams can visualize user feedback and iterate on designs. By facilitating collaboration, organizations can harness the collective intelligence of their teams, leading to more comprehensive insights and better decision-making. This collaborative environment will not only enhance the quality of analysis but also promote a culture of shared knowledge and continuous improvement.

10.7 Enhanced Data Storytelling

Data storytelling will become a critical component of data visualization, as organizations seek to convey insights in a compelling and relatable manner. By combining visual elements with narrative techniques, data storytellers can guide audiences through complex datasets, highlighting key findings and implications. This approach not only makes data more engaging but also helps to contextualize information, making it easier for stakeholders to understand the significance of the data. As organizations recognize the power of storytelling in data communication, we can expect to see a greater emphasis on crafting narratives that resonate with audiences and drive action. This focus on storytelling will enable organizations to connect emotionally with their data, fostering a deeper understanding and commitment to data-driven initiatives.

The future of data visualization is bright, with advancements in technology set to create more immersive, interactive, and user-friendly experiences. By integrating AI, AR/VR, real-time analytics, NLP, and enhanced customization, organizations will be better equipped to harness the power of their data. As these features become more prevalent, data visualization will not only enhance decision-making but also foster a culture of data-driven insights across all levels of an organization. Embracing these innovations will be crucial for businesses looking to stay competitive in an increasingly data-centric world. Ultimately, the evolution of data visualization will empower organizations to unlock the full potential of their data, driving growth, innovation, and success in the years to come. By prioritizing these advancements, organizations can ensure that they are not only keeping pace with technological changes but also leveraging them to create meaningful impact and value.

11. CONCLUSION

Data visualization plays a transformative role in business development, serving as a critical bridge between raw data and actionable insights. In an era where data is generated at an unprecedented rate, the ability to effectively visualize this information is paramount for organizations seeking to unlock its full potential. By translating complex datasets into intuitive visual formats, businesses can enhance their decision-making processes, improve operational efficiency, and ultimately gain a competitive advantage in their respective markets.

With the advent of advanced tools and technologies, the transformation of data into actionable insights has become more accessible than ever. These tools enable organizations to sift through vast amounts of information, identifying patterns, trends, and anomalies that may otherwise go unnoticed. For instance, businesses can utilize sophisticated data visualization software to create interactive dashboards that provide real-time insights into key performance indicators (KPIs). This capability allows decision-makers to monitor their operations continuously, enabling them to respond swiftly to changing conditions and make informed choices that drive growth.

As the demand for real-time data and communication tools continues to rise, the future of data visualization promises to drive further innovation across industries. Organizations are increasingly recognizing the importance of timely insights in maintaining a competitive edge. In sectors such as finance, logistics, and healthcare, where rapid decision-making is critical, the ability to visualize data in real-time can significantly impact outcomes. For example, financial institutions can leverage real-time data visualization to monitor market fluctuations and adjust investment strategies accordingly, while logistics companies can track shipments and optimize delivery routes based on live data feeds.

Moreover, the integration of emerging technologies such as artificial intelligence (AI), machine learning (ML), augmented reality (AR), and natural language processing (NLP) into data visualization tools is set to revolutionize the way businesses interact with their data. AI and ML can automate the analysis process, providing predictive insights that help organizations anticipate future trends and make proactive decisions. AR and VR technologies offer immersive experiences that allow users to explore data in 3D environments, enhancing understanding and engagement. Meanwhile, NLP enables users to query data using natural language, making it easier for non-technical stakeholders to access and interpret information.

The future of data visualization is not just about improving the aesthetics of data presentation; it is about creating a more collaborative and inclusive environment for data-driven decision-making. Enhanced customization options will allow users to tailor visualizations to their specific needs, ensuring that insights are relevant and actionable. This level of personalization empowers teams to engage with data more effectively, fostering a culture of collaboration and shared knowledge.

In conclusion, data visualization is a powerful tool that plays a pivotal role in business development. By transforming complex data into clear, actionable insights, organizations can improve efficiency, enhance decision-making, and gain a competitive advantage. As the demand for real-time data and innovative communication tools continues to grow, the future of data visualization holds immense potential for driving innovation across industries. Embracing these advancements will enable businesses to harness the power of their data, unlocking new opportunities for growth and success in an increasingly data-driven world. Ultimately, organizations that prioritize effective data visualization will be better positioned to navigate the complexities of the modern business landscape and leverage insights for strategic advantage.

REFERENCES

Abdulla, A., Naim, A., Muniasamy, A., Mohammed, A. B., Bilfaqih, S. M., & Sabahath, A. (2024). Optimizing business insights data visualization applications in sales forecasting, marketing analytics, and financial reporting. *Advances in Business Information Systems and Analytics*, 103–124. DOI: 10.4018/979-8-3693-6537-3.ch006

Bahuguna, P. C., Srivastava, R., & Tiwari, S. (2023). Two-decade journey of green human resource management research: A bibliometric analysis. *Benchmarking*, 30(2), 585–602. DOI: 10.1108/BIJ-10-2021-0619

Bandi, A., & Fellah, A. (2017). Crafting a data visualization course for the tech industry. *Journal of Computing Sciences in Colleges*, 33(2), 46–56.

Chy, M. K. H., & Buadi, O. N. (2023). Role of data visualization in finance. *American Journal of Industrial and Business Management*, 13(08), 841–856. DOI: 10.4236/ajibm.2023.138047

Elsisi, M., Tran, M.-Q., Mahmoud, K., Mansour, D.-E. A., Lehtonen, M., & Darwish, M. M. F. (2021). Towards secured online monitoring for digitalized GIS against cyber-attacks based on IoT and machine learning. *IEEE Access : Practical Innovations, Open Solutions*, 9, 78415–78427. DOI: 10.1109/ACCESS.2021.3083499

Gröger, G., & Plümer, L. (2012). CityGML – Interoperable semantic 3D city models. [ISPRS]. *ISPRS Journal of Photogrammetry and Remote Sensing*, 71, 12–33. DOI: 10.1016/j.isprsjprs.2012.04.004

Gurram, R. T. (2024). The evolution of data visualization tools and their impact on business decision-making : A historical analysis. *International Journal of Scientific Research in Computer Science. Engineering and Information Technology*, 10(6), 467–473. DOI: 10.32628/CSEIT24106192

Kelly, J. P. (2017). Televizual: Data visualization in industry and academia. DOI: 10.59350/hz092-wt871

Lal, R., Deb, N., & Gogoi, D. M. (2024). Assessing the role of digital data visualization tools in the advertising industry for informed business decision-making. In *Advances in Business Information Systems and Analytics* (pp. 189–208). DOI: 10.4018/979-8-3693-6537-3.ch009

Lande, O. B. S., Johnson, E., Adeleke, G. S., Amajuoyi, C. P., & Simpson, B. D. (2024). The role of data visualization in strategic decision making: Case studies from the tech industry. *Computer Science & IT Research Journal, 5*(6), 1374–1390. DOI: 10.51594/csitrj.v5i6.1223

Mourtzis, D., Zogopoulos, V., Katagis, I., & Lagios, P. (2018). Augmented Reality based Visualization of CAM Instructions towards Industry 4.0 paradigm: A CNC Bending Machine case study. *Procedia CIRP*, 70, 368–373. DOI: 10.1016/j.procir.2018.02.045

Panghal, R. (2024). The role of data visualization in decision making – case of D-mart. *International Journal For Multidisciplinary Research*, 6(3), 19630. Advance online publication. DOI: 10.36948/ijfmr.2024.v06i03.19630

Rustemi, E., & Tahiri, M. (2022). *The role of visualization in understanding data*. 28-31. DOI: 10.5281/ZENODO.7125689

Seyi-Lande, B., Johnson, O., Adeleke, E., Amajuoyi, G. S., & Simpson, C. P. (2024). The role of data visualization in strategic decision making: Case studies from the tech industry. *Computer Science & IT Research Journal*, 5(6), 1374–1390. DOI: 10.51594/csitrj.v5i6.1223

Zhao, Y., & Dyer, E. B. (2024, June 10). Data visualization renarrated: Probing the role of renarrating in data visualization reimagining. *Proceedings of the 18th International Conference of the Learning Sciences - ICLS 2024*. DOI: 10.22318/icls2024.847189

Chapter 3
An Effective Data Visualization Overview and Impact

Vijayalakshmi P. S.
https://orcid.org/0000-0003-4561-1908
Dr. N.G.P. Arts and Science College, India

Poorana Senthilkumar S.
https://orcid.org/0000-0001-5731-2337
Dr. N.G.P. Arts and Science College, India

Rajan John
College of Engineering and Computer Science, Jazan University, Saudi Arabia

ABSTRACT

The modern world generates a tremendous amount of data every day. Additionally, when evaluating data for specific trends, it can occasionally be challenging to spot patterns of the data left in the raw format. This is avoided by the use of data visualization. This data visualization identifies it easier to understand, view, and interpret the data by providing a clean, organized graphical visualization of the data. When working in data, it might be difficult to completely explain the information it is only provided in tabular format. When compared to a table and a CSV file holding the data, this makes correlations, patterns, and trends simpler to observe. In this chapter, the authors show how to visualize data using Python and several modules. The primary aim is to access high data and interpret it to show emerging areas and patterns more quickly. This is mainly important because it comes in massive amounts of information and data analysis, as the big amount of data can be debilitating in the absence of efficient visualization methods.

DOI: 10.4018/979-8-3693-7868-7.ch003

I.INTRODUCTION

The process of turning information into visually appealing elements, such as graphs or maps, is known as data visualization. This makes it easier to draw conclusions from the data. Finding correlations, trends, and outliers in big data sets is the primary goal of data visualization. Statistics graphics, information visualization, and information graphics are frequently used interchangeably. The skills of data-centric practitioners in data visualization are a reflection of recent advancements in computer systems and highly visual design concepts. They also produce insightful and relevant outcomes that support decision-making (Asamoah, 2022). Data visualization is one step in implementing the scientific method, which states that findings can only be made from material that has been collected, examined, and modelled. One element of data architecture presentation is data visualization, which is a field dedicated to finding, locating, altering, preparing, and communicating data in an efficient manner. Business schools worldwide can determine which software applications are the most valuable to devote time and money in to prepare their students for employment opportunities by using the knowledge gathered by experimenting with various visualization tools (Diamond & Mattia, 2017). The visualization of data is crucial for almost all professional areas. CEOs use it, researchers use it to research advancements in intelligent machines (AI), and instructors use it to display exam results to students. It is also essential to big data initiatives. As businesses accumulated massive volumes of data, they needed a way to quickly and easily get an assessment of their data. Visualization tools were the most effective in providing meaningful information. Advanced analytics need visualization for similar reasons. It is also necessary for big data projects. Businesses required a method to swiftly and simply obtain an evaluation of their data as they gathered enormous amounts of it. The best techniques for delivering insightful data were those that involved visualization. Visualization is necessary for advanced analytics for similar reasons. A scientist who works with data must be able to analyses the outputs of complex machine learning as well predictive analytics algorithms in order to track outcomes and make sure the models are operating as intended. Data represented graphically or pictorially, which makes it easier to understand and interpret (Srivastava, n.d.). looked into the application of data iteration in production-ready machine learning models. The design of data plays an equally important role in machine learning as that of models, serving as a source of inspiration for research on producing data and future tool development (Hohman et al., 2020). Data visualization turns complex data sets into aesthetically pleasing representations that are considerably easier for the average individual to understand. This may entail a variety of visual assistance, such as: pie, line, Bar, and many types of diagrams are available.

Graphs: Histograms and scatter plots etc.,

Maps: Heat maps an d geographical maps, etc.

The interactive platforms are dashboards that integrate many visual aids.

Increasing access to information and interpretation is the primary goal of visualization, allowing users to identify relationships, developments, and outliers more rapidly. This is particularly important for big data because the sheer volume of information accessible can be crippling in the absence of effective visualization techniques. Data visualization is a powerful tool for enhancing understanding and communication of complex data. It entails putting data into a graphical or visual format to facilitate comprehension and interpretation (Sadiku et al., 2016; Wang et al., 2020; Ward, Grinstein, & Keim, 2015). In this chapter, discussed about interpretation data Visualization in python libraries , and also explored the benefits, merits, demerits of visualizing data.

II. IMPORTANCE OF DATA VISUALIZATION

Every kind of data visualization tool has merits and demerits of its own, and the appropriate tool for a given use case will rely on the user's experience level and requirements Pavlopoulos, Wegener, & Schneider, 2008; Parbat, Dwivedi, & Vyas, 2010). Visualization provides an easy and better way to give information around the world by using visual information. Even though business experts come from a variety of backgrounds and domains, visualizations should be accessible to all. When company insights are visualized, employees can act upon them and make decisions more readily. These are but a handful of the many kinds of data visualization methods that are out there (Cao & Cui, 2016; Furmanova et al., 2020). The type of data being analyzed, the conclusions that are wanted, and the intended audience will all influence the data visualization technique selection. In business, data visualization is mostly used to data evaluation, share insights, and make defensible decisions. In order to comprehend consumer preferences, competition activity Market analysis (Ajibade & Adediran, 2016) comprises data analysis as well as market trends. The technique of classifying consumers based on shared characteristics such as actions, preferences, and demographics is known as customer segmentation (Kumar & Belwal, 2017). Network diagrams, graphs with bars, line charts, and scatter plots are a few of the various information visualization techniques and instruments used in customer segmentation (Fiaz et al., 2016). These are employed for the purpose of visualizing client behavior and demographics in addition to connections among various customer categories. Visualizations have many applications in business. Here are a couple such examples:

- They assist in determining the factors affecting the behavior of consumers.

- They identify products and services that need to be improved.
- They improve stakeholders' recall of data.
- They are able to project income or sales quantities. • They help businesses choose the ideal times and places to display specific products.

In the area of social sciences, data visualization is frequently employed (Berson & Berso, 2009) for data analysis and insight sharing. Bar charts, graphs of lines, scatter graphs, and heat maps are some of the data visualization techniques used in survey analysis, which is the process of examining survey data to understand attitudes, habits, and opinions. Charts with lines, graphs of bars, and dashboard application are some of the data visualization tools used in trend analysis (Womack, 2014), which is the process of analyzing data to identify trends and patterns across time.

2.1 Types of Data for Visualization

Accurate data in visualization is important to market research and it allows for the visualization of numerical as well as categorical information, which boosts insights and lowers the possibility of analysis patterns. Thus, the following categories apply to data visualization:

Numerical Data
The categorical Data

Figure 1. Data visualization categories

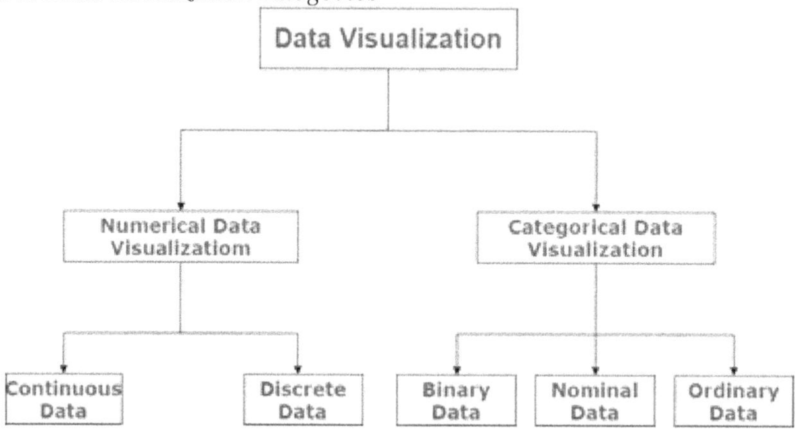

2.2 Types of Data Visualization Techniques

A strong tool for converting complex data into visually clear representations is data visualization. Data visualization can be accomplished through a variety of methods, each having unique advantages and uses.

1. The bar Charts: A traditional method, bar charts are useful for comparing various categories or showing changes over a period of time. They display data values using either vertical or horizontal bars.
2. Line Diagrams: Line charts, which connect data points with lines to display trends and patterns across time, make it simple to see relationships and fluctuations.
3. Pie Diagrams: These circular diagrams show how every group contributes to the total by dividing data into parts according to their proportions.
4. Scatter Plots: Plotting individual data points onto a graph to reveal patterns or clusters is a useful technique for examining relationships between variables.
5. Heat Map: Heat maps make it easy to quickly identify high and low values inside a dataset by using color changes to display variables in a matrix as well as table format.
6. Geographic Maps: By employing colored zones or markers to display information on a map layout, geographic maps facilitate the visualization of geographical data.
7. Tree maps: To effectively depict hierarchical structures and illustrate the relative proportions of various components, tree maps use nested rectangles inside bigger rectangles.
8. Network Diagrams: Using nodes to represent entities and edges to indicate links, these diagrams are ideal for showing relationships between elements such as social networks with organizational hierarchies.

Depending on the type of dataset and the sought insights, each technique has a distinct function.

Figure 2. Data Visualization in Analytics

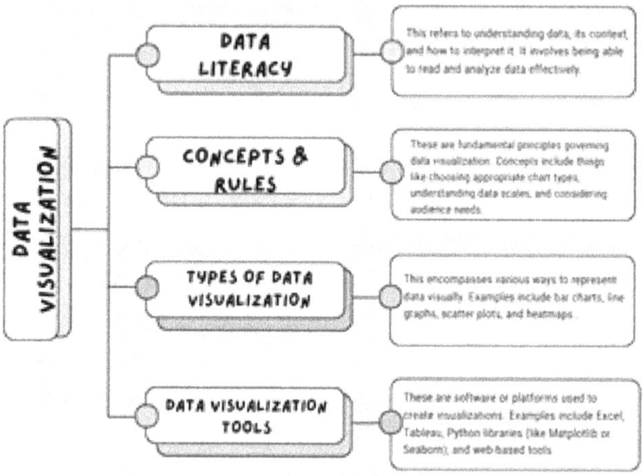

2.3 Efficient Data Visualization

The effectiveness and impact of the evaluation can be increased by following a few guidelines for data visualization. Here are some important points to remember:

1. Know your audience: Before creating any visualizations, it's critical to ascertain who will be seeing the information. Modify the images to suit their needs and preferences.
2. Maintain simplicity: Avoid cluttering the visualizations with unnecessary features or excessive information. Layout should be made simpler, and the main focus should be on articulating the most important findings.
3. Choose pertinent charts and graphs: For various types of data, different visualization strategies are required. Select the chart or graph that best and most accurately represents the data.
4. Use color strategically: Colors can help with comprehension, but they must be used carefully. Make sure the colors are select have a purpose and don't detract from the message are want to convey.
5. Sequencing is important: Make sure the parts are arranged logically to prevent the reader from becoming confused.
6. Provide context: Provide viewers with sufficient background information to ensure that the visualizations are accurately and easily understood.

7. Clearly labelled elements and titles: Make sure that all of the labels and names for the components of each visualization are clear.

Following these recommendations will help us create visually appealing data representations that improve analysis and understanding without being too distracting for the viewer.

2.4 Data Visualization across Different Sectors

1. Health Care: Improving patient outcomes and operational efficacy in the healthcare industry requires data visualization. Hospitals can use visualizations, for example, to track patient wait times and identify bottlenecks in the emergency room. This may lead to efficient utilization of information and faster patient wait times in order to improve patient outcomes, comprehend patient data and patterns, and make well-informed decisions, healthcare personnel need to have access to data visualization tools (Shneiderman, Plaisant, & Hesse, 2013).
2. Marketing: Data visualization is revolutionary when it is used for analyzing customer behavior and marketing performance. Presenting data from many sources, such as social media networks then website analytics, allows marketers to identify trends, understand consumer preferences, and choose the best marketing strategies. Points, which are lines, or bars can be used to graphically depict numerical data in order to visually communicate a quantitative assertion. (De Datos, 2021).
3. Finance: Experts in the area of finance can quickly and accurately evaluate complex financial data with the help of data visualization. Investment companies, for example, can use interactive charts to show the evolution of stock prices or compare the performance of multiple investment portfolios visually. As a result, they are better equipped to see trends or anomalies, which may affect the investments they make.
4. Manufacturing: Data visualization helps manufacturers optimize their operations by effectively tracking key performance indicators (KPIs). When production line data, such rate of throughput as well defect rates, are clearly displayed, managers can identify inefficiency in the process promptly and take remedial action.
5. Technology: Data visualization techniques are critical to the technology industry's ability to analyses the vast amounts of data generated by people and machines alike.

For example, data visualizations enable cybersecurity professionals to spot patterns in network traffic more quickly and respond quickly to threats.

These case studies demonstrate how data visualization techniques may be used successfully by companies across many industries.

It's clear that businesses who want to thrive in the extremely competitive climate of today need to make investments in superior data analysis through visually appealing imagery.

III. THE BENEFITS OF DATA VISUALISATION

The benefits of data visualization include the following:

Actionable conclusions: A wide spectrum of personnel within an organization can understand the images presented in business intelligence displays. This helps people make decisions more quickly, get better insights, and assimilate information more quickly.

Analyzing complex relationships: Sophisticated technology for data visualization can demonstrate complex relationships between measurements and data points, allowing an organization to make data-driven choices faster.

Fascinating experiences: Data dashboards that are visually appealing and clearly communicate the information will hold the attention of the audience.

Accessibility: By making information more accessible and understandable, visualization tools let both semi-technical and non-data scientist people interpret and analyses data.

Communication: On interactive dashboards, users can click on various sections of the data to get more details. This is extremely beneficial for people who are less informed about the subject matter represented by the data.

IV. THE SHORTCOMINGS OF DATA VISUALISATION

While data visualization has many advantages, there are a number of potential drawbacks as well, including the following:

Complexity: A extremely complicated visualization could appear congested or make it difficult to discern important details. Furthermore, as tools get more complicated, users need to be trained on how to use them properly to prevent creating the wrong visual representation of the data they are using.

The potential for miscommunication: When interpreting complex graphics, users of visualization tools may make mistakes—even with the greatest of intentions.

Security and privacy of data: Users need to think about the privacy and security of the data they are visualizing. The security of the data being utilized could be jeopardized by a platform that is vulnerable to cyberattacks, or it could be using a data set that isn't consistent with data privacy laws.

Prejudice: This is essential to carefully test visualizations and the data are based on to make sure bias isn't there, either knowingly or unknowingly. Refusing to do this could make those analyses less credible. For instance, a biased data visualization may result from a data set with omits important population demographics.

V. TYPICAL USE CASES FOR DATA VISUALIZATION

The following are some examples of data visualization use cases:

Marketing and sales: According to market and research on customers firm eMarketer, digital advertising in the United States will cost $264 billion by 2023. By 2027, that amount is anticipated to surpass $390 billion. Marketing teams need to be particularly aware of where their website traffic comes from and how their online sites make money, considering the amount of money that goes into advertising. The use of data visualization prepares it easier to see how the marketing initiatives impact traffic in patterns on time.

The political sphere: The physical map that shows the states, counties, or other geographic areas that the candidates received the most votes for is a popular application of data visualization in politics.

Medical care: This Choropleth map are a common tool utilized by healthcare practitioners to visualize critical health data. Geographical regions or areas that are given a certain color in connection to a numerical variable are displayed on a choropleth maps. Professionals can view how an indicator, such the death rate from heart disease, varies over certain geographic locations by using choropleth maps.

Researchers: Scientists and researchers can learn more from their experiments and other acquired data by using scientific visualization, or SciVi.

Wealth: Finance experts must keep an eye on the performance of their investments while deciding whether to buy or sell. Candlestick charts are a useful tool for finance professionals to assess price movements over time. They show data on expenditures, derivatives, currency, bonds, stocks, and commodities. By analyzing price fluctuations over time, financiers along with information analysts can spot trends.

Transport: In order to establish a based-on data supply chain and identify the most cost-effective shipping routes, shipping businesses employ visualization tools.

Researchers and data scientists: Typically, data professionals create visualizations to display the data to a specific audience or for their own purpose. They make use of the selected programming languages' and tools' visualization libraries. Researchers and data scientists often employ proprietary technologies for complex statistical analysis or freely available programming languages like Python. Visualizations help academics and data scientists comprehend data sets better and see developments or patterns that they might have missed otherwise.

VI.DATA VISUALIZATION USING PYTHON

Plotting libraries such as Matplotlib, Seaborn, and numerous more are available in Python and offer a variety of capabilities that allow users to create visually appealing, personalized, and educational graphs that show data in the most direct and efficient manner possible.

6.1 The Python Libraries:" Matplotlib and Seaborn"

The Python libraries utilized for visualization of data include Matplotlib, Seaborn and so on. They come with built-in structures for graphing more types of data. Although graphs can be embedded into programs using Matplotlib, statistical graphs are the main use case for Seaborn.The two well-known Python visualization packages, Matplotlib, Seaborn, are contrasted in the below table 1.

Table 1. Matplotlib vs Seaborn

Matplotlib	Seaborn
The Basic graph plotting is line charts and bar charts.	It can do sophisticated visualizations with lesser commands and is primarily used for statistics of visualization.
It primarily uses arrays and datasets.	It is compatible with whole datasets.
Seaborn handles the entire dataset for a single unit and is far more structured and functionals than Matplotlib.	Matplotlib functions well with frames and data arrays. It views the figures and aces as objects.
Seaborn is typically utilized for statistical analysis and having many built-in themes.	For exploratory data analysis, Matplotlib works well with NumPy and Pandas and offers greater customization.

Figure 3. Types of data visualization

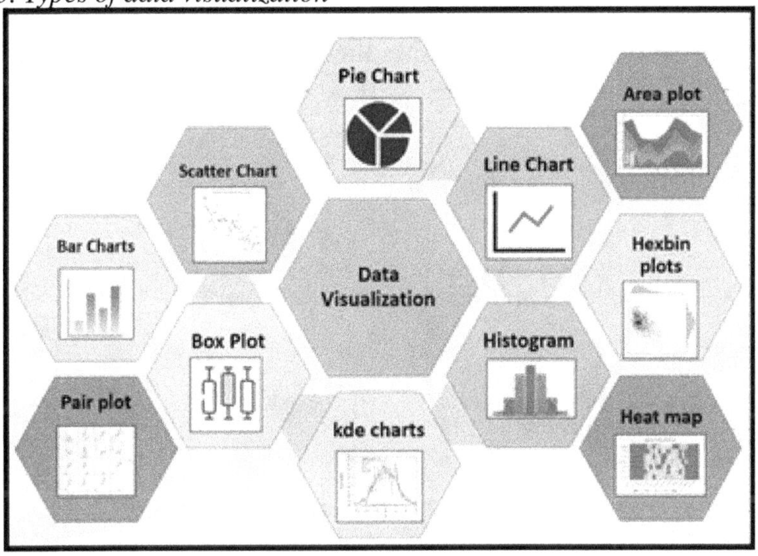

When interacting the data, it might be fully comprehending the information if it is just presented in tabular format. To visualise or display our data graphically in order to comprehend what exactly it represents, as well as to better clean and choose appropriate models for it. This makes connections, patterns, and trends easier to see than they would be in the table or CSV file containing the data.

Data visualisation is the process of visually expressing our data to identify patterns and relationships. There are several Python modules available for data visualisation, including Matplotlib, Seaborn, Plotly, and others.

The field of data analysis that deals with the visual depiction of data is called data visualisation. It depicts data graphically and is a useful tool for communicating conclusions drawn from data.

To obtain a visual representation of our data by using data visualisation. The human mind processes and comprehends material more easily when it is presented in the form of images, maps, and graphs. Large data sets make it difficult to view all of the information , to even process and comprehend it manually. In these situations, data visualisation is very helpful in representing both huge and small data sets.

6.2 Line Charts

The line chart constitutes a graphic in which the data points are joined with a straight line in order to depict the information. Every data point as well as marker in a lines chart is drawn and joined by curves otherwise lines. Let's think about India's agriculture yield, measured in tonnes per hectare. Using this data, let's create a line graph to show how crop yield varies over time. First, import the libraries Seaborn and Matplotlib.

Figure 4. Import of necessary libraries

```
import matplotlib.pyplot as plt
import seaborn as sns
```

6.2.1Using Matplotlib

The yield of crops is represented by random data points.

Figure 5. Plotting crop yields

```
crop_yields=[0.456,0.567,0.7891,0.890,0.901,0.972,0.9875,0.8666]
plt.plot(crop_yields)
```

```
[<matplotlib.lines.Line2D at 0x7d7554d0dc00>]
```

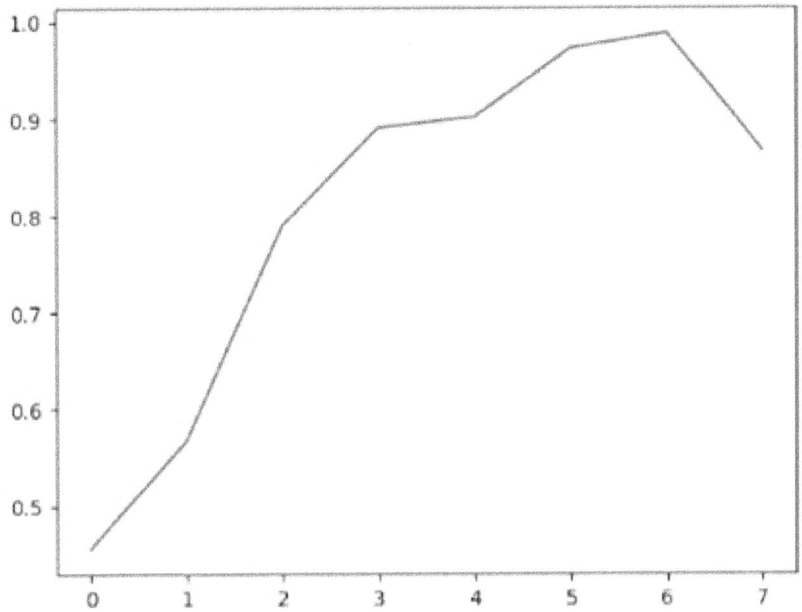

Also include the x-axis numbers to further clarify the graph's meaning.

Figure 6. Axis values

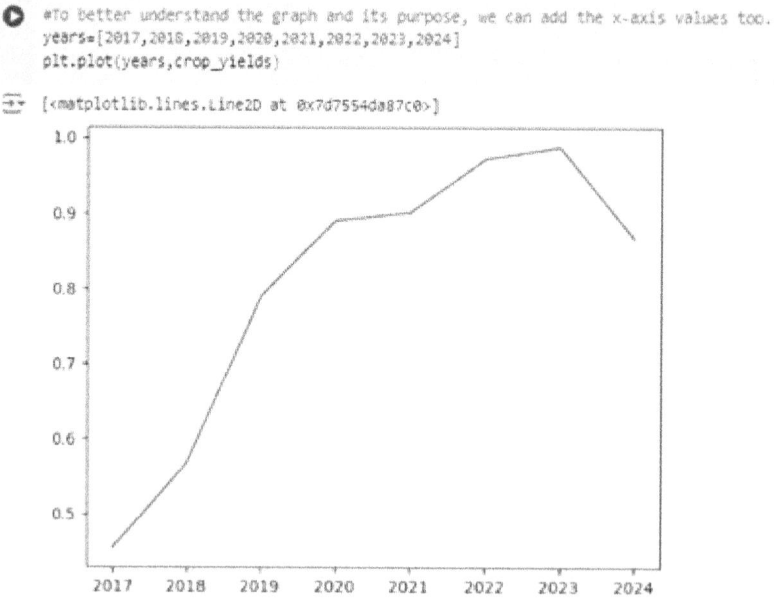

Now that the axes have labels, illustrate what each axis stands for.

Figure 7. Axis and labels

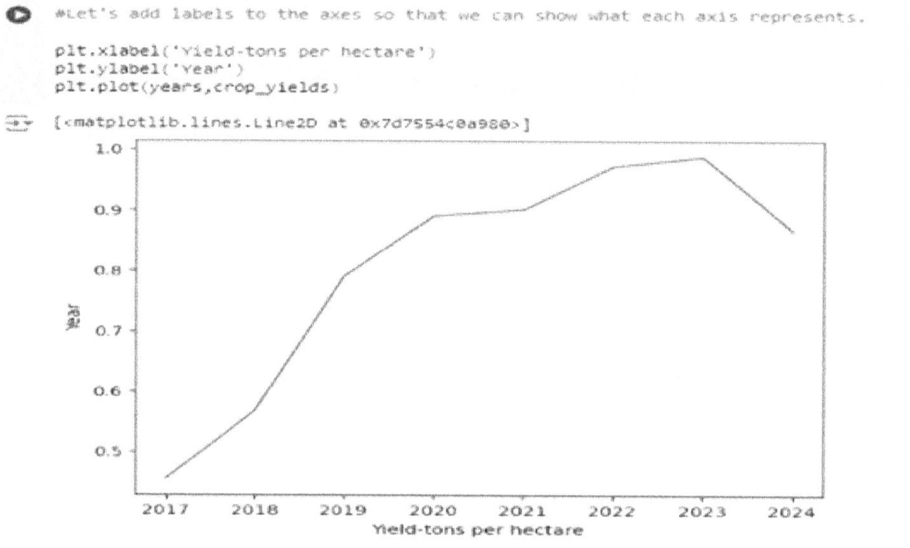

Simply use the Pl. Plot method once for every set of data to plot them on the same graph. Let's utilize this to compare, on the same graph, the yields of vegetables and crops.

Figure 8. Plotting multiple graphs

```
years = range(2015,2022)
crop=[0.457,0.344,0.452,0.452,0.789,0.879,0.982]
vegg=[0.987,0.456,0.678,0.432,0.987,0.654,0.987]

plt.xlabel('Year')
plt.ylabel('Yield-tons per hectare')
plt.plot(years,crop)
plt.plot(years,vegg)
```

```
[<matplotlib.lines.Line2D at 0x7d7554c0ab00>]
```

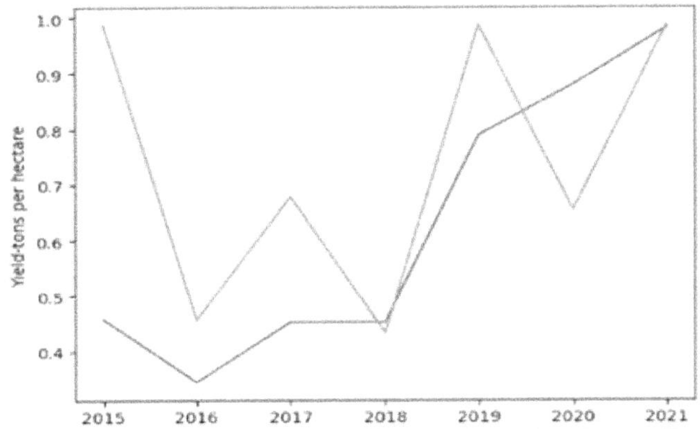

A legend explaining the meaning of the lines in our graph can be included. Give the graph a label so that people can understand whatever plotting.

Figure 9. Comparing crops and veg

```
years = range(2015,2024)
crop=[0.457,0.344,0.452,0.452,0.789,0.879,0.982,0.9765,0.9966]
vegg=[0.987,0.456,0.678,0.432,0.987,0.654,0.987,0.9761,0.9865]

plt.xlabel('Year')
plt.ylabel('Yield-tons per hectare')
plt.plot(years,crop)
plt.plot(years,vegg)
```

```
[<matplotlib.lines.Line2D at 0x7d7554935d50>]
```

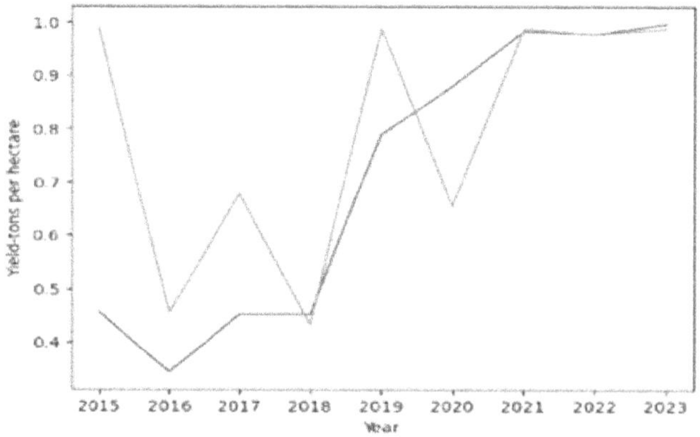

Figure 10. Multiple graphs

```
'''We can add a legend which tells us what each line in our graph means.
To understand what we are plotting, we can add a title to our graph.'''


years = range(2015,2024)
crop=[0.457,0.344,0.452,0.452,0.789,0.879,0.982,0.9987,0.1202]
vegg=[0.987,0.456,0.678,0.432,0.987,0.654,0.987,0.9934,0.1244]

plt.xlabel('Year')
plt.ylabel('Yield-tons per hectare')
plt.plot(years,crop)
plt.plot(years,vegg)

plt.title('Crop  yields in India')
plt.legend(['crop','vegg'])
```

```
<matplotlib.legend.Legend at 0x7d7554967760>
```

Figure 11. Plotting multiple graphs

```
<matplotlib.legend.Legend at 0x7d7554967760>
```

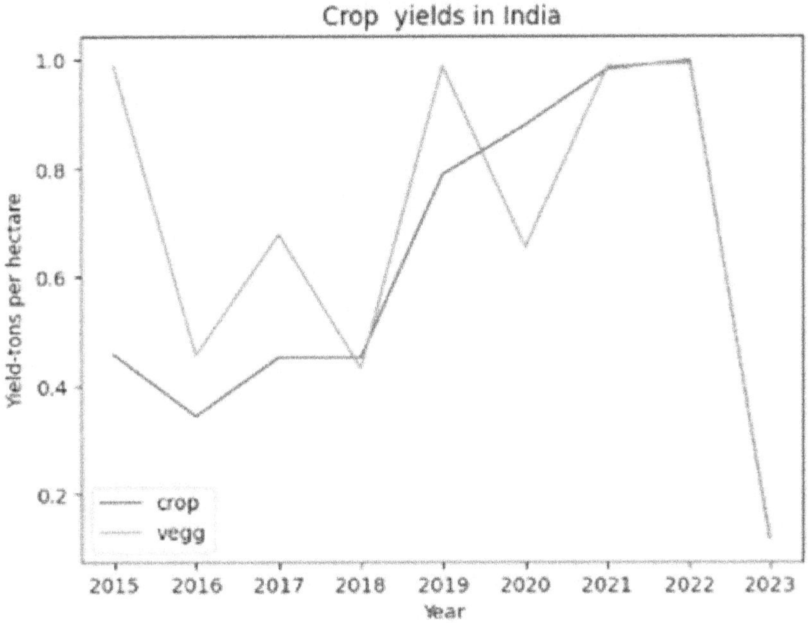

Using the marker option, use markers to highlight every point of data on our graph. Matplotlib has a wide variety of marker shapes, including square, diamond, cross, circle, and more.

Figure 12. Using markers code

```
'''To show each data point on our graph, we can highlight them with markers using the marker argument.
 Many different marker shapes like a circle, cross, square, diamond, etc. are provided by Matplotlib.'''

plt.plot(years,crop,marker='o')
plt.plot(years,vegg, marker='x')


years = range(2015,2024)
crop=[0.457,0.344,0.452,0.452,0.789,0.879,0.982,0.9987,0.1202]
vegg=[0.987,0.456,0.678,0.432,0.987,0.654,0.987,0.9934,0.1244]

plt.xlabel('Year')
plt.ylabel('Yield-tons per hectare')
plt.plot(years,crop)
plt.plot(years,vegg)

plt.title('Crop  yields in India')
plt.legend(['crop','vegg'])
```

Figure 13. Visual Using markers

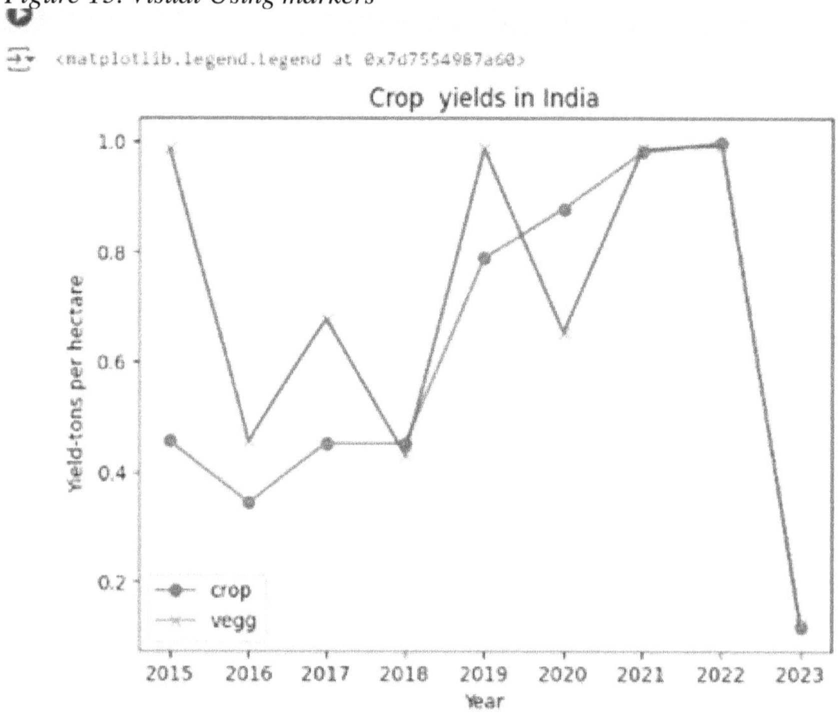

To alter the dimension of the figures, use the Pl. Figure function.

6.2.2 Using Seaborn

Use some of the Seaborn library's basic styles to quickly and easily create gorgeous charts. The sns.set_style function can be used to apply these worldwide.

Figure 14. White grid in seaborn

```
'''Using Seaborn
An easy way to make your charts look beautiful is to use some default styles from the Seaborn library.
These can be applied globally using the sns.set_style function.'''

sns.set_style('whitegrid')

plt.plot(years,crop,marker='o')
plt.plot(years,vegg, marker='x')


years = range(2015,2024)
crop=[0.457,0.344,0.452,0.452,0.789,0.879,0.982,0.9987,0.1202]
vegg=[0.987,0.456,0.678,0.432,0.987,0.654,0.987,0.9934,0.1244]
plt.xlabel('Year')
plt.ylabel('Yield-tons per hectare')
plt.plot(years,crop)
plt.plot(years,vegg)

plt.title('Crop  yields in India')
plt.legend(['crop','vegg'])
```

Figure 15. Using Seaborn white grids

```
<matplotlib.legend.Legend at 0x7d75548b6380>
```

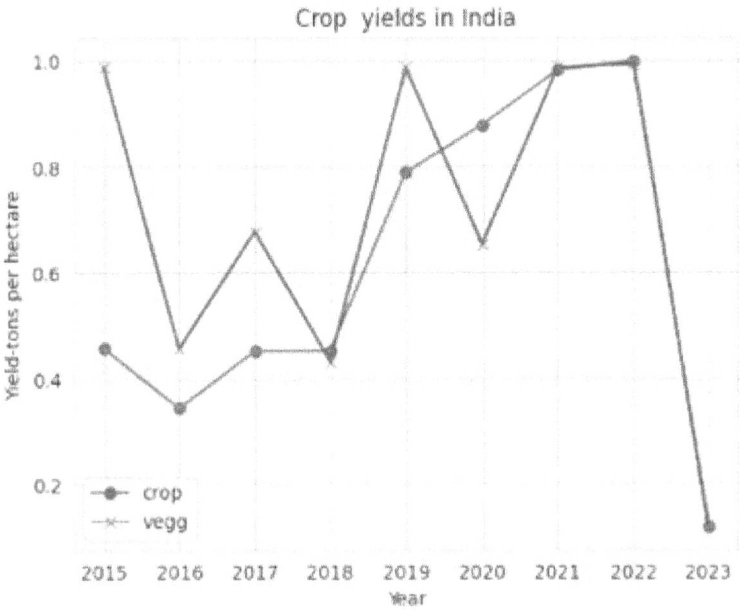

To alter the backdrop colour to a darker hue, also utilise the darkgrid option.

Figure 16. Using Seaborn data grids

```
#we can also use the darkgrid option to change the background color to a darker shade.

sns.set_style('darkgrid')

plt.plot(years,crop,marker='o')
plt.plot(years,vegg, marker='x')


years = range(2015,2024)
crop=[0.457,0.344,0.452,0.452,0.789,0.879,0.982,0.9987,0.1202]
vegg=[0.987,0.456,0.678,0.432,0.987,0.654,0.987,0.9934,0.1244]

plt.xlabel('Year')
plt.ylabel('Yield-tons per hectare')
plt.plot(years,crop)
plt.plot(years,vegg)

plt.title('Crop  yields in India')
plt.legend(['crop','vegg'])
```

Figure 17. Using dark grid in Seaborn

```
<matplotlib.legend.Legend at 0x7d755473feb0>
```

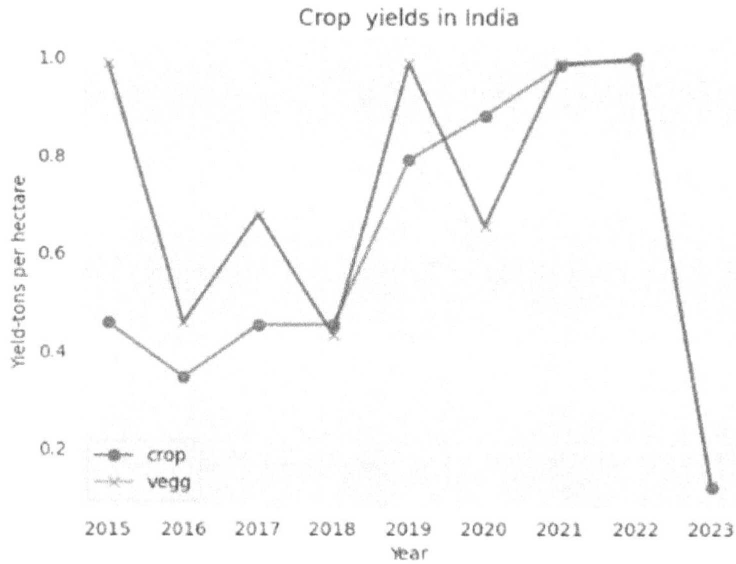

6.4 Bar Graphs

A bar graph is a useful tool for representing categorical information. A bar graph represents data by using bars, which show classification on the x-axis and value on the y-axis. Bar graphs display data that falls into a particular category using bars of different heights.

Figure 18. Bar graphs

```
'''Bar Graphs
When you have categorical data, you can represent it with a bar graph. A bar graph plots data with the help of bars,
which represent value on the y-axis and category on the x-axis.
Bar graphs use bars with varying heights to show the data which belongs to a specific category.'''


years=range(2015,2024)

crop=[0.45,0.55,0.23,0.56,0.78,0.89,0.95,0.99,0.99]
vegg=[0.4,0.5,0.7,0.5,0.6,0.9,0.7,0.8,0.9]

plt.bar(years,crop)

plt.xlabel('Year')
plt.ylabel('Yield-tons per hectare')
```

Figure 19. Bar graph

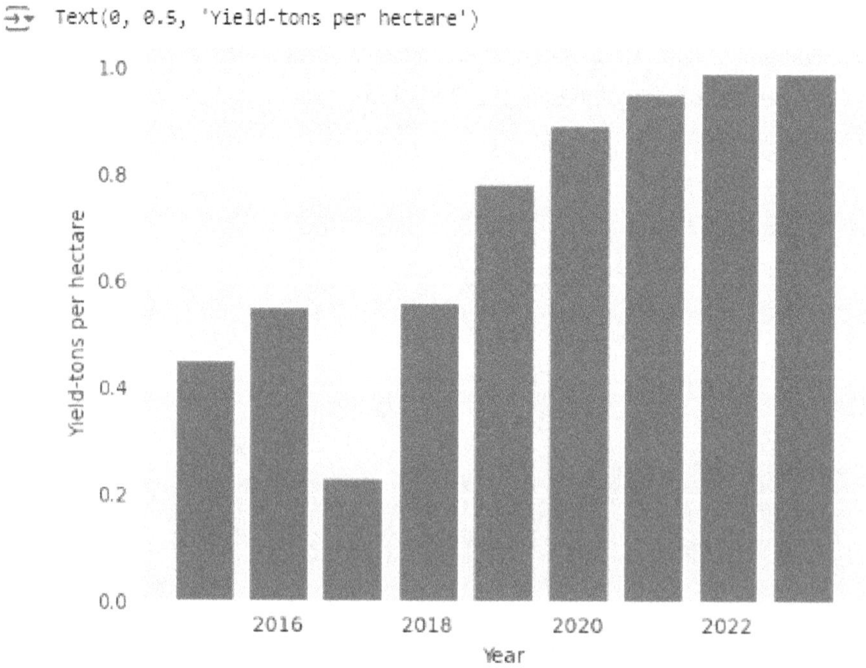

Bars can also be stacked on top of one another. Now let's visualise the crop and vegetable Statistics.

Figure 20. Bar graph with stack bars

```
#We can also stack bars on top of each other. Let's plot the data for apples and oranges.

years=range(2015,2024)

crop=[0.45,0.55,0.23,0.56,0.78,0.89,0.95,0.99,0.99]
vegg=[0.4,0.5,0.7,0.5,0.6,0.9,0.7,0.8,0.9]
plt.bar(years,crop)

plt.xlabel('Year')
plt.ylabel('Yield-tons per hectare')

plt.bar(years,crop)
plt.bar(years,vegg, bottom=crop)
```

Figure 21. Plotting stacked bar graphs

```
<BarContainer object of 9 artists>
```

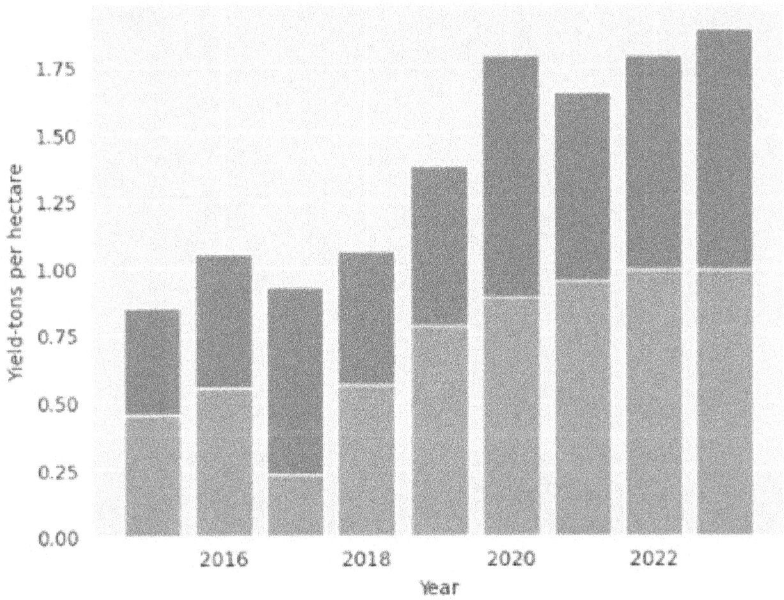

Figure 22. Iris Dataset

```
df=sns.load_dataset('iris')
df
```

	sepal_length	sepal_width	petal_length	petal_width	species
0	5.1	3.5	1.4	0.2	setosa
1	4.9	3.0	1.4	0.2	setosa
2	4.7	3.2	1.3	0.2	setosa
3	4.6	3.1	1.5	0.2	setosa
4	5.0	3.6	1.4	0.2	setosa
...	...	...	...	...	...
145	6.7	3.0	5.2	2.3	virginica
146	6.3	2.5	5.0	1.9	virginica
147	6.5	3.0	5.2	2.0	virginica
148	6.2	3.4	5.4	2.3	virginica
149	5.9	3.0	5.1	1.8	virginica

150 rows × 5 columns

Figure 23. Tips dataset

```
[ ] df1=sns.load_dataset('tips')
    df1
```

	total_bill	tip	sex	smoker	day	time	size
0	16.99	1.01	Female	No	Sun	Dinner	2
1	10.34	1.66	Male	No	Sun	Dinner	3
2	21.01	3.50	Male	No	Sun	Dinner	3
3	23.68	3.31	Male	No	Sun	Dinner	2
4	24.59	3.61	Female	No	Sun	Dinner	4
...	...	...	...	...	...	...	...
239	29.03	5.92	Male	No	Sat	Dinner	3
240	27.18	2.00	Female	Yes	Sat	Dinner	2
241	22.67	2.00	Male	Yes	Sat	Dinner	2
242	17.82	1.75	Male	No	Sat	Dinner	2
243	18.78	3.00	Female	No	Thur	Dinner	2

244 rows × 7 columns

To see how an average bill amount changes on various days of the week, create a bar chart. To accomplish this, use plt.bar after calculating the day-wise averages. Additionally, the barplot function in the Seaborn library has the ability to compute averages automatically.

Figure 24. Plotting averages of each bar

```
[ ] '''We can draw a bar chart to visualize how the average bill amount varies across different days of the week.
    We can do this by computing the day-wise averages and then using plt.bar.
    The Seaborn library also provides a barplot function that can automatically compute averages.'''

    sns.barplot(x='day',y='total_bill',data=df1)

<Axes: xlabel='day', ylabel='total_bill'>
```

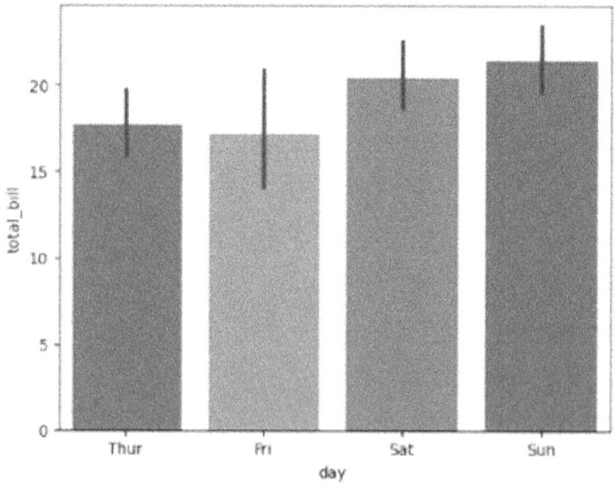

The hue option can be used to compare bar charts side by side. The third attribute mentioned in this argument will serve as the basis for the comparison.

Figure 25. Plotting multiple bar graphs

```
[ ] sns.barplot(x='day',y='total_bill', hue='sex',data=df1)

<Axes: xlabel='day', ylabel='total_bill'>
```

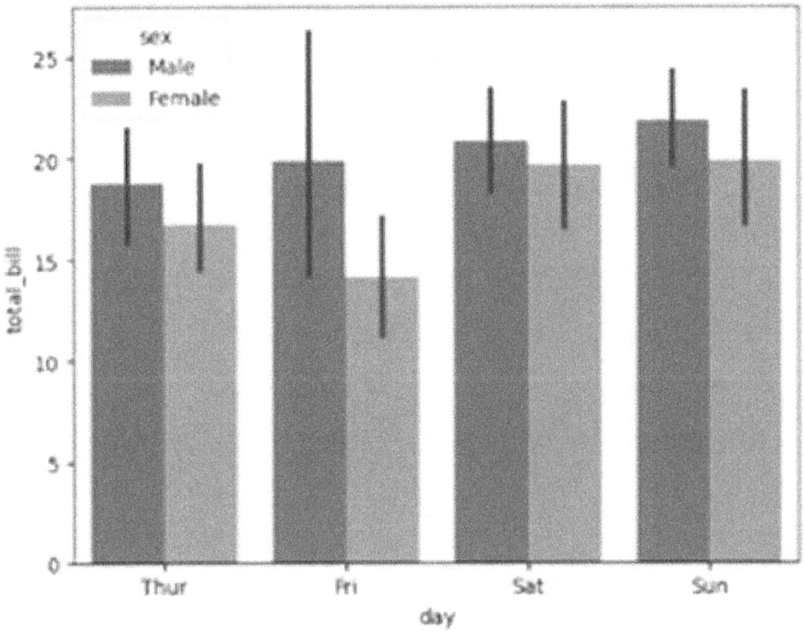

By changing the axis, you may make the bars horizontal.

Figure 26. Horizontal bar graphs

```
sns.barplot(x='total_bill', y='day', hue='sex', data=tips_df)
```

```
<matplotlib.axes._subplots.AxesSubplot at 0x2054af1b250>
```

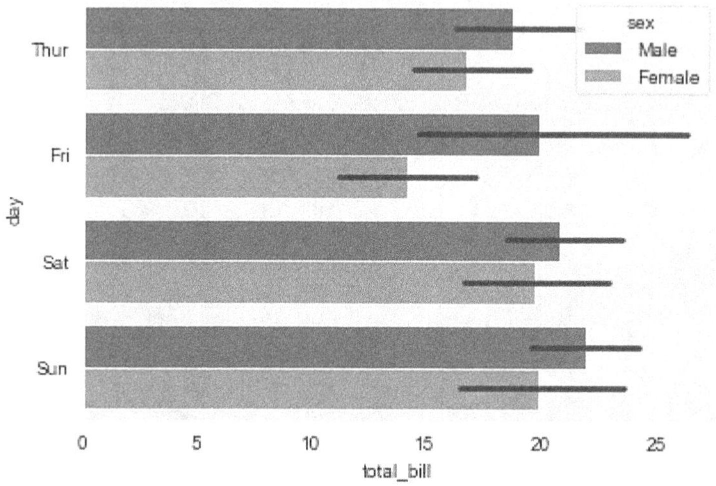

6.4 Histograms

A diagram with bars that shows data fluctuating over a range is called a histogram. It displays the variance along the x-axis as well as the heights of the values that fall within a range along the y-axis. Data can be plotted over a range of values using histograms. To display the data for each range, they utilise a bar chart. Once more, let's plot histograms using the "Iris" information, which include floral data.

Figure 27. Iris dataset in histogram

```
'''Histograms
A Histogram is a bar representation of data  that varies over a range. It plots the height of the data belonging
to a range along the y-axis and the range along the x-axis. Histograms are used to plot data over
a range of values. They use a bar representation to show the data belonging to each range.
 Let's again use the 'Iris' data which contains information about flowers to plot histograms.'''

plt.title('Distribution of Sepal width')
plt.hist(df.sepal_width,bins=5)
```

Now, let's plot a histogram using the hist() function.

Figure 28. Plotting histograms

```
plt.title('Distribution of Sepal width')
plt.hist(df.sepal_width,bins=5)

(array([11., 46., 68., 21.,  4.]),
 array([2.  , 2.48, 2.96, 3.44, 3.92, 4.4 ]),
 <BarContainer object of 5 artists>)
```

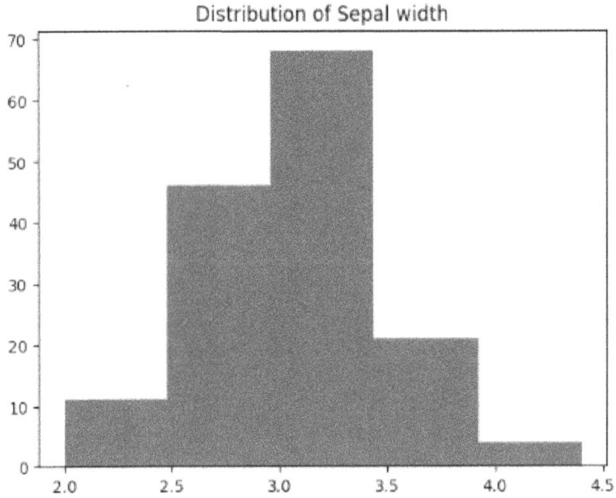

6.5 Scatter Plots

Scatter plots are to exhibit multiple variables are present at different coordinates and utilise scatter plots. The data is scattered across the graph rather than confined within a range. In a scatter plot, two or more elements are shown, with a distinct colour assigned to each. Let's use the "Iris" dataset to make a scatter plot.

Figure 29. Iris Dataset

```
flowers_df = sns.load_dataset("iris")
```

```
flowers_df
```

	sepal_length	sepal_width	petal_length	petal_width	species
0	5.1	3.5	1.4	0.2	setosa
1	4.9	3.0	1.4	0.2	setosa
2	4.7	3.2	1.3	0.2	setosa
3	4.6	3.1	1.5	0.2	setosa
4	5.0	3.6	1.4	0.2	setosa
...	...	...	...	...	...
145	6.7	3.0	5.2	2.3	virginica
146	6.3	2.5	5.0	1.9	virginica
147	6.5	3.0	5.2	2.0	virginica
148	6.2	3.4	5.4	2.3	virginica
149	5.9	3.0	5.1	1.8	virginica

150 rows × 5 columns

Let's start by counting the variety of flower species that exist.

Figure 30. Unique flower species

```
flowers_df.species.unique()
```

```
array(['setosa', 'versicolor', 'virginica'], dtype=object)
```

Let's attempt to plot the data using a line chart.

Figure 31. Plotting line chart

```
plt.plot(flowers_df.sepal_length, flowers_df.sepal_width)
```

```
[<matplotlib.lines.Line2D at 0x2054a78b7c0>]
```

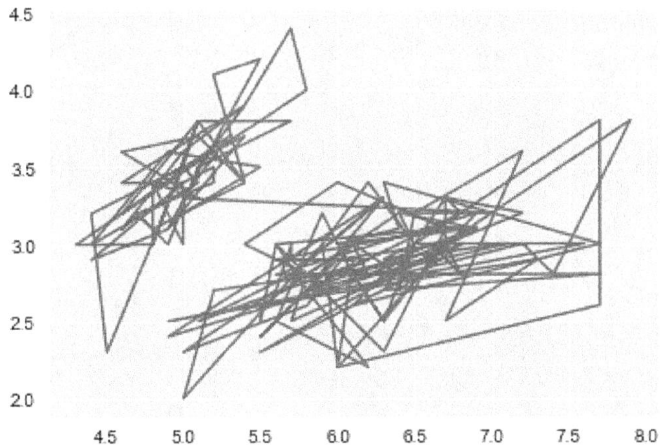

It's not very informative, this. The relationship between several data pieces is impossible for us to determine.

Figure 32. Scatter plot

```
sns.scatterplot(x=flowers_df.sepal_length, y=flowers_df.sepal_width)
```

```
<matplotlib.axes._subplots.AxesSubplot at 0x2054a958820>
```

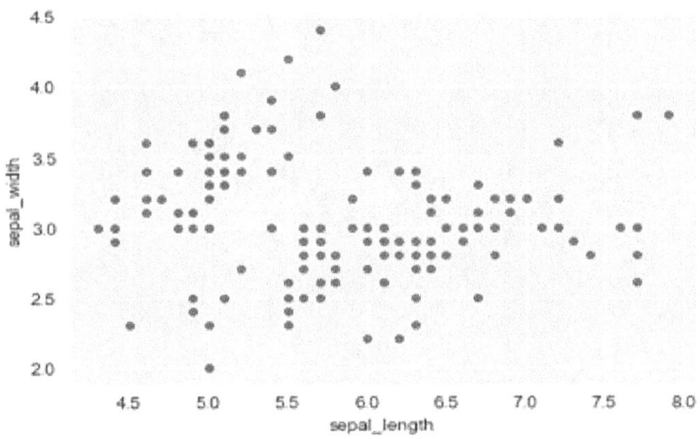

This is far superior. However, still unable to distinguish between distinct data points that belong to various categories. It will use the hue of the flower species to colour the dots.

Figure 33. Scatter plot with multiple colors

```
sns.scatterplot(x=flowers_df.sepal_length, y=flowers_df.sepal_width, hue=flowers_df.species, s=70);
```

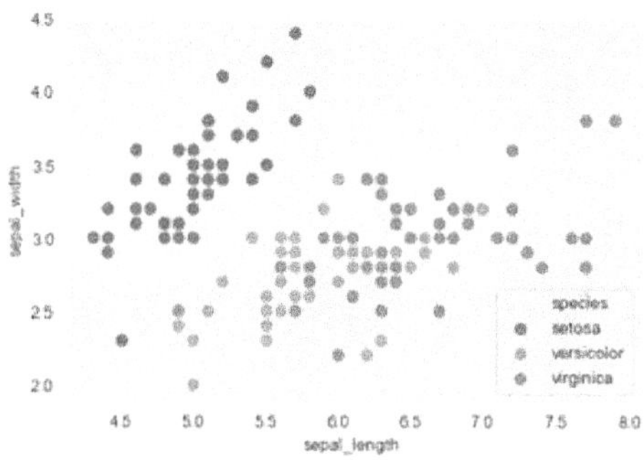

The plotting functions in Matplotlib are used internally by Seaborn, thus it can alter the figure using functions plt.figure and plt.title.

Figure 34. Dimensions of scatter plot

```
plt.figure(figsize=(12, 6))
plt.title('Sepal Dimensions')

sns.scatterplot(x=flowers_df.sepal_length,
                y=flowers_df.sepal_width,
                hue=flowers_df.species,
                s=100);
```

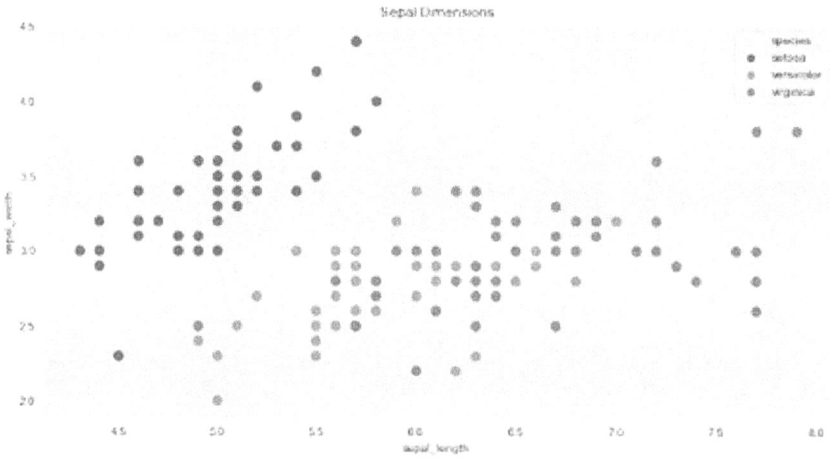

6.6 Heat Maps

Heatmaps are a useful tool for visualising slow changes in data or behavioural changes. It represents various values with different colours. It can determine how the occurrence varies by looking at how these colours vary in terms of hue, intensity, etc. Let's visualise monthly passenger foot traffic at an airport over a 12-year period using heatmaps derived from the Seaborn flight dataset.

Figure 35. Flights dataset

```
flights_df = sns.load_dataset("flights").pivot("month", "year", "passengers")
flights_df
```

year	1949	1950	1951	1952	1953	1954	1955	1956	1957	1958	1959	1960
month												
January	112	115	145	171	196	204	242	284	315	340	360	417
February	118	126	150	180	196	188	233	277	301	318	342	391
March	132	141	178	193	236	235	267	317	356	362	406	419
April	129	135	163	181	235	227	269	313	348	348	396	461
May	121	125	172	183	229	234	270	318	355	363	420	472
June	135	149	178	218	243	264	315	374	422	435	472	535
July	148	170	199	230	264	302	364	413	465	491	548	622
August	148	170	199	242	272	293	347	405	467	505	559	606
September	136	158	184	209	237	259	312	355	404	404	463	508
October	119	133	162	191	211	229	274	306	347	359	407	461
November	104	114	146	172	180	203	237	271	305	310	362	390
December	118	140	166	194	201	229	278	306	336	337	405	432

The flights_df dataset, which is presented above, displays the monthly foot traffic at each airport for the years 1949 through 1960. The numbers show how many travellers via the airport there were (in thousands). Let's visualise the aforementioned data using a heatmap.

Figure 36. Plotting heatmap

```
plt.title("No. of Passengers (1000s)")
sns.heatmap(flights_df)
```

```
<matplotlib.axes._subplots.AxesSubplot at 0x2054c1feaf0>
```

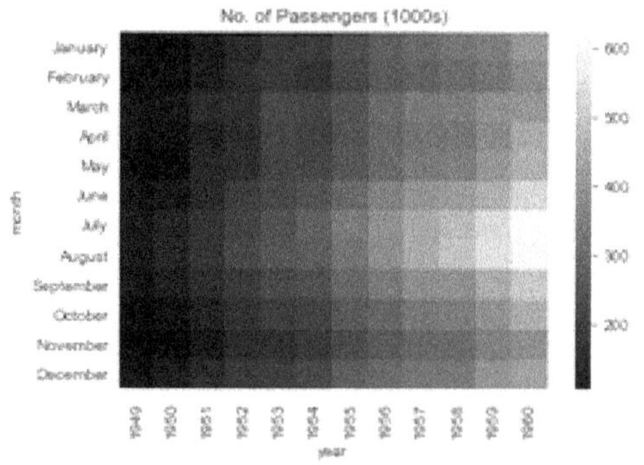

The airport sees more foot traffic the brighter the colour. Based on the graph, it may deduce that:

1. In any given year, July and August have the most annual foot traffic.
2. Every year, more people visit. Every month in the year will see more foot traffic than it did in the past. Now let's adjust the heatmap's hue to blue and show the actual values.

Figure 37. Plotting heatmap with values

```
plt.title("No. of Passengers (1000s)")
sns.heatmap(flights_df, fmt="d", annot=True, cmap='Blues')
```

```
<matplotlib.axes._subplots.AxesSubplot at 0x2054c2dc850>
```

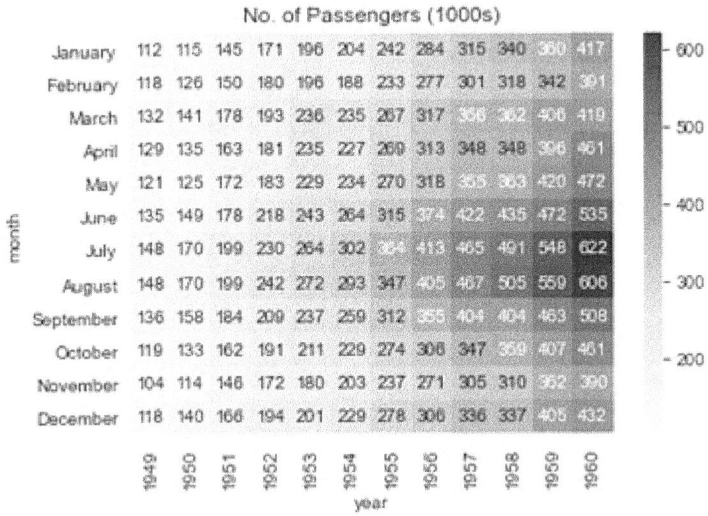

VII. CONCLUSION

In many different businesses, data visualisation has emerged as a vital tool for efficient data processing. Users are able to swiftly comprehend patterns, correlations, and insights that could otherwise be missed by viewing complex information in a visual format. In this post, we've covered the value of data visualization in data analysis as well as many methods for producing powerful visualizations. Additionally, we've outlined typical mistakes to avoid and ideal practices to adhere to while creating visualizations. You may make sure that your visualizations accurately, compellingly, and understandably convey the data by following these recommendations.

Also looked at case studies that showed off effective data visualization applications in a range of industries. Organizations in a variety of industries, including marketing, finance, and healthcare, are utilizing the power of images to obtain insightful information and make wise decisions.

Python data visualization was briefly discussed. Many additional cutting-edge techniques like interactive dashboards and augmented reality experiences, which will significantly improve our capacity to analyses and comprehend complicated datasets, as technology continues to evolve quickly.

REFERENCES

Ajibade, S. S., & Adediran, A. (2016). An overview of big data visualization techniques in data mining. *International Journal of Computer Science and Information Technology Research*, 4(3), 105–113.

Asamoah, D. (2022). Improving data visualization skills: A curriculum design. *International Journal of Education and Development Using Information and Communication Technology*, 18(1), 213–235.

Berson, I. R., & Berso, M. J. (2009). Making sense of social studies with visualization tools. *Social Education*, 73(3), 124–126.

Cao, N., & Cui, W. (2016). Overview of text visualization techniques. In *Introduction to text visualization* (pp. 11–40). Springer. DOI: 10.2991/978-94-6239-186-4_2

Diamond, M., & Mattia, A. (2017). Data visualization: An exploratory study into the software tools used by businesses. *Journal of Instructional Pedagogies*, 18, 1–13.

Fiaz, A. S.. (2016). Data visualization: Enhancing big data more adaptable and valuable. *International Journal of Applied Engineering Research: IJAER*, 11(4), 2801–2804.

Furmanova, K., Gratzl, S., Stitz, H., Zichner, T., Jaresova, M., Lex, A., & Streit, M. (2020). Taggle: Combining overview and details in tabular data visualizations. *Information Visualization*, 19(2), 114–136. DOI: 10.1177/1473871619878085

Hohman, F., Wongsuphasawat, K., Kery, M. B., & Patel, K. (2020, April). Understanding and visualizing data iteration in machine learning. In *Proceedings of the 2020 CHI Conference on Human Factors in Computing Systems* (pp. 1–13). ACM. DOI: 10.1145/3313831.3376177

Kumar, S. M., & Belwal, M. (2017). Performance dashboard: Cutting-edge business intelligence and data visualization. In *2017 International Conference on Smart Technologies for Smart Nation (SmartRechCon)* (pp. 1–6). IEEE. DOI: 10.1109/SmartTechCon.2017.8358558

Parbat, B., Dwivedi, A. K., & Vyas, O. P. (2010). Data visualization tools for WSNs: A glimpse. *International Journal of Computer Applications*, 2(1), 14–20. DOI: 10.5120/617-868

Pavlopoulos, G. A., Wegener, A. L., & Schneider, R. (2008). A survey of visualization tools for biological network analysis. *BioData Mining*, 1(1), 1–11. DOI: 10.1186/1756-0381-1-12 PMID: 19040716

Sadiku, M. N. O. (2016). Data visualization. *International Journal of Engineering Research and Advanced Technology*, 2(12), 11–16.

Shneiderman, B., Plaisant, C., & Hesse, B. W. (2013). Improving healthcare with interactive visualization. *Computer*, 46(5), 58–66. DOI: 10.1109/MC.2013.38

Srivastava, D. (n.d.). An introduction to data visualization tools and techniques in various domains. Unpublished manuscript.

Wang, Z. (2020). Cheat sheets for data visualization techniques. In *Proceedings of the 2020 CHI Conference on Human Factors in Computing Systems* (pp. 1–13). ACM. DOI: 10.1145/3313831.3376658

Ward, M. O., Grinstein, G., & Keim, D. (2015). *Interactive data visualization: Foundations, techniques, and applications*. CRC Press. DOI: 10.1201/b18379

Womack, R. (2014). Data visualization and information literacy. *IASSIST Quarterly*, 38(1), 12–17. DOI: 10.29173/iq619

Chapter 4

Analysis of Crime Against Women Data Using Machine Learning and Statistical Methods

P. Tamilarasi
https://orcid.org/0000-0001-9788-4129
Sri Sarada College for Women, India

R. UmaRani
Sri Sarada College for Women, India

T. JayaSudha
https://orcid.org/0009-0001-4754-1125
Sri Sarada College for Women, India

Yusliza Yusoff
Universiti Teknologi Malaysia, Malaysia

C. KumuThini
https://orcid.org/0000-0001-9554-1106
Dr. N.G.P. Arts and Science College, India

ABSTRACT

Analyzing, cleaning, manipulating, and modelling datasets to conclude the data they include is the process known as data analytics. Qualitative and quantitative data analysis are two more categories into which data analytics may be separated. The scientific and mathematical study of algorithms is known as machine learning (ML). Crime against women has grown to be a major issue. Numerous nations are

DOI: 10.4018/979-8-3693-7868-7.ch004

always working to avoid this offence, which is something that must be done. Crimes against women have increased dramatically in recent years. Every year, a massive dataset is created based on the reporting of crimes. To a certain extent, this data can help us prevent crime by analyzing and forecasting it. The crime rate against women is predicted in this chapter using a variety of statistical techniques, including the correlation coefficient ANOVA, and hypothesis testing with ML models in Python, including linear regression. The results are finally presented based on the performance of the ML algorithms using evolution metrics, such as MAE, MSE, and R2.

INTRODUCTION

Research in fields like statistics, computer science, and intelligence, as well as practical advancements in fields like science, engineering, the public sector, business, social sciences, and lifestyle, are all being driven by data analytics, which is acknowledged as a vital and evolving scientific discipline. In data analytics, methodologies vary based on organisational objectives and involve extracting and classifying data in order to uncover and analyse behavioural data and trends. Predictive data Analytics which used for forecasting

- ✓ Prescriptive analytics is used in simulation and optimisation;
- ✓ descriptive analytics is used in business intelligence and data mining;
- ✓ diagnostic analytics is mostly used to identify the cause of previous problems.

Predictive data analytics focused at predict expected outcomes based on historical information using systematic methods like statistics and Machine Learning. Descriptive analytics is a statistical method that is used to search and summarizes historical data to identify patterns or meanings. Prescriptive analytics is used to finding the best actions from given data which also includes predictive and prescriptive analytics. Diagnostic analytics is advanced analytics that focuses on explaining why something has happened based on data analysis. The below figure1 show different types of data analytics.

Figure 1. Types of data analytics

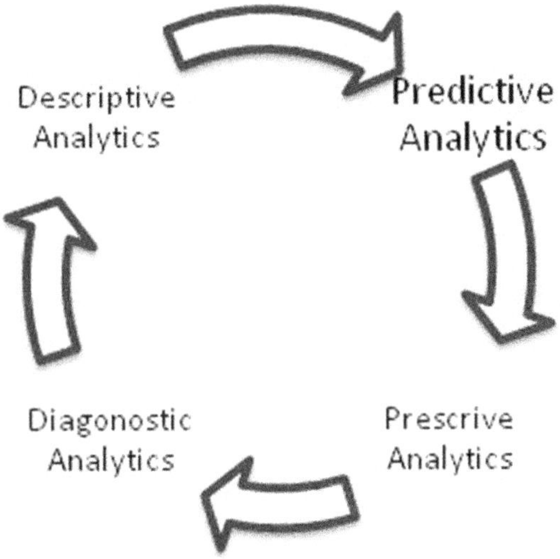

MACHINE LEARNING APPROACH

A set of algorithms for computer programs is known as machine learning (ML). It does not require human intervention to learn and adjust to new facts. This is an artificial intelligence segment that retains its innate algorithms. Three primary categories of machine learning exist: supervised, unsupervised, and reinforcement learning. The most widely used machine learning model is supervised learning. It is the most easy to detect and the simplest to apply. It's comparable to educating children using flashcards. An entirely new paradigm will be able to be seen by the supervised learning algorithm, which will also be able to assign a suitable label to it. A aspect of supervised learning that lacks labels is called unsupervised learning. This algorithm is equipped with tools to identify the qualities of data and reads a large amount of data. A subset of machine learning is augmentation learning. The best course of action to maximise credit under a given set of circumstances is addressed. Many programs and organisations utilise it to track it in a specific context or determine what is a desirable, achievable conduct. Augmentation learning differs from supervised learning in that in supervised learning, the algorithm is trained with a véridique response because the tutelage data contains response keys. In contrast, in a reinforcement study, there are no response keys, and even the reinforcement mediator makes decisions about what will be presented in the assigned work. From the lack of training datasets, it is spring to gain knowledge from it. Below figure 2 shows categories of Machine learning.

Figure 2. Vary types of approaches in machine learning

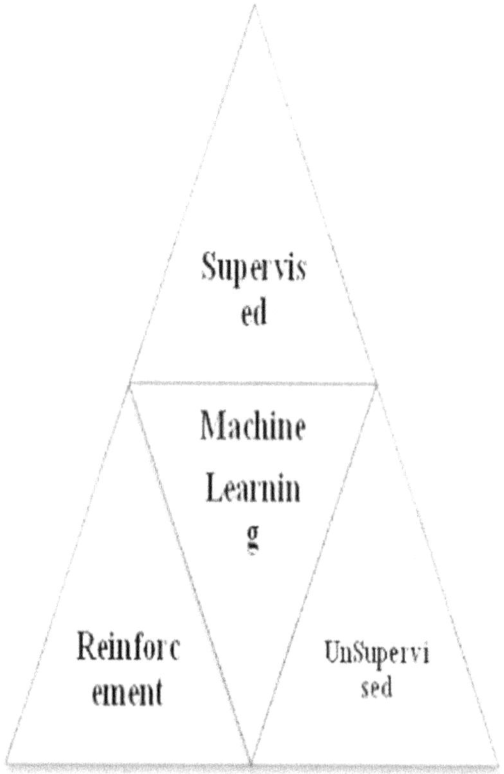

One of the nation's top worries at the moment is women's safety. The following is a list of violent crimes against women: rape, dowry threats, and killings. Although this violence has occurred in the past, it is still happening now. These kinds of issues ought to be discussed and taken seriously. A lot of analytics work has been set aside and used for predict deterrence, offence recognition, and the completion of a few forms of violence against women in India. Various machine learning techniques are used to reliably predict crimes against women.

Machine Learning Based Applications and It's Algorithms

The primary development in artificially intelligent algorithms is the derivation of the picture. Convolution neural networks analyse items within a picture or re-organise it. Example: Facebook uses machine learning algorithms to extract your face. One fascinating and entertaining use of machine learning is speech recognition. Numerous businesses worldwide are utilising machine learning and deep learning to process vast volumes of voice data in order to extract sound characteristics, as demonstrated by Siri, Alexa, Google Home, and other systems. For many businesses, the recommendation system has proved essential. Additionally, this system serves as a platform for Facebook adverts.

Generally Utilized Machine Learning Models

Linear regression

One key model in machine learning is these types of linear regression. By forming a line connecting the data points, it is used to transfer the values of numerical input data to numerical output data. Put it simply. The linear model is used to construct the link between an independent variable and a dependent variable it is also identified by a linear equation.

Logistic Regression

When the input data is of the binary kind, this model runs. Similar to other regression models, the logistic regression is a predictive model as well. The primary purpose of this model is to provide information and specifics on the relationship between dependent binary data and one or more independent variables.

Ridge Regression

Edge relapse occurs at the moment when there is an increased link between independent elements, which is another appropriate device. It is perceived as a regularization technique and is utilized to decrease the trouble of the shape. It's anything but a small preference measure that builds the imitation less organised to overgood using a predisposition lattice.

Lasso Regression

It is the same as lasso regression, another often used framework for aggregating the inconvenient techniques. It functions in this way by ignoring the relapse coefficient's overall makeup. In contrast to edge regression, the coefficient rate occurs closer to zero in this explanation.

Polynomial Regression

With a direct structure, the polynomial relapse measure is a nonlinear record. This describes how to fit a square stake with a circular aperture like a violin. While using a non-straight arch, it's anything but a connected road to a few straight relapses (it's anything but a direct relapse even though amid complicated sovereign elements). When information values are already presented in a nonlinear manner, it is employed. The model duplicates these data points using a linear model and transforms them into the polynomial skin of a specific scale.The most notable example of this is the bent polynomial line that follows them rather than the straight line observed in a direct relapse. However, this model may be prone to overfitting, therefore check the bending in the last section to prevent an unusual appearance.

Decision Trees

The result is obtained in a tree structure using the decision tree model. it is applied without any restrictions. one kind of supervised technique is this one. which, by identifying the proper procedure to fracture the data foundation on a range of scenarios into a tree formation, is utilised in both classification and regression models. the ultimate goal is to use the grasp the obtain state to predict an event or importance.

Support Vector Machine

The primary use of this model is to locate the hyper planes inside the N-dimensional region. There are several potential hyper planes that might be chosen to split the two data modules. Finding the planes with the largest border—that is, the maximum space between the data of the two modules—is the primary goal. Maximise the reinforcement that edge remoteness has provided so that anticipated data values may be categorised with further confidence.

Naive Bayes

One algorithm is not Naive Bayes. It is a collection of several categorisation formulas. Another term for these algorithms is Bayes. Bayes' Naive Theorem. Each pair of traits is split individually, and they are all combined under the same premise.

Clustering

One of the main categories of machine learning algorithms is clustering. In order to make the data more closely associated to one cluster than the data value is a shift to that group, it is used to divide the population or data points into different collections. There are two types of clustering procedures. 1. Strict grouping 2. Soft grouping. Every data value in hard cluster types is either completely fitted inside the cluster or not. In soft cluster approaches, each data value is put in prospect or probability. Subsequent clusters are separated into several categories, including as density, distribution, and catered models.

Density Based Cluster

These tactics have clusters that are shaped to help in front of the information esteem densities that are shown in the information opening. Areas that exhibit a high degree of agreement with the information values found in that area are considered clusters. The information values that fall into the wretched region—that is, the segment where there are very few information values—are interpreted as anomalies or disturbances. This strategy's cluster framing might have abstract shapes. Density-based bunching models' viewpoint is the outcome.

DBSCAN

Group information focusses, or DBSCANs, are collectively reliant on the separation metric and guidelines for the smallest total quantity of information focusses. It gains the least amount of attention and two limiting Eps. Eps demonstrate how to seal the information that is considered to be confidential. The standard practice for the smallest amount of attention should be to acknowledge that the area is a remote location.

OPTICS

Other than emphasising one of the shortcomings of the previous model—namely, the inability to build bunches as of information of any strength—this is identical in technique to DBSCAN. It recognises two additional boundaries: get to fitness separation and emphasise reserved quality. If the goal is to focus by assigning the lowest possible rating scale, then centre distance is also important. The ideal centre space and separation cost measure to employ for slyly calculating the distance between two focusses is accomplish ability save. In the reach ability field, one item to consider is if the rate remnants are sufficient when one information point has a centre point.

HDBSCAN

One type of thickness support bunching approach that may be used to expand the DBSCAN style by converting it to different levelled grouping strategies is called HDBSCAN.

Hierarchical Clustering

Hierarchical Clustering (This is likewise distinguished as Bottom-Up technique) or part (dissonant portray as Top-Down strategies) the gathering support on the save assessment. In an Agglomerative gathering, each mark of information proceeds collectively, in the first place, set the gathering deliberate. Problematic is the clashing of Agglomerative, this is beginning sharp through every one of the situations with a solitary group and separate them to create extra bunches. These strategies produce a space climate of each introduced bunch and accomplish the relationship among the gathering dependent on the state of the connection. The gathering of the focuses is representing through a dendrogram. There are different classifications of linkages

Single Linkage: In this linkage-type, the space among the two gatherings is the express save among positions in the people two gatherings.
Complete Linkage: In these sorts of complete linkage, the breadth including the two gatherings is the most extreme space including the position in people two gatherings.
Normal Linkage: In the linkage kind of normal the space among the two groups is the mediocre hold of each top in the gathering into each position in an alternate bunch.

Fuzzy Clustering

The assignment of the information dab in a portion of the gatherings isn't urgent in fluffy bunching. Now, singular information tips can be found a way into an extra than a solitary gathering. It offers the outcome as the probability of the information esteems fit into each bunch. One sort of technique carried out in fluffy grouping has been Fuzzy c-implies bunching. This strategy is connected in the movement to be the K-Means bunching and it is changing in the contemplations that are embroiled in the computation like fuzzifier and relationship goals.

K-NN

One of the simplest methods for machine learning is K-NN. That's a type of supervised learning process. The K-NN model spots new information to the kind that is most commonly associated with the open kind and anticipates similarities between the new event or information and realistic material. Using a KNN approach, each new piece of information is supplied, and the most recent data is arranged according to similarities. This suggests that additional information may be easily described into a respectable suite categorisation using the K-NN computation. K-NN is an algorithm that operates without parametric assumptions, meaning it doesn't generate any conjecture regarding underlying data. It is also known as a languid student calculation because, rather than focussing on the direction given explicitly, it provides the dataset and, at the order's mark, delivers an adventure on it. At the guiding stage, the KNN model only provides the dataset. Later, when it acquires new data, it describes that data to a group that is an exceptional arrangement similar to the newly acquired data.

Random Forest

A popular machine learning technique called Random Forest has been fitted with supervised algorithms. It may be applied to machine learning tasks including both regression and classification. This is founded on the idea of group learning, which is the process of combining several classifiers in order to solve a multipart problem and improve the way the approaches are presented. According to its name, "Random Forest is the classifier that being contained some decision trees on a variety of subsets of the specified a dataset and acquires the standard to progress the prognostic correctness of that dataset."Rather of depending on a single decision tree, the random forest aggregates the predictions from each tree and determines the final output by weighing the predictions' prevalence. The forest's increased tree cover helps to ensure higher accuracy and minimises the risk of overfitting.

LITERATURE SURVEY

Today, a number of academics intended to develop different systematic methods for predicting crimes. The dataset characteristics serve as the foundation for the error-free outcomes. A variety of data mining strategies were developed by author L. Ahuja (2019) in order to estimate the prevalence of crime against women. To estimate the crime rate against women in India and improve the accuracy of the crime rate prediction, S. Bhowmick (2019) presented linear regression machine learning approaches. To forecast India's crime rate against women, author Rishabh Singh (2021) using k-means clustering technique. The authors H. Chen and W. Chung (2004) used several data mining approaches to create a framework centred on crime. The author employed three models—eradication, identification, and network analysis—to expand this research. In order to detect four types of offenses—fraud, traffic violence, criminal violence, and crime in a web—Prabakaran, S., and Mitra, S. (2018) employed several mining algorithms.To forecast crime, analyst Javideh M. R (2011) uses clustering methods and neural networks. These methods allow criminal data to be automatically entered into the database of law enforcement. In order to anticipate the precise crime location with a high chance of crime occurrences, the researcher Shiju Sathyadevan, M.S. (2014) devised a KNN classification method. In order to predict crime patterns, the clinician Sudha Bhauvaneswari N. (2019) used clustering and classification techniques. She also used link analysis to examine the actions of the individual. Akila D. [9], the author, used the WEKA tool's clustering using Euclidian distance to predict and reduce the number of infractions in metropolitan urban regions. To determine accuracy on criminal data based on correlation coefficient, the authors McClendon, L., & Meghanathan, N. (2019) used two distinct regression models: Linear, Additive, and Decision Stump.To verify the accuracy and effectiveness of the various machine learning algorithms, researcher Smriti Sehgal (2017) conducted a comparative analysis. Using the logistic model, experimenter Dahai Liu (2013) makes educated guesses about the offence rate. Using crime data from Vancouver, the author Joshi Sused (2020) used KNN and decision tree algorithms to forecast accuracy. The researcher Zhao X. (2017) uses a pattern of the spatiotemporal technique to determine the crime in a certain location. In order to identify the major crime type in a given region and forecast the crime rate using several sorts of models, such as regression and decision trees, the tester Saltos G. (2017) employed LSOA code.

PROPOSED METHODOLOGIES

Many statistical methods are proposed in this chapter with the simple linear regression Techniques. The below-given figure 3 shows the workflow of crime analysis methods of this paperwork.

Figure 3. Work flow of crime analysis

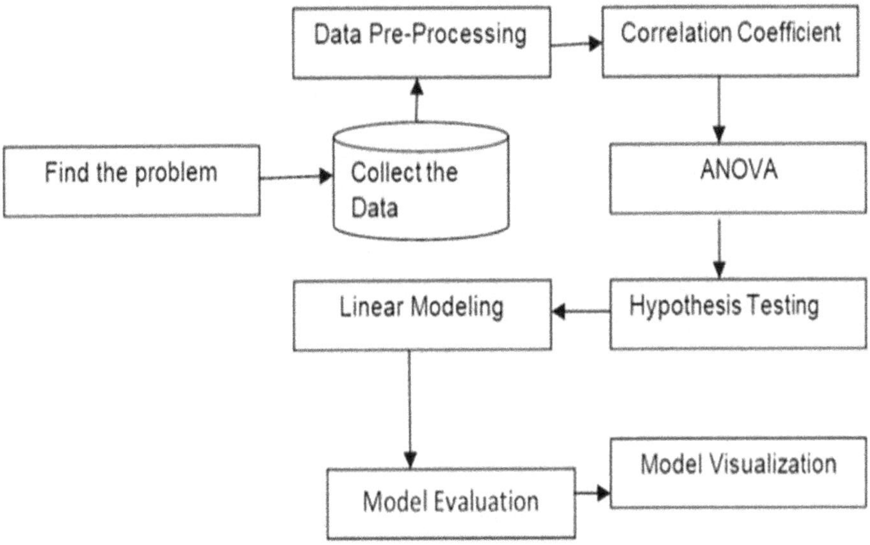

Data Pre-processing

Information pre-processing is utilized in Machine Learning; it's anything but basic work that helps improve the greatness of data to empower the withdrawal of huge understanding from the information. Information pre-processing strategies in Machine Learning followed the arrangement of masterminding (cleanout and sort) the natural information to make it's anything but development and planning Machine Learning model. In simple words, information cleaning is an information mining strategy that is utilized in Machine Learning. That makes over crude information with a logical and understandable configuration. There are various cleaning techniques are following for data cleaning. Information cleaning is the underlying technology that is mandatory in Data pre-processing. In this strategy, the focal notification is on the end of anomalies diminishing reiteration, overseeing lost information, rowdy information, figured injustice, and finding inside the information. Information mix has been the strategy to help when the information is together from broadened information induction and altogether is incorporation to shape unremitting data. This steady data is later than achieve data attack support in examination and information research. Data analytics has been a work that is coordinated to take an incredible number of messages. At the point when administration with the colossal size of messages, seeing is troublesome in such personality. In power to obtain staggering of this, we orchestrate messages diminishing position.

It is necessities to augment the analysis costs, extra room ability, and abatement information extra room.

Statistical Approaches: Correlation Coefficient and Its Types

Correlation can simply implicit as co relation. To delineate, Correlation is the association among 2 or greater than 2 attributes. When one variable values alter, it affects the remaining variable significance then correlation occur between that two attributes. The correlated assessment can be going in the similar direction or opposite direction. If the correlation between only two variables this is called a simple correlation. Correlation is divided as five categories such as

- +ve correlation values should be >0.05
- -ve correlation values > -0.05
- perfectly +ve correlation should be 1
- perfectly -ve correlation should be -1
- 0 correlation and linear correlation is 0.

Positive Correlation

The Positive correlation is an association between 2 variables in that both variables increasing the same direction. A positive correlation exists when one variable gets a negative value and other variables also get a negative direction, or one variable gets a positive value and the other variable also gets a positive value. Positive value indicates +1.

Figure 4. Value based correlation

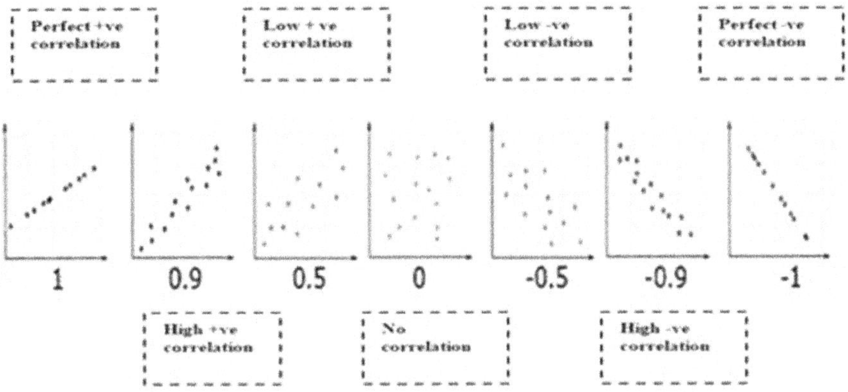

Above figure 4 shows different types of correlation based on the values.

Negative Correlation

The negative correlation is a relationship between 2 variables if one variable gets a negative direction and another variable also gets a positive direction. The negative correlation represents the value -1.

No Correlation or Zero Correlation

When no liaison occurs between 2 attributes then zero values exit. This type of correlation is called zero correlation. Correlation is articulated visually. It is expressed by using a scatter gram which is used to draw a plot for a variable opposite to another variable on a chart. When a scatter gram is used to draw it does not bother which erratic goes x-axis and goes on y-axis. Correlation usually behaves with two attribute values and these attribute values are used for drawing a figure. Fix which attribute values travel in both axes draw a cross at the tip where the 2 scores overlapped. In statistics, the correlation has three types, Pearson's correlation, Spearman correlation, and Kendall rank correlation. Below figure 5 illustrates the correlation using a scatter gram.

Figure 5. Plot for correlation using scatter gram

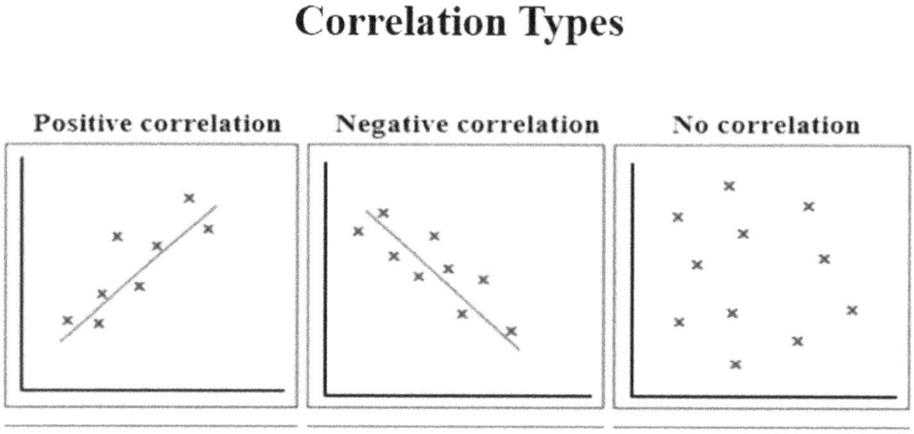

Pearson-r Correlation Approach

This kind of correlation is depending on statistics used to work out the level of the liaison among linear interrelated attributes. For exemplar, calculate the two elements are linked to one other in the reserve bazaar. The following below formula represents correlation of Pearson.

$$r = \frac{N\sum xy - \sum(x)(y)}{\sqrt{[N\sum x^2 - \sum(x^2] - [N\sum y^2 - \sum(y^2]]}} \tag{1}$$

Here element r signifies the correlation of Pearson and element N represents the amount of desirability in the data set. Attribute xy represents an addition of products of two scores then x denotes the addition of x variables and y denotes the addition of y scores. x^2, y^2 process the addition of squared values.

Spearman Correlation Approach

This is the non-parametric analysis type of correlation that is accustomed to determine the stage of association among two elements. It was established by Spearman that why it's called using the name Spearman correlation. This spearman correlation doesn't assume any hypothesis regarding the allocation of the information and which is the correct correlation study when the elements are considered on a scale that is at least ordinal. Given the below formula used to calculate the Spearman correlation.

$$p = 1 - \frac{6\sum d_i^2}{n(n^2 - 1)} \tag{2}$$

From the above formula, di represents the variation of xi, and yi then n represents the size of observations in the particulars.

Kendall Rank Correlation Approach

This category of correlation analysis is used in non-parametric, which deals with the potency of dependence amongst two factors. If consider, a and b as for test sample n denotes sample range then b value calculated by using n (n-1)/2. The subsequent rule computes the rank correlation of Kendall.

$$\tau = \frac{n_c - n_d}{\frac{1}{2}n(n-1)} \tag{3}$$

In the above rule, nc represents the capacity of concordant and nd represents the size of discordant.

Analysis of Variance Approach (ANOVA)

This approach is the way of verdict the dissimilarity along with two or more than two mean values. It is a tool with various types of statistical methods which are helped to test the significant variation of attributes. ANOVA also predicts the authority of independent attribute has the dependent element in regression. In the early years, t and z tests were used then invented the ANOVA by Ronald Fisher which is an extension of t and z. ANOVA was also used to call the name Fisher analysis of variance. It further classified two categories one-way and two-way analysis.

Approaches of ANOVA One-Way Techniques

This class of approach is familiar for discover statistically substantial diversity among means of greater than or equal to two self-determining clusters. Below specified principle applied to detect single-way ANOVA.

$$F = \frac{MST}{MSE} \tag{4}$$

$$MST = \frac{\sum_{I=1}^{K}\left(\frac{T_I^2}{n}_i\right) - G^2/_n}{k - 1} \tag{5}$$

MSE=

$$\frac{\sum_{i=1}^{k}\sum_{j=1}^{n_i} Y_{ij}^2 - \sum_{i=1}^{k}(T_i^2/n_i)}{n-k} \qquad (6)$$

Here F is an Analysis of Variance Coefficient, MST represents the sum of squares when occurs error.MSE stands for the mean sum of the square it is also calculated at the time of errors.

Approaches of ANOVA Two-Way Method

Two ways ANOVA derived from one way ANOVA type. When population categorized with a single feature that time one way ANOVA used. If ANOVA has two factors ANOVA gives a better result than one way. In two ways ANOVA, the sample should be in equal size.

Figure 6. Rules of two ways ANOVA

Rules for Two Way ANOVA

Source of variation	*Sum of squares (SS)*	*Degrees of freedom (d.f)*	*Mean square (MS)*	*F-ratio*
Between columns treatment	$\sum\frac{(T_j)^2}{n_j} - \frac{(T)^2}{n}$	$(c-1)$	$\frac{SS\ \text{between columns}}{(c-1)}$	$\frac{MS\ \text{between columns}}{MS\ \text{residual}}$
Between rows treatment	$\sum\frac{(T_i)^2}{n_i} - \frac{(T)^2}{n}$	$(r-1)$	$\frac{SS\ \text{between rows}}{(r-1)}$	$\frac{MS\ \text{between rows}}{MS\ \text{residual}}$
Residual or error	Total SS − (SS between columns + SS between rows)	$(c-1)(r-1)$	$\frac{SS\ \text{residual}}{(c-1)(r-1)}$	
Total	$\sum X_{ij}^2 - \frac{(T)^2}{n}$	$(cr-1)$		

Factors and its explanation of figure 6 listed below.
c = Total range of column
r =Total rows range, MS = Residual of columns and rows
Here Residual = Total ss = ss between col and ss between row (7)

Hypothesis Approach

Hypothesis gives the outcome in statistical form and decides by assessment data. This test was mostly conducted through experimental and prepared the report regarding population factor. A hypothesis is an assumption that exploits variation amongst duo or more than duo factors. Hypothesis testing is classified into six types. It is explained below one by one.

Simple

It represents the all features linked through the allocation are stated. This kind of hypothesis explains relationships along with tandem factors. Ex considers study well as independent element and while scoring pass percentage as a dependent element.

Complex

Complex types of the hypothesis will test the alliance values between more than 2 dependent and one independent component. Ex if have fruits then get shinny skin and more vitamins to good health.

Directional

This class of hypotheses implemented by an analyzer to check the predicted value's positive or negative change among a couple of elements. Ex four years a kid having a good food its IQ power is good at the age of five, compared to not taking proper food kid.

Non Directional

This type of testing does not forecast the direction of the variation or relationship among groups. Ex if conducting Memory test between college and higher secondary students cannot predict the way of relationship among them.

H0 or Null

This gives a contradictory report and when there is no relationship between both dependent and independent variables. It is denoted as "H0" and this represents the negative statement.

Associative and Causal Hypothesis

An Associative hypothesis is used when one variable result affects some other variable and contributory suggestion recommended reason and effect relations of duplet or more than duplet factor.

Hypothesis: One Sampled T-Test Approach

This hypothesis test is a statistical method. This method helps us to predict whether test observations are created via a process with an exact mean or not. Upper and lower tailed implemented at the time of mean variation.

$$t = \frac{\overline{x} - \mu}{s\overline{x}}$$

here

$$\overline{x} = \frac{s}{\sqrt{n}} \tag{8}$$

Since the above rule
$\overline{x}$ = Mean
s^2 = Variation
n = sample size
μ = mean of Population
t = t quintile along with (n-1) degree of freedom

Evaluating the Machine Learning Models Performance

Evaluation is inevitable for detect the machine learning algorithm's performance based on its accuracy value. Evaluation metrics fluctuate based on the predicament. The linear regression model is usually used for these types of metrics and the objective of the linear regression holds information only. Errors show how the algorithm is fixed and performed while prediction. The main work of the metrics is to find the contrast of intention data and predicted one.

Evaluation of Regression

Following figure 7 express the metrics types and its equations

Figure 7. Evaluation metrics for the machine learning model

Evaluation Metrics

$$MAE = \frac{1}{N}\sum_{i=1}^{N} |y_i - \hat{y}|$$

$$MSE = \frac{1}{N}\sum_{i=1}^{N} (y_i - \hat{y})^2$$

$$RMSE = \sqrt{MSE} = \sqrt{\frac{1}{N}\sum_{i=1}^{N} (y_i - \hat{y})^2}$$

$$R^2 = 1 - \frac{\Sigma(y_i - \hat{y})^2}{\Sigma(y_i - \bar{y})^2}$$

Where,
$\hat{y}$ – predicted value of y
$\bar{y}$ – mean value of y

Regression is an ml model, coded by using statistical and regression that predicts the significant variation among elements. These predicted values contingent on the independent. Below specified equation for the regression

$$Y = \theta_{1\,+}\, \theta_{2\,.}\, X \tag{9}$$

X is an input variable
Y is a labelled to the data
These values are represents the intercept and coefficient of X.

RESULT AND DISCUSSIONS

The below figure8 has given the correlation values for the crime data 2001 to 2012.

Figure 8. Pearson correlation coefficient for crime data

```
[-0.45499746 -0.47186688 -0.45901314 ... -0.40743572 -0.40239439
 -0.3956554 ]]

In [14]: print(df.corr())
          2001      2002      2003  ...      2010      2011      2012
2001  1.000000  0.977338  0.918542  ...  0.823178  0.799310  0.796995
2002  0.977338  1.000000  0.953900  ...  0.858739  0.836965  0.832542
2003  0.918542  0.953900  1.000000  ...  0.852503  0.838167  0.834020
2004  0.949967  0.977338  0.976470  ...  0.915796  0.901220  0.898917
2005  0.935116  0.969198  0.972490  ...  0.921202  0.905677  0.901155
2006  0.925369  0.956625  0.962252  ...  0.938835  0.924750  0.922344
2007  0.910327  0.937866  0.937807  ...  0.959183  0.945412  0.942079
2008  0.882838  0.905192  0.906292  ...  0.979517  0.969155  0.965402
2009  0.854270  0.881700  0.882302  ...  0.992687  0.985671  0.982738
2010  0.823178  0.858739  0.852503  ...  1.000000  0.994944  0.992546
2011  0.799310  0.836965  0.838167  ...  0.994944  1.000000  0.996515
2012  0.796995  0.832542  0.834020  ...  0.992546  0.996515  1.000000

[12 rows x 12 columns]

In [15]:
```

Table 1. Midpoint and standard deviation values for ANOVA

Categories of Crimes	Mid values(Mean)	Standard Deviation
AWI To Outrage	1295.74	1744.88
Cruelty By Husband Or Relatives	3043.63	4621.06
Dowry Death	235.23	446.49
Immoral Traffic(Prevention)Act	73.23	134.80
Indecent Representation Of Women(Prevention)Act	4.03	12.10
Insult To The Modesty Of Women	262.09	661.31
Kidnapping & Abduction	1093.20	1642.47
Rape	712.09	820.81

The above table1 contains the crime data values for mean and standard deviation for analysis of variance, figure 9 shows the sample crime dataset and figure 10 visualize the crime details in state-wise.

Figure 9. Crime dataset for ANOVA

	2001	2002	2003	2004	2005	2006	2007	2008	2009	2010	2011	2012	crime type	STATE
0	871	1002	946	1016	935	1049	1070	1257	1188	1362	1442	1341	RAPE	Andhra Pradesh
1	33	38	31	42	35	37	48	42	59	47	42	46	RAPE	Arunachal Pradesh
2	817	970	1095	1171	1238	1244	1437	1438	1631	1721	1700	1716	RAPE	Assam
3	888	1040	985	1390	1147	1232	1555	1302	929	795	934	927	RAPE	Bihar
4	959	992	898	969	990	995	982	978	976	1012	1053	1034	RAPE	Chhattisgarh

```
5]: df.boxplot('2012',by='STATE')
```

Figure 10. Box plot for 2012 state-wise crime details

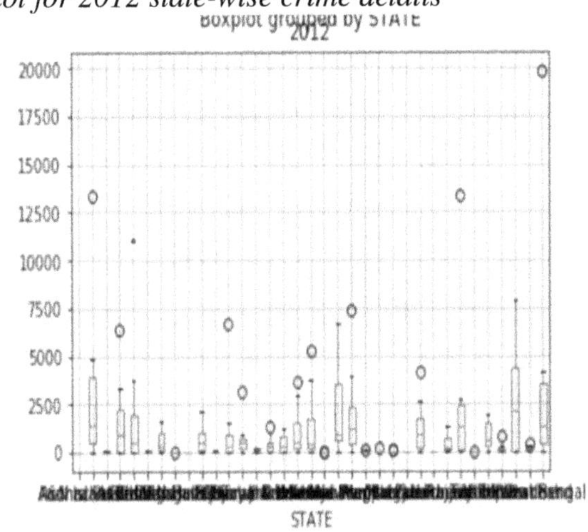

Based on the one way ANOVA the following f and p values for crime against women data is f=0.49161045236192025 and p =0.6185056796954008

To predict the crime rate against women in 2012, this approach was implemented to test the hypothesis and it has given the following output. Since the below figures 11 and 12 show the one sampled t-test and rejecting null hypothesis testing results for the crime dataset.

Figure11. P-value for one sampled t -test

```
In [42]: print(p_value)
0.002247522250471508
```

Figure12. Checking whether hypothesis is null or not

```
n [44]: if p_value < 0.05:
   ...:     print("we are rejecting null hypothesis")
   ...: else:
   ...:         print("we are accepting null hypothesis")
ie are rejecting null hypothesis
```

From the above result, there is a change between the sample mean and population means so the null hypothesis is rejected here. Predict the crime rate of crime against women data set using linear regression we get the following output and evaluating model using metrics of MAE, MSE, R2.Table 2 gives the metric results using a regression model.

Table. 2 Evolution details for regression

Regression	Absolute error value of Mean	Squared Error value of mean	Value of R^2
Linear Regression	.5693	.6724	.97530

Figure 13. Metric evaluation comparisons

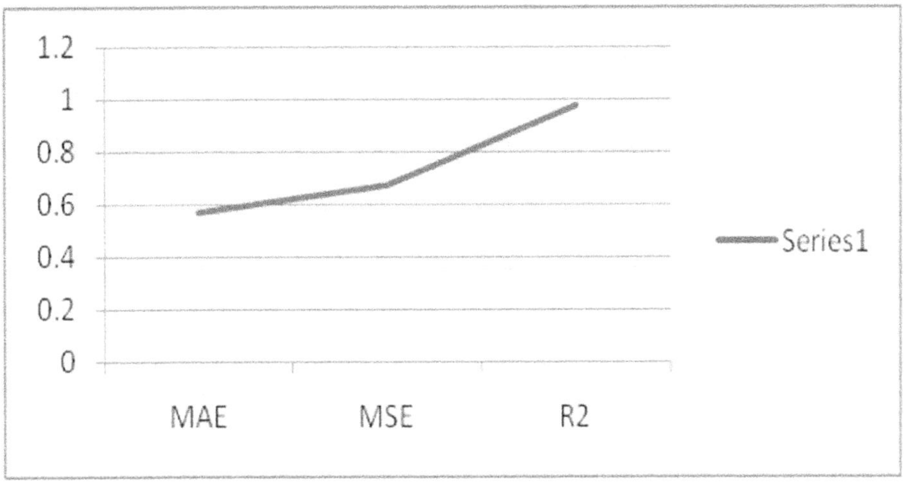

The figure 13 visualizes the metric results for crime analysis.

CONCLUSION

This chapter work was done by using the dataset from 2001 to 2012. Several modules can be used to implement while performing this analysis. The data set is not efficient when it was collected as raw. Pre-processing was broadly used to prepare the data for efficient use. The main objectives of the data analysis are efficient and get the result with higher accuracy. Now a day's technologies are also very helpful to predict crime accurately. In this work, the linear regression was performed with less error, based on the R2 values the prediction has given higher accuracy. This type of prediction will be helpful to the police department to control the significant crime in a hotspot area, In the future; we can predict the crime rate using various types of regression Techniques.

REFERENCES

Ahuja, L. (2019). *Crime against women: Analysis and prediction using data mining techniques*. Big Data, Cloud and Parallel Computing.

Akila, D. (2019). *Crime against women (CAW) analysis and prediction in Tamilnadu police using data mining techniques. International Journal of Recent Technology and Engineering*.

Bhauvaneswari, N. S. (2019). *Data mining techniques to analyze and predict crimes*. IJRTE.

Bhowmick, S. (2019). *Analysis of crimes against women in India using regression*. IJEAT.

Chung, H. (2004). *Crime data mining: A general framework and some examples*. ACM SIGPLAN.

Javideh, M. R. (2011). Detecting and investigating crime by means of data mining: A general crime matching framework. *Procedia Computer Science*.

Joshi, S. (2020). Crime analysis through machine learning. *ic-ETITE*.

Lawrence. (2015). Using machine learning algorithms to analyze crime data. *MLAIJ*.

Liu, D. (2013). Burglary crime analysis using logistic regression. *International Conference on Human Interface and the Management of Information (HIMI)*.

McClendon, L. (2015). *Using machine learning algorithms to analyze crime data*. MLAIJ. DOI: 10.5121/mlaij.2015.2101

Mitra, S. (2018). Survey of analysis of crime detection techniques using data mining and machine learning. *Journal of Physics:IOP Conf Series*.

Rishabh, S. (2021). *K-means clustering analysis of crimes on Indian women*. ASPG.

Saltos, G., & Cocea, M. (2017). An exploration of crime prediction using data mining on open data. *International Journal of Information Technology & Decision Making*, 16(5), 1155–1181. DOI: 10.1142/S0219622017500250

Sathyadevan, M. S. (2014). *Crime analysis and prediction using data mining*. ICN-SC. DOI: 10.1109/CNSC.2014.6906719

Sehgal, S. (2017). A review: Crime analysis using data mining techniques and algorithms. *International Conference on Computing Communication and Automation*.

Singh, R. (2021). *K-means clustering analysis of crimes on Indian women*. ASPG.

Zhao, X. (2017). Exploring transfer learning for crime prediction. *ICDMW*.

Chapter 5
Intelligent Decision Model Based on Deep Reinforcement Learning for Soccer Games Outcome Prediction Using Optimal Feature Extraction and Optimization

V. Thamilarasi
https://orcid.org/0000-0002-5866-0074
Sri Sarada College for Women, India

R. Roselin
Sri Sarada College for Women, India

Kirti H. Wanjale
Vishwakarma Institute of Technology, India

P. Pushpa
https://orcid.org/0009-0002-8275-2814
East China University of Technology, China

DOI: 10.4018/979-8-3693-7868-7.ch005

ABSTRACT

In this study, the authors propose an intelligent decision model, the deep reinforcement learning for soccer games outcome prediction (DRL-SGO), using optimal feature extraction and optimization. Initially, they design a feature extraction model based on DenseNet to extract soccer games domain knowledge, including recency and rating features, from the given dataset. Subsequently, they use the artificial rabbit optimization (ARO) algorithm to optimize features, selecting the best among a multitude of options. Additionally, they employ deep reinforcement learning (DRL) techniques to enhance the accuracy of predicting soccer game outcomes. Finally, they validate the performance of the proposed DRL-SGO model using the 2017 soccer prediction challenge dataset. Remarkably, the DRL-SGO model achieved an accuracy of 93.991%, precision of 89.169%, recall of 90.537%, and F-measure of 89.843%, showcasing its impressive predictive in the realm of soccer game outcome forecasting.

1. INTRODUCTION

The world's most popular sport soccer has improved in athleticism and strategy. Soccer tactical optimization is transitioning from coaches' intuition to AI and deep reinforcement learning (Ji et al., 2021). In this strategic age, cutting-edge technology and soccer games will alter how teams plan, adapt, and succeed. To enhance techniques, soccer coaches employed subjective appraisals, stories, and trial-and-error. Strategic optimization has here thanks to big data, advanced computers, and machine learning. Deep reinforcement learning, a subset of machine learning, is perfect for soccer games because it extracts insights from large data sets and optimizes decision-making in dynamic contexts (Voigt et al., 2023). Deep reinforcement learning-based smart decision models optimize soccer tactics in this study. Such novelty is needed as soccer becomes more competitive and fine-tuning approaches can make or break team. DRL AI can help coaches and teams make better decisions, adapt to changing game situations, and gain a tactical advantage over their opponents. More than a sport, soccer is a dynamic mix of skill, strategy, and teamwork (Protevi, 2023). Soccer success depends on individual skill and team strategy to outmaneuver opponents. Soccer tactical optimization involves refining game play techniques, formations, and decision-making to maximize field results (Yeung & Fujii, 2023). Tactical optimization is crucial, especially as teams become more advanced. The current game requires an ordered development that incorporates technology, not just traditional coaching (Chen, 2023). This research investigates how intelligent decision models, particularly deep reinforcement learning ones, can improve soccer teams' tactics. Soccer strategies have evolved via creativity and adaptation. Historically, coaches developed game strategies using intuition, experience, and observation (Barraclough et al., 2023). Traditional tactical methods are limited by cognitive biases, individuality, and lack of capacity to examine massive quantities in real time. Player statistics and in-game measures are more accessible in modern soccer. This data is too large and complex to analyze. Traditional procedures fail to maximize information, preventing teams from making decisions based on data.

Artificial intelligence in soccer strategy changes tactical optimization (O'Brien & O'Keeffe, 2022). Machine learning-based AI computers can comprehend subtle patterns, find hidden relationships, and handle massive datasets faster than humans. Soccer teaching can become more scientific and data-driven with these possibilities. Recent soccer machine learning applications include player performance analysis and injury prediction (Jin et al., 2022). DRL, which blends deep neural networks with reinforcement learning, allows models of decision-making to learn the best approaches through trial and error, like soccer. Machine learning's deep reinforcement learning subset excels in consecutive decision-making in dynamic environments (Kedir et al., 2022). It uses deep neural networks to learn complex representations and reinforcement learning techniques to optimize agent actions based on environmental feedback. This combination of technologies can revolutionize soccer tactical decision-making. Soccer's fluidity, volatility, and need for real-time response match DRL's strength (Lan & Shin, 2023). DRL-based intelligent decision models allow coaches to use algorithms to assess, adjust, and optimize strategy over games and season.

Soccer has changed significantly throughout time. Cutting-edge technologies have changed the tactical environment. This section analyzes the technological advances that have shaped soccer strategies. Video analysis revolutionized soccer's tactical strategy (Wang & Chen, 2022). Sports code, Catapult Vision, and Nacsport give coaches new ways to evaluate match footage (Deuker et al., 2023). Coaches use frame-by-frame analysis to understand player movements, defensive systems, and trends that inform tactical adjustments. Video analysis speeds up post-match assessments and allows instant tactical alterations during clashes (Chhabra et al., 2023). GPS monitoring gadgets and wearable have revolutionized player performance data analysis (Dovgan, 2023). Due to the quantity of data, trainers may personalize training, assess player fitness, and optimize training techniques (Cossich et al., 2023). Evaluations of performance and tactical analysis show a player's strengths and allow strategic modifications (Kenwright, 2023). Data analytics is crucial to modern soccer strategies (Mozgovoy et al., 2021). Modern decision-making relies on mathematical models and machine learning. Coaches use anticipated goals (xG) measures to uncover goal scoring patterns and opponent defense deficiencies. Data analytics gives teams a competitive edge by providing evidence-based insights and facilitating dynamic match and tactical preparation (Grover et al., 2018).

Technology goes beyond physical training to include VR and simulation. Coaches use these technologies to simulate match circumstances in training. VR lets players practice complicated game situations in a controlled setting. This immersive method improves decision-making under duress, spatial awareness, and tactical understanding, making the team more adaptable and resilient. Tactical simulations have reached new heights with AI. AI-powered algorithms forecast opponent plans and tactical patterns from massive datasets (Rønningen, 2021). Intelligent decision models replicate game scenarios to help coaches anticipate and counter opposition tactics. Teams use AI and coaching intuition to take a more sophisticated and tactical approach to matches, combining technology's analytical power with coaching's experience. These technical advances have changed how teams prepare, strategize, and compete on the pitch, mirrored in soccer's tactical evolution.

Our contributions. Presented is an intelligent decision model, the deep reinforcement learning for soccer games outcome prediction (DRL-SGO), incorporating optimal feature extraction and optimization techniques. The commitments of the proposed DRL-SGO model are illustrated as follows.

1. To begin, we have created a DenseNet-based feature extraction model that is used to extract features like recency and ratings from the provided dataset that are relevant to soccer games.
2. Artificial rabbit optimization (ARO) algorithm is used to optimize features, ensuring that the best ones from a set of options are chosen.
3. Besides, the profound support learning (DRL) technique is acquainted with foresee soccer match results, in this way upgrading the general expectation precision of the model.
4. At last, the presentation of the proposed DRL-SGO model is thoroughly assessed utilizing the 2017 soccer forecast challenge dataset. Various metrics, including accuracy, precision, recall, and F-measure, are employed to validate the model's performance with respect to soccer game outcome prediction.

The rest of this paper is organized as follows. Section 2 gives the review of recent works related to the soccer games outcome prediction using intelligent decision models. Section 3 provides the detailed working process of proposed DRL-SGO model with the detailed mathematical models. The results and comparative analysis of proposed and existing soccer games outcome prediction models have discussed in the Section 4. Finally, the paper concludes in Section 5.

2. RELATED WORKS

2.1 State-of-Art Studies

A data based deep reinforcement learning system was used to optimize player behavior in important soccer match scenarios where passing or dribbling is prohibited. The training policy network-based architecture helps players and coaches make better judgments by comparing their conduct policy to the optimal policy. The player can foul, pass, shoot, or risk losing possession to the other team. After evaluating 104 matches, the optimal policy network considerably raises mean rewards to 0.45, greater than the behavior policy's obtained expected objectives (-0.1). They use off-policy policy gradient reinforcement learning to optimize soccer game objectives. The study suggests expanding the framework's evaluation to encompass all on-the-ball events, such as dribbles and passes, to make it more relevant for soccer match analysis (Rahimian, Oroojlooy, & Toka, 2021).

An end-to-end deep reinforcement learning framework focused on deriving optimal decisions from actual team behaviors in soccer matches. The framework initially analyzes team strategies by assessing propensities for selecting ball destination locations using deep learning. It then determines optimal tactics based on the collective locations of all players on the pitch. The optimization framework continually highlights the optimal space for the ball, maximizing its potential contribution to the team's long-term success. Unlike counterfactual reasoning, the study directly derives optimal policies for moving the ball, showcasing the expected improvement in goal difference if teams adapted their behavior. The study represents the first attempt to utilize reinforcement learning to maximize expected possession outcomes across the entire soccer pitch. A potential future direction is expanding the framework to capture individual player contributions, enabling adaptation to team-specific optimal strategies at an individual level (Rahimian et al., 2022).

Reinforcement Learning (RL) is applied to the very small size soccer (VSSS) category, a robotic soccer environment. Utilizing multi-agent and self-play techniques, the study demonstrates RL's capability to learn both control and strategic aspects within this context. The learning process is analyzed by comparing two training methods: self-play and training against a hand-coded heuristic from PequiMecânico's VSSS-EMC. PequiMecânico's best approach, the self-play model wins 84%, beating the hand-coded heuristic. The unified strategy for control and strategic decision-making overcomes hierarchical solutions and shows RL's capacity to handle both simultaneously. Implementing the model on real robots, fine-tuning for sim-to-real transfer, and using Imitation Learning to emulate PequiMecânico's heuristic behavior before RL self-play are future possibilities this method improves training efficiency and allows heuristic analysis of final behavior (Brandão et al., 2022).

The study emphasizes soccer decision-making and data analysis above imaginary scenarios. The proposed method simulates soccer "what if" problems using data-driven machine learning models. An event-based soccer simulation compliant with the OpenAI GYM API uses the models to simplify difficult human physics and ball interactions. The study introduces tools for exploring and gaining insights into soccer, including calculating risk/reward ratios for action sequences, manually defining playing criteria, and discovering strategies through Reinforcement Learning. The simulation-based methodology offers a practical means to delve into various aspects of soccer decision-making, providing a valuable framework for analysis and exploration beyond traditional data-centric approaches. (Mendes-Neves et al., 2021)

Most existing match analysis has relied on simple variable descriptions and associations, often lacking practicality for coaches and teams. Advanced analyses, typically driven by computer scientists, may lack practicality and adoption by coaches. Applied machine learning alongside trainers and analytics could handle more interacting variables, providing teams with faster and more useful information. Future sports scientists must increase machine learning and knowledge representation as data analysis becomes more sophisticated. To evaluate machine learning data and trends, multi-disciplinary approaches including computing research groups and football-savvy sports scientists are needed (Herold et al., 2019).

Information based deep reinforcement learning architecture to help offensive and defense players choose optimal possession actions. The training policy network-based approach helps players and coaches evaluate real and ideal policies for decision-making. Sports pros can optimize offensive and defensive strategies using possession attributes and state representation. Analysis of 104 matches from 11 teams shows that the optimal policy network considerably boosts offensive and defensive mean rewards. Defensive teams should react dependent on location, while attacking teams should shoot more in half-spaces. Teams are ranked by their ability to choose optimal actions. Future research could use multi-agent reinforcement learning to optimize opponent teams' policies and consider game context attributes for better results. Limitations include focusing on on-ball defensive actions and not knowing teams' positioning decisions or strategy. (Rahimian & Toka, 2023)

The study underscores the versatility of reinforcement learning in various artificial intelligence applications, emphasizing its role in team collaboration and decision-making within virtual human swarms. Football, as a group sport, uniquely encapsulates both individual and group intelligence, making it an ideal scenario for investigating multi-intelligence collaboration. The research delves into the intricacies of team collaboration and gaming issues within the specific context of football, employing reinforcement learning to address the complex dynamics of cooperation and competition among intelligent entities. The study aims to unravel the intricate relationships between individual and group intelligences within virtual human swarms by utilizing reinforcement learning in the context of football. The all encompassing nature and fierce elements of football give a rich proving ground to creating successful multi-knowledge preparing models. The examination looks for not exclusively to improve how we might interpret group joint effort in a particular climate yet in addition to contribute significant experiences that might actually reach out to more extensive applications in multi-specialist frameworks and man-made reasoning fields. (Mo et al., 2022)

The evolving landscape of team sports performance analysis presents exciting opportunities with the increasing availability of data. The incorporation of big data technologies in soccer research holds promise for addressing key challenges. This advancement may lead to novel methods and a more comprehensive theoretical understanding of tactical team performance in elite soccer. The machine learning approaches, primarily led by computer science research groups, suggest future collaborations between computer and sports scientists for more relevant applications. The integration of big data technologies calls for adjustments in university curricula to equip students with the necessary background to comprehend and utilize these techniques effectively. (Rein & Memmert, 2016)

A groundbreaking framework integrates machine learning and artificial intelligence to the strategies employed in professional soccer. Markov decision for learning offensive behaviors with probabilistic model checking, the framework facilitates reasoning about modeled policies. Notably, the study addresses challenges such as learning missing intended end locations and sparsity issues through predictive modeling and a hierarchical Bayesian approach. The framework is applied to two use cases: evaluating shot policies and optimizing defensive strategies against specific opponents. Although the model's correctness lacks strong guarantees, it offers valuable insights for tactical analysis, aiding coaches in training sessions and game preparation. The approach, while currently agnostic over opponents, holds promise for broader applications in other team sports, leveraging existing domain knowledge. Limitations include the need for explicit modeling of opponent behaviors and potential enhancements in contextual state space and policy evaluation assumptions. Overall, the framework pioneers the integration of learning and reasoning for nuanced insights into soccer strategies. (Karakaya et al., 2022)

Soccer, a globally cherished sport, has undergone significant evolution, transitioning from a purely physical exertion-based game to one heavily reliant on pre-planned decision-making, particularly in the context of league standings. The system, applicable beyond soccer, serves as a generic tool for various sports, aiming to enhance decision support for managers and coaches in player selection. The system's adaptability across sports underscores its potential to revolutionize decision support for team management in diverse athletic disciplines. By using soft computing techniques, particularly artificial intelligence and neural networks, this innovative approach aligns with the demand for data-driven insights in sports analytics, offers tool for informed decision-making in dynamic sporting environments. (Vijay Fidelis & Karthikeyan, 2022)

2.2 Research Gaps

Soccer games outcome prediction plays a crucial role in several domains, with implications extending across diverse industries. In the sports betting sector, accurate predictions are essential for both bookmakers and bettors, guiding informed decisions on wager placements. Additionally, outcome predictions contribute significantly to fan engagement, adding excitement as enthusiasts anticipate and discuss potential match results involving their favorite teams. Soccer coaches and teams leverage predictive models to analyze opponents' strengths and weaknesses, aiding in the formulation of strategic game plans, including player positioning, tactics, and overall strategies. In the realm of fantasy sports, where participants assemble virtual teams, outcome predictions serve as valuable guide for optimizing team selections. Beyond the fan-centric sphere, predictive analytics in soccer outcomes also influences broadcasting and media, enhancing the narrative provided by sports analysts and commentators with statistical insights and pre-match predictions. Berrar et al. (2019) introduced two novel methodologies for constructing predictive features from soccer match data, denoting them as recency feature extraction and rating feature learning. The application of these techniques to the 2017 soccer prediction challenge dataset resulted in the creation of two distinct learning sets: the recency feature learning set and the rating feature learning set. Both datasets can be conveniently represented in tabular or matrix form, facilitating subsequent supervised learning. To explore these datasets, the authors initially employed k-nearest neighbor (k-NN) learning, well-established approach in machine learning. Nonetheless, they additionally explored different avenues regarding troupes of outrageous inclination helped trees (XGBoost) for result expectation. Quite, the best model that could be concluded on time was the k-NN model prepared on the rating highlight learning set.

One common test emerges from the mind boggling elements of soccer matches, described by complex collaborations among players. Simulated intelligence arrangements, especially profound learning methods like brain organizations, demonstrate significant in consequently learning multifaceted examples and connections inside the information, empowering models to adjust to the nuanced elements of soccer. Another test originates from the high dimensionality of soccer match datasets, which frequently contain various factors. AI uses feature extraction techniques like Principal Component Analysis (PCA) or autoencoder to address this issue. These techniques make it easier to identify the features that are most important and reduce the complexity of the data. Worldly elements and groupings in soccer occasions present extra obstacles, as the request for activities can fundamentally impact results. Artificial intelligence, through the use of recurrent neural networks (RNNs) and long short-term memory (LSTM) organizations, really models successive conditions in the information, permitting expectation models to think about the sequential request of occasions. AI addresses this challenge through imputation techniques and robust training methods, ensuring the mitigation of the impact of incomplete or noisy data on prediction accuracy. Non-linearity and intricate interactions between features pose further challenges, and AI responds with the deployment of kernel methods, support vector machines, and deep learning architectures like multi-layer perceptron. These techniques effectively model complex, nonlinear relationships and capture intricate feature interactions within the data. Imbalances in the distribution of outcomes (win, lose, and draw) within soccer data may result in biased models. AI strategies such as oversampling, undersampling, or employing different cost functions during training are used to rectify class imbalances, ensuring fair representation of all outcomes. The interpretability of profound learning models, frequently saw as "secret elements," represents a test. Simulated intelligence procedures, including logical computer based intelligence techniques like SHAP values or consideration components in brain organizations, are consolidated to give bits of knowledge into the elements impacting the model's forecasts. To resolve the above issues, we plan the accompanying examination goals.

1. Configuration, carries out, and assesses cutting edge profound learning customized for soccer match result expectation. This incorporates investigating creative designs and advancing model boundaries to upgrade the limit with respect to catching mind boggling examples and connections inside the unique setting of soccer matches.
2. Research and carry out ideal element extraction procedures, with an emphasis on techniques to successfully distinguish and focus on important elements inside high-layered soccer datasets.
3. Create and evaluate progressed transient demonstrating strategies to catching the successive conditions inborn in soccer occasions. It is utilized to work on the model's capacity to think about the sequential request of activities and improve expectation precision in unique game situations.
4. Investigate and implement robust training strategies to deal with issues caused by noisy or incomplete soccer match datasets. This includes investigating ascription procedures and high level preparation systems to work on the model's strength to information flaws, prompting more dependable and generalizable result forecasts.

3. PROPOSED METHODOLOGY

3.1 Overview of Proposed DRL-SGO Model

The general framework plan of the proposed DRL-SGO (Profound Support Learning for Soccer matches Result) model, as portrayed in Figure 1, gives a thorough structure to the precise expectation of soccer match results. The 2017 soccer prediction challenge dataset is meticulously preprocessed in the first step to address missing values, normalize the data, and deal with outliers, resulting in a clean and standardized dataset for subsequent analysis. Following information preprocessing, DenseNet, brain network design eminent for its thick associations between layers, is utilized for highlight extraction. Explicitly intended to catch Recency elements and Rating highlights from the soccer match dataset, DenseNet assumes a critical part in removing pertinent data fundamental for anticipating game results. During the feature optimization phase, the artificial rabbit optimization (ARO) algorithm is used to further improve the model's performance. The picked ARO calculation is known for its proficiency in exploring complex component spaces. The result of this streamlining system is a bunch of elements considered ideal for adding to the model's prescient precision. In this manner, the chose ideal elements are coordinated into the soccer match result expectation stage utilizing profound support learning (DRL) strategies. DRL, picked for its flexibility to consecutive information and dynamic conditions, is utilized to group game results into classes like win, misfortune, or draw. The bits of knowledge acquired from the streamlined elements effectively work on the exactness of expectations, offering progressed abilities in determining soccer match results. It holds likely applications in sports examination, wagering methodologies, and training experiences inside the powerful scene of soccer matches.

Figure 1. Overall system design of proposed DRL-SGO model for soccer game outcome prediction

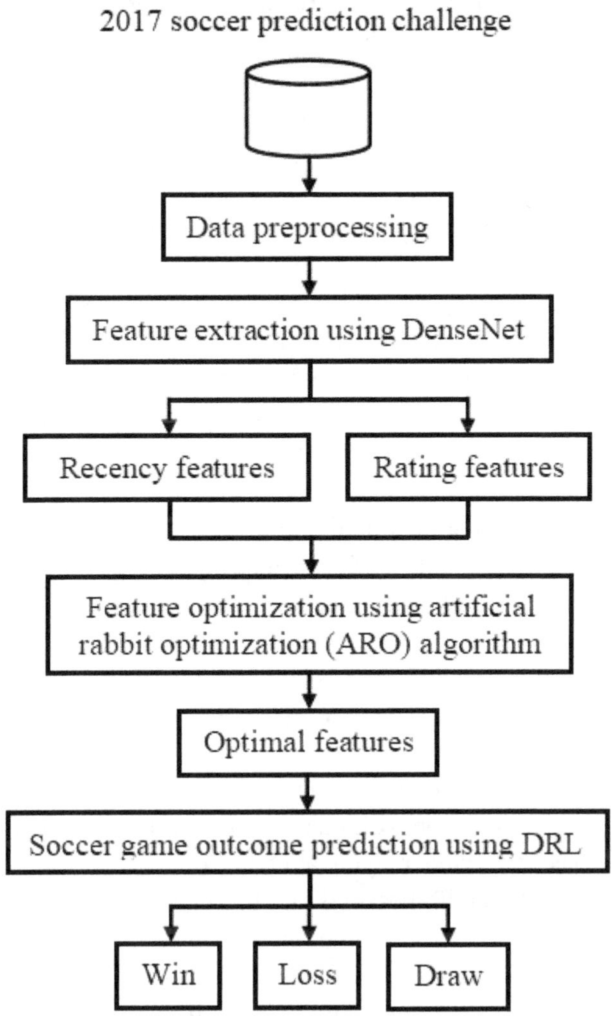

3.2 Feature Extraction

In our methodology, we have made an element extraction model in view of DenseNet, a brain network engineering known for its thick associations between layers. From the provided dataset, this model aims to extract soccer-specific domain knowledge. DenseNet, in this specific situation, is used to show highlights addressing each match utilizing four particular component bunches for each group included.

1. The principal highlight bunch is the "going after strength," which evaluates a group's ability in scoring objectives. This element epitomizes the hostile capacities of a group and gives significant bits of knowledge into its objective scoring potential during a match.
2. The subsequent component bunch is the "guarded strength," zeroing in a group's ability to forestall objectives by the rival. This element offers a measurement for a group's protective ability, showing its capacity to impede the rival group's objective scoring endeavors.
3. The third feature group, "home advantage," is used to evaluate the home venue's attacking and defensive strengths. It catches the impact of playing at the group's home ground, influencing both hostile and protective parts of the game.
4. The fourth component bunch, "strength of resistance," effectively qualifies going after and guarded qualities, as well as home benefit, according to the nature of the resistance. This feature group acknowledges that a team's performance is significantly influenced by the opponent's strength.

To additionally refine the quantitative portrayal of a group's presentation, we characterize four extra highlights, each catching explicit parts of a group's capacity to score and forestall objectives both at home and away scenes.

1. "Home going after strength" mirrors a group's capability in scoring objectives while playing at its home scene. A higher worth connotes a more grounded hostile exhibition at home.
2. "Home guarded shortcoming" connotes a group's weakness in forestalling objectives at its home scene. A higher worth demonstrates a higher weakness to yielding objectives while playing at home.
3. "Away going after strength" measures a group's capacity to score objectives while playing at the rival's scene. A value that is higher suggests a better offensive performance away from home.
4. "Away protective shortcoming" addresses a group's weakness in forestalling objectives at the rival's scene. A higher worth recommends a higher weakness to yielding objectives while playing ceaselessly.

These highlights on the whole give a nuanced and far reaching portrayal of a group's presentation elements, enveloping hostile and protective capacities both at home and away scenes, and considering in the strength of the resistance. This element extraction model establishes the groundwork for resulting examinations and expectations with regards to soccer match results. DenseNet varies from convolutional neural networks (CNNs) by laying out thick associations between layers. Here, each layer gets input from the first layer as well as from every previous layer.

This thick network design works with highlight reuse and improves the model's capacity to catch multifaceted examples in the information. DenseNet is used to extract essential domain knowledge from the dataset and represent it in this setting.

- DenseNet is applied to address every soccer match utilizing four particular element bunches for each group. These feature groups are essential for predicting game outcomes because they capture various aspects of a team's performance.
- The four feature groups are home advantage, attacking strength, defensive strength, and opposition strength. Every one of these component bunches gives an exceptional viewpoint in a group's capacities and considers factors, for example, hostile and protective ability, home-field advantage, and the nature of the resistance.
- To additionally refine the portrayal, four quantitative highlights are characterized for each group. These highlights catch a group's presentation with regards to scoring and forestalling objectives at both home and away settings.
- DenseNet is utilized to process highlights like home going after strength, home protective shortcoming, away going after strength, and away guarded shortcoming. These highlights offer itemized experiences into group's hostile and cautious elements in game situations.
- The thick network in DenseNet guarantees that the model can successfully catch conditions and connections among the different highlights, making a rich portrayal of soccer match. This portrayal, enveloping different parts of group execution, fills in as an establishment for resulting stages in the expectation model.

3.3 Feature Optimization

The artificial rabbit optimization (ARO) calculation is a nature-enlivened enhancement calculation that draws motivation from the rummaging conduct of hares looking for food. ARO is intended to effectively investigate arrangement spaces and close ideal answers for streamlining issues. ARO is motivated by the searching way of behaving of bunnies. In nature, bunnies adjust their scrounging procedures to find food sources productively. Likewise, the calculation tries to adaptively investigate the arrangement space to track down ideal arrangements. The calculation keeps a populace of fake hares, each addressing an expected arrangement in the hunt space. These rabbits move around the solution space to investigate and take advantage of various areas. A vital component of ARO is its versatile inquiry system. Based on their individual experiences and the collective knowledge of the population as a whole, the rabbits in the population dynamically adjust the balance between exploration and exploitation. Both local and global search strategies are incorporated into ARO. Bunnies investigate the nearby neighborhood of their ongoing situation to take advantage of promising regions, and they additionally participate in worldwide investigation to find new districts with the potential for improved arrangements. The optimization problem's objective function is used to evaluate each rabbit's position's fitness. The bunnies plan to expand or limit this wellness capability, contingent upon the idea of the advancement issue. ARO utilizes a memory instrument to hold data about the verifiable execution of each hare. This permits the memorable calculation promising regions in the pursuit space and guide future investigation towards those districts. Hares in ARO adjust their ways of behaving and development methodologies after some time in view of their singular achievement and the outcome of the whole populace. This versatile learning component upgrades the calculation's capacity to join to ideal arrangements. In this specific situation, ARO can be utilized to choose the most important elements from a bigger arrangement of expected highlights. The algorithm explores different subsets of features and evaluates their performance based on a fitness criterion. Features that contribute to better performance are retained, and the process iterates until an optimal or near-optimal set of features is identified.

In ARO calculation, each emphasis refreshes the number of inhabitants in the bunnies' situation as per the standards of the gave strategy and afterward it is exposed to the goal capability's appraisal. As the methodology proceeds, the pursuit specialists of the hare's positions, which address the arrangements, improve. A randomized site inside the looking through space is delegated to each situation initially populace:

$$Ev_u = KV + random(1, \mathrm{dim}antion) \times [YB - KV]u = 1{:}M_{Ev} \tag{1}$$

where Rbi means the area of each hare, UB and LB signify the upper and lower limits of the plan factors, NRb and faint are, correspondingly, the quantity of bunnies in the populace and the quantity of the factors that are being assessed. Each looking for hare decides to switch positions with another looking for creature picked arbitrarily from the multitude and embrace interruption, according to the AROA's diversion scrounge strategy.

$$MEv_l(iteration + 1) = Ev_h(iteration) + \left(Ev_l(iteration) - Ev_h(iteration)\right) \times xn + MSA \times round \left(\tfrac{1}{2} \times \left(\tfrac{5}{100} + e_u\right)\right), l, h = 1{:}M_{Ev}, h \neq l \tag{2}$$

$$Xn = f \times \left(w - w\left(\tfrac{iteration-1}{iteration_{max}}\right)^2\right) \times \sin(2\tau e_2) \tag{3}$$

$$f(h) = \begin{cases} 1 if h = t(\varphi) \\ o else \end{cases}, h = 1{:}\dim and \varphi = 1{:}\left[e_3, \dim antion\right] \quad (4)$$

$$T = randperm(\dim), m_1 \approx M(0,1) \quad (5)$$

where iter demonstrates to the ongoing emphasis, Rbk and NRbk are the old and new areas of the kth hare, NDS is the standard capability connected with ordinary dissemination, rand perm is a randomizing change capability, r1, r2, and r3 are three irregular numbers close enough [0, 1], and Itermax addresses the greatest cycles number. A hare regularly uncovers various passages close to its home to act as haven while dodging hunters.

$$v_l, h(iteration) = Ev_l(iteration) \times (1 + H.G) \quad (6)$$

$$l = 1{:}M_{ev} and h = 1{:}\dim \quad (7)$$

$$G = e_4 \times \frac{iteration_{\max} - iteration + 1}{iteration_{\max}} \quad (8)$$

$$T(h) = \begin{cases} 1 if h = l \\ 0 else \end{cases} h = 1{:}\dim \quad (9)$$

where r4 seems to be a randomly chosen number between [0, 1], bk,j is the jth burrow of the kth rabbit, and H is the hiding value, which progressively falls from 1 to 1/Itermax as a function of the current iteration. These burrows are initially built in a rabbit's bigger surroundings based on this trait. To remain, rabbits need to find a safe location to stay. They select a hole at random from those they must hide in to remain undetected.

$$MEv_l(iter + 1) = Ev_l(iter) + An \times \left(e_5 \times v_l, n(iter)\right) l = 1{:}MEv. \quad (10)$$

The kth rabbit's location is altered as following if detour forage or randomly hiding are effective:

$$Ev_l(iter + 1) = \begin{cases} Ev_l(iter) d\left(Ev_l(iter) \leq d\left(MEv_l(iter + 1\right)\right) \\ MEv_l(iter + 1) d\left(Ev_l(iter) \geq d\left(MEv_l(iter + 1\right)\right) \end{cases} \quad (11)$$

The energy model is accustomed to demonstrating the abuse stage portrayed by randomized camouflage. The energy factor can be characterized as follows:

$$QR(iter) = 4 \times 1m\frac{1}{e} \times \left(1 - \frac{iter}{iter_{\max}}\right) \quad (12)$$

ARO is suitable for feature selection in machine learning and data analysis tasks due to its adaptability and capacity to efficiently explore solution spaces. The algorithm is useful for fine-tuning feature sets for improved model performance because it is able to strike a balance between exploration and exploitation.

3.4 Soccer Game Outcomes Prediction

The use of deep reinforcement learning (DRL) procedures in foreseeing soccer match results includes coordinating high level calculations that join profound brain networks with standards of support learning. Inside the support learning system, the DRL model goes about as a specialist, drawing in with the climate of soccer matches and mentioning forecasts in view of gotten objective facts. These perceptions, addressing the condition of the climate, include a scope of elements like group insights, player exhibitions, and other context oriented data pertinent to match results. The DRL model defines an action space and the possible predictions it can make about a game's outcome. The model's subsequent interactions are influenced by how accurate these predictions are. A feedback mechanism that directs the learning process assigns rewards or penalties to the model based on how accurate its predictions are. Profound brain networks act as vital parts inside the DRL model, working as powerful function approximates capable of capturing complex and non-linear relationships in the input data. The preparation cycle includes an equilibrium of investigation, where the model investigates different forecast techniques, and double-dealing, where the model applies learned information to make further developed expectations. DRL models succeed in undertakings requiring consecutive dynamic after some time, making them appropriate for catching the worldly viewpoints and movement of occasions during soccer matches. The flexibility of DRL models considers move realizing, where information acquired in anticipating results in a single setting can be adjusted to upgrade expectations in various situations, adding to further developed exactness across different soccer match settings. In essence, the employment of DRL techniques in soccer game outcomes prediction represents a sophisticated approach to learning optimal strategies, leveraging the capabilities of deep neural networks within the dynamic and complex environment of soccer matches.

The DRL specialist utilizes an epsilon-covetous arrangement to perform characterization activity in light of bunches of information. The open computer based intelligence climate prospects a specialist's activity and afterward assesses the awards for the specialist in like manner. The specialist's memory stores this whole experience. Toward the finish of clump culmination, the DRL specialist tests a cluster of memory from its experience replay cradle, alters the Y-esteem by Y-organization, assesses the misfortune, and performs back-proliferation to update the loads. Modern performance was achieved by our updated model, which successfully differentiated between fraudulent and non-fraudulent digital transactions. The exemplary model of the DRL comprised of single-specialist RL. A limited DRL is characterized as a record <P, U, F, X>, the definition contains P as a decent arrangement of states in a climate, a limited arrangement of specialist activities U, the state likelihood capability F: P × U × P → [0, 1] and the award capability ρ: P × U × P → r. At each different time step s, the state xt∈X characterizes a climate. In addition, it doesn't express anything concerning the well established outcomes of this arrangement. The reward function is presumptively limited. Also, the educational experience doesn't work with the single component vector. Here, the capability of change likelihood "f" is refreshed with the progress capability

$$F{:}P \times U \rightarrow P \tag{13}$$

The arrangement characterizes the specialist's way of behaving which makes sense of how the specialist acknowledges its activities in the present. By and large, a strategy or manage might be either deterministic or stochastic. The determined condition for stochastic is I: P × U → [0, 1] and for deterministic is I: P → U. In the event that a strategy doesn't change over the long haul, it is called fixed. The specialist's fundamental objective is to find a superior strategy that expands with an assumption for limited return γ for each state p.

$$r^{\pi}(P) = e\left\{ \sum_{s=0}^{\infty} \gamma^{K} R_{s} + 1 p_{0} = p, \pi \right\} \tag{14}$$

The expectation is taken into account for the number of possible transition states under the policy when the discount factor is between 0 and 1. The rebate factor γ can be depicted as catching and expanding vulnerability in potential compensations. A drawn out benefit acquired by a specialist is communicated by the bring r back.

The meaning of Y (an ideal) Y-capability as . The Bellman optimality fulfills the accompanying condition.

$$Y^{*}(State\, p,\ action\ U)$$

$$= \sum p' \in F(p, u, p')\rho(p, u, p')\ where\ \{p{:}\forall\in\ , u \in U\} \tag{15}$$

As per ideal activity reward is gotten by taking u of p, which is a demonstrated or anticipated brief prize summation, and increasing it by the limited and most invaluable worth that is reachable from the following consecutive state. Once is accessible, the exact arrangement, which works on the return, can be assessed. It picks an activity in each express that expands the ensuing potential compensation. The ideal Y-esteem is communicated as follows.

$$\pi^*(p) = \arg Max_u Y^*(p, u) \tag{16}$$

At the point when different exercises accomplish the most noteworthy Y-esteem, any of them can be picked and the methodology will stay ideal. All things considered, the argmax administrator was deciphered as a boundary for choosing great explanation. A policy is said to be greedy in the Y-function it improves or maximizes. There are processes finished in two stages, for example, dissecting and the voracious arrangement in . An iterative approximation procedure is referred to as Y-learning. At each time step, Q begins gaining from erratic of Y-capability, and it investigate the advances the Y capability is refreshed after each progress detectable.

$$Y_{s+1}(p_s, U_s) = Y_s(y_s, U_s) + \alpha_s R_{s+1} + \gamma Max\, U' Y_s(y_{s+1}, u') - Y_s(p_s, u_s) \tag{17}$$

We signifies the distinction between the ongoing appraisal and the best y-worth of and for which the worth refreshed or assessed Here, the new assessment is created by the bellman, i.e., applied to in the state and activity pair. The benefit of learning rate $\gamma \in (0, 1]$ can be shifted over the long haul in discrete mode, and as a rule, it diminishes after some time. In the event that a specialist keeps on attempting exercises with nonzero probabilities in every one of the states, then, at that point, it very well may be called investigation and afterward cleaned.

4. RESULTS AND DISCUSSION

In this section, we present the results and comparative analysis of proposed and existing soccer games outcome prediction models. To validate the performance of proposed DRL-SGO model through the publically available 2017 soccer prediction challenge dataset. The working process of proposed model is implemented on Python programming language. The results or proposed DRL-SGO model is compared with the existing models such as PageRank (Hubáček et al., 2019), dynamic with hybrid Bayesian network (DHBN) (Constantinou, 2019), hierarchical poison log-linear (HPLL) (Tsokos et al., 2019), k-NN+rating features (k-NN+Ra), and XGBoost+recency features (XGB+Re) (Berrar et al., 2019). The exhibition can be approving through the different quality measurements (exactness, accuracy, review, F-measure, and ranked probability score (RPS)) and blunder measures (mean square mistake (MSE) and root mean square blunder (RMSE)).

4.1 Dataset Description

To validate the performance of proposed DRL-SGO model through the publically available 2017 soccer prediction challenge dataset. Three datasets are available for this challenge, starting with the initial training set, which has already been provided to all participants. An updated training set is scheduled to be released on 22 March 2017 CET, allowing participants to refine their predictive models with the most recent match data from leagues still in progress by the crucial 30 March 2017 deadline. The initial training set encompasses match data from over 200,000 soccer matches played across 52 leagues, starting from the 2000/2001 season, with a focus on leagues whose seasons have concluded. This dataset serves as the foundation for participants to develop their predictive models. Alongside the updated training set, a test version is also promptly provided to participants for testing their data processing workflows. Moreover, a forecast set, containing matches from continuous seasons highlighted in the refreshed preparation information and played following the 30 Walk 2017 cutoff time, is made accessible on 22 Walk 2017 CET. The test spins around foreseeing the results of these matches, giving members a unique expectation challenge. The prediction and the updated training set contribute to refining and evaluating participants' predictive models for this special issue.

4.2 Results Analysis of Quality Measures

Table 1 presents a comprehensive comparison of quality measures between the proposed soccer game outcome prediction model and existing models across various testing and training samples. The accuracy comparison of different soccer game outcome prediction models across varied testing and training samples is presented in Figure 2, shows the performance metrics for each model under different scenarios. The models considered include PageRank (Hubáček et al., 2019), DHBN (Constantinou, 2019), HPLL (Tsokos et al., 2019), k-NN+Ra (Berrar et al., 2019), XGB+Re (Berrar et al., 2019), and the proposed DRL-SGO model. Across the range of training/testing sample splits, the models exhibit varying degrees of accuracy. Notably, the DRL-SGO model consistently outperforms its counterparts, achieving the highest accuracy across all sample splits. Specifically, DRL-SGO demonstrates accuracy percentages of 93.235%, 93.896%, 94.025%, 94.235%, and 94.563% for the training/testing splits. In comparison to XGB+Re, DRL-SGO showcases a consistent increase in accuracy ranging from approximately 6.57% to 6.77% across the different sample splits. Similarly, when compared to k-NN+Ra, DRL-SGO exhibits percentage-wise improvements ranging from 13.14% to 13.34%.

Table 1. Quality measure comparison for proposed and existing soccer game outcome prediction models with different testing/training samples

Models	**Training/Testing samples**					**Training/Testing samples**				
	70/30	**75/25**	**80/20**	**85/15**	**90/10**	**70/30**	**75/25**	**80/20**	**85/15**	**90/10**
	Accuracy (%)					**Precision (%)**				
PageRank [32]	60.391	61.052	61.181	61.391	61.719	53.179	52.724	51.724	50.608	48.391
DHBN [33]	66.959	67.620	67.749	67.959	68.287	60.747	60.292	59.292	58.176	55.959
HPLL [34]	73.528	74.189	74.318	74.528	74.856	68.316	67.861	66.861	65.745	63.528
k-NN+Ra [31]	80.097	80.758	80.887	81.097	81.425	75.885	75.430	74.430	73.314	71.097
XGB+Re [31]	86.666	87.327	87.456	87.666	87.994	83.454	82.999	81.999	80.883	78.666
DRL-SGO	93.235	93.896	94.025	94.235	94.563	91.023	90.568	89.568	88.452	86.235
	Recall (%)					F-measure (%)				
PageRank [32]	45.641	45.428	45.119	44.819	44.537	49.122	48.805	48.196	47.538	46.384
DHBN [33]	54.726	54.514	54.205	53.905	53.623	57.580	57.258	56.634	55.959	54.766
HPLL [34]	63.812	63.599	63.290	62.990	62.708	65.987	65.661	65.027	64.338	63.116
k-NN+Ra [31]	72.898	72.685	72.376	72.076	71.794	74.361	74.032	73.389	72.690	71.444
XGB+Re [31]	81.983	81.770	81.461	81.161	80.879	82.712	82.380	81.729	81.022	79.757
DRL-SGO	91.069	90.856	90.547	90.247	89.965	91.046	90.712	90.055	89.340	88.061
	RPS (%)									
PageRank [32]	26.616	26.482	26.184	25.991	25.604					
DHBN [33]	23.125	22.975	22.889	22.777	22.748					
HPLL [34]	24.053	23.919	23.621	23.428	23.041					
k-NN+Ra [31]	20.562	20.412	20.326	20.214	20.185					
XGB+Re [31]	21.490	21.356	21.058	20.865	20.478					
DRL-SGO	15.236	15.105	15.023	14.895	14.652					

The proposed DRL-SGO model's remarkable accuracy across diverse training/testing samples underscores its robustness and superior predictive capabilities. The consistent upward trend in accuracy, coupled with notable advantages over existing models, positions DRL-SGO as a highly effective and reliable approach for soccer game outcome prediction. These outcomes confirm the viability of utilizing profound support learning with ideal element extraction in upgrading the exactness of soccer match expectations, offering important experiences for sports examination, wagering systems, and training choices.

Figure 2. Accuracy comparison with different testing/training samples

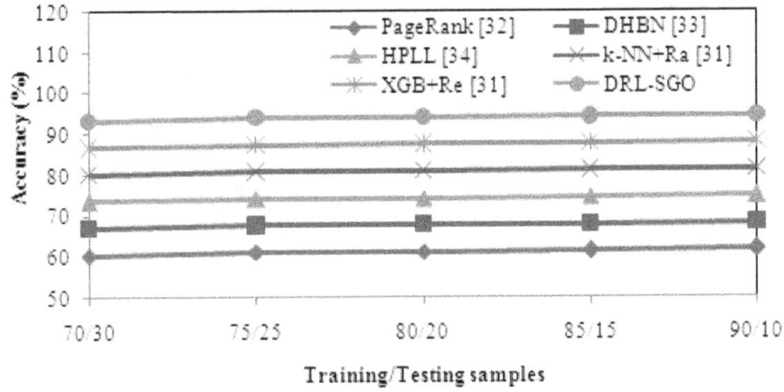

Fig. 3 presents a point by point correlation of accuracy measurements among different soccer match result forecast models across various preparation and testing tests. DRL-SGO shows the precision values of 91.023%, 90.568%, 89.568%, 88.452%, and 86.235%, respectively. When contrasted with the second-most elevated performing model, XGB+Re, DRL-SGO shows rate wise increments going from around 7.57% to 7.87% across the different example parts. Essentially, when contrasted with k-NN+Ra, DRL-SGO shows rate wise enhancements going from 15.14% to 15.44%. The proposed DRL-SGO model's ability to accurately predict positive soccer game outcomes is demonstrated by consistently superior precision metrics. The notable advantages over existing models affirm the model's ability to minimize false positives and enhance precision across diverse training and testing scenarios. These results emphasize the robustness and reliability of the DRL-SGO approach, positioning it as a valuable tool for precise soccer match outcome predictions.

Figure 3. Precision comparison with different testing/training samples

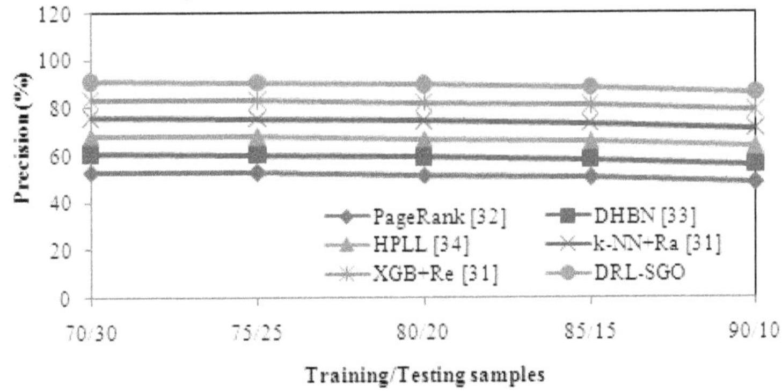

Figure 4. Recall comparison with different testing/training samples

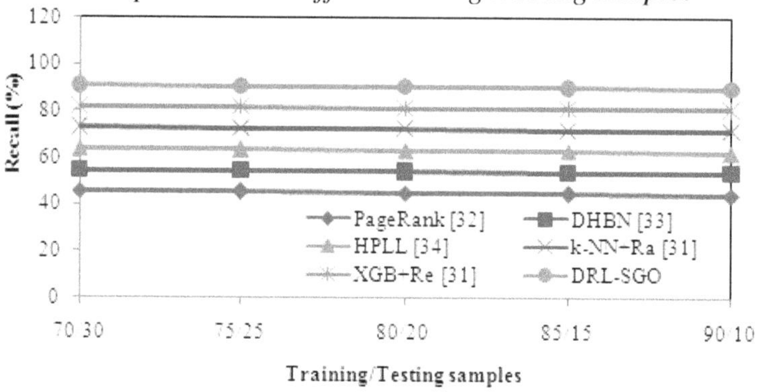

In Figure 4, a detailed comparison of recall metrics is presented for various soccer game outcome prediction models across different training and testing samples. DRL-SGO demonstrates recall values of 91.069%, 90.856%, 90.547%, 90.247%, and 89.965%, respectively, showcasing its effectiveness in capturing a high proportion of true positive predictions. In comparison to the second-highest performing model, XGB+Re, DRL-SGO demonstrates increases ranging from approximately 9.09% to 9.39% across the different sample splits. Similarly, when compared to k-NN+Ra, DRL-SGO displays improvements ranging from 18.17% to 18.47%. The consistently superior recall metrics of the proposed DRL-SGO model emphasize its ability to effectively identify and capture a substantial portion of actual positive outcomes in soccer game predictions. The notable advantages over existing models underscore the model's capability to minimize false negatives and enhance recall across diverse training and testing scenarios. These results affirm the robustness and reliability of the DRL-SGO approach, positioning it as a valuable tool for comprehensive soccer match outcome predictions.

Figure 5. F-measure comparison with different testing/training samples

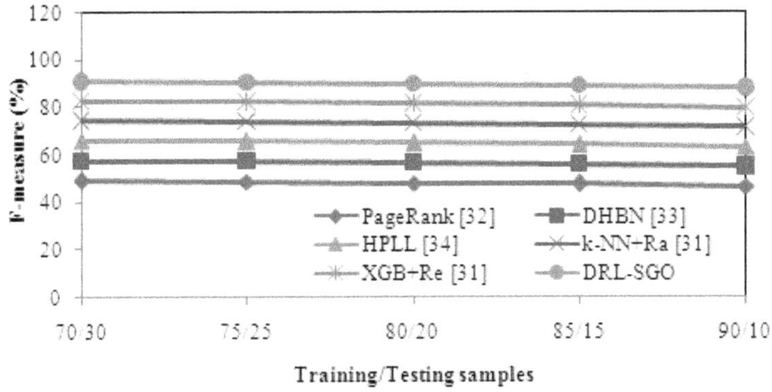

Figure 5 illustrates a comprehensive comparison of F-measure metrics for various soccer game outcome prediction models across different training and testing samples. Specifically, DRL-SGO demonstrates F-measure values of 91.046%, 90.712%, 90.055%, 89.340%, and 88.061%, respectively. In contrast with different models, XGB+Re, DRL-SGO displays increments going from around 8.33% to 8.70% across the different example parts. When contrasted with k-NN+Ra, DRL-SGO shows rate wise upgrades going from 16.69% to 17.06%. The reliably predominant F-measure measurements of the proposed DRL-SGO model feature its viability in accomplishing a reasonable accuracy and review, offering an exhaustive assessment of its prescient capacities. The eminent benefits over existing models confirm the model's capacity to give precise and solid forecasts across different preparation and testing situations. In the context of soccer match outcome predictions, these results emphasize the robustness and overall performance excellence of the DRL-SGO approach.

In Figure 6, a point by point examination of Positioned Likelihood Score (RPS) measurements is introduced for different soccer match result expectation models across various preparation and testing tests. DRL-SGO shows RPS values of 15.236, 15.105, 15.023, 14.895, and 14.652, respectively. Analyzing the increment and reduction in RPS, DRL-SGO features significant upgrades contrasted with different models. In contrast with the second-most minimal RPS model, k-NN+Ra, DRL-SGO shows diminishes going from roughly 25.70% to 26.35% across the different sample splits. When compared to the highest RPS model, PageRank, DRL-SGO displays decreases ranging from approximately 42.66% to 43.82%. The consistently superior RPS metrics of the proposed DRL-SGO model underscore its effectiveness in providing well-calibrated probability forecasts for soccer match outcomes. The notable advantages over existing models affirm the model's ability to generate more accurate and reliable probability estimates, contributing to improved decision-making in the context of soccer game outcome predictions.

Figure 6. RPS comparison with different testing/training samples

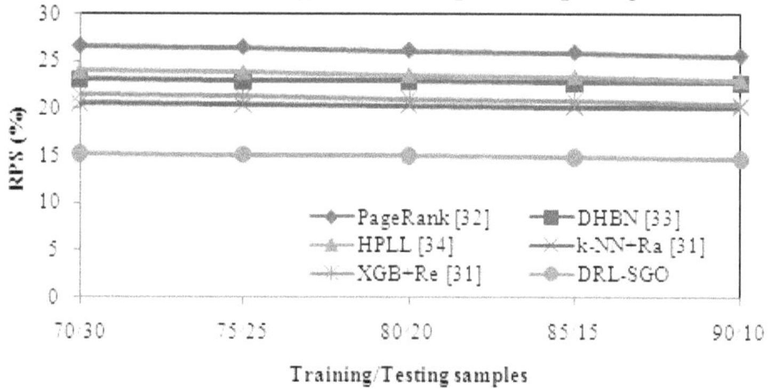

Table 2. Overall quality measure comparison of proposed and existing soccer game outcome prediction models

Models	Values in %				
	Accuracy	Precision	Recall	F-measure	RPS
PageRank [32]	61.146	51.325	45.109	48.009	26.175
DHBN [33]	67.715	58.894	54.194	56.439	22.903
HPLL [34]	74.284	66.463	63.280	64.826	23.612
k-NN+Ra [31]	80.853	74.031	72.366	73.183	20.340
XGB+Re [31]	87.422	81.600	81.451	81.520	21.049
DRL-SGO	93.991	89.169	90.537	89.843	14.982

Table 2 provides a comprehensive overview of the overall quality measures for proposed and existing soccer game outcome prediction models, encompassing accuracy, precision, recall, F-measure, and RPS. DRL-SGO model consistently outshines other models in accuracy, achieving an impressive 93.991%. Compared to the second-highest accuracy model, XGB+Re, DRL-SGO exhibits a substantial percentage-wise increase of approximately 6.569%. In precision, DRL-SGO demonstrates superior performance with 89.169%, shown its ability to make accurate positive predictions. Compared to XGB+Re, the model with the second-highest precision, DRL-SGO displays an increase of approximately 7.569%. DRL-SGO excels in recall, achieving a remarkable 90.537%, indicating its proficiency in capturing a substantial proportion of actual positive outcomes. Compared to XGB+Re, the model with the second-highest recall, DRL-SGO demonstrates an increase of approximately 8.086%. With an F-measure of 89.843%, DRL-SGO achieves a balanced blend of precision and recall. In comparison to XGB+Re, the second-highest F-measure model, DRL-SGO shows an increase of approximately 8.423%. RPS is impressively low for DRL-SGO at 14.982%, indicating its accuracy in generating well-calibrated probability forecasts. Compared to k-NN+Ra, the model with the second-lowest RPS, DRL-SGO exhibits a significant decrease of approximately 26.086%. From Fig. 7 shows the results affirm the superior predictive capabilities of the proposed DRL-SGO model across a spectrum of quality measures. Its consistently high accuracy, precision, recall, and F-measure, coupled with low RPS, shown its effectiveness in providing accurate and well-calibrated predictions for soccer game outcomes.

Figure 7. Average results on quality measure of proposed and existing soccer game outcome prediction models

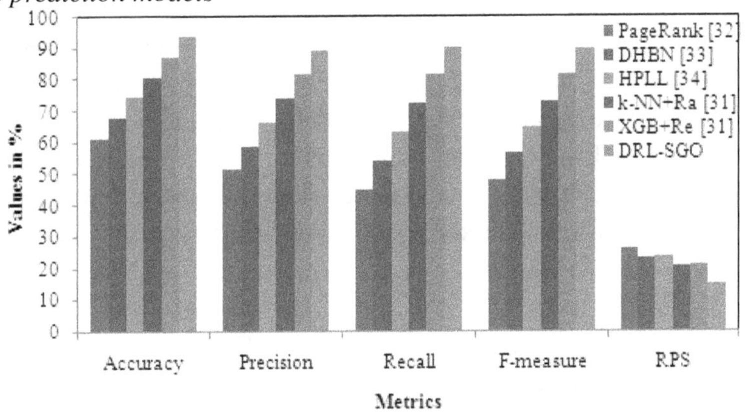

Table 3. Error measure comparison for proposed and existing soccer game outcome prediction models with different testing/training samples

Models	Training/Testing samples					Training/Testing samples				
	70/30	75/25	80/20	85/15	90/10	70/30	75/25	80/20	85/15	90/10
	MSE					RMSE				
PageRank [32]	0.063	0.060	0.058	0.056	0.053	0.251	0.245	0.241	0.237	0.230
DHBN [33]	0.058	0.054	0.052	0.050	0.047	0.240	0.233	0.229	0.224	0.218
HPLL [34]	0.052	0.049	0.047	0.045	0.042	0.228	0.221	0.216	0.212	0.204
k-NN+Ra [31]	0.046	0.043	0.041	0.039	0.036	0.215	0.208	0.203	0.198	0.190
XGB+Re [31]	0.041	0.038	0.036	0.034	0.031	0.202	0.194	0.189	0.183	0.175
DRL-SGO	0.035	0.032	0.030	0.028	0.025	0.188	0.179	0.173	0.167	0.158

Table 4. Average error measure comparison

Models	MSE	RMSE
PageRank [32]	0.058	0.241
DHBN [33]	0.052	0.229
HPLL [34]	0.047	0.216
k-NN+Ra [31]	0.041	0.203
XGB+Re [31]	0.036	0.189
DRL-SGO	0.03	0.173

4.3 Results Analysis of Error Measures

Table 3 shows a comprehensive comparison of error measures for various soccer game outcome prediction models, providing insights into their performance across different testing and training samples. Fig. 8 displays the MSE values for various soccer game outcome prediction models, including both existing models and the proposed DRL-SGO model. Across all training/testing sample scenarios, the proposed DRL-SGO model consistently outperforms the existing models in terms of MSE, demonstrating its superior predictive accuracy. DRL-SGO achieves progressively lower MSE values compared to the other models. For instance, when comparing DRL-SGO to XGB+Re, which has the second-lowest MSE values, the decreases range from approximately 23.53% to 28.57% across the different training/testing sample splits. These outcomes propose that the DRL-SGO model shows an outstanding improvement in limiting forecast blunders contrasted with the current models. The abatements highlight the adequacy of the proposed approach in giving precise forecasts to soccer match results. The predictable pattern of diminishing MSE values for DRL-SGO across fluctuating example parts supports its powerful exhibition. In functional terms, lower MSE values show that the forecasts produced by DRL-SGO are nearer to the genuine results, exhibiting the model's capacity to catch the fundamental examples in soccer match information all the more precisely. The proposed model's prevalent presentation, as confirmed by the decreases in MSE, features its true capacity for upgrading the dependability and accuracy of soccer match result expectations.

Figure 8. MSE comparison with different testing/training samples

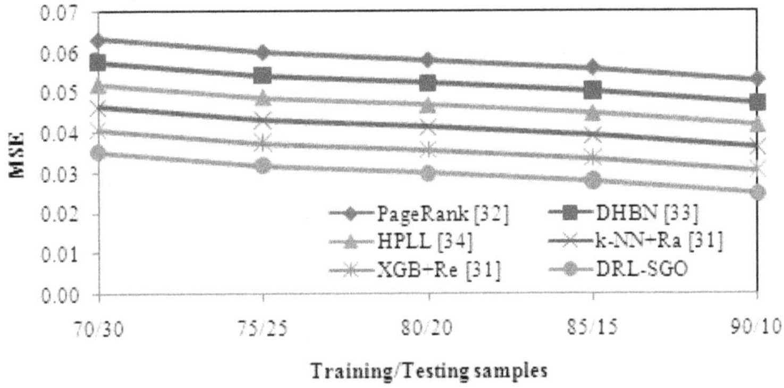

Figure 9. RMSE comparison with different testing/training samples

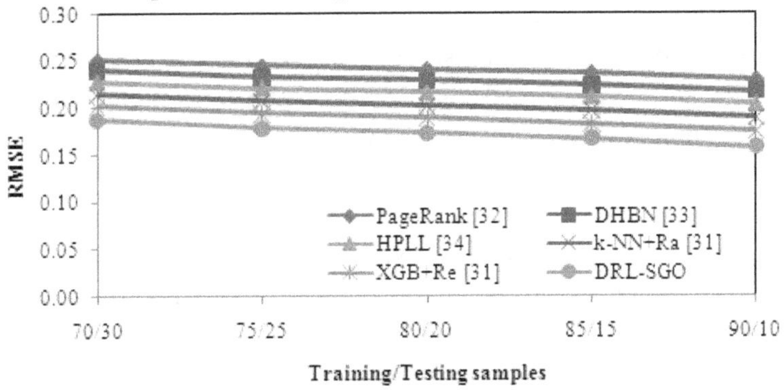

Figure 9 represents the RMSE correlation among different soccer match result expectation models across various preparation and testing tests. It gives a visual portrayal of RMSE values, a critical measurement for evaluating the accuracy of expectation models. DRL-SGO reliably displays lower RMSE values contrasted with the current models across all preparation/testing test situations. For example, in contrast with XGB+Re, the model with the second-most minimal RMSE values, DRL-SGO exhibits rate wise reductions going from around 12.87% to 17.39% across various example parts. The proposed model's practical significance is emphasized by its lower RMSE values, which indicate that the predictions made by DRL-SGO are closer to the actual outcomes.

Figure 10. Average results on error measure of soccer game outcome prediction models

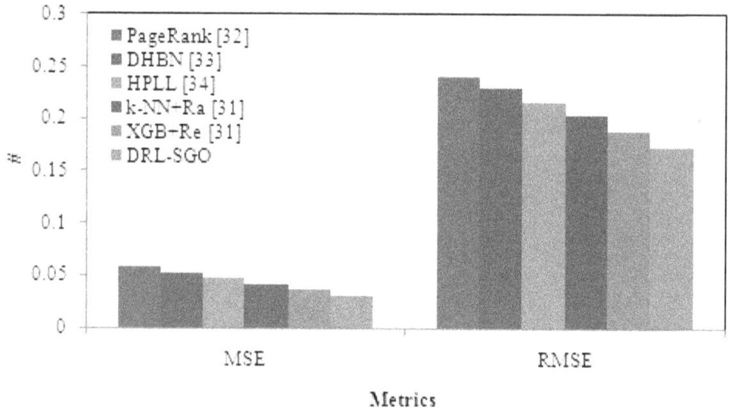

Table 4 presents an average error measure comparison among various soccer game outcome prediction models, encompassing MSE and RMSE values. In terms of average MSE values, the DRL-SGO model consistently demonstrates superior performance compared to the other models, indicative of its ability to minimize prediction errors effectively. Similarly, regarding average RMSE, DRL-SGO maintains lower error measures, signifying enhanced precision in predicting soccer game outcomes. For instance, in contrast to XGB+Re, the model with the second-lowest average MSE and RMSE, DRL-SGO exhibits decreases ranging from approximately 16.67% to 28.57% for MSE and 8.33% to 18.52% for RMSE across different sample scenarios.

5. CONCLUSION

We introduce an intelligent decision model, the deep reinforcement learning for soccer games outcome prediction (DRL-SGO), integrating optimal feature extraction and optimization. Leveraging DenseNet, our feature extraction model captures essential soccer game domain knowledge, encompassing recency and rating features, extracted from the provided dataset. The artificial rabbit optimization (ARO) algorithm plays a pivotal role in optimizing features, meticulously selecting the most advantageous among a plethora of options. Employing the deep reinforcement learning (DRL) significantly enhances the precision of predicting soccer game outcomes. To assess the efficacy of our DRL-SGO model, we conducted validation using the 2017 soccer prediction challenge dataset. Notably, from a quality measure perspective, the DRL-SGO model achieved remarkable accuracy at 93.991%, precision of 89.169%, recall of 90.537%, and an impressive F-measure of

89.843%. These results underscore the model's proficiency in the domain of soccer game outcome forecasting. Additionally, examining error measures, the DRL-SGO model exhibited a low MSE of 0.03 and RMSE of 0.173. These outcomes further reinforce the model's exceptional predictive capabilities in the intricate landscape of soccer game outcome forecasting.

REFERENCES

Barraclough, S., Piggott, D., Till, K., Kerr, A., & Emmonds, S. (2023). Creating a shared mental model of performance: Coaches' perspectives of key position-specific soccer actions. *International Journal of Sports Science & Coaching*.

Berrar, D., Lopes, P., & Dubitzky, W. (2019). Incorporating domain knowledge in machine learning for soccer outcome prediction. *Machine Learning*, 108(1), 97–126. DOI: 10.1007/s10994-018-5747-8

Brandão, B., De Lima, T. W., Soares, A., Melo, L., & Maximo, M. R. (2022). Multiagent reinforcement learning for strategic decision making and control in robotic soccer through self-play. *IEEE Access : Practical Innovations, Open Solutions*, 10, 72628–72642. DOI: 10.1109/ACCESS.2022.3189021

Chen, Z. (2023). Artificial intelligence-virtual trainer: Innovative didactics aimed at personalized training needs. *Journal of the Knowledge Economy*, 14(2), 2007–2025. DOI: 10.1007/s13132-022-00985-0

Chhabra, G., Kumar, S., Gupta, S., & Nagpal, P. (2023). Machine Learning for Individual Performance Analysis and Sports Analytics. In *Artificial Intelligence to Analyze Psychophysical and Human Lifestyle* (pp. 113–127). Springer Nature Singapore. DOI: 10.1007/978-981-99-3039-5_10

Constantinou, A. C. (2019). Dolores: A model that predicts football match outcomes from all over the world. *Machine Learning*, 108(1), 49–75. DOI: 10.1007/s10994-018-5703-7

Cossich, V. R., Carlgren, D., Holash, R. J., & Katz, L. (2023). Technological Breakthroughs in Sport: Current Practice and Future Potential of Artificial Intelligence, Virtual Reality, Augmented Reality, and Modern Data Visualization in Performance Analysis. *Applied Sciences (Basel, Switzerland)*, 13(23), 12965. DOI: 10.3390/app132312965

Deuker, A., Wittkugel, J., Dublin, Y., Klatt, S., Körner, S., Vogt, T., . . . Klemp, M. (2023). Analyzing the effect of reduced field sizes on tactical behaviour in 11 versus 11 football practice. In World Congress on Science and Football 2023: Enhance Performance Engage Society (p. 240).

Dovgan, N. (2023). The Pivotal Role of Technology in Enhancing Athletic Performance: Insights and Future Directions. DOI: 10.2139/ssrn.4602857

Grover, V., Chiang, R. H., Liang, T. P., & Zhang, D. (2018). Creating strategic business value from big data analytics: A research framework. *Journal of Management Information Systems*, 35(2), 388–423. DOI: 10.1080/07421222.2018.1451951

Herold, M., Goes, F., Nopp, S., Bauer, P., Thompson, C., & Meyer, T. (2019). Machine learning in men's professional football: Current applications and future directions for improving attacking play. *International Journal of Sports Science & Coaching*, 14(6), 798–817. DOI: 10.1177/1747954119879350

Hubáček, O., Šourek, G., & Železný, F. (2019). Learning to predict soccer results from relational data with gradient boosted trees. *Machine Learning*, 108(1), 29–47. DOI: 10.1007/s10994-018-5704-6

Ji, B., Wang, Y., Song, K., Li, C., Wen, H., Menon, V. G., & Mumtaz, S. (2021). A survey of computational intelligence for 6G: Key technologies, applications and trends. *IEEE Transactions on Industrial Informatics*, 17(10), 7145–7154. DOI: 10.1109/TII.2021.3052531

Jin, J., Rong, D., Pang, Y., Ye, P., Ji, Q., Wang, X., Wang, G., & Wang, F. Y. (2022). An agent-based traffic recommendation system: Revisiting and revising urban traffic management strategies. *IEEE Transactions on Systems, Man, and Cybernetics. Systems*, 52(11), 7289–7301. DOI: 10.1109/TSMC.2022.3177027

Karakaya, A., Ulu, A., & Akleylek, S. (2022). GOALALERT: A novel real-time technical team alert approach using machine learning on an IoT-based system in sports. *Microprocessors and Microsystems*, 93, 104606. DOI: 10.1016/j.micpro.2022.104606

Kedir, N. S., Somi, S., Fayek, A. R., & Nguyen, P. H. (2022). Hybridization of reinforcement learning and agent-based modeling to optimize construction planning and scheduling. *Automation in Construction*, 142, 104498. DOI: 10.1016/j.autcon.2022.104498

Kenwright, B. (2023). Data collection during active gameplay: Unveiling a multifaceted portrait of the individual. In *Games as Stealth Assessments* (pp. 192–219). IGI Global. DOI: 10.4018/979-8-3693-0568-3.ch008

Lan, D., & Shin, I. (2023). Boosting in-transit entertainment: Deep reinforcement learning for intelligent multimedia caching in bus networks. *Soft Computing*, 27(24), 1–17. DOI: 10.1007/s00500-023-09354-8

Mendes-Neves, T., Mendes-Moreira, J., & Rossetti, R. J. (2021, September). A data-driven simulator for assessing decision-making in soccer. In *EPIA Conference on Artificial Intelligence* (pp. 687-698). Cham: Springer International Publishing. DOI: 10.1007/978-3-030-86230-5_54

Mo, X., Hu, B., Xu, C., & Yang, Y. (2022, December). Research on virtual human swarm football collaboration technology based on reinforcement learning. In *2022 IEEE 21st International Conference on Ubiquitous Computing and Communications (IUCC/CIT/DSCI/SmartCNS)* (pp. 357-364). IEEE. DOI: 10.1109/IUCC-CIT-DSCI-SmartCNS57392.2022.00062

Mozgovoy, M., Preuss, M., & Bidarra, R. (2021). Team sports for Game AI benchmarking revisited. *International Journal of Computer Games Technology*, 2021, 1–9. DOI: 10.1155/2021/5521877

O'Brien, K. A., & O'Keeffe, M. (2022). Reimagining the role of technology in sport officiating: How artificial intelligence (AI) supports the design and delivery of ecologically dynamic development processes. *Managing Sport and Leisure*, 1–13. DOI: 10.1080/23750472.2022.2126996

Protevi, J. (2023). Esprit de Corps and thinking on (and with) your feet: Standard, enactive, and poststructuralist aspects of relational autonomy and collective intentionality in team sports. *The Southern Journal of Philosophy*, 61(S1), 24–38. DOI: 10.1111/sjp.12525

Rahimian, P., Oroojlooy, A., & Toka, L. (2021, October). Towards optimized actions in critical situations of soccer games with deep reinforcement learning. In 2021 IEEE 8th International Conference on Data Science and Advanced Analytics (DSAA) (pp. 1-12). IEEE. DOI: 10.1109/DSAA53316.2021.9564207

Rahimian, P., & Toka, L. (2023). A data-driven approach to assist offensive and defensive players in optimal decision making. *International Journal of Sports Science & Coaching*.

Rahimian, P., Van Haaren, J., Abzhanova, T., & Toka, L. (2022). Beyond action valuation: A deep reinforcement learning framework for optimizing player decisions in soccer. In 16th Annual MIT Sloan Sports Analytics Conference. MIT.

Rein, R., & Memmert, D. (2016). Big data and tactical analysis in elite soccer: Future challenges and opportunities for sports science. *SpringerPlus*, 5(1), 1–13. DOI: 10.1186/s40064-016-3108-2 PMID: 27610328

Rønningen, M. H. (2021). The genesis of data-driven decision-making in the world of soccer tactics: deciphering the potential of big data (Master's thesis, University of Agder).

Saklani, A. (2023). Integrating technology into physical education: Exploring the dynamics of AI, virtual reality, apps, and wearables for an enhanced educational odyssey.

Tsokos, A., Narayanan, S., Kosmidis, I., Baio, G., Cucuringu, M., Whitaker, G., & Király, F. (2019). Modeling outcomes of soccer matches. *Machine Learning*, 108(1), 77–95. DOI: 10.1007/s10994-018-5741-1

Vijay Fidelis, J., & Karthikeyan, E. (2022). Optimization of Artificial Neural Network Parameters in Selection of Players for Soccer Match. In *Sustainable Advanced Computing: Select Proceedings of ICSAC 2021* (pp. 275-288). Singapore: Springer Singapore. DOI: 10.1007/978-981-16-9012-9_23

Voigt, L., Friedrich, J., Grove, P., Heinrich, N., Ittlinger, S., Iskra, M., Koop, L., Michirev, A., Sparascio, S., & Raab, M. (2023). Advancing judgment and decision-making research in sport psychology by using the body as an informant in embodied choices. *Asian Journal of Sport and Exercise Psychology*, 3(1), 47–56. DOI: 10.1016/j.ajsep.2022.09.006

Wang, J., & Chen, J. (2022). Design and Research of Dynamic Evolution System in Football Tactics Under Computational Intelligence. *Mathematical Problems in Engineering*, 2022, 2022. DOI: 10.1155/2022/3772236

Yeung, C. C., & Fujii, K. (2023). A Strategic Framework for Optimal Decisions in Football 1-vs-1 Shot-Taking Situations: An Integrated Approach of Machine Learning, Theory-Based Modeling, and Game Theory. arXiv preprint arXiv:2307.14732.

Chapter 6
Foundations and Obstacles of Deep Learning in Healthcare

Lakshmi Devi S.
https://orcid.org/0000-0002-6190-3452
Sri Krishna Adithya College of Arts and Science, India

Vijaya Lakshmi P. S.
https://orcid.org/0000-0003-4561-1908
Dr. N.G.P. Arts and Science College, India

Satheesh Kumar Nataraj
University of Technology Bahrain, Bahrain

ABSTRACT

Proven results show that deep learning (DL) plays a key role in smart manufacturing and logistic supply chain management. DL was effective in the healthcare sector because of its capacity to manage vast amounts of complex data with little assistance from humans. To improve the quality of care and health for patients, physicians, and other healthcare workers, deep learning (DL) is being implemented in the current healthcare system. It was discovered that DL was useful for diagnosing illnesses, detecting acute diseases, analyzing images, finding new drugs, delivering drugs, and monitoring smart health. This chapter offers a cutting-edge analysis of the DL foundations, challenges, and applications in healthcare systems to meet multi-objective aims.

DOI: 10.4018/979-8-3693-7868-7.ch006

1. INTRODUCTION

The subfield of machine learning is known as deep learning. With the increasing use of machine learning methodologies in healthcare, we may see a time when data, analysis, and creativity work together to benefit enormous numbers of people inadvertently. The effectiveness of previously unavailable treatment alternatives may soon be increased by the widespread use of machine learning (ML)-based applications loaded with real-time patient information from numerous healthcare systems across multiple countries (Vyas & Bhargava, 2021; Huang, Jagota, Espinoza-Muñoz, & Flores-Albornoz, 2021).

As medical technology advanced, the biomedical field ushered in the big data age, which in turn gave rise to computational medicine, which is powered by artificial intelligence technology. To advance the advancement of precision medicine, people must extract the useful information found in these massive biological data sets. Traditionally, machine learning techniques are used to extract biomedical data and identify features from the data. These techniques typically depend upon the feature engineering and subject-matter expertise of specialists, which takes a lot of time and resources. Deep learning is a cutting-edge branch of machine learning that, in contrast to standard methods, can automatically discover robust and sophisticated features from raw data with no having to look for feature engineering. Deep learning has been explored for its applications in drug discovery, genomics, medical imaging, and electronic health records. It is suggested that deep learning has a clear benefit in optimizing the use of biomedical information while raising the standard of medical care. Deep learning has many potential applications and is becoming more and more significant in the medical profession. Nonetheless, there are also issues and difficulties with deep learning in cognitive physical health, such as heterogeneity, interpretability, lack of data, and data privacy. The examination and discourse around these issues offer a framework for enhancing the utilization of deep computing in the field of medicine.

Deep learning can be used to generate the current state of patients based on their raw data or through their historical records. Because of this feature, it can be applied to several domains, including the security of the cybercrime sector and the healthcare system. Nonetheless, it is essential to the healthcare system, particularly for young people and the elderly, and as of late, seniors are more likely to live alone. Taking the facts into account, deep learning is essential for progress.

These days, the death rate from cardiovascular disease (CD) rises daily. Due to annoyance, wearables are not preferred by children or the elderly. In these situations, deep learning is used to collect data while wearables can locate or identify patients' conditions in real time. These days, acute illnesses like diabetes, Alzheimer's disease, cancer, genetic disorders, and respiratory illnesses can be reduced by implementing intelligence in the healthcare system. This is made possible by computational learning systems, SHM, IoT, and skilled medical professionals who can identify a patient's condition in real-time and have the necessary knowledge to predict a patient's future state.

The medical survey estimates that approximately 30% of people have a cardiovascular condition. Since smart health monitoring combines IoT, artificial intelligence, and health monitoring devices, we can argue that computational learning and robotic learning are employed in this process. In today's modern healthcare system, the SHM is essential. Healthcare systems use artificial intelligence to implement machine learning software and algorithms. The data employed in machine learning forms the basis for artificial intelligence outcomes. Essentially, the game finds this out.

When patient data cannot be detected by IoTs or smart health monitoring devices, computational learning is used in the healthcare system. These algorithms, sometimes referred to as artificial intelligence or machine learning, can identify behavioral data and create their models. It is the process by which an artificial neural network of an animal (AI) is created using CNN and ANN, and it functions in two ways: Algorithms are literal in nature, and deep learning can be used to create "black boxes." Unlike nonlinear old approaches, which need patients to attend unwelcome hospital visits, deep learning operates on the foundation of linear methods. This allows patients to interact with doctors computationally.

2. LITERATURE REVIEW

The smart wellness tracking network and healthcare services have made substantial use of deep learning and machine learning in recent times. The health data produced by different IoMT technology and sensors were analyzed using DL and ML. Cloud networks and cloud services have been used to handle and store these health data. These intricate health data are analyzed using ML and DL to accomplish multi-objective tasks. By the end of 2020, there will be over 50 billion gadgets in the medical field, all of which will provide numerous security concerns, as predicted by Mohammad Ali et al. He claims that in addition to being utilized for threat detection in cybercrime, DL/ML is also employed for the collection of large data (Al-Garadi, Mohamed, Al-Ali, Du, Ali, & Guizani, 2020).

Imran Ahmed et al. recently published a study in which they discussed the use of data obtained from an IP-based RGB camera installed at a height of 4 meters to capture patients' top views and data captured at the Institute of Management Science, Peshawar. The purpose of this data collection is to identify patient discomfort based on patient movement. This camera aids in determining the degree of patient discomfort. The degree of discomfort is determined from the top using deep learning algorithms, or models. (e Mask R-CNN 19 is used on the patients to identify them.

These experiments employ a variety of evaluation metrics, including the TPR, FPR, TNR, and MCR, as well as the FDR and TDR for video records. (The average performance of the patient's body's organs as seen in the movies is compiled and shown in Table 1. It is evident that the model, with an FPR of 7% and an MCR of 4%, could identify the discomfort (Ahmed, Jeon, & Piccialli, 2021).

After computer vision became successful, image processing saw the first use of deep learning in clinical data, particularly in the examination of brain Magnetic Resonance Imaging (MRI) scans for identifying Alzheimer's disease and its variants (Liu, Liu, Cai, et al., 2014; Brosch & Tam, 2013). CNNs have been utilized in other medical areas to automatically divide cartilage and identify the likelihood of osteoarthritis by inferring an ordered arrangement of low-field knees MRI data (Prasoon, Petersen, Igel, et al., 2013). This solution outperformed a state-of-the-art approach employing manually picked 3D multi-scale features, albeit using 2D photos. Additionally, deep learning has been used to differentiate between malignant as well as benign breast nodules using ultrasound images (Cheng, Ni, Chou, et al., 2016) and to segment lesions related to multiple sclerosis using multi-channel 3D MRI (Yoo, Brosch, Traboulsee, et al., 2014). In the meantime, Gulshan et al. (2016) obtained excellent specificity and sensitivity across about 10,000 test photos concerning qualified ophthalmologist annotations when using CNNs to diagnose diabetic retinopathy in retina fundus photographs. Over a large data set of 130,000 images (1942 biopsy-labeled test images), CNNs also achieved performances on par with 21 board-certified dermatologists in classifying biopsy-proven clinical specimens of various kinds of skin cancer (Esteva, Kuprel, Novoa, et al., 2017).

3. DEEP LEARNING FOUNDATIONS

The discipline of medical health has ushered in the big data era with the explosive increase of physiological data and the swift growth of medical and computer technology in recent years (Miotto, Li, Kidd, & Dudley, 2016). Computational medicine started to emerge as a novel field in this setting. Computational healthcare is a multidisciplinary discipline that combines medicine, biological sciences, mathematics, and other subjects. It is based on large biomedical information as well as computer technology. By evaluating large amounts of data, it applies artificial intelligence to comprehend the underlying principles and physiological mechanisms of human diseases and offers helpful advice and information for clinical diagnosis, illness prognosis, and healthcare services. Using the pharmaceutical business as an example, new medication research has historically been plagued by lengthy timelines, significant costs, and a high failure rate. The field of medical health has begun to transition into the age of intelligence and digitization, as evidenced by computational medicine research, which can finish preclinical drug development and research in an average of 1-2 years with a high success rate and low use of resources.

However, it is challenging to efficiently harvest the rich information hidden beneath biological datasets due to their high dimension, jumble, noise, and sparsity. Consequently, to process vast volumes of biomedical data and produce useful information, a suitable strategy is required. Deep learning is currently regarded as a shining gem in the artificial intelligence field of machine learning. Deep learning, a subfield of machine learning, has demonstrated efficacy in fields such as computer vision (He, Zhang, Ren, & Sun, 2016), natural language processing (Lan, Chen, Goodman, et al., 2020), and speech recognition (Abdel-Hamid, Mohamed, Jiang, et al., 2014), outperforming more typical machine learning techniques. Feature engineering is a machine learning technique that involves the artificial use of expert and domain knowledge to extract features from data, which are then further analyzed using machine learning models (e.g., random forest, support vector machine, etc.). Big data has made manual extraction inadequate and biased, making it unable to develop a high-performing model for particular jobs.

Figure 1. Deep learning applications

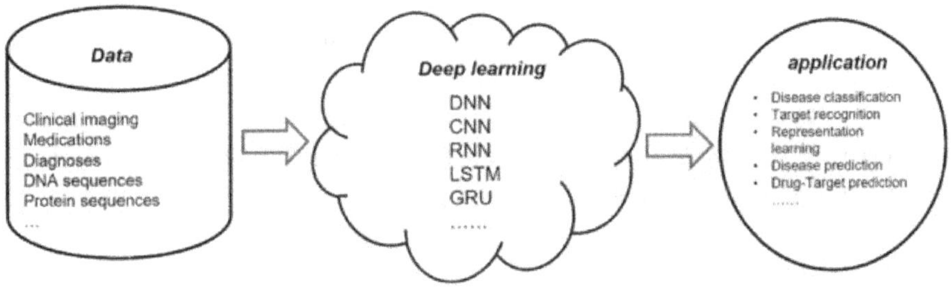

Deep learning increases time and resource effectiveness by eliminating the need for manual feature extraction, in contrast to typical machine learning techniques. Neural networks, which are made up of neurons, are used to implement deep learning. Large numbers of neurons make up each layer of a neural network, with the output of one layer being considered to be the input of the one below it. The neural network can transform the original input into the output by connecting the layers and using the nonlinear processing technique.

4. DEEP LEARNING ALGORITHMS

4.1 Deep Learning

Deep learning is a kind of machine learning that analyzes data using a layered algorithmic design. It is sometimes referred to as hierarchical learning and deep structured learning.

Deep learning models use a cascade of layers to filter input, with each layer building on the output of the one before it to produce new findings. As more data is processed by deep learning models, their accuracy increases. This is because the models learn from past performance to improve their capacity to identify patterns and connections.

The way that biological neurons interact with one another in the animal brain to process information offers a rough model for deep learning. Every layer of nodes after that is activated in response to stimuli from nearby neurons, much like electrical signals go through living things' cells.

Deep learning models are based on artificial neural networks (ANNs), where each layer is assigned a distinct part of a transformation task and data may pass through the layers several times to optimize and refine the final result.

The mathematical translation operations that convert unprocessed input into useful output are carried out by these "hidden" layers.

With the use of this multi-layered approach, deep learning models can accomplish a variety of classification tasks, including the detection of minute abnormalities in healthcare images, the grouping of patients into risk-based cohorts based on shared characteristics, and the highlighting of correlations between symptoms as well as outcomes within large amounts of unstructured data.

4.2 Algorithms in Deep Learning

Hundreds of millions of neurons and over 100,000 connections between each other make up the human brain, which serves as the model for machine learning, which includes deep learning. Artificial Neural Network is the name of the deep learning technique. The input layer, hidden layer, as well as output layer, are the three layers that make up the neural network, as depicted in Figure 2. Multiple neurons make up each layer, and the concealed layer could have multiple layers. The number of neurons in the output layer of neural networks varies depending on the type of task being performed. For instance, in the three-classification problem, the output layer consists of three neurons, each of which represents the likelihood of falling into a particular group.

Figure 2. Neural network

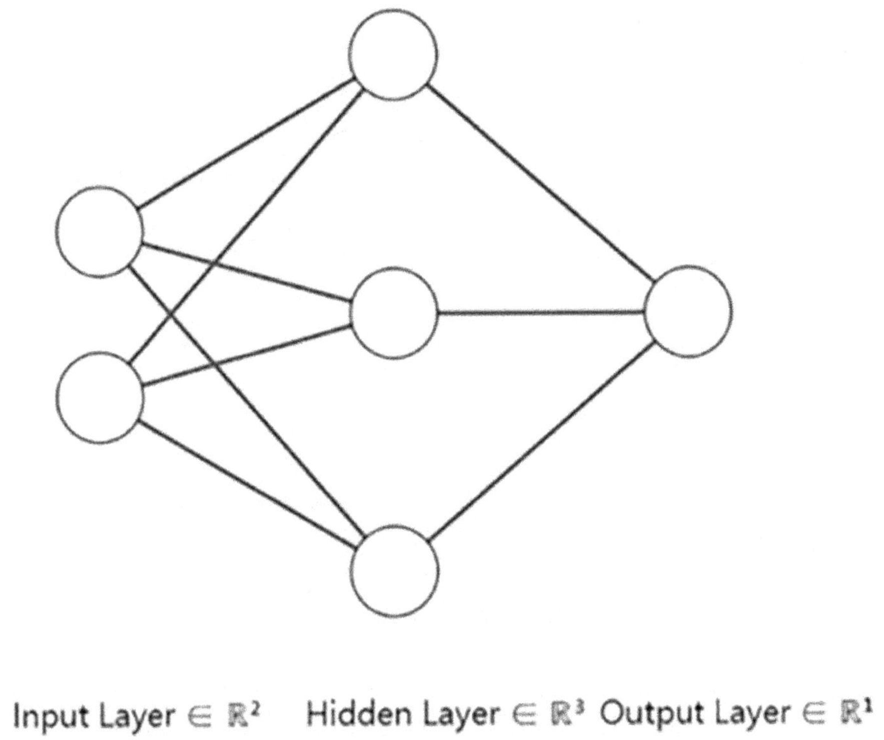

To demonstrate the neuron's calculating technique, we provide an example of a neuron in the layer that is hidden. The neuron's calculation is as follows, as seen in Figure 3.

Figure 3. Neuron's calculation

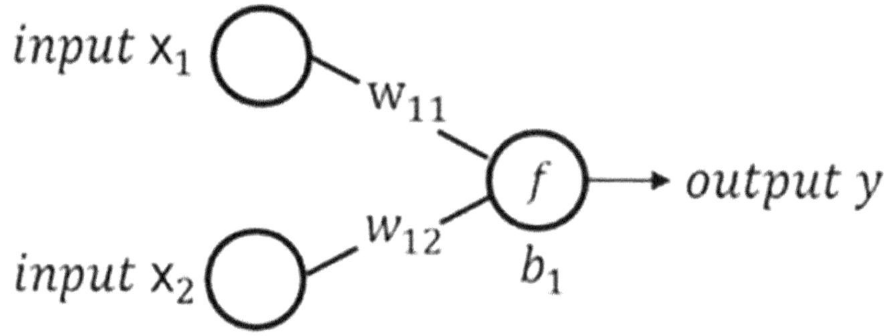

The following is the neuron calculation equation:

where f is the activation function to apply a nonlinear transformation to the neuron's output, xj is the neuron's jth input, y is its output, wij is the weight of the ith neuron and the jth input, and bi is the ith neuron's bias. The sigmoid, ReLU, tanh, softmax, and other common activation functions are among them.

Both the forward and backward propagation algorithms are essential to the neural network's training. When data is propagated through the input layer through the output layer, the neural network computes the intermediate parameters of each neuron sequentially. This process is known as forward propagation. Backpropagation is the term used to describe the neural network's parameter optimization procedure. By using gradient descent, the neural network's parameters are changed by the intermediate variables that are determined through forward propagation.

Table 1. Types of Neural networks

Neural networks	Advantages	Disadvantages	Biomedical tasks
Fully connected neural network	It is widely used at the end of the other neural network models to integrate features and make predictions	It is not easy to process high-dimensional data	Combined with other neural networks, it is widely used in many fields
Convolutional neural network	It can extract highly abstract and complex features from images	It has too many parameters, and the training speed is slow	It is suitable for processing imaging-related tasks, such as clinical imaging
Recurrent neural network	It has a memory function and can effectively process data about sequence and time	Training procedure is difficult and computationally intensive	It is suitable for processing sequence related biomedical data, such as DNA sequence, protein sequence, electronic health records
Autoencoder	It can perform unsupervised learning without using labeled data	It needs a pretraining phase	It is suitable for feature dimensionality reduction or learning effective features from data, such as clinical imaging and genomics
Deep belief network	It can be used for both supervised learning and unsupervised learning	The training process is computationally intensive	It is suitable for automatic feature extraction tasks, such as genomics and drug development

Fully Connected Neural Network

As the name suggests, as illustrated in Figure 4, a neural network with full connectivity is one in which every neuron in every layer is fully connected. The input layer, hidden layer, and output layer make up a fully linked neural network. Receiving input data is the responsibility of the input layer. For feature extraction, the hidden layer is made up of numerous neural network layers. The final prediction outcome is output by the output layer.

Figure 4. A neural network with full connectivity

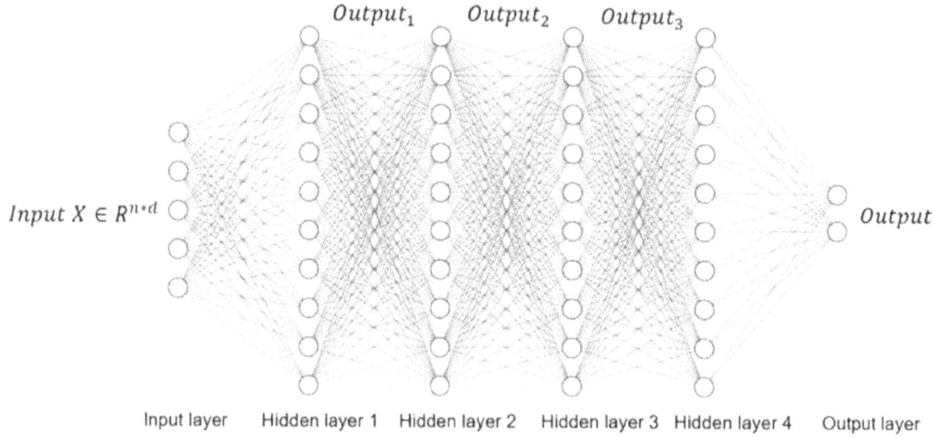

Convolutional Neural Network

The convolutional neural network, or CNN, has improved significantly in image recognition in recent years. Convolutional neural networks use weight sharing and local connections, which lowers the network's complexity and allows it to use the image as input straight away. Two key qualities of the convolution neural network are as follows: first, the features taken from the image are continuous as well as nondeformable; second, the features extracted are more abstract and complex depending on the convolution layer. The convolution layer, pooling layer, and fully linked layer make up the convolution neural network. Filters make up the convolution layer. Every filter is the size of a tiny window. To extract features from the image, these tiny windows move across it. To extract higher-quality features and increase the model's accuracy and robustness, the learned features are then subsampled via a pooling procedure. Ultimately, the prediction result is output by the completely connected layer. Figure 5 illustrates a convolutional neural network system for lung pattern recognition.

Figure 5. Convolutional neural network

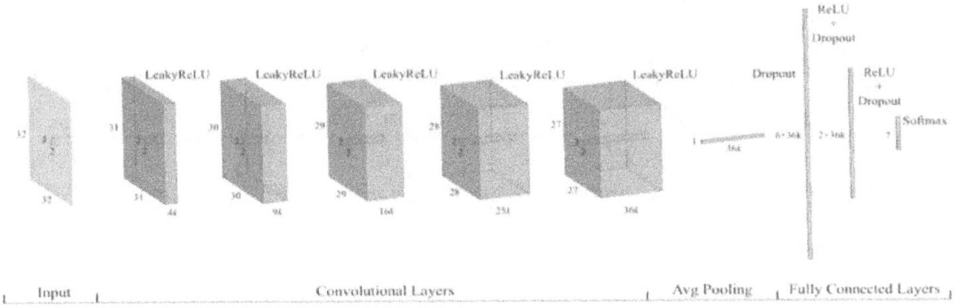

5. DISADVANTAGES AND FUTURE CHALLENGES

The primary driver of progress in the medical profession has been deep learning; yet, there are several drawbacks, such as the requirement for massive amounts of data for recognition and result generation, which can occasionally be unachievable. These computational techniques are more expensive since bulky data might be complex and generate complex data models. Because of this, not everyone can apply it, and as a result, they are unable to fully profit from this strategy. Deep learning: Because of the volume of data used in training and testing, deep learning is more likely to contain errors. Data can occasionally become inconsistent, which is caused by constant updating.

Undoubtedly, DL learning is becoming more and more significant in various fields, but it still faces some difficulties. To begin with, this kind of learning is not interpretable, necessitates large amounts of data, can occasionally struggle with direct symbols and decision-making help, and has trouble with natural languages. Since deep learning techniques need a lot of data, processing that data is more challenging and takes more time and storage space. Only medical professionals with the necessary understanding of language grammar and patient health data can comprehend the study of deep learning technologies

Security Issues in DL

Because of their flimsy architecture, Internet of Things devices are vulnerable to privacy breaches, jamming, spoofing, denial of service (DoS), and man-in-the-middle malware assaults. Attacks using spoofing and Sybil are also frequent. For security, there are numerous DL-based frameworks in the public domain. While there exist models for malware detection, secure offloading, access control, and authentication based on deep learning, they are not very accurate or quick to learn, and they come with a significant computational and communication cost in addition to the possibility of unsupervised learning. Large-scale IoT systems require stronger security measures, including blockchain technology (Kumar, Jagota, & Shabaz, 2021; Bhola, Soni, & Cheema, 2020). ML approaches include supervised approaches, unsupervised approaches, semi-supervised approaches, and RL methods based on IoT security learning (Bhola, Shabaz, Dhiman, Vimal, Subbulakshmi, & Soni, 2021). Additionally, supervised, unsupervised, and semi-supervised DL learning are distinguished.

One of the primary obstacles to changing healthcare is still obtaining knowledge and useful insights from complicated, high-dimensional, and heterogeneous biomedical data. In contemporary biomedical research, a multitude of data formats have emerged, including text, imaging, -omics, electronic health records, and sensor data. These formats are typically complex, heterogeneous, poorly annotated, and unstructured. To extract useful and reliable features from the data, traditional data mining and statistical learning techniques usually require feature engineering first. Based on these resilient and effective features, prediction or clustering models are then constructed. When dealing with complex data and insufficient topic expertise, there are several obstacles on both sides. New and efficient methods for obtaining end-to-end learning models from complex data are made possible by the most recent developments in deep learning technologies. Based on the analyzed work, we suggest that deep learning approaches could be the vehicle for translating big biomedical data into improved human health.

The practical use of deep learning in healthcare is still beset by several unresolved issues, even with the encouraging outcomes that may be achieved using deep architectures. We draw special attention to the following significant problems:

- ***Volume of data:*** A collection of computationally intensive models is referred to as deep learning. Fully linked multi-layer neural networks are a common example, in which a large number of network parameters must be accurately predicted. The abundance of data available is the foundation for achieving this aim. A general rule of thumb is to have at least a tenth of the number of samples used as parameters in the network, even though there are no strict standards about the minimum amount of training documents. The following is also one of the main causes why deep learning works so well in fields like computer vision, speech recognition, and natural language processing where massive amounts of data are easily collected. As a result, we are unable to build an extensive deep-learning model with as many patients as we would like. Furthermore, comprehending illnesses and their variations is far more difficult than other tasks like voice or picture recognition. As a result, from the standpoint of big data, a significantly greater quantity of medical data than other media would be required to train a reliable and strong deep-learning model.

- ***Quality of Data*:** In contrast to other fields where data are clear and organized, healthcare information is incredibly inconsistent, unclear, noisy, and lacking. It is difficult to train a robust deep learning algorithm with such large and diverse data sets and must take into account several factors, including data sparsity, redundancy, and missing values.
- ***Temporality:*** The diseases constantly advance and change in a nondeterministic fashion across time. Many deep learning models now in use, including those that have been suggested for the medical field, however, are based on the assumption of static vector-based inputs, which makes it difficult for them to handle time. Creating deep learning methods that can manage periodic healthcare data is a crucial task that calls for the creation of original solutions.
- ***Domain complexity*:** The challenges in the fields of biology and health care are more complicated than those in other application domains (such as image and audio analysis). The diseases are very diverse, and the etiology and progression of the majority of them are still completely unknown. Furthermore, we are unable to request as many patients as we would want because the number of patients in a realistic clinical context is typically limited.
- ***Interpretability***: Despite their effectiveness in many application areas, deep learning models are frequently seen as opaque. In the healthcare industry, algorithmic performance is not the only factor that matters; the rationale behind the algorithms' operation is equally significant, even though this may not be an issue in other, more deterministic areas like picture annotation. Indeed, demonstrating which phenotypes are influencing the predictions through model interpretability is essential to persuading medical practitioners to follow the recommendations made by the predictive system.
- ***Feature enrichment:*** Since there are only so many patients in the world, we must collect as much information as we can on each one to better understand them and come up with creative ways to process them all at once. EHRs, social media (Correia, Li, & Rocha, 2016; Nikfarjam, Sarker, O'Connor, et al., 2015), wearable technology, surroundings, surveys, online communities, genome profiles, omics data (such as proteomes), and so on are among the data sources that must be used to generate such features. An essential and difficult research problem would be how to exploit such extremely varied data and integrate them effectively into a deep learning model. To the best of our knowledge, however, no research has been done that tries to use deep learning to integrate various kinds of medical data sources

- ***Federated inference*:** Every clinical facility has a unique patient demographic. In this context, developing a deep learning model that uses patients from several sites while protecting their private information becomes a critical challenge. Therefore, another key research area that will interact with other mathematical disciplines like cryptography (e.g., homomorphic encryption (Gilad-Bachrach, Dowlin, Laine, et al., 2016) and safe multiparty computation (Yao, 1982)) will involve developing deep models in this federated context in a secure fashion.
- ***Model privacy*:** When scaling deep learning, privacy is a major concern (e.g. using cloud computing services). Tramèr et al.'s recent work (Tramèr, Zhang, Juels, et al., 2016) has shown how vulnerable Machine Learning (ML)-as-a-service, or "predictive analytics," is to several standard models, including deep neural networks. The attack respects all access control and authentication protocols, but it violates the model and individual privacy by inferring parameters or training data using publicly accessible Application Program Interfaces (APIs). The privacy community is aware of this problem, thus researchers have created a guiding framework known as "differential privacy" (Dwork, 2011; Leoni, 2012) to guarantee that individual samples in training data cannot be distinguished from one another based on their functional outputs (McSherry & Talwar, 2007). However, simplistic approaches may not be able to sufficiently protect or render outputs useless, which makes developing differential privacy solutions that are realistically useful nontrivial. As an illustration, Chaudhuri et al. (2011) created differential private techniques to safeguard the logistic regression model's training parameters. Because there are more parameters to protect, maintaining the secrecy of deep learning models is considerably more difficult, while recent work has made significant progress in this area (Abadi, Chu, Goodfellow, et al., 2016; Phan, Wang, Wu, et al., 2016; Shokri & Shmatikov, 2015). However, with all the private data that deep models are expected to handle in clinical applications, the use of intelligent tools for next-generation health care must take these dangers into account and try to establish a differential privacy standard.
- ***Expert knowledge*:** When it comes to health care issues, the specialist knowledge currently available for medical issues is important. Integrating expert knowledge into deep learning to steer it in the proper direction is an important research topic because of the scarcity of medical data and the different quality issues associated with it. To maximize the overall performance of the systems, trustworthy content that may be included in the deep architecture should be extracted from online medical encyclopedias and PubMed abstracts, for instance. Additionally, due to its capacity to leverage both labeled and unlabeled samples, semi-supervised learning—an efficient strategy

to learn from a huge amount of unlabeled samples with only a few labeled samples—would be of considerable potential.

- ***Temporal modeling*:** Given the significance of time in various healthcare-related issues, particularly those about EHRs and monitoring devices, it is imperative to train a time-sensitive deep learning model to enhance patient comprehension and facilitate prompt clinical decision support. Thus, temporal deep learning is essential for resolving issues in the medical field. We anticipate that RNNs and memory-coupled designs (Hermann, Kocisky, Grefenstette, et al., 2015) contribute significantly to the development of more advanced clinical deep architectures to achieve this goal.
- ***Interpretable modeling*:** When it comes to healthcare issues, model performance, and interpretability are equally crucial. It is improbable that clinicians will embrace a system they do not comprehend. Deep learning models are widely used due to their exceptional capabilities. However, the creation of trustworthy and dependable systems heavily depends on how to interpret and make more comprehensible the findings produced by these models. Research directions, in our opinion, will encompass both ways to assist the networks with current tools that explain the predictions of data-driven systems (Ribeiro, Singh, & Guestrin, 2016; The Michael J. Fox Foundation, 2016) and algorithms to explain the deep models (Lei, Barzilay, & Jaakkola, 2016).

Even if deep learning has outperformed machine learning in the realm of medicine and health, there are still certain issues and difficulties. Here, we address some of the issues and difficulties that follow and highlight potential solutions.

Insufficient Data

Data is the driving force behind deep learning. Neural networks typically have a large number of parameters that must be learned, updated, and optimized from the data. As the big data era advances, enough data are available to support the development of deep learning. As a result, deep learning has been very successful in many data domains, including computer vision, natural language processing, and picture recognition. Nonetheless, medical datasets are typically constrained and skewed in the realm of healthcare. Deep learning is not easily applied in this subject because there are considerably more health samples than sickness cases, or because the quantity of photos in each category is not uniform.

Inadequate data will restrict deep learning's ability to optimize its parameters and cause overfitting. While the learned model performs well on the training set, it performs appallingly poorly on never-before-seen data. The model has a low capacity for generalization. Regularization and dropout are typically the two approaches used to address overfitting. Moreover, an expanding dataset is another popular strategy to reduce overfitting. Data augmentation is a technique used in clinical imaging to increase dataset sizes. Creating new images by techniques including translation, rotation, clipping, scaling, contrast modification, and more is known as data augmentation. For instance, enhancing the data on a limited dataset of histology images of breast cancer increases the model's resilience.

The issue of inadequate data can also be effectively resolved by transfer learning. Transfer learning refers to the process wherein a model gains sufficient experience on one task before applying its newly acquired knowledge to a similar activity and fine-tuning its parameters. For instance, it can apply the neural network model to the problem of tiny sample medical photos once it has been trained on a large number of natural photographs. Transfer learning is a successful strategy, as demonstrated by numerous trials. For instance, transfer learning from computer-aided diagnosis datasets to large-scale annotated natural picture datasets (ImageNet) is useful in studies.

Multimodal learning has gained popularity as a solution to this issue in recent years. When many forms of data are used as input, such as genomic data, medical imaging, and electronic health records, multimodal learning can learn multiple types of data at once. Various models are constructed based on the properties of various data kinds. Ultimately, the data is combined to produce the model capability. For instance, fundus pictures and clinical reports were used to identify retinal microaneurysms. Training neural networks under severely uneven data distribution are resolved by combining expert subject knowledge with visual data.

Model Interpretability

Deep learning's inability to explain itself makes it a "black box" in many cases. In certain domains, like image identification, the absence of interpretability could not pose a significant issue. Nonetheless, the interpretability of models is crucial in the healthcare industry. Because doctors will accept a model's conclusions and make suitable decisions if it can furnish them with adequate and trustworthy information. At the same time, an interpretable model can give patients a thorough knowledge.

A few scholars have been investigating neural network interpretative issues. an optimization technique to visualize gene sequence categorization by extracting features or patterns. According to statistical physics, data privacy is a crucial component of the medical and health industries. There will be terrible repercussions if patient data is misused, abused, or used improperly. As is well known, training deep learning models necessitates a vast quantity of representative datasets. These datasets have great value, but they can also be quite delicate.

Many researchers in computational medicine have created deep learning models recently and made them available to the public for usage. The deep learning model has a large number of parameters, some of which can include sensitive data. It is possible for some individuals with hidden agendas to meticulously craft attacks on deep learning models. They can violate the privacy of the patients and the model by deriving these parameters from the deep learning model and even deriving sensitive information from the dataset. a homomorphic encryption method to address the issue of data leaks. The information in the data can be recovered by the countermeasures network generation. When neural networks are being trained, their settings may allow information from the training set to leak out.

Researchers have been investigating deep learning safety in the last few years. An approach that combines deep learning and differential privacy is the differential privacy random gradient descent algorithm. They increased the computational efficiency of differential privacy in deep learning by creating new technologies. A differential privacy projection in the input layer, an effective gradient technique, and other technologies are examples of these. Their approach is flexible and can be used to address the privacy issue in deep learning with a wide range of traditional optimization strategies.

Owing to the rapid expansion of data, several users are opting to store their data on cloud platforms, posing issues for deep learning in cloud computing when processing data from many data owners. Two strategies to safeguard deep learning privacy have been developed to address the issue of collaborative deep learning in cloud computing. There are two types of schemes available: the basic scheme uses multi-key fully homomorphic encryption, while the advanced scheme combines fully homomorphic encryption with a double decryption process. They have demonstrated the security of the two systems in preserving multi-key privacy on encrypted data.

Sensitive information contained in patient data poses obstacles to the research and implementation of deep learning in computational medicine, creating a vicious cycle. Large amounts of patient private data are held by hospitals and researchers; if these data are disclosed, it could result in unimaginable losses and negative effects. Conversely, hospitals and researchers are reluctant to provide their patient data and information due to concerns about data leaks, which could result in the issue that deep learning is unable to utilize vast amounts of data.

Heterogeneity

There is a great deal of variety in the healthcare data. Both structured and unstructured data exist. Furthermore, the healthcare sector's data are low-quality, noisy, and high-dimensional.

The presence of such disparate data makes it challenging to select an appropriate deep-learning model. We are aware that neural networks require processing to transform their input data into a numerical value. Researchers should first think about the issue of how to correctly preprocess the structured and unstructured biomedical data before training the neural networks.

Thus, one of the difficulties in using deep learning in the medical industry is analyzing these data. Medical imaging datasets have been the subject of investigation by certain researchers. Li et al. (2020) conducted a thorough annotation of medical images by utilizing anatomical and pathological aspects. Their work successfully addressed the issue of a short data sample size by extending the dataset's label. The findings demonstrate the much greater diagnostic accuracy of the algorithms trained on the heavily annotated medical imaging datasets.

6. CONCLUSION

Deep learning is used in computational medicine to solve problems in drug discovery, genetics, clinical imaging, and electronic health records. By processing large amounts of biomedical data with deep learning, medical professionals may better advise patients and raise standards of care by extracting valuable insights from the data. This article also highlights the issues and difficulties associated with using deep learning in computational medicine. It offers a guide and means of enhancing the future use of deep learning in the medical and health fields.

REFERENCES

Abadi, M., Chu, A., & Goodfellow, I.Deep learning with differential privacy. *Proceedings of the 2016 ACM SIGSAC Conference on Computer and Communications Security*, 308–18. DOI: 10.1145/2976749.2978318

Abdel-Hamid, O., Mohamed, A.-R., Jiang, H., Deng, L., Penn, G., & Yu, D. (2014). Convolutional neural networks for speech recognition. *IEEE/ACM Transactions on Audio, Speech, and Language Processing*, 22(10), 1533–1545. DOI: 10.1109/TASLP.2014.2339736

Ahmed, I., Jeon, G., & Piccialli, F. (2021). A deep-learning-based smart healthcare system for patient's discomfort detection at the edge of Internet of things. IEEE Internet of Things Journal, 8(13).

Al-Garadi, M. A., Mohamed, A., Al-Ali, A. K., Du, X., Ali, I., & Guizani, M. (2020). A survey of machine and deep learning methods for Internet of things (IoT) security. IEEE Communications Surveys & Tutorials, 22(3), 1646–1685. DOI: 10.1109/COMST.2020.2988293

Bhola, J., Shabaz, M., Dhiman, G., Vimal, S., Subbulakshmi, P., & Soni, S. K. (2021). Performance evaluation of multilayer clustering network using distributed energy efficient clustering with enhanced threshold protocol. *Wireless Personal Communications*. Advance online publication. DOI: 10.1007/s11277-021-08780-x PMID: 34456513

Bhola, J., Soni, S., & Cheema, G. K. (2020). Genetic algorithm based optimized leach protocol for energy efficient wireless sensor networks. *Journal of Ambient Intelligence and Humanized Computing*, 11(3), 1281–1288. DOI: 10.1007/s12652-019-01382-3

Brosch, T., & Tam, R. (2023). Manifold learning of brain MRIs by deep learning. Med Image Comput Comput Assist Interv, 16, 633–40. DOI: 10.1007/978-3-642-40763-5_78

Chaudhuri, K., Monteleoni, C., & Sarwate, A. (2011). Differentially private empirical risk minimization. *Journal of Machine Learning Research*, 12, 1069–1109. PMID: 21892342

Cheng, J.-Z., Ni, D., Chou, Y.-H., Qin, J., Tiu, C.-M., Chang, Y.-C., Huang, C.-S., Shen, D., & Chen, C.-M. (2016). Computer-aided diagnosis with deep learning architecture: Applications to breast lesions in US images and pulmonary nodules in CT scans. *Scientific Reports*, 6(1), 24454. DOI: 10.1038/srep24454 PMID: 27079888

Correia, R. B., Li, L., & Rocha, L. M. (2016). Monitoring potential drug interactions and reactions via network analysis of instagram user timelines. *Pacific Symposium on Biocomputing*, 21, 492–503. DOI: 10.1142/9789814749411_0045 PMID: 26776212

Dwork, C. (2011). Differential privacy. In *Encyclopedia of Cryptography and Security* (pp. 338–340). Springer. DOI: 10.1007/978-1-4419-5906-5_752

Esteva, A., Kuprel, B., Novoa, R. A., Ko, J., Swetter, S. M., Blau, H. M., & Thrun, S. (2017). Dermatologist-level classification of skin cancer with deep neural networks. *Nature*, 542(7639), 115–118. DOI: 10.1038/nature21056 PMID: 28117445

Gilad-Bachrach, R., Dowlin, N., & Laine, K.CryptoNets: applying neural networks to encrypted data with high throughput and accuracy. *International Conference on Machine Learning*, 201–10.

Gulshan, V., Peng, L., Coram, M., Stumpe, M. C., Wu, D., Narayanaswamy, A., Venugopalan, S., Widner, K., Madams, T., Cuadros, J., Kim, R., Raman, R., Nelson, P. C., Mega, J. L., & Webster, D. R. (2016). Development and validation of a deep learning algorithm for the detection of diabetic retinopathy in retinal fundus photographs. *Journal of the American Medical Association*, 316(22), 2402–2410. DOI: 10.1001/jama.2016.17216 PMID: 27898976

He, K., Zhang, X., Ren, S., & Sun, J. (2016). *Deep residual learning for image recognition.2016 IEEE Conference on Computer Vision and Pattern Recognition (CVPR)*. IEEE. DOI: 10.1109/CVPR.2016.90

Hermann, K. M., Kocisky, T., & Grefenstette, E. (2015). Teaching machines to read and comprehend. *Adv Neural Inf Process Syst*, 201, 1693–701.

Huang, X., Jagota, V., Espinoza-Muñoz, E., & Flores-Albornoz, J. (2021). Tourist hot spots prediction model based on optimized neural network algorithm. *International Journal of System Assurance Engineering and Management*. Advance online publication. DOI: 10.1007/s13198-021-01226-4

Kumar, M. N., Jagota, V., & Shabaz, M. (2021). Retrospection of the optimization model for designing the power train of a formula student race car. *Scientific Programming*, 2021, 9. DOI: 10.1155/2021/9465702

Lan, Z., Chen, M., Goodman, S., Gimpel, K., Sharma, P., & Soricut, R. (2020). *ALBERT: A lite bert for self-supervised learning of language representations.In ICLR 2020? Eighth International Conference on Learning Representations*. La Jolla: ICLR.

Lei, T., Barzilay, R., & Jaakkola, T. (2016). Rationalizing neural predictions. DOI: 10.18653/v1/D16-1011

Leoni, D. (2012). Non-interactive differential privacy: a survey. *Proceedings of the First International Workshop on Open Data*, 40–52. DOI: 10.1145/2422604.2422611

Liu, S., Liu, S., & Cai, W.Early diagnosis of Alzheimer's disease with deep learning. *International Symposium on Biomedical Imaging*, 1015–18. DOI: 10.1109/ISBI.2014.6868045

McSherry, F., & Talwar, K. (2007). Mechanism design via differential privacy. *48th Annual IEEE Symposium on Foundations of Computer Science*, 94–103.

Miotto, R., Li, L., Kidd, B. A., & Dudley, J. T. (2016). Deep patient: An unsupervised representation to predict the future of patients from the electronic health records. *Scientific Reports*, 6(1), 26094–26094. DOI: 10.1038/srep26094 PMID: 27185194

Nikfarjam, A., Sarker, A., O'Connor, K., Ginn, R., & Gonzalez, G. (2015). Pharmacovigilance from social media: Mining adverse drug reaction mentions using sequence labeling with word embedding cluster features. *Journal of the American Medical Informatics Association : JAMIA*, 22(3), 671–681. DOI: 10.1093/jamia/ocu041 PMID: 25755127

Phan, N., Wang, Y., & Wu, X.Differential privacy preservation for deep auto-encoders: an application of human behavior prediction. *Proceedings of the Thirtieth AAAI Conference on Artificial Intelligence,* 1309–16. DOI: 10.1609/aaai.v30i1.10165

Prasoon, A., Petersen, K., & Igel, C. (2013). Deep feature learning for knee cartilage segmentation using a tri-planar convolutional neural network. *Medical Image Computing and Computer-Assisted Intervention : MICCAI.*, 16, 246–253. PMID: 24579147

Ribeiro, M. T., Singh, S., & Guestrin, C. (2016). Why should I trust you? Explaining the predictions of any classifier. *ACM Conferences on Knowledge Discovery and Data Mining*, 1135–44. DOI: 10.18653/v1/N16-3020

Shokri, R., & Shmatikov, V. (2015). Privacy-preserving deep learning. *Proceedings of the 22nd ACM SIGSAC Conference on Computer and Communications Security,* 1310–21.

The Michael J. Fox Foundation for Parkinson's Research. (2016). Subtyping Parkinson's disease with deep learning models. https://www.michaeljfox.org/foundation/grant-detail.php?grant_id=1518

Tramèr, F., Zhang, F., & Juels, A.Stealing machine learning models via prediction apis. *USENIX Security Symposium.*

Vyas, S., & Bhargava, D. (2021). Smart Health Systems. Singapore: Springer. DOI: 10.1007/978-981-16-4201-2

Yao, A. C. (1982). Protocols for secure computations. *23rd Annual Symposium on Foundations of Computer Science (SFCS 1982)*, 160–4. DOI: 10.1109/SFCS.1982.38

Yoo, Y., Brosch, T., & Traboulsee, A. Deep learning of image features from unlabeled data for multiple sclerosis lesion segmentation. *International Workshop on Machine Learning in Medical Imaging*, 117–24. DOI: 10.1007/978-3-319-10581-9_15

Chapter 7
Data Science In Healthcare

T. Jayasudha
https://orcid.org/0009-0001-4754-1125
Sri Sarada College for Women, India

R. Uma Rani
Sri Sarada College for Women, India

P. Tamilarasi
https://orcid.org/0000-0001-9788-4129
Sri Sarada College for Women, India

ABSTRACT

Cardiovascular disease (CVD) has been the leading reason of death up to this point. Cardiovascular illness must be diagnosed as soon as possible to save patients' lives. The intention of this research is identifying the most important features to predict CVD by using feature selection method, and find out the most effective classification model to forecast cardiovascular diseases. This study makes use of patient datasets from the UCI repository for prediction. For data scaling, Min-Max Scaler is employed. Data transformation is accomplished using the label encoding technique. The Z-score method is applied to handle the outlier. The most essential features were picked using the chi square approach. For classification, logistic regression, support vector machine, naive bayes, decision tree, and boosted random forest were employed. The achievement was assessed by applying confusion matrix, accuracy, recall, F1 score, and precision, and ROC. Among five classifiers, boosted random forest classifier achieved the highest accuracy (87.3%).

DOI: 10.4018/979-8-3693-7868-7.ch007

1. INTRODUCTION

1.1 Data Science

Data science is a multidisciplinary domain that uses a multiple approaches and techniques to obtain knowledge and clarity from data. To analyse complicated data sets, it blends ideas from mathematics, computer science, statistics, and domain-specific expertise.

1.2 Relationship Between Data Science, Machine Learning, Deep Learning and AI

Based on data science, machine learning (ML) and deep learning (DL) are two different methods that use data to create intelligent systems. Artificial intelligence (AI) includes both machine learning (ML) and deep learning (DL), with the goal of developing structure that can execute activities that would usually need human-like skill. Figure 1 illustrate the relationship between DS, ML, DL, AI.

Figure 1. Relationship Between DS, ML, DL, and AI

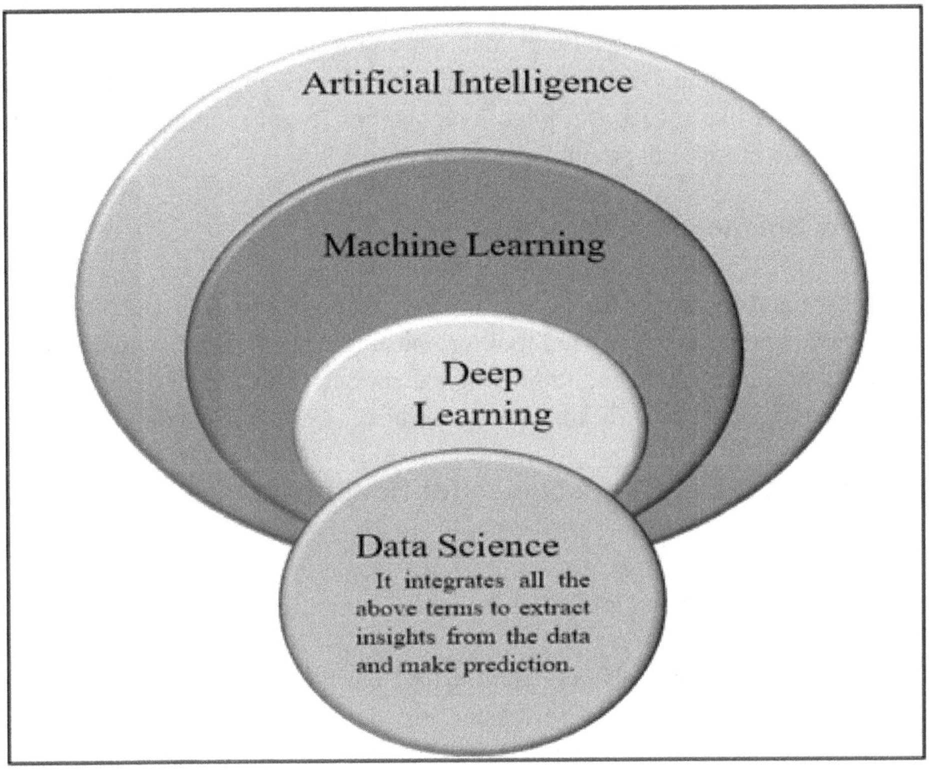

Artificial Intelligence (AI):

- **Definition:** A more general term referring to the method of replicating human intelligence in machines so that those machines are able to perform operations that would commonly require human intellect.
- **Relation to Data Science:** In order to improve decision-making and automate procedures, AI systems can use the fundamental facts and insights provided by data science.

Machine Learning (ML):

- **Definition:** A division of artificial intelligence that concentrates on statistical methods and algorithms that allow computer process and interpret data to learn from and make predictions or judgements.
- **Relation to Data Science:** Data science frequently uses machine learning (ML) techniques for pattern recognition and predictive modelling. Data scientists build models that can generalise from training data to new data using machine learning (ML) methods.

Deep Learning (DL):

- **Definition:** A subfield of machine learning that applies multilayer neural networks to analyse big datasets and simulate intricate patterns.
- **Relation to Data Science:** DL is frequently applied to data science tasks like speech and picture recognition. Significant amounts of data and processing power are needed.

1.3 Data Science in Healthcare

Integrating data science technology is driving a rapid change in the healthcare sector. Data science is now a vital tool for boosting clinical decision-making, expediting medical research, and improving patient outcomes due to the increasing digitization of patient records, diagnostic instruments, and clinical data.

1.4 Innovations in Data Science for Healthcare

a. Machine Learning and Predictive Analytics:

Machine learning models have transformed the healthcare sector by offering predictive analytics that aid in forecasting the development of diseases, patient readmissions, and treatment outcomes. For instance, models like neural networks, Random Forests, and Support Vector Machines (SVM) have been effectively used to forecast the beginning of diabetes, cardiovascular disease, and even the return of cancer. Predictive analytics make early interventions possible, raising patient recovery rates and lowering medical expenses.

b. Deep Learning in Medical Imaging:

In medical imaging, data science has made one of the biggest contributions to healthcare. Convolutional neural networks (CNNs), in particular, have shown enormous promise in the diagnosis of diseases from imaging data, including CT scans, MRIs, and X-rays.

c. Natural Language Processing (NLP)

To mine and comprehend unstructured healthcare data, including doctor reports, electronic health records (EHRs), and clinical notes, natural language processing (NLP) is essential. NLP is especially helpful in finding patterns in patient histories that human practitioners would miss, giving a more complete picture of a patient's health.

d. Big Data Analytics for Population Health Management

By employing big data analytics, healthcare institutions can handle enormous volumes of both structured and unstructured data, combining data from genomics, wearable technology, EHRs, clinical trials, and more. These massive datasets offer population-level information that may be utilised to forecast outbreaks, spot patterns, and create public health campaigns. For instance, big data played a crucial role in monitoring the COVID-19 pandemic's virus transmission, allocating medical resources, and determining the effectiveness of treatment.

1.5 Applications of Data Science in Healthcare

Data science has a significant influence on healthcare, changing the way that treatment is provided and leading to better patient outcomes.

a. Disease Diagnosis and Prevention

Predictive models are useful in identifying patients who are prone to developing heart disease, diabetes, cancer, etc. Some instances are:

✓ **Heart Disease Prediction:** To evaluate the risk of heart disease, machine learning algorithms examine patient variables such as blood pressure, and cholesterol levels.
✓ **Cancer detection:** To increase the chances of an early diagnosis, AI algorithms, particularly deep learning methods are employed to discover malignant cells in imaging data such as MRIs and mammograms.

b. Drug Development and Discovery

To predict the behaviour of novel pharmaceuticals, data science analyses enormous quantities of biological information, including chemical compounds, proteomics, and genomes. This helps to speed up the drug discovery process.

✓ **AI in therapeutic Design:** Algorithms identify possible adverse effects and forecast the efficacy of therapeutic candidates, avoiding the need for costly and time-consuming laboratory testing.

- ✓ **Clinical Trials:** Trial protocol optimisation and participant selection are made easier with the use of data-driven models.

c. Optimizing Hospital Operations

Hospitals may optimise personnel, cut down on wait times, and enhance patient care overall by evaluating data on patient admissions, treatment durations, and resource usage. Utilisations consist of:

- ✓ **Resource Allocation:** Based on the demands of patients in real time, predictive analytics assists hospitals in allocating resources such as ICU beds, ventilators, and staff.
- ✓ **Patient Flow Management:** Hospitals may effectively handle patient admissions, discharges, and transfers by using data-driven insights to manage patient flow.

d. Fraud Detection and Risk Management

Healthcare organisations can detect and stop fraudulent activity, including insurance fraud and false claims, with the use of data science.

- ✓ **Insurance Claim Fraud Detection:** Data-driven solutions are designed to automatically identify inflated claims or suspect billing trends and send them for more investigation.
- ✓ **Risk management:** Healthcare companies evaluate risks, such as malpractice or noncompliance with regulations, using data analytics and implement preventative actions.

1.6 Challenges of Data Science in Healthcare

a. Data Privacy and Security

Safeguarding sensitive patient data protection and security is a major issue in healthcare data science. "Stringent regulations, such as the Health Insurance Portability and Accountability Act (HIPAA) in the US, mandate the protection of patient data in the healthcare industry.

b. Data Integration and Quality

Data analysis in the healthcare industry is sometimes hampered by noisy, inconsistent, or incomplete data. Clinical decision support systems and trustworthy machine learning models depend on consistent, high-quality data.

c. Bias and Fairness in AI Models

The Standard of machine learning models is based on the caliber of the training data. Health disparities can be made worse by biased healthcare data, such as the under-representation of particular demographic groups, which can result in unfair or erroneous projections.

Ensuring that the data is representative of all groups and developing fair algorithms are necessary to promote equality in healthcare.

1.7 Cardiovascular Disease

Cardiovascular disease continues to be the key reason of mortality globally, affecting millions of people. Early detection of CVD is therefore crucial. Swift identification of heart-related diseases may lessen the possibility of death (Ntiloudi et al., 2016). A broad range of conditions, including atherosclerosis, hypertension, and heart failure, are included under the umbrella term "CVD" (Aryal et al., 2020). Cardiovascular disease can clog blood vessels, leading to a heart attack, angina, or stroke. Few typical CVD types are:

1. **Coronary artery disease:** Narrowing or blockage of the coronary arteries, which frequently results in angina or heart attacks, is known as coronary artery disease (CAD).
2. **Heart attack (myocardial infarction):** Causes damage when blood flow is cut off to a portion of the heart muscle.
3. **Heart failure:** A ailment in which the heart is unable to pump blood effectively, resulting in exhaustion, breathing difficulties, and oedema.
4. **Arrhythmia:** An irregular heartbeat, such as bradycardia, tachycardia, or atrial fibrillation.
5. **Hypertensive Heart Disease:** Coronary artery disease, and Heart failure are among the conditions brought on by high blood pressure.
6. **Cardiomyopathy**: Heart muscle disease labelled as cardiomyopathy leads to more difficult for the heart to supply blood, which increases the risk of heart failure.
7. **Peripheral artery disease:** artery narrowing, usually in the legs, resulting in discomfort, numbness, and a higher chance of having a heart attack or stroke.

8. **Stroke:** A stroke is the result of disrupted blood movement to a portion of the brain, which kills brain cells. It may be hemorrhagic (caused by bleeding) or ischaemic (caused by blockages).
9. **Congenital Heart Disease:** A term used to describe structural heart problems that manifest from birth and can vary in severity from simple to severe.
10. **Rheumatic Heart Disease:** Rheumatic fever, which results from untreated streptococcal infections, damages the heart valves.
11. **Aortic Aneurysm**: Aortic aneurysms are weak spots or bulges in the aortic wall that have the potential to burst and release potentially fatal amounts of blood.
12. **Valvular heart disease:** The term "valvular heart disease" denotes, the condition affecting one or more of the heart's valves, such as prolapsed mitral valve or aortic stenosis.

An increased risk of cardiovascular disease (CVD) is linked to several behavioural and physiological risk factors, including excessive alcohol, caffeine use, smoking, physical inactivity, pre-existing heart illnesses, and obesity (Shah et al., 2020). When processing medical data, it can be challenging to forecast cardiovascular sickness. Numerous risk factors, including elevated blood pressure, hyperlipidemia, and irregular heartbeats, may make it challenging to diagnose cardiovascular illness.

By analysing vast amounts of medical data to enhance patient care, treatment outcomes, and healthcare operations, data science plays a revolutionary role in the healthcare field. It makes it possible to identify at-risk groups, provide individualised treatment regimens, and diagnose diseases early thanks to methods like machine learning and predictive analytics. The efficiency, accuracy, and accessibility of healthcare are eventually improved by data science, which also improves hospital administration, lowers expenses, and fosters advancements in telemedicine and medication research. Machine learning approaches have proven to be more accurate and quicker at predicting diseases in the healthcare sector (Mohan et al., 2019).

1.8 Research Contribution

- The clinical traits of patients with cardiovascular disease were examined to forecast the condition.
- Determining which characteristics are most crucial for CVD prediction.
- Pre-processing the data to ensure optimal performance of the classifier by eliminating redundant information and handling missing data.
- Choosing the best variables to classify CVD.
- Using many classifiers including boosted random forest to forecast CVD.
- Comparing the performance of the various ML algorithms to see which one is most effective at predicting CVD.

2. RELATED WORKS

Spencer et al. (2020) integrated the ML algorithm with feature selection technology, and the resulting model achieved an accuracy of 85% by combining the BayesNet algorithm with chi-square feature selection.

The Coronary Artery Disease (CAD) dataset was used by Nasarian E, Abdar M, et al. (2020) along with occupational and environmental factors. Using the suggested feature selection strategy, the SMOTE and XGBoost classifiers have obtained an 81.23% classification accuracy.

An ensemble of classifiers is used by B. C. Latha et al. (2019) to examine the accuracy of heart illness forecast. Training and testing were conducted using the Cleveland heart ailment dataset from the UCI machine learning public library. For the tests, the ensemble algorithms majority voting, boosting, bagging, and stacking were used. When the feature set FS2 was deployed to the stack of MLP, Naïve Bayes, Bayes Net, C4.5, and PART using a random tree, 80.21% accuracy was seen.

An approach known as cluster-based DT learning (CDTL) was used by Magesh and Swarnalatha (2021). The SVM, random forest (RF), DT, and linear models were the baseline techniques used to compare the performance of the suggested strategy. A higher prediction accuracy of 89% was attained when CDTL and RF were combined. The CDTL-RF forecast accuracy achieved 89% after feature processing, which is a 12% improvement over the non-CDTL approach.

The Artificial Neural Network (ANN) technique was proposed in (Cheng & Chiu, 2017) for the categorisation of carotid artery stenting (CAS) disease. From the Taiwan Nation Health Insurance Research Database (NHIRD), 317 patient records were consumed to create and evaluate an artificial neural network (ANN) model with 13 input characteristics. The model's performance displayed 89.4% sensitivity and 82.5% accuracy.

Pathak and Valan (2020) presented an analytical model for heart disease analysis based on fuzzy logic and DT. The recommended technique successfully forecasts heart disease and enhances classification accuracy. The suggested approach achieved 88% accuracy. Just eight patient features are used in the suggested method to diagnose heart illness.

Research Gap

Currently, the boosted random forest algorithm is not commonly employed for cardiovascular disease classification. While some researchers use either random forest or boosted models, boosted random forest remains underutilized. This study aims to fill that gap.

Additionally, I will select the best features for classifying cardiovascular disease using the Chi-Square test. I plan to create new combinations of models by integrating the Chi-Square test with various classification algorithms. Furthermore, I will compare the performance of multiple classifiers to evaluate whether the Boosted Random Forest achieves superior accuracy.

3. WORKFLOW

This investigation aims to explore the impact of variable selection method on enhancing the classification of cardiovascular disease. Figure 2 depicts the flow of various strategies.

- ✓ First step is downloading open-source UCI cardiovascular disease dataset.
- ✓ The next step is pre-processing, which involves data cleaning, data transformation, data scaling.
- ✓ Next step is feature selection. Chi-square test approach is used to establish the important attributes for CVD classification.
- ✓ Later, logistic regression, decision tree, SVM, Naive Bayes, and boosted random forest algorithms are applied for classification.

Figure 2. Work Flow of CVD classification frame work

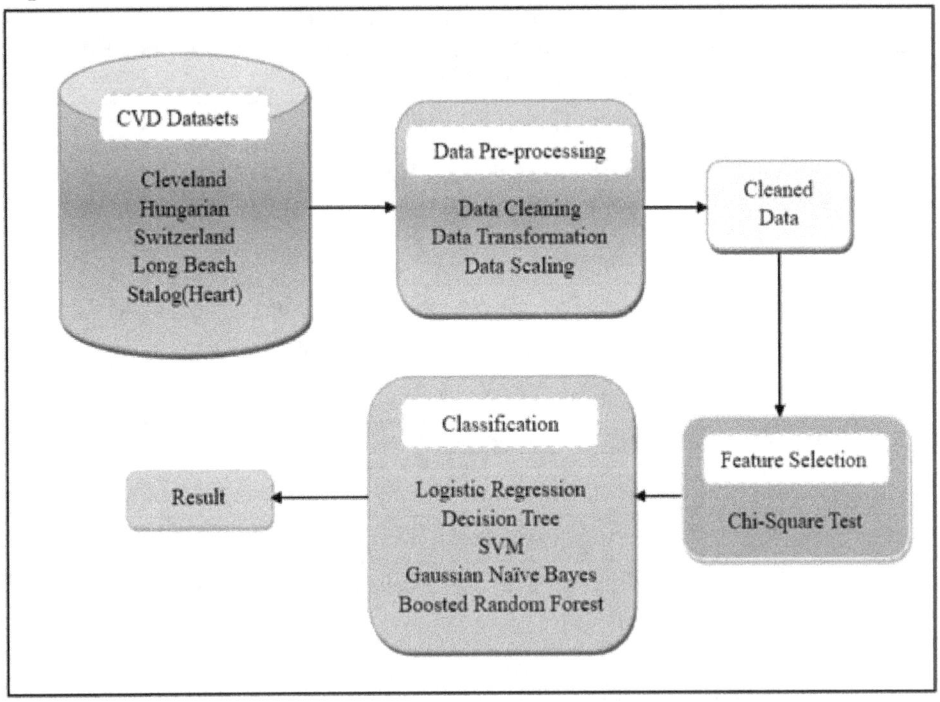

3.1 Dataset Description

I have used data from the UCI Machine Learning warehouse for this research project.

Here, 12 common features (11 predictors; 1 class) such as sex, chest pain type, resting blood pressure, etc. are merged from 5 cardiac datasets.

These datasets are:

- Cleveland: 303 records
- Hungarian: 294 records
- Switzerland: 123 records
- Long Beach VA: 200 records
- Stalog Heart Data Set: 270 records

Figure 3 shows the features' names and their descriptions.

Figure 3. Attributes details

S. No	Attribute Name	Description
1	Age	Age of the patient [years]
2	Sex	Sex of the patient [Male/Female]
3	ChestPainType	There are four different types of chest pain: [TA: Typical Angina, ATA: Atypical Angina, NAP: Non-Anginal Pain, ASY: Asymptomatic]
4	RestingEGC	Resting electrocardiogram results [Normal: Normal, ST: having ST-T wave abnormality, LVH: showing probable or definite left ventricular hypertrophy]
5	RestingBP	Resting blood pressure level [mm Hg]
6	Cholesterol	Patient's total cholesterol level in milligram per deciliter (mg/dl)
7	FastingBS	Fasting blood sugar [1: if Fasting BS > 120 mg/dl, 0: otherwise]
8	MaxHR	Maximum heart rate achieved [Numeric value between 60 and 220]
9	Oldpeak	When compared to rest, exercise causes ST depression. Oldpeak = ST [Numeric value measured in depression]
10	ExerciseAngina	Agnosia was discovered after exercising. [Y: Yes, N: No]
11	ST Slope	The slope of the peak exercise ST segment [Up: upsloping, Flat: flat, Down: down sloping]
12	HeartDisease	Output class. If this value is 0, there is no risk of cardiovascular disease. If value is 1, there is a chance of cardiovascular disease.

3.1.1 Exploratory Data Analysis

In pandas, the describe () function is used to obtain a representation of key statistics on data frame for numeric (and optionally other) datatypes. It is good for quickly understanding the data distribution and stats of our dataset. Figure 4 illustrates the statistical distribution of the features.

Here is the general output we get as a numeric column in describe ().

✓ **Count:** Count of non-NA elements.

- ✓ **Mean:** Average of the values.
- ✓ **Standard Deviation(std):** Spread of the values.
- ✓ **Min:** The smallest value.
- ✓ **Maximum (max):** Largest value.
- ✓ **25th percentile (25%)**: Value below which 25% of the data fall.
- ✓ **50th percentile (50%)**: 50th percentile.
- ✓ **75th percentile (75%):** Value below which that the bottom 75% of dataset fall.

Figure 4. Statistical distributions of the features

	Age	Sex	Chest Pain Type	Resting BP	Cholesterol	Fasting BS	Resting ECG	Maximum Heart Rate	Exercise Angina	Oldpeak	ST slope	Heart Disease
count	1190.000000	1190.000000	1190.000000	1190.000000	1190.000000	1190.000000	1190.000000	1190.000000	1190.000000	1190.000000	1190.000000	1190.000000
mean	53.720168	0.763866	3.232773	132.153782	210.363866	0.213445	0.698319	139.732773	0.387395	0.922773	1.624370	0.528571
std	9.358203	0.424884	0.935480	18.368823	101.420489	0.409912	0.870359	25.517636	0.487360	1.086337	0.610459	0.499393
min	28.000000	0.000000	1.000000	0.000000	0.000000	0.000000	0.000000	60.000000	0.000000	-2.600000	0.000000	0.000000
25%	47.000000	1.000000	3.000000	120.000000	188.000000	0.000000	0.000000	121.000000	0.000000	0.000000	1.000000	0.000000
50%	54.000000	1.000000	4.000000	130.000000	229.000000	0.000000	0.000000	140.500000	0.000000	0.600000	2.000000	1.000000
75%	60.000000	1.000000	4.000000	140.000000	269.750000	0.000000	2.000000	160.000000	1.000000	1.600000	2.000000	1.000000
max	77.000000	1.000000	4.000000	200.000000	603.000000	1.000000	2.000000	202.000000	1.000000	6.200000	3.000000	1.000000

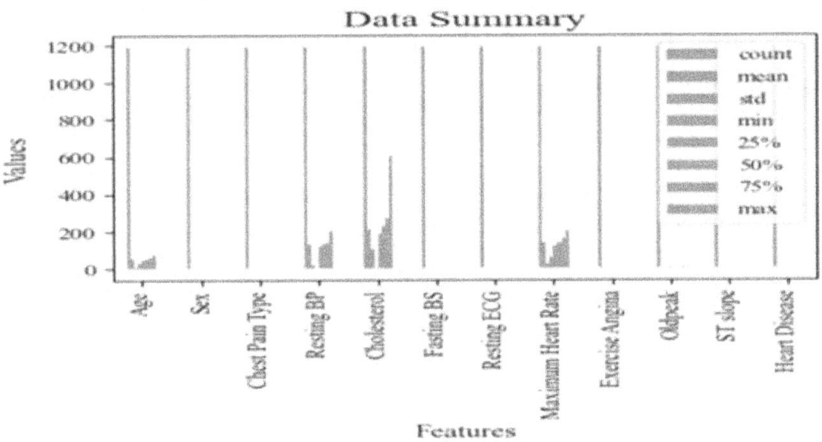

The distribution of target feature is displayed in figure 5. There were 55.3% patients with CVD, and 44.7% doesn't have CVD.

Figure 5. Class distribution

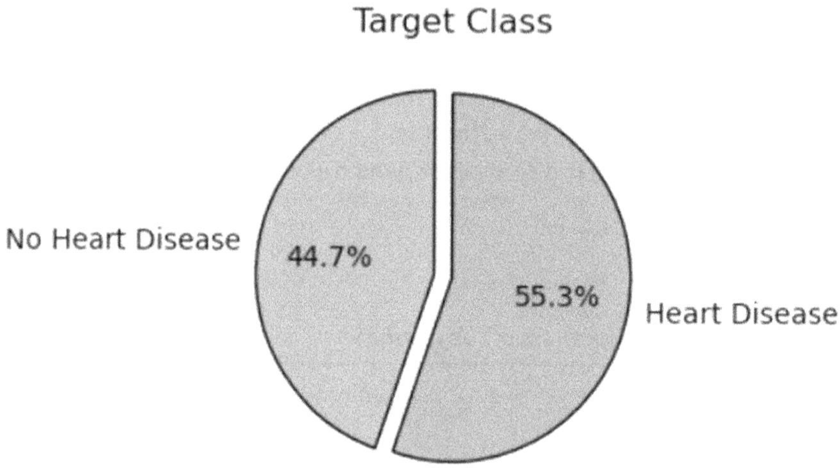

Figure 6 plots categorical features such ST-slope, exercise-induced angina, resting ECG, fasting blood sugar, and kind of chest pain. Male patients accounted for 90.2% of those with cardiovascular disease. ASY-type chest pain suggests a substantial chance of cardiovascular illness (392); 170 out of 508 patients with cardiovascular disease had fasting blood sugar. According to the ST Slope statistics, a flat slope denotes a very high risk of cardiovascular disease. The LVH level and ST level account for 20.9% and 23.0% of heart disease, respectively, based on the resting electrocardiogram.

Figure 6. Categorical features

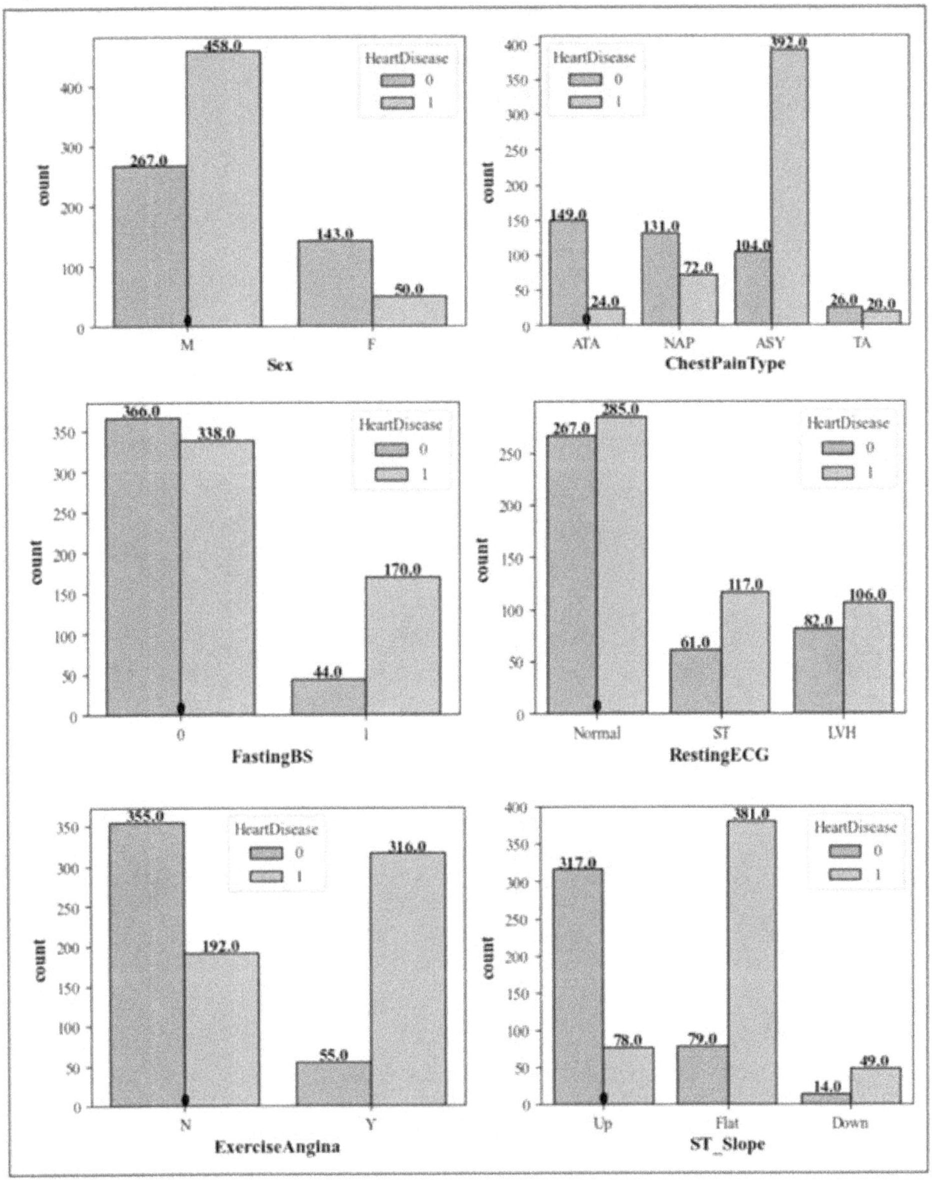

The figure 7 shows the plot of numerical features such as age group, resting BP, cholesterol, maximum heart rate, and old peak value. The age range of most cardiovascular patients is 40–70. Resting blood pressure values between 100 and 170, old peak values 0–4, maximum HR readings of 100–180, and cholesterol levels between 160 and 340 are the most likely to suggest heart disease.

Figure 7. Numerical features

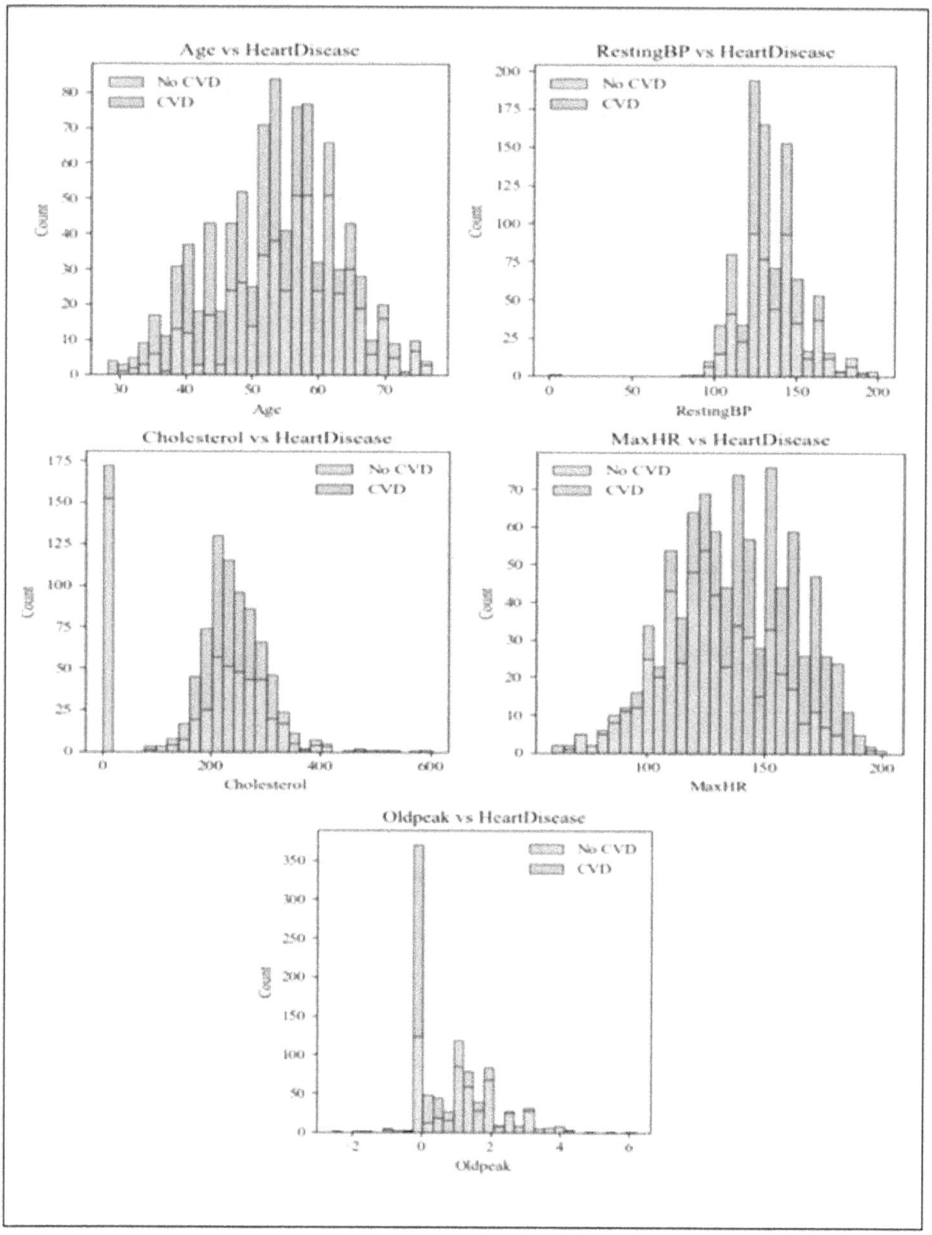

3.2 Data Pre-Processing

3.2.1 Handling Missing Values

A method for filling in missing values in a dataset is called data filling. Incomplete data is a usual obstacle problem in datasets due to several factors, such as measurement faults, data loss, or simply because certain information was not collected. Imputation methods help to handle missing data by estimating or predicting the values that are missing based on the observed data. In this study, missing values are substituted with the mean of the non-missing values in the same column. The formula for mean is (Eq 1):

$$Mean = (\Sigma x\_i)/n \tag{1}$$

Where:

- x_i: The i-th data point
- n: The total number of data points

3.2.2 Encoding

The encoding refers to the transformation of categorical data into a numerical format that can be effectively used by algorithms. This alteration is crucial because maximum machine learning models need numerical input to execute computations and make predictions. In this study, label encoding is used for encoding the categorical data.

3.2.3 Data Normalization

The data normalization is a pre-processing method employed to rescale the values of numeric features in a dataset to a standard range. The goal of normalization is to bring all the variables to a uniform scale, avoiding features with larger scales from dominating the learning process compared to features with smaller scales. In this work min-max scaling is used for normalization. Using this method, the features are scaled to a given range, ordinarily between 0 and 1. The formula for min-max is (Eq 2):

$$X - X_{min}$$

x normalized =

$$\frac{x - x_{min}}{x_{max} - x_{min}} \quad (2)$$

$x_{\max} - x_{\min}$

Where:

- The normalized value is represented by " x normalized ".
- The feature's initial value is represented by x.
- The feature's minimal value is denoted by x_{min}.
- *The feature's maximum value is denoted by* x_{max}.

In this work, chi-square test technique is used to identify the importance of features. This statistical strategy can be used to evaluate the significant association between two categorical variables. Figure 8 shows pseudocode of chi-square method working process.

Figure 8. Chi-Square Method Pseudocode

1. Import necessary libraries.
2. Load your dataset into a DataFrame.
3. Do data pre-processing.
4. Initialize an empty list to store Chi-Square scores
   chi2_scores = []
5. For each feature in the dataset (excluding the target variable)
   - Create a contingency table between the feature and the target variable (CVD).
   - Perform the Chi-Square test using chi2_contingency.
   - Store the Chi-Square score in chi2_scores list.
6. Create a DataFrame for Chi-Square scores:
   - chi2_results = DataFrame (columns = ['Feature', 'Chi-Square Score'])
   - For each feature and its corresponding score in chi2_scores:
     Append the feature and score to chi2_results.
7. Plot the features against their Chi-Square scores.

Figure 9. Chi-Square Score

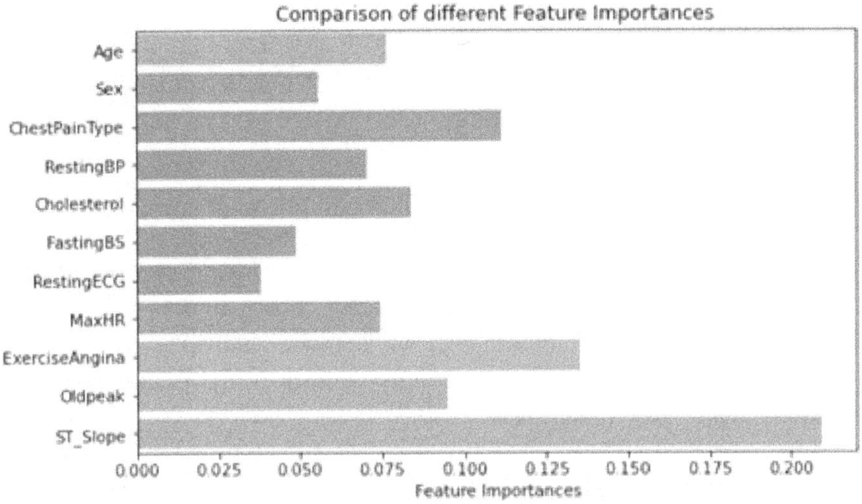

Figure 9 shows that ST_Slope, ExcerciseAngina, ChestpainType, Oldpeak, Cholesterol, Age, MaxHR, and RestingBP were the most important features to classify cardiovascular disease. RestingECG, FastingBS, and Sex were the less important features for detecting CVD.

3.4 Classification

The following classification algorithms are applied to the pre-processed dataset:

3.4.1 Logistic Regression

The sigmoid function, which admits input as independent factors and outputs a possibility value between 0 and 1, is used in logistic regression for binary classification.

3.4.2 Decision Tree

A decision tree is an implementation of a tree-like graph with probable outcomes that include resource codes, purpose, and chance event outcomes. It illustrates an algorithm that is made up of a conditional control statement.

3.4.3 Support Vector Machine

A supervised learning technique called SVM organizes data into one of two groups after taking a look at it. SVM categorizes data points by mapping the input data to an extended-dimensional feature space.

3.4.4 Boosted Random Forest

A machine learning technique called "boosted random forest" combines random forest and boosting to enhance model performance. For each data point, boosted random forests generate predictions using a single model, known as a weak learner. They then allocate higher weights to wrongly classified data points, construct a second model, and repeat the process.

3.4.5 Gaussian Naive Bayes

In order to accomplish classification, Naive Bayes classifiers estimate the likelihood of the input dataset. Each variable in the given data is assessed independent of the others. A strong possibility class is the output class of a mentioned instance.

4. CLASSIFICATION RESULT

All the dependent factors were utilised to predict CVD except Sex, FastingBS and RestingECG features. Many machine learning methods are used for disease classification.

Logistic Regression:

Figure 10. Performance of Logistic Regression

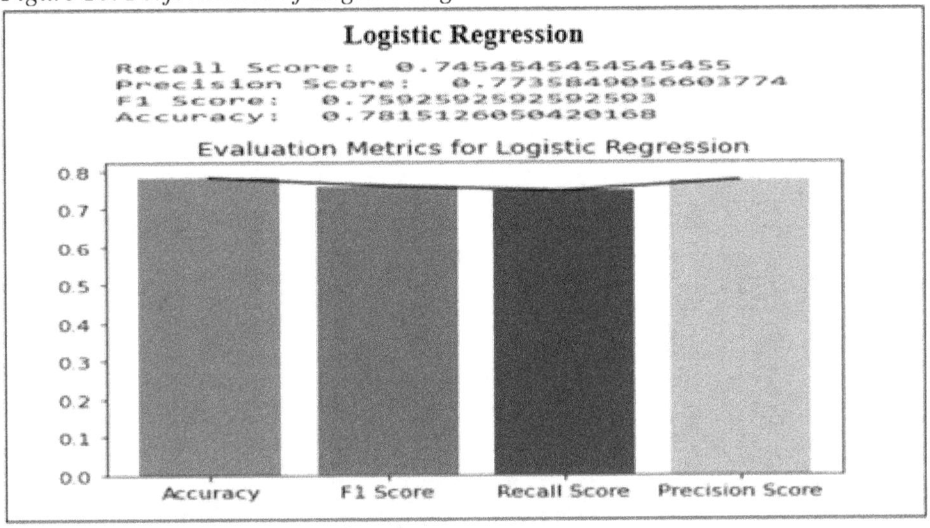

Figure 10 illustrate the accuracy, F1 score, recall score and precision score of logistic regression classification. The accuracy measure of logistic regression is 78.1%, the recall score is 74.5%, the precision value is 77.3%, and the F1 result is 75.9%. Tabel 1 shows the parameters, which are used in logistic regression.

Table 1. Parameters used in Logistic Regression

Parameters	Description
penalty: 'l2'	Regularization type
C: 1.0	Inverse of regularization strength
solver: 'lbfgs'	Optimization algorithm
max_iter: 100	Maximum number of iterations for the solver
tol: 1e-4	Tolerance for stopping criteria
fit_intercept: True	Whether to include an intercept
class_weight: 'balanced'	Handle class imbalance
random_state: None	No fixed seed for reproducibility

Decision Tree:

Figure 11 shows the accuracy, F1 rate, recall score and precision value of decision tree classification. The accuracy rate of decision tree is 84.0%, the recall score is 87.2%, the precision value is 80%, and the F1 result is 83.4%. Table 2 presents the parameters utilized in the Decision Tree algorithm.

Figure 11. Performance of Decision Tree

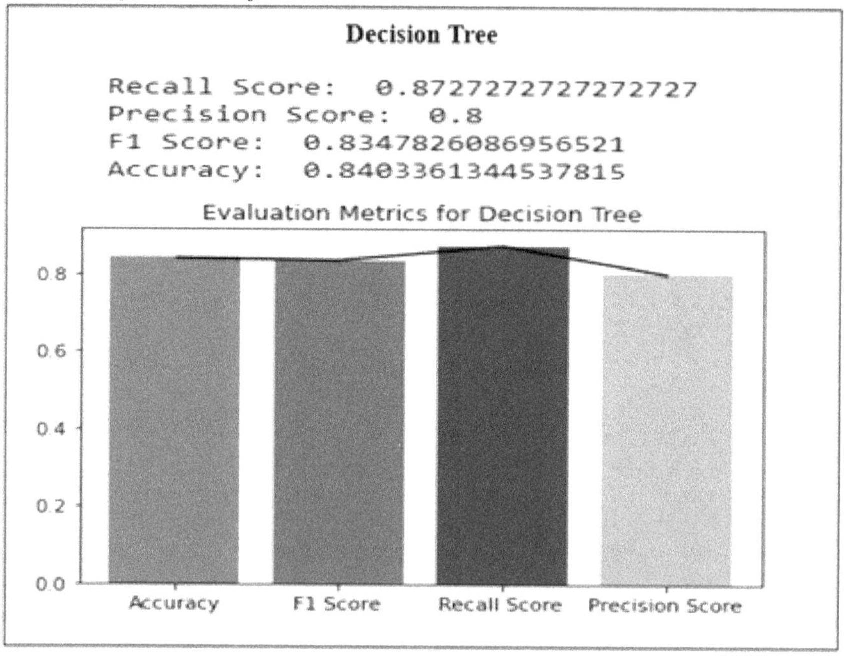

Table 2. Parameters used in Decision Tree

Parameters	Description
criterion='gini'	Quality of a split
max_depth=5	Set maximum depth
min_samples_split=2	Minimum samples to split
min_samples_leaf=1	Minimum samples at leaf
max_features='sqrt'	Features to consider
class_weight='balanced'	Handle class imbalance
random_state=42	For reproducibility

Support Vector Machine:

The accuracy value, F1 score, recall value and precision score of the SVM classification are shown in figure 12. The accuracy score of SVM is 75.6%, the recall score is 72.7%, the precision rate is 74%, and the F1 value is 73.3%. Table 3 displays the main parameters employed in the SVM algorithm.

Figure 12. Performance of SVM

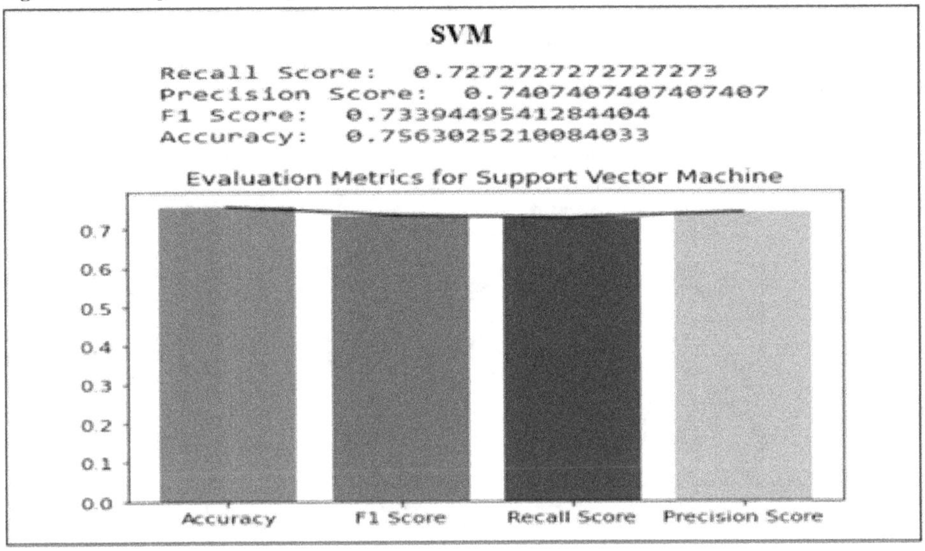

Table 3. Parameters used in SVM

Parameters	Description
C=1.0	Regularization parameter
kernel='rbf'	Kernel type
degree=3	Degree of the polynomial kernel function
gamma='scale'	Kernel coefficient
class_weight='balanced'	Handle class imbalance
random_state=42	Controls the randomness of the estimator for reproducibility
max_iter= -1	Maximum number of iterations

Boosted Random Forest:

Figure 13 illustrate the accuracy value, F1 score, recall value and precision rate of boosted random forest classification. The accuracy rate of boosted random forest is 87.3%, recall score is 89.3%, the precision value is 87.9%, and the F1 rate is 88.6%. Table 4 outlines the parameters utilized in the boosted random forest algorithm.

Figure 13. Performance of Boosted Random Forest

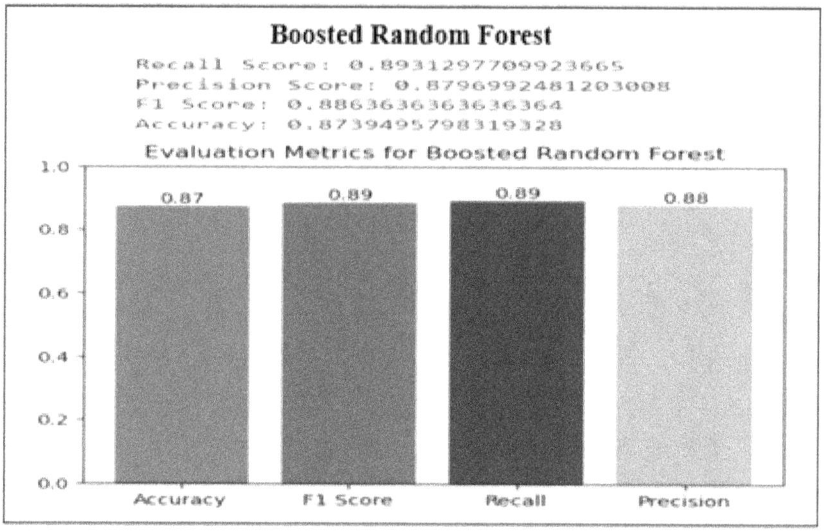

Table 4 Parameters used in boosted random forest

Parameters	Description
n_estimators = 100	Number of boosting rounds
max_depth =3 to 10	Maximum depth of a tree
min_samples_split =2	Minimum number of samples required to split an internal node
bootstrap = True	Whether bootstrap samples are used
learning_rate =0.1	Step size shrinkage

Gaussian Naive Bayes:

Figure 14. Performance of Gaussian Naive Bayes

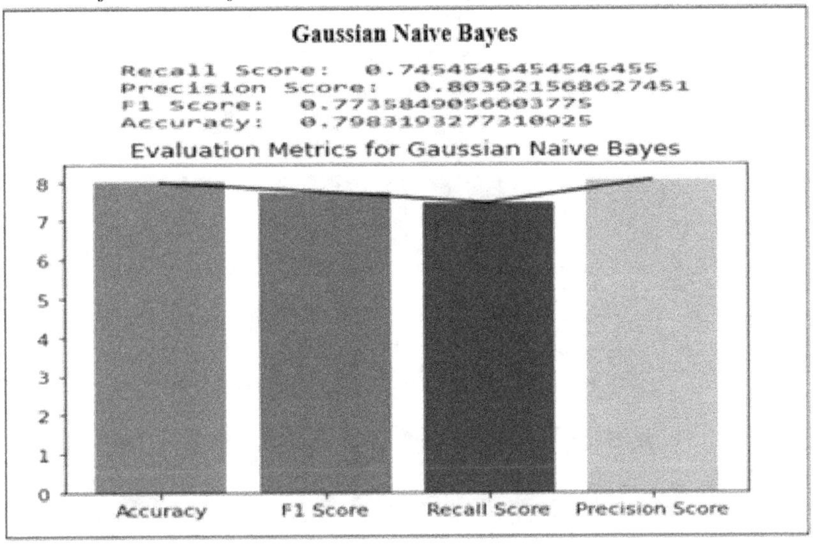

Figure 14 shows the accuracy rate, F1 rate, recall score and precision score of gaussian naive bayes classification. The accuracy of naive bayes is 79.8%, the recall score is 74.5%, the precision result is 80%, and the F1 value is 77.3%. Table 5 highlights the parameters applied in the gaussian naïve bayes.

Table 5. Parameters used in Gaussian Naive Bayes

Parameters	Description
Priors = None	Prior probabilities of the classes
var_smoothing =1e-9	Portion of the largest variance of all features added to variances for stability

Figure 15. Comparison classification algorithms

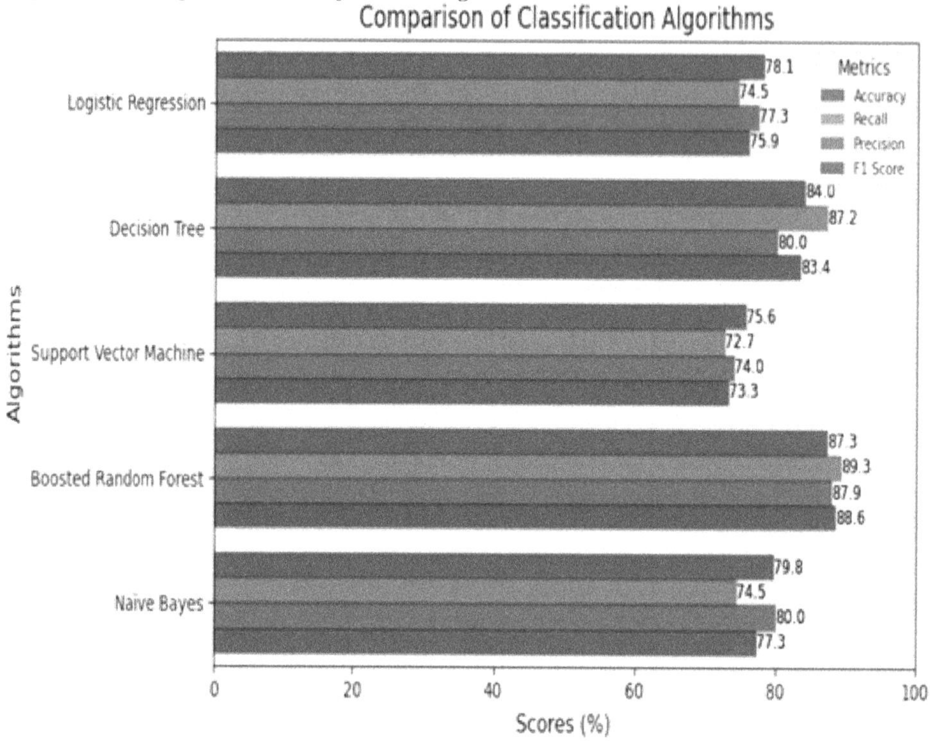

The figure 15 compares the performance of all the classifiers. The accuracy of logistic regression is 78.1%, decision tree is 84.0%, SVM is 75.6%, gaussian naïve bayes is 79.8%, and boosted random forest is 87.3%. Among all the classifiers, boosted random forest achieved the best accuracy of 87.3%.

The confusion analysis table for the best performance is shown in figure 16. The amount of true positive cases is 117, true negative cases are 91, false negative case are 14, and false positive cases are 16.

Figure 16. Confusion Matrix of BRF

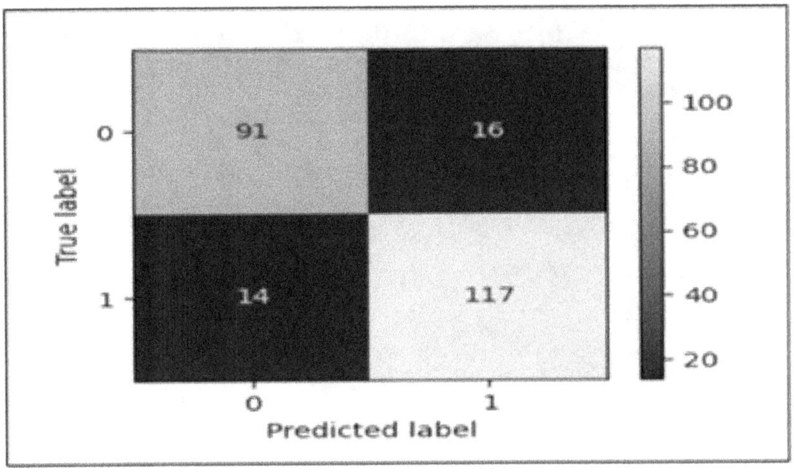

The area under the curve value is shown in figure 17.

Figure 17. ROC of BRF

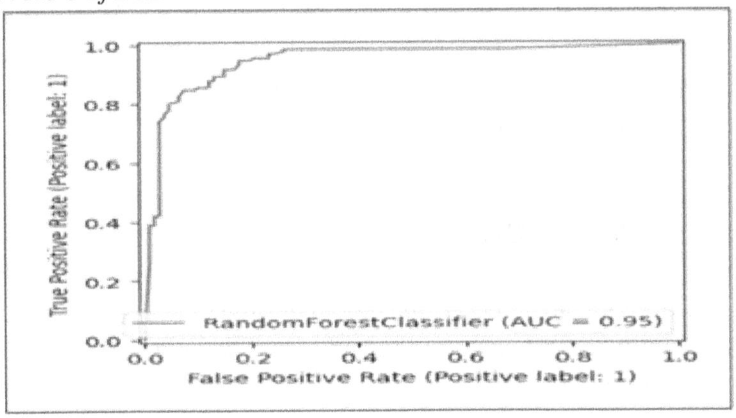

Figure 18. CVD prediction system

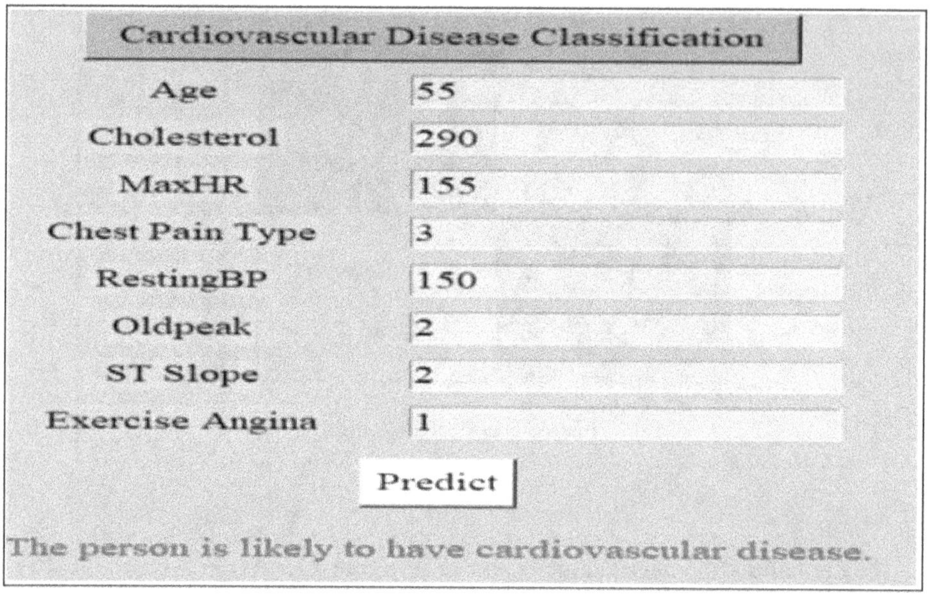

Figure 18 shows that the patient with Age, Cholesterol, MaxHR, Chest Pain Type, RestingBP, Oldpeak, ST Slope, and Exercise Angina values of 55, 290, 155, 3, 150, 2, 2, and 1respectively has cardiovascular disease. This predictive system used boosted random forest classifier for prediction.

5. RESULTS AND DISCUSSION

Cardiovascular sickness is becoming one among the main reason of death, hence the forecasting of this condition must be considered while analysing clinical data. In terms of gender distribution, men made up larger percentages (90.2%) of those with CVD. ASY-type chest pain suggests a substantial chance of cardiovascular illness (392); 170 out of 508 patients with cardiovascular disease had fasting blood sugar. According to the ST Slope data, 381 patients had cardiovascular disease. The majority of individuals (285 out of 256) with a normal resting ECG reading had cardiovascular disease. Ages 40–70 make up the majority of cardiovascular patients. Resting blood pressure values between 100 and 170, old peak values of 0–4, max HR readings of 100–180, and cholesterol levels between 160 and 340 are the most likely to indicate heart disease. The best eight features were selected for CVD classification using chi-square method. This study used five machine learning techniques for CVD classification. The boosted random forest model with the chi-square feature selection technique scored the highest accuracy..

6. COMPARATIVE ANALYSIS

Table 6 shows the comparative performance of proposed work with the other studies.

Table 6. Accuracy comparison with other studies

Reference	Feature selection	Approach	Accuracy %
Spencer et al. (2020)	Chi-squared	Bayes Net Classifier	85.0
R. Aggrawal & Pal (2020)	Sequential Feature Selection	Random Forest	86.67
Takci (2018)	Relief Method	SVM (Linear kernel)	84.81
Kodati et al (2018)	-	Naive Bayes	83.70
Buscema et al. (2013)	-	TWIST Algorithm	84.14
Rubini et al. (2021)	-	Random Forest Linear Regression SVM (Using Linear Kernel Function) SVM (Using Radial Basis Kernel Function) Naïve Bayes	84.81 83.82 74.05 58.57 54.08
Tomar and Agarwal (2014)	F-Score Feature Selection	LSTSVM	85.90
Proposed work	**Chi-squared**	**Boosted Random Forest**	**87.3**

Spencer et al. (2020) predict heart disease using the chi-squared feature selection method and Bayes net classifier with 85.0% accuracy. R. Aggrawal et al. (2020) classified the data using sequential feature selection and random forest with 86.67% accuracy. Using the reliefF method and SVM (linear kernel) Takci (2018), showed 84.81% accuracy. Kodati et al (2018) used a Naive Bayes algorithm with an accuracy of 83.7% on CVD dataset. Buscema et al. (2013) classified the data using TWIST Algorithm with an accuracy of 84.14%. Rubini (2021) classified the data using random forest, linear regression, SVM (Using Linear Kernel Function), SVM (Using Radial Basis Kernel Function), Naïve Bayes. The best result was obtaining using random forest with 84.81% accuracy. Tomar and Agarwal (2014) used LSTSVM with an accuracy of 85.9%. While Comparing with our result, the boosted random forest accuracy is better than other works.

7. CONCLUSION AND FUTURE STUDY

Cardiovascular illness is a foremost issue in medical data assessment since it has become one of the main roots of death. The data scaling and transformation processes were carried out using Min-Max scaler and label encoding, respectively. This paper's major goal is to use feature selection approach to increase the accuracy of cardiovascular disease prediction, for that the chi-square test technique is used to find the most significant features. For classification, five supervised classification strategies were applied. The boosted random forest obtained the highest accuracy (87.3%) out of all of them. Our work suggests combining the chi-square test feature selection technique with the boosted random forest model to anticipate cardiac illness with the highest level of accuracy. In the coming years, machine learning and deep learning approaches will be able to anticipate more diseases.

REFERENCES

Aggrawal, R., & Pal, S. (2020). Sequential feature selection and machine learning algorithm-based patient's death events prediction and diagnosis in heart disease. *SN Computer Science*, 1(6), 1–8. DOI: 10.1007/s42979-020-00370-1

Aryal, S., Alimadadi, A., Manandhar, I., Joe, B., & Cheng, X. (2020). Machine learning strategy for gut microbiome-based diagnostic screening of cardiovascular disease. *Hypertension*, 76(5), 1555–1562. DOI: 10.1161/HYPERTENSIONAHA.120.15885 PMID: 32909848

Buscema, M., Breda, M., & Lodwick, W. (2013). Training with Input Selection and Testing (TWIST) Algorithm: A significant advance in pattern recognition performance of machine learning. *Journal of Intelligent Learning Systems and Applications*, 5(1), 29–38. DOI: 10.4236/jilsa.2013.51004

Cheng, C., & Chiu, H. (2017). An artificial neural network model for the evaluation of carotid artery stenting prognosis using a National-Wide Database. *Proceedings of the 39th Annual International Conference of the IEEE Engineering in Medicine and Biology Society (EMBC),* 2566–2569. DOI: 10.1109/EMBC.2017.8037381

Kodati, S. (2018). Analysis of heart disease using data mining tools Orange and Weka. *Global Journal of Computer Science and Technology*, 18(1), 1–9. DOI: 10.17487/GJCSCT/18.1.1

Latha, C. B. C., & Jeeva, S. C. (2019). Improving the accuracy of prediction of heart disease risk based on ensemble classification techniques. *Informatics in Medicine Unlocked*, 16, 100203. Advance online publication. DOI: 10.1016/j.imu.2019.100203

Magesh, G., & Swarnalatha, P. (2021). Optimal feature selection through a cluster-based DT learning (CDTL) in heart disease prediction. *Evolutionary Intelligence*, 14(2), 583–593. DOI: 10.1007/s12065-019-00336-0

Mohan, S., Irumalai, C., & Srivastava, G. (2019). Effective heart disease prediction using hybrid machine learning techniques. *IEEE Access : Practical Innovations, Open Solutions*, 7, 81542–81554. DOI: 10.1109/ACCESS.2019.2923707

Nasarian, E., Abdar, M., Fahami, M. A., Alizadehsani, R., Hussain, S., Basiri, M. E., Zomorodi-Moghadam, M., Zhou, X., Pławiak, P., Acharya, U. R., Tan, R. S., & Sarrafzadegan, N. (2020). Association between work-related features and coronary artery disease: A heterogeneous hybrid feature selection integrated with balancing approach. *Pattern Recognition Letters*, 133, 33–40. DOI: 10.1016/j.patrec.2020.02.010

Ntiloudi, D., Giannakoulas, G., Parcharidou, D., Panagiotidis, T., Gatzoulis, M. A., & Karvounis, H. (2016). Adult congenital heart disease: A paradigm of epidemiological change. *International Journal of Cardiology*, 218, 269–274. DOI: 10.1016/j.ijcard.2016.05.046 PMID: 27240150

Pathak, A. K., & Valan, J. A. (2020). A predictive model for heart disease diagnosis using fuzzy logic and decision tree. In *Smart Computing Paradigms: New Progresses and Challenges* (pp. 131–140). Springer. DOI: 10.1007/978-981-13-9680-9_10

Rubini, P. E., & Subasini, C. A. (2021). A cardiovascular disease prediction using machine learning algorithms. *Annals of R.S.C.B.*, 25(2), 904–912. https://www.researchgate.net/publication/350312435

Shah, D., Patel, S., & Bharti, S. K. (2020). Heart disease prediction using machine learning techniques. *SN Computer Science*, 1(6), 1–6. DOI: 10.1007/s42979-020-00365-y

Spencer, R., Abtah, F., & Abdelhamid, N. (2020). Exploring feature selection and classification methods for predicting heart disease. *Digital Health*, 6, 1–10. DOI: 10.1177/2055207620914777 PMID: 32284873

Takci, H. (2018). Improvement of heart attack prediction by the feature selection methods. *Turkish Journal of Electrical Engineering and Computer Sciences*, 26, 1–10. DOI: 10.3906/elk-1611-235

Tomar, D., & Agarwal, S. (2014). Feature selection based Least Square Twin Support Vector Machine for diagnosis of heart disease. *International Journal of Bio-Science and Bio-Technology*, 6(2), 69–82. DOI: 10.14257/ijbsbt.2014.6.2.07

Chapter 8
Survey on Data Science Application on Healthcare Analysis

S. Hemalatha
https://orcid.org/0009-0005-0397-8738
Panimalar Engineering College, India

Krithick Ajay S.
Panimalar Engineering College, India

ABSTRACT

The application of data science is revolutionizing healthcare, spurring advances in tailored care, diagnosis, and treatment. This survey offers a thorough review of data science's role in healthcare, with a particular emphasis on its applications in drug development, genomics, predictive analytics, medical imaging, and patient care management. The ability of key data science approaches, such as big data analytics, machine learning, deep learning, and natural language processing, to handle large amounts of complicated healthcare data is examined. In addition to highlighting new developments like precision medicine and AI-driven health monitoring, the study also addresses difficulties, such as data privacy, model interpretability, and integration of disparate data sources. In the end, this research highlights how data science has the capacity to revolutionize patient outcomes, streamline healthcare processes, and promote innovation in the medical industry.

DOI: 10.4018/979-8-3693-7868-7.ch008

1. INTRODUCTION

The introduction of data science technology has resulted in a rapid transformation of the healthcare sector in recent years. This change is enabling major advancements in disease prediction, diagnosis, and treatment in addition to empowering healthcare providers to handle and analyze enormous volumes of patient data. To understand data from a variety of sources, including wearable technology, medical imaging, and electronic health records (EHRs), data science blends a range of cutting-edge approaches, including machine learning (ML), deep learning (DL), and natural language processing (NLP). These developments are a part of a broader trend toward data-driven healthcare, which could advance precision medicine, better patient outcomes, and streamline the delivery of healthcare. The processing, analysis, and application of medical data to patient care are being revolutionized by the introduction of data science into the healthcare industry. Healthcare systems create huge amounts of data from different sources, including electronic health records (EHRs), medical imaging, laboratory tests, and genomics. There is great potential for improving the accuracy and effectiveness of medical judgments with the help of these varied data streams. Personalized healthcare is being transformed by the application of data science approaches, including machine learning (ML) and deep learning (DL), which is enabling the construction of predictive models for disease diagnosis, treatment planning, and outcome prediction.

The computer vision techniques, one of the main fields benefiting from data science, medical imaging has made great progress. Medical practitioners can now analyze complicated pictures, such CT scans, MRIs, and X-rays, more accurately thanks to deep learning-based techniques, which help with early disease identification and lowers human error. In addition to imaging, data science is advancing genomics and drug discovery by using algorithms to sort through enormous databases in search of biomarkers and possible treatment targets.Similar to this, deep learning algorithms—more specifically, Convolutional neural networks (CNNs)—have transformed medical imaging. CNNs are capable of identifying minute patterns in imaging modalities including CT, MRI, and X-rays. When it comes to tasks like tumor detection, disease classification, and anatomical structure segmentation, these models frequently perform better than conventional diagnostic methods. In addition, sophisticated methods such as GAN-DRR (Generative Adversarial Networks with Digitally Reconstructed Radiographs) are enhancing the quality of reconstructed pictures, helping radiologists to more accurately visualize intricate structures. These AI-driven imaging techniques have the potential to decrease diagnostic delays and improve treatment outcomes by improving early diagnosis and decreasing human error.

Data science is progressing not only in imaging but also in drug development and genomics. Large-scale genomic databases can now be analyzed by researchers to find possible biomarkers for diseases or therapeutic targets thanks to big data analytics and machine learning. These methods are accelerating the process of developing new pharmaceuticals, cutting down on the time required to test them, and customizing medications to fit certain genetic profiles—a crucial component of precision medicine.

Predictive analytics is another use of data science in healthcare; it forecasts patient outcomes using both historical and current data. Predictive models, for example, can identify those who are at risk for chronic diseases like diabetes, cancer, and cardiovascular disorders. This allows for early interventions and more individualized treatment approaches. In this situation, trends can be analyzed and predictions of therapy response, illness progression, or even hospital readmissions can be made using machine learning algorithms trained on huge datasets. By enabling doctors to provide proactive treatment instead of reactive, they can increase patient satisfaction and efficiency. But even with its enormous promise, there are a number of obstacles to overcome before data science can be fully integrated into healthcare. Data security and privacy are important concerns since health information is sensitive. Maintaining adherence to laws like GDPR and HIPAA is essential for safeguarding patient data. The interpretability of machine learning models, sometimes known as the "black box" problem, presents another difficulty. Clinical trust and acceptance may be hampered by the fact that many sophisticated models—particularly deep learning networks—provide remarkably accurate predictions but are opaque about their decision-making process. It is also common for healthcare data to be heterogeneous, coming from several sources such as labs, hospitals, and wearable technology. Harmonizing these disparate datasets to produce a single platform for analysis is still a technical challenge.

As the field of healthcare continues to expand, the current advancements in data science will undoubtedly pave the way for more tailored and efficient patient care. This survey intends to investigate the numerous uses of data science in the medical field, talk about the difficulties encountered, and point out new developments that will influence the field's future. The sector is changing as a result of data science's incorporation into healthcare since it promotes personalized medicine, predictive analytics, and improved diagnostic accuracy. Healthcare practitioners can now process and extract insights from large and complicated datasets thanks to cutting-edge methods like machine learning, deep learning, and big data analytics.

These advancements are contributing to more proactive patient care, breakthroughs in medical imaging, and quicker drug discovery and genomics research. To fully realize the promise of data science, however, obstacles including data privacy, model interpretability, and the difficulty of connecting disparate healthcare data sources must to be resolved. It is anticipated that as AI-driven technologies and data-driven methodology advance, patient outcomes will be enhanced and that the effectiveness and reach of healthcare delivery systems will be completely transformed on a global scale. Although there is a lot of room for innovation, prudent and efficient use of these game-changing technologies will require constant cooperation between data scientists, healthcare practitioners, and policymakers.

This chapter discuss the fundamentals of statistics are covered, and important machine learning approaches are examined, ranging from simple supervised and unsupervised learning to sophisticated strategies like deep learning and ensemble approaches. The importance of data visualization in sharing insights, the difficulties associated with big data technologies, and real-world applications in a range of industries are also covered in this chapter. The last half of the article discusses the ethical ramifications and new developments that may influence data science in the future, highlighting the necessity of ethical and progressive methods in the industry.

2. LITERATURE SURVEY ON CORE CONCEPTS AND TECHNIQUES IN DATA SCIENCE

In this section concentrates on, the integration of statistics, domain specific knowledge and computer science techniques used for the extracting the information in data. Core concepts and knowledge are essential for extracting the data from the large volume and even from the complex data information. This survey part outlines the elements of data science techniques used so far for the purpose of data collection, preparing the data, exploring the data, modelling the information, visualization of data and theirs applications usages etc.

Data collection is the initial stage of any data science process, (Mayer-Schönberger & Cukier, 2013) initiated the survey for collecting the data with the support of various methods like web scraping, sensors and APIs etc. Later the availability of big data supports for transformation of data collection from the different data sets was suggested by the (Chaudhuri et al., 2011), (Kotsiantis et al., 2006) has done the work of data cleaning or wrangling after the handling of missing values. Batini et al. (2009) stated the effective cleaning processes which enhance the readability of data.

Exploratory of Data Analysis (EDA) is coming under the Data Exploration for classifying the structure and pattern on the data. (Tukey, 1977) employed in data characteristics of EDA and statically analysis. (Behrens, 1997) discussed the visualization of data in EDA with relationships on data by adding the hypothesis generation. Cheng et al. (2019) given the roles of visualization tools for making the complex datasets are essential for the data driven decision making process.

Modern techniques like machine learning supports for the data science to more development with the classification of data using the supervised learning and unsupervised learning. (Jordan & Mitchell, 2015) discussed the Machine learning supports for the data science development with several algorithms. (Hastie et al., 2009) was discussed how the algorithms such as regression, neural network and decision trees are using in supervised learning also discussed the classification of data using the unsupervised learning . (LeCun et al., 2015) deep learning with enhanced model accuracy and complexity supports for processing the unstructured data even if it is images as well as in text . (Few, 2009) has given the data visualization from the data science, which help to communicate on the data effectively with the support of modern tools and techniques like bar chart, plots, dash boards etc, this information supports for the stakeholders to get clear understanding on complex data relationships . Cairo (2013) has done the review about the effective visualization for the strategic decision and influence the data interpretation.

Later the applications of the data science were used in many industries like healthcare, retail, finance and marketing for classifying the data in their filed. In the health care (Davenport & Prusak, 1998) used the predictive analysis for disease forecasting and medicine classification. (Kumar & Ravi, 2016) has elaborated the financial sector usage of the data science for fraude detection and risk assessments. (Chong et al., 2017) was discussed about the data science usage for the retailers for the inventory management and segmentation for operational efficiency. (Sankaran et al., 2020) has proposed the data science with the Integration of latest technologies like Internet of Things for collect the real time data across the domains. Ahmed et al. (2021) has made the data science applied in to APIs for cloud based services, data aggregate data. Enhanced machine learning techniques for web scraping has suggested by the (Wang et al., 2023).

Next stage of data science is data preparation, Khalaf et al., has made the literature survey on automated data cleaning techniques for handle the missing data and outliers. Data normalization and data transformation techniques for ensuring the data compatibility and analysis purpose was proved by the Meyer et al., 2020. The authors Bertels et al. enhanced the reliability of data set by integration of data quality frameworks. Later Interactive visualization, such as visual analytics tools are enriched the EDA to allow the data scientist to uncover the pattern effectively was discussed by the Kirk 2019 .The recent studies done by the Almalki et al., 2022, to explore the analysis to derive the meaningful data from the large data sets. Raffel et al., 2020 discussed the supervised and unsupervised learning techniques of machine learning for the domains of natural language processing and computer vision. In advanced the automated machine learning platforms has model the building process for making the non experts.

Effective communication among the data is needed for the data visualization, for interactive visualization in the deeper was suggested by the Elmqvist et al., 2018. **Storytelling** with data for the impact of visualization of decision making process was discussed by Few, **2020.** Finally the applications of data science have expanded across the various industries. In the health care domain, the data science is employed the predictive analysis, treatment plans, patient outcomes are discussed by the (Sharma et al., 2023). Jain et al., 2021 was discussed the machine learning techniques for fraud detection and risk management for making the critical role in financial sector. Data science techniques was used in the retail section for inventory optimization and customer behaviour analysis for making the shopping experiences was proposed by the Choudhury et al., 2022. Even in the Transportations application Khan et al., 2023 was proposed the route optimization, predictive maintenance across the sectors.

In the year 2021, World Health organization has made the research on health care systems for better understanding of COVID -19 and efficiency of the vaccines. For that the rapid development of the data science techniques were supported for the data classification of the heath care domain. With the adoption of telemedicine explore the heath care delivery, disease management and mental health was proposed by the by Monaghesh, E., & Hajizadeh, A. (2020).Troiano, G., & Nardi, A. (2021).

The health care research finds out the list about the vaccine hesitancy, misinformation, improve the public health. Esteva, A., et al. (2021) has discussed the health care incorporates with the AI and machine learning for diagnostic of medicine and image analysis. Even the Data science technology was added in to the health care field of radiology, pathology and cardiology for detecting the cancer, heart diseases. Health care research has put more effort on anxiety, depression and other mental health issues during the pandemic period. Pfefferbaum, B., & North, C.S. (2020). Nalbandian, A., et al. (2021) has done work on the remote mental health interventions and therapy for health tools. Millett, G.A., et al. (2020), has pointed out, during the COVID -19 the health care disparities al issues. Mishra, T., et al. (2020) proposed the support of wearable devices for continuous health monitoring has grown significantly. This research enhanced to focus on chronic conditions disease like diabetes, heart disease remotely. This literature survey outlines the foundational elements of data science, focusing on data collection, preparation, exploration, modeling, visualization, and applications in health care domain as summaries in the table 1.

Table 1. Survey of data analysis in healthcare

S. No	Authors	Techniques	Advantages	Disadvantages
1	Mayer-Schönberger & Cukier (2013)	Data Collection (Surveys, Web Scraping, APIs, Sensor Data)	Diverse data collection from multiple sources	Requires efficient strategies for large data volumes
2	Chaudhuri et al. (2011)	Big Data Collection	Allows for extensive data collection from various sources	Data privacy and storage concerns
3	Kotsiantis et al. (2006)	Data Preparation (Data Cleaning, Wrangling)	Enhances data quality, leading to more reliable analysis	Time-consuming and resource-intensive
4	Batini et al. (2009)	Data Quality Framework	Improves reliability of datasets and subsequent analysis	Difficult to implement in large, heterogeneous datasets
5	Tukey (1977)	Exploratory Data Analysis (EDA), Descriptive Statistics	Helps identify patterns and relationships in data	Limited in providing insights beyond basic trends
6	Behrens (1997)	Data Visualization for EDA	Simplifies complex data for better understanding	Visualization may oversimplify or miss key details
7	Cheng et al. (2019)	Advanced Data Visualization Tools	Enhances comprehension of large, complex datasets	Requires specialized tools and expertise
8	Jordan & Mitchell (2015)	Machine Learning (Supervised, Unsupervised, Reinforcement)	Enables predictive models and decision-making capabilities	Can be computationally expensive and requires large training datasets
9	Hastie et al. (2009)	Regression, Decision Trees, Neural Networks, Clustering	Versatile algorithms for various prediction and classification tasks	Requires expertise in selecting appropriate algorithms
10	LeCun et al. (2015)	Deep Learning for Unstructured Data	High accuracy in complex tasks like image and text analysis	Requires extensive computational power and large datasets
11	Few (2009)	Data Visualization Techniques (Bar Charts, Scatter Plots)	Clear communication of data-driven insights	Static visualizations may not be interactive
12	Cairo (2013)	Storytelling with Data	Influences decision-making effectively through visual narratives	Can be biased if not representing the full dataset
13	Davenport & Prusak (1998)	Predictive Analytics in Healthcare	Enhances personalized treatment and disease forecasting	Potential for data bias, affecting outcomes
14	Kumar & Ravi (2016)	Machine Learning for Fraud Detection and Risk Assessment	Improves accuracy in identifying fraudulent activities	Difficult to maintain models as fraud tactics evolve

continued on following page

Table 1. Continued

S. No	Authors	Techniques	Advantages	Disadvantages
15	Chong et al. (2017)	Customer Segmentation, Inventory Management in Retail	Optimizes operational efficiency	Requires continuous data updates for accurate segmentation
16	Sankaran et al. (2020)	IoT for Real-Time Data Collection	Real-time monitoring across domains	Raises concerns about data security and device interoperability
17	Ahmed et al. (2021)	APIs for Cloud-Based Data Access	Seamless data aggregation from multiple sources	Can create dependency on third-party services
18	Wang et al. (2023)	Web Scraping Enhanced by Machine Learning	Efficient and accurate data extraction	Legal and ethical concerns regarding data usage
19	Khalaf et al. (2019)	Automated Data Cleaning Techniques	Reduces manual efforts in cleaning large datasets	May not handle complex data inconsistencies
20	Meyer et al. (2020)	Data Normalization and Transformation	Ensures compatibility for further analytical processing	Potential loss of data variance or key patterns during normalization
21	Bertels et al. (2021)	Data Quality Frameworks	Increases the reliability and usability of datasets	Complex to implement across multi-source data
22	Kirk (2019)	Interactive Visualizations in EDA	Enables dynamic exploration of complex datasets	Requires sophisticated tools and technical expertise
23	Almalki et al. (2022)	Statistical Techniques for Exploratory Data Analysis	Provides deeper insights into large datasets	May be complex for non-statisticians
24	Raffel et al. (2020)	Transfer Learning in Machine Learning	Allows use of pre-trained models, speeding up development	Transfer learning may not perform well on drastically different tasks
25	H2O.ai (2023)	Automated Machine Learning (AutoML)	Simplifies model-building for non-experts	Limited customization and optimization of models
26	Elmqvist et al. (2018)	Interactive and Sophisticated Visualizations	Enhances user engagement with data through interactivity	May require high computing power and software tools
27	Few (2020)	Storytelling with Data for Decision Making	Facilitates better understanding and engagement with data	Risk of narrative bias, oversimplifying the data
28	Sharma et al. (2023)	Predictive Analytics in Healthcare	Improves patient outcomes through data-driven decision-making	Requires high-quality data and specialized analytics tools
29	Jain et al. (2021)	Fraud Detection in Finance using Machine Learning	Enhances detection of fraudulent transactions	Models may become outdated as fraud tactics evolve

continued on following page

Table 1. Continued

S. No	Authors	Techniques	Advantages	Disadvantages
30	Choudhury et al. (2022)	Inventory Optimization and Customer Behaviour Analysis	Personalizes customer experiences and improves retail operations	Depends on accurate, real-time data feeds
31	Khan et al. (2023)	Route Optimization, Predictive Maintenance in Transportation	Improves operational efficiency and reduces downtime	Requires constant data collection and updates
32	Monaghesh, E., & Hajizadeh, A. (2020)	Telemedicine for Chronic Disease Management	Expands healthcare access, especially during the pandemic	Limited by technology access and infrastructure
33	Troiano, G., & Nardi, A. (2021)	Public Health Communication, Vaccine Hesitancy	Improves public trust and vaccination rates	Challenging to combat widespread misinformation
34	Esteva, A., et al. (2021)	AI and Machine Learning for Medical Diagnostics	Enhances diagnostic accuracy in radiology and pathology	High computational costs and dependence on large datasets
35	Pfefferbaum, B., & North, C.S. (2020)	Remote Mental Health Interventions (Online Therapy, Digital Tools)	Expands access to mental health support, especially post-pandemic	May lack personal touch and therapeutic efficacy compared to in-person care
36	Nalbandian, A., et al. (2021)	Long COVID Research (Symptoms, Treatment, Burden)	Addresses the long-term effects of COVID-19 on patient health	Ongoing research with evolving findings
37	Millett, G.A., et al. (2020)	Healthcare Disparities (Race, Socioeconomic Status, COVID-19)	Highlights healthcare inequities, improving targeted interventions	Difficult to resolve systemic healthcare issues
38	Mishra, T., et al. (2020)	Wearable Devices for Health Monitoring	Provides continuous health tracking and early detection of diseases	Privacy concerns, data security, and reliance on technology

3. PRACTICAL APPLICATIONS OF HEALTH CARE CASE STUDIES

Data science applications are spread across all the domains like finance, marketing, various industries automation etc. This filed has enhanced in to human health care for enhance the patient care with predictive analysis and hospital readmission etc. Even in the health care the feature dimensions are planned how to treat the patient with the genetic and life style data by using the deep learning techniques. Health care data science support for decision making about the patient health care by monitoring the medical care, operational efficiency and extract the information from the large data set. One of the applications of the health care using data science is predictive analysis where the models are analysis with the machine learning model using patient data .Predictive model creates the electronic health records and lifestyle factors to access the patient information like diseases. Another application of health care is personalized medicine which takes the treatment of individual patient, based on the lifestyle, genetic and environmental factors. By analysing the image analysis from the large data set, the predictive analysis could able to support for the cancer patient treatment in advance.

Health care operation supports for the patient to reduce the waiting time by using the data science optimization, where the predictive analysis support for the doctor to give information about the patient from the history of data . Even the decision making supports for the health care to take the advance decision about the patient health treatment. The effective implementation of data science towards the health care should follow the predefined structure which make clear objective of the case study and done the predictive analysis of the diseases with the support of image analysis, later the Electronic health record, clinical notes and lab tested results are must be maintained in advance. Then the pre-processing is done with removal of redundant data, missing value and integrating of multiple sources.

Followed by the exploratory data analysis should be done with visualization of data and understanding the trends and previous patterns for which machine learning algorithm supported to make the best EDA. Once such a model is created, that is deployed in the health care system with the hospital and monitoring the decision making done by the professional are right which includes the data privacy, bias etc . Finally feedback system is collected from the professional to refine the system model.

Here's the algorithm for implementing healthcare data science, organized into distinct stages:

Stage 1: Define Objectives
Stage 2: Data Collection
Stage 3: Data Preparation
Stage 4: Exploratory Data Analysis (EDA)
Stage 5: Model Development
Stage 6: Implementation and Integration
Stage 7: Monitor and Optimize
Stage 8: Address Ethical Considerations
Stage 9: Reporting and Visualization

During the stage of data objective definition, for the health care systems, first need to identify the objective followed by outcomes of the goal, and operation cost, diagnosis accuracy need to indentify. This could be done with the support of predictive analysis about the individual patient hospital operations. The objective provides the clear idea about the system operation also help to organizing the product development stages. The next stage after objective is called organizations, which arrange the data set needed for the analysis. This uses the Electronic Health Records (ERH) with medical images. The next stage of organizing is data pre-processing, the collected data has used for pre-processing where the information are check and removed the duplicate records, redundant record, unwanted data, classification of data based on the category for analysis etc .The final outcome of this stage is clear data with all category of easies information available. Then it could be used for EDA. During the stage of model development, the system models were developed using the supervised and unsupervised algorithms in machine learning techniques. The collected data are trained based on the algorithm and purpose of the methods. Electronic health record allows the data to make use for decision making systems.

Last three stages are supported for checking the developed product test cases, ethical consideration, and final report generation. Monitoring stage continuously oversight the system effectiveness, tracking the system how it supported for real world applications usage. Ethical consideration follows the data privacy ethical concern; ensure compliance and HIPAA protection etc. Final stages of report are visualization which demonstrate the communication among the data set and create the dashboard to plot the representation. This healthcare algorithm is common to all the system development which supports for effective development of Heath care with data science.

4. ETHICS AND FUTURE TRENDS IN DATA SCIENCE

Since the data science were used in all decision making process at different sectors, the ethical consideration is also to be consider when decide the decision. Always the ethical consideration ensures the transparency, fairness and accountability without any algorithms bias even the data are leads to discriminatory outcomes. Predictive algorithms is plays a vital role on making the transparency among the justice. Even though the automated decision support system were implemented in the system model should insist the ethical consideration about the fairness in data science. Data privacy is also a part of the ethics in health care data science, as a volume of data increases which support the data privacy, not to reveal the data to other parties, securing sensitive data by using the data store on cloud access with latest security feature. Data security could be support by use of encryption and decryption data on the cloud services which thwart from the cyber threats. When the modern technologies used in the data science like AI, IoT and Edge computing, also need to follow the ethical consideration. Current AI follows the ethics in positive global aspects. Auto ML simplify the model for making the data science with ethics.

5. CONCLUSION

A thorough grasp of data science's fundamental ideas and methods is crucial for both practitioners and scholars as the field continues to transform industries and spur innovation. From data collection to sophisticated machine learning, this chapter has described the essential phases in the data science process in the healthcare industry and emphasized the tools and techniques that allow for the discovery of significant insights. Additionally, it has emphasized the significance of ethical issues and the continuous advancement of data science tools. This chapter gives readers the tools they need to traverse the intricacies of data science and contribute to its responsible and significant application in a variety of disciplines by fusing fundamental knowledge with real-world applications. In order to ensure that data-driven judgments are both creative and just, data science will need to strike a balance between ethical responsibilities and technical developments.

REFERENCES

Ahmed, M., Khan, M., & Anwar, A. (2021). Analyzing the Impact of API on Data Collection in Cloud-Based Applications. *Journal of Cloud Computing (Heidelberg, Germany)*, 10(1), 15–24.

Almalki, M. (2022). Statistical Techniques in Data Exploration: A Comprehensive Review. *International Journal of Data Science and Analytics*, 15(2), 102–118.

Bating, C., & Scannapieco, M. (2009). Data Quality. In Data Management and Data Quality.

Behrens, J. T. (1997). Principles and procedures of exploratory data analysis. *Psychological Methods*, 2(2), 141–149. DOI: 10.1037/1082-989X.2.2.131

Bertels, S. (2021). Data Quality Frameworks: A Review and Future Directions. *Journal of Database Management*, 13(3), 45–58.

Bollen, J., Mao, H., & Zeng, X. (2011). Twitter Mood Predicts the Stock Market. *Journal of Computational Science*, 2(1), 1–8. DOI: 10.1016/j.jocs.2010.12.007

Breiman, L. (1996). Bagging Predictors. *Machine Learning*, 24(2), 123–140. DOI: 10.1007/BF00058655

Cairo, A. (2013). *The Functional Art: An Introduction to Information Graphics and Visualization*. New Riders.

Chaudhuri, S., Dayal, U., & Narasayya, V. (2011). Data Warehousing and Business Intelligence: A Survey. *ACM Computing Surveys*, 45(4), 1–43.

Chong, A. Y. L. (2017). Predicting online shopping behaviour using data mining techniques. *International Journal of Retail & Distribution Management*, 45(4), 382–402.

Choudhury, A. (2022). Data Science Applications in Retail: A Systematic Review. *Journal of Retailing and Consumer Services*, 66, 102923.

Cram, D. (2021). *Data Communication: A Pragmatic Approach*. Routledge.

Davenport, T. H., & Prusak, L. (1998). *Working Knowledge: How Organizations Manage What They Know*. Harvard Business Press.

Dhar, V. (2013). Data Science and Prediction. *Communications of the ACM*, 56(12), 64–73. DOI: 10.1145/2500499

Elmqvist, N. (2018). The Role of Interactive Visualization in Data Science. *Information Visualization*, 17(3), 201–207.

Esteva, A. (2021). A guide to deep learning in healthcare. *Nature Medicine*, 27(1), 15–25. PMID: 30617335

Few, S. (2009). *Now You See It: Simple Visualization Techniques for Quantitative Analysis*. Analytics Press.

Few, S. (2012). *The Functional Art: An Introduction to Information Graphics and Visualization*. Analytics Press.

Few, S. (2020). *Storytelling with Data: A Data Visualization Guide for Business Professionals*. Wiley.

Friedman, J. H. (2001). Greedy Function Approximation: A Gradient Boosting Machine. *Annals of Statistics*, 29(5), 1189–1232. DOI: 10.1214/aos/1013203451

Gandomi, A., & Haider, M. (2015). Beyond the Hype: Big Data Concepts, Methods, and Analytics. *International Journal of Information Management*, 35(2), 137–144. DOI: 10.1016/j.ijinfomgt.2014.10.007

Goodfellow, I., Bengio, Y., & Courville, A. (2016). *Deep Learning*. MIT Press.

H2O.ai. (2023). Automated Machine Learning: Best Practices and Implementation. H2O.ai Whitepaper.

Han, J., Pei, J., & Kamber, M. (2011). Data Mining: Concepts and Techniques. Elsevier.

Hastie, T., Tibshirani, R., & Friedman, J. (2009). *The Elements of Statistical Learning: Data Mining, Inference, and Prediction*. Springer. DOI: 10.1007/978-0-387-84858-7

Hochreiter, S., & Schmidhuber, J. (1997). Long Short-Term Memory. *Neural Computation*, 9(8), 1735–1780. DOI: 10.1162/neco.1997.9.8.1735 PMID: 9377276

Hyndman, R. J., & Athanasopoulos, G. (2018). *Forecasting: Principles and Practice*. OTexts.

Igarashi, A., & O'Connell, A. (2020). *Data Visualization: A Practical Introduction*. Princeton University Press.

Jain, A. (2021). Machine Learning in Finance: Applications and Challenges. *Journal of Financial Services Research*, 59(2), 245–262.

Jordan, M. I., & Mitchell, T. M. (2015). Machine learning: Trends, perspectives, and prospects. *Science*, 349(6245), 255–260. DOI: 10.1126/science.aaa8415 PMID: 26185243

Jurafsky, D., & Martin, J. H. (2021). *Speech and Language Processing: An Introduction to Natural Language Processing, Computational Linguistics, and Speech Recognition* (3rd ed.). Pearson.

Khalaf, O. A. (2019). Automating Data Cleaning: An Overview of Methods and Challenges. *Data Science and Engineering*, 4(4), 295–307.

Khan, A. (2023). Data Science in Transportation: Opportunities and Applications. *Transportation Research Part C, Emerging Technologies*, 138, 103584.

Kirk, A. (2019). *Data Visualisation: A Handbook for Data Driven Design*. SAGE Publications.

Knaflic, C. N. (2015). *Storytelling with Data: A Data Visualization Guide for Business Professionals*. Wiley. DOI: 10.1002/9781119055259

Kotsiantis, S. B. (2006). Data Preprocessing for Supervised Learning. *International Journal of Computational Science*, 1(2), 111–117.

Kreps, J., Narkhede, N., & Rao, J. (2011). Kafka: A Distributed Messaging System for Log Processing. *Proceedings of the NetDB*.

Kumar, A., & Ravi, V. (2016). A survey of data mining techniques for fraud detection. *Journal of Network and Computer Applications*, 75, 120–134.

LeCun, Y., Bengio, Y., & Haffner, P. (2015). Gradient-based learning applied to document recognition. *Proceedings of the IEEE*, 86(11), 2278–2324. DOI: 10.1109/5.726791

Lee, J., Kao, H. A., & Yang, S. (2014). Service Innovation and Smart Analytics for Industry 4.0 and Big Data Environment. *Procedia CIRP*, 16, 3–8. DOI: 10.1016/j.procir.2014.02.001

Mayer-Schönberger, V., & Cukier, K. (2013). *Big Data: A Revolution That Will Transform How We Live, Work, and Think*. Houghton Mifflin Harcourt.

Meyer, P. J. (2020). Data Normalization Techniques for Improved Model Performance. *Data Science Journal*, 19(1), 10.

Millett, G. A., Jones, A. T., Benkeser, D., Baral, S., Mercer, L., Beyrer, C., Honermann, B., Lankiewicz, E., Mena, L., Crowley, J. S., Sherwood, J., & Sullivan, P. S. (2020). Assessing differential impacts of COVID-19 on black communities. *Annals of Epidemiology*, 47, 37–44. DOI: 10.1016/j.annepidem.2020.05.003 PMID: 32419766

Mishra, T., Wang, M., Metwally, A. A., Bogu, G. K., Brooks, A. W., Bahmani, A., Alavi, A., Celli, A., Higgs, E., Dagan-Rosenfeld, O., Fay, B., Kirkpatrick, S., Kellogg, R., Gibson, M., Wang, T., Hunting, E. M., Mamic, P., Ganz, A. B., Rolnik, B., & Snyder, M. P. (2020). Pre-symptomatic detection of COVID-19 from smartwatch data. *Nature Biomedical Engineering*, 4(12), 1208–1220. DOI: 10.1038/s41551-020-00640-6 PMID: 33208926

Monaghesh, E., & Hajizadeh, A. (2020). The role of telehealth during COVID-19 outbreak: A systematic review based on current evidence. *BMC Public Health*, 20(1), 1193. DOI: 10.1186/s12889-020-09301-4 PMID: 32738884

Nalbandian, A., Sehgal, K., Gupta, A., Madhavan, M. V., McGroder, C., Stevens, J. S., Cook, J. R., Nordvig, A. S., Shalev, D., Sehrawat, T. S., Ahluwalia, N., Bikdeli, B., Dietz, D., Der-Nigoghossian, C., Liyanage-Don, N., Rosner, G. F., Bernstein, E. J., Mohan, S., Beckley, A. A., & Wan, E. Y. (2021). Post-acute COVID-19 syndrome. *Nature Medicine*, 27(4), 601–615. DOI: 10.1038/s41591-021-01283-z PMID: 33753937

Ngai, E. W., Hu, Y., Wong, Y. H., Chen, Y., & Sun, X. (2011). The Application of Data Mining Techniques in Financial Fraud Detection: A Classification Framework and an Academic Review of Literature. *Decision Support Systems*, 50(3), 559–569. DOI: 10.1016/j.dss.2010.08.006

O'Neil, C. (2016). *Weapons of Math Destruction: How Big Data Increases Inequality and Threatens Democracy*. Crown Publishing Group.

Pfefferbaum, B., & North, C. S. (2020). Mental health and the COVID-19 pandemic. *The New England Journal of Medicine*, 383(6), 510–512. DOI: 10.1056/NEJMp2008017 PMID: 32283003

Raffel, C. (2020). Exploring the Limits of Transfer Learning with a Unified Text-to-Text Transformer. *Journal of Machine Learning Research*, 21(140), 1–67.

Raghupathi, W., & Raghupathi, V. (2014). Big Data Analytics in Healthcare: Promise and Potential. *Health Information Science and Systems*, 2(1), 1–10. DOI: 10.1186/2047-2501-2-3 PMID: 25825667

Sankaran, A. (2020). The Role of IoT in Data Collection and Analysis: Opportunities and Challenges. *Journal of Internet of Things*, 1, 45–56.

Sharma, M. (2023). Data Science Applications in Healthcare: A Review of Recent Trends. *Health Informatics Journal*, 29(1), 22–34.

Solove, D. J. (2020). *Understanding Privacy*. Harvard University Press.

Strauch, C. (2011). *NoSQL Databases. Lecture Notes*. Stuttgart Media University.

Troiano, G., & Nardi, A. (2021). Vaccine hesitancy in the era of COVID-19. *Public Health*, 194, 245–251. DOI: 10.1016/j.puhe.2021.02.025 PMID: 33965796

Tukey, J. W. (1977). *Exploratory Data Analysis*. Addison-Wesley.

Wang, Y. (2023). Advanced Web Scraping Techniques for Big Data Collection. *Journal of Web Engineering*, 22(1), 12–30.

Wedel, M., & Kannan, P. K. (2016). Marketing Analytics for Data-Rich Environments. *Journal of Marketing*, 80(6), 97–121. DOI: 10.1509/jm.15.0413

Wolpert, D. H. (1992). Stacked Generalization. *Neural Networks*, 5(2), 241–259. DOI: 10.1016/S0893-6080(05)80023-1 PMID: 18276425

Zaharia, M., Chowdhury, M., Franklin, M. J., Shenker, S., & Stoica, I. (2010). Spark: Cluster Computing with Working Sets. *Proceedings of the 2nd USENIX conference on Hot topics in cloud computing*.

Chapter 9
Data Analytics and Visualization Tools and Applications

Harishchander Anandaram
https://orcid.org/0000-0003-2993-5304
Amrita School of Artificial Intelligence, India

Rakheeba Taseen
https://orcid.org/0009-0007-4514-6002
Presidency University, India

Haseeba Yaseen
https://orcid.org/0000-0002-7963-0915
Vasavi College of Engineering, India

Anup Bhange
KDK College of Engineering, India

Nidhya M. S.
https://orcid.org/0000-0002-1290-4520
Dayananda Sagar University, India

ABSTRACT

Data visualisation allows for the visual representation of data and information. Trends and changes in data may be seen with the use of data visualisation tools and visual data analysis using visual elements. The basic goal of data visualisation is to help people better comprehend and examine data—that is, to comprehend the outcomes of their processing—by transforming it into a visual environment. Humans have the quickest cognitive pathway in the visual canal. This is why visual data is more

DOI: 10.4018/979-8-3693-7868-7.ch009

appealing than text or audio data. It is common for quick data processing, analysis, and presentation to become more important in daily life in this era of digital data overproduction. Processing tools and visual data analysis undergo continual upgrading as a result of the two-way communication between developers, managers, and users. With that in mind, this chapter will examine and contrast the efficiency of the various visual data analysis and visualisation techniques available today.

I. INTRODUCTION

Data visualisation allows for the visual representation of data and information. Trends and changes in data may be seen with the use of data visualisation tools and visual data analysis using visual elements. The basic goal of data visualisation is to help people better comprehend and examine data—that is, to comprehend the outcomes of their processing—by transforming it into a visual environment. Humans have the quickest cognitive pathway in the visual canal. This is why visual data is more appealing than text or audio data. It is common for quick data processing, analysis, and presentation to become more important in daily life in this era of digital data overproduction. Processing tools and visual data analysis undergo continual upgrading as a result of the two-way communication between developers, managers, and users. With that in mind, this chapter will examine and contrast the efficiency of the various visual data analysis and visualisation techniques available today.

Data has grown exponentially across all industries due to our immersion in digital life. Data in the digital global environment is growing at an exponential rate, and the term "Big Data" has emerged to characterise these enormous quantities. Data analytics is the process of analysing data sets to make decisions based on business information with the help of specialised software and systems. When compared to traditional databases, Big Data offers new insights to businesses and organisations by changing the way new values are produced from data. It also helps to understand the hidden values in large amounts of data and poses new challenges, such as how to store and manage such large amounts of data. With the use of analytics, companies can learn more about their customers, which in turn helps them create more effective ads, more tailored content, and higher profits. Through the use of visual representations, data visualisation makes it easier to see patterns and trends in large amounts of numerical data.

Businesses may swiftly absorb massive amounts of data pertaining to their operations with the help of data analytics. With the ability to discover relationships across multi-dimensional datasets, business leaders may make educated and game-changing decisions. By making use of visual aids like charts, maps, and graphs, data visualisation methods help company executives make sense of large amounts of data.

Companies may get a greater understanding of consumer sentiment data, uncover opportunities, and provide new offerings using customer analytics. Businesses may get useful insights into their operations with the use of customised analytics dashboards, which can lead to increased sales and efficiency. Graphical representation of strategic data source-derived marketing patterns, consumer behaviour, demand changes, sales, and prices

Analysts, managers, and anybody else involved in managing and making use of big data for operational purposes might benefit from visual data analysis (VDA), a method for preparing and showing data that helps make the data more understandable. In order to aid in decision-making and understand as much meaningful information as possible, data visualisation tools are of special importance to big data analysts (Kennedy, 2016). Technology is advancing at a dizzying rate, driven mostly by information technology (IT) applications, but also by data analysis and the increasing use of visualisation, or the presentation of information in a more appealing visual manner (Aybeyan, 2021). The ability of the human brain to rapidly memorise visual representations and data gathered from the environment is the foundation of visualisation, which relies on the speed with which humans perceive visual forms. Finding methods and techniques to make everyday human existence easier is becoming an increasingly important focus of science. Market data visualisation tools compete with one another according to the premise that they are "closer" to user needs. Easy to use. The importance of choosing the correct choice is growing at a time when everything is changing at a rapid pace. When it's understood that making a poor choice is preferable than doing nothing at all, the need of data visualisation tools for effective decision making becomes crystal evident. All of this has led to a proliferation of visual data analysis and data visualisation solutions in today's software marketplaces. Developers are on the lookout for user-friendly tools that are simple and content-friendly, but consumers really do have it better when it comes to tools that are easy to use.

II. ASSOCIATED TASKS

Many researchers and analysts are always adding new features to the top tools for visual data analysis and data visualisation, while also regularly using their skills. We will examine the most popular approaches, methodologies, and resources used by researchers and analysts working with big data in order to synthesise a portion of their findings. Thanks to the proliferation of accessible, user-friendly tools for interactive visual data analysis, progress in this field has been accelerated. Using a design technique, Minatogawa et al. created a tool to aid in the search for new business models. The customer-driven artefact leverages Big Data analytics to facilitate improvements in business models by measuring the success of company business models using indicators. The findings demonstrate that the artefact was useful in the ongoing and proactive process of developing the business model. The artefact helps to democratise techniques of business model innovation and big data analytics outside of large organisations, even if it is accessible to the small company environment, despite its foundation in technological notions. Particularly in the corporate world, big data and visualisation make it easier to make decisions and mediate innovations, as well as to produce results from large-scale statistical procedures (Vinicius, Franco, Rampasso, & Anholon, 2022).

Visual study on the Hajj ritual's organisation in Mecca, Saudi Arabia, was conducted by Alharthi et al. They stress the significance of visualising huge data via graphs and tables. Their studies primarily include the planning of religious ceremonies as well as the services that are needed and those that are provided. The organisers relied on the data collected from the pilgrims' individual studies to make decisions about the Hajj. This paper demonstrates how to enhance certain services by using big data visualisation based on more detailed service visualisation. The study's findings make it clear that standard map visualisations don't give information centred on enhancing services via timely and appropriate action. In order to identify issues and direct decision-makers towards appropriate evaluation, which may enhance services, sophisticated visual data analysis methods are required (Alharthi, Krotov, & Bowman, 2017). An outstanding method for investigating the elements impacting the media and the public at large was developed by Kennedy et al. In order to raise public awareness of the usefulness of data visualisation, the study suggests, among other things, merging the paradigms of media and communication studies with those of human-computer interaction (HCI). A call for improved public visual data comprehension and interpretation across demographics is made in the paper's conclusion (Kennedy, 2016). The difficulties in implementing effective data visualisation strategies were investigated by Jagadish et al. It not only defines a plethora of big data ideas and how to visualise them, but it also delves into the difficulties of big data visualisation and discusses how big data is an inevitable part of today's society, businesses, and public life (Jagadish, Gehrke, Labrinidis, Papakonstantinou, & Patel, 2014). Cloud computing's potential in visualisation was investigated by Ventartaman et al., who also made forecasts about the VDA's use and the new data centre constellation. The foundation of this process analysis of big data visualisation is the provision of business information for efficient and timely decision-making. In order to provide better performance and scalable business information to various organisations, the paper acknowledges the need of building a big data infrastructure. It is shown that cutting-edge big data infrastructure tools and technologies are used, together with the NIST (National Institute for Technology Standards) architecture. Through detailed case studies of several production instances, the benefits of data visualisation are shown. Put simply, the article makes a significant contribution by offering insightful information on how organisations may use big data to build a scalable infrastructure that can make better, more informed choices (Venkataraman, 2012). Written by G. Rushton. is now in the early stages of laying the groundwork for GIS spatial analysis, which will allow for better data processing in the future and better health-related decision-making. In a nutshell, the map-based methods discussed in the article mark the birth of contemporary data visualisation and have an impact on public health in the US generally (Rushton, 2003). Large volumes of heterogeneous data pertaining to big data, their processing tools, analysis, and decision-making approaches are reached by Kumar and Singh in their article. This data is structured, unstructured, or semi-structured. The influence of big data on healthcare and the use of different technologies, including Hadoop, to investigate the theoretical framework of data analysis form the basis of their study. Hadoop and MapReduce are the technologies that form the basis of the study (Maninder & Kumar, 2019). Debus R. displays extensive details and a variety of features on Power BI boards for data visualisation. Outlines the rationale for processed data serving as the ultimate representation of the process. Using numerous examples, the article demonstrates the benefits of data analysis in decision making, and it presents Power BI's research advantages, such as its user interface, the ability to consolidate multiple data sources (Excel, CSV, XML, Text), interactive reports and map mapping, and the integration with R, Python, and SQL (Roxane, 2020). Of course. The merit of stressing the ability to do statistical analysis using visualised findings is supported by G and Everitt B in SAS research articles. In addition, the paper explains why and how the SAS tool is important for processing massive data. Divergent diagrams, basic regression, correlation, and SAS procedures are also covered in the work (Der & Everitt, 2006). In Mani's studies. Feri and M. An essential component of large data analysis is the visualisation of S data. This study looks at the best practices for visualising huge data, with an emphasis on interactive procedures. An analyst conducting an interactive visualisation session has the option to request several visualisations, with each succeeding visualisation expanding upon the ones that came before. Integrating distributed data processing systems with visualisation systems allows for efficient processing of big data sets, and even interactive visualisation of smaller data sets may be included in the study. In order to minimise the visualisation delay time, the search for alternatives is also prioritised. All of this is seen as a conclusion that may be a solution to future needs, as a springboard for analysts to get new experiences that would boost their productivity (Murali Mani, 2017). There are a lot of other researchers that have used visual data analysis tools for large data and had great results. This is why we'll take a look at what the most popular tools for VDA and viz have to offer.

III. RESOURCES FOR FACILITATING DATA ANALYTICS AND VISUALISATION

Without a question, data visualisation is a buzzing new area of study that data scientists and those who put this knowledge into practice are very interested in since it promises to lead to more insightful, quicker, and more efficient observations—the very ingredients for data penetration. And they'll be able to assist their companies make better, faster, and more practical judgements. Consequently, it is crucial to show the data in a way that makes use of novel approaches, primitives like colours, components, and dimensions, and analyses that impact the data's representativeness. Several visualisation tools have been created and used due to the fact that data visualisation, particularly in large data, requires familiarity with both design and data as well as fundamental statistical concepts. Some of them would be singled out by us.

The Public Tableau

When it comes to visual data analysis and visualisation, Tableau is among the top ranked tools according to the Gartner group. There are a number of versions of this highly regarded visualisation tool, and one of them is Tableau Public, which is open to the public but has restricted features. The straightforward design and ease of use of the tool make it stand out. Tableau Public makes it simple and fast to create visualisations of any kind, even without knowing how to code. Paying for a licence and getting the full paid edition will get you access to all of the software's functionality. The premium Tableau edition opens up many more options, and it also allows you to integrate data types that are native to formats like Excel or PDF. When it comes to visualising massive data, Tableau Public is your best choice. Not only that, but it also allows for interactive data analysis between the data and the visualisations, making tables, lists, and maps a breeze (Tableau Software, 2022).

a. Tableau Public

Tableau Public allows users to merge or connect tables and data. Group and cluster attributes allow for the editing of data. Many different types of organisations, both public and private, utilise Tableau Public. On the web, you may distribute your own data visualisations to others. Sharing the data with mobile devices that are tool-compatible is also possible (Ohmann & Floyd, 2015). When data becomes large enough (on the scale of five bytes), online data analysis may be done without transferring any data thanks to Tableau Live's simple connection to Hive (Big Data Business Intelligence) resources. Big data and data warehouse investments are safe-guarded by Tableau Live's design. Through direct connections to the operational database in memory, Tableau is also able to visualise big datasets. With Tableau, you can quickly and easily analyse massive amounts of data, including hundreds of millions of rows, and take use of its streaming features. The primary capabilities of the Tableau tool include the following: annotating tables, changing views, dragging and dropping, a Tableau Reader for data viewing, data visualisations, data reduction at intervals, interactive table creation, data exchange, data highlighting and filtering, spreadsheet sharing, data notifications, automatic display of new features, and security permissions at any level.

b. Yellowfin Bi

One analytics software that focuses on spreadsheets and visual analysis is Yellowfin BI. With its wealth of pre-made spreadsheets, it offers a contemporary solution for data visualisation. Because of how it is structured, the tool helps users perform better. A variety of supplementary tools, including the potential for automatic insight, built-in explanations, and contextual analysis, are available from the manufacturer. Several resources and relational databases, including Hadoop and NoSQL, may be effortlessly connected to the tool. Quicker replies to requests based on key performance indicators are also possible using the capabilities offered by the tool (Yellowfin, 2021). Among the many useful features of the Yellowfin BI tool are the following: on-demand visualisation; answers derived from machine learning; and visualisations that are both simple to comprehend and show. One other perk of this application is that it allows you to isolate certain data points in a spreadsheet and get focussed results by choosing or omitting them. You also have full control over how those data points are visualised. The HTML5-based mobile app supersedes the original app in the latest version of the utility (6.3). The programme updates its findings in real time when it identifies data changes automatically (Yellowfin BI, 2022).

c. SAP Cloud Analytics

Companies in the planning and analysis of their own oversights and decisions may benefit greatly from SAP ANALYTICS CLOUD, a data visualisation tool for business research. At any point during processing, different data might be utilised again and again. Sharing documents in PDF format is a simple way for SAP Analytics Cloud users and external collaborators to work together in a hands-on way (SAP, 2022).

we can show our data properly with the help of SAP Cloud Analytics Story's many professional, interactive, important list, and other object-based features. Personalising data and adding bookmarks to key views for future investigation are both made possible by applying custom filters to widgets and spreadsheets. You may set temporary reminders, assign tasks, and track their progress using the built-in calendar. You may transfer data in PDF format without dynamic capabilities or with full dynamic aspects while using the programme. All the while, it safeguards businesses by granting access permissions to owners and users, either alone or in groups.

d. Oracle Cloud for Analytics

Organisations of any size may benefit from ORACLE ANALYTICS CLOUD, a data visualisation platform that combines analytics with joint reporting. The machine learning capabilities of the technology make it possible to intuitively visualise data and uncover essential information. A big perk of ORACLE ANALYTICS CLOUD is that it processes data in plain language, meaning that users don't need to be coding experts to find and analyse the data that interests them. Also, ORACLE ANALYTICS CLOUD gives a far more in-depth look at company data via scenario simulations and multidimensional data analysis (Oracle, 2022). One of the many benefits of the ORACLE ANALYTICS CLOUD tool is its capacity to automatically generate visualisations via the identification of methods based on machine learning in big data analysis. The tool's user-friendly interface offers consistent data analysis across different data visualisation methodologies and approaches.

e. The DOMO

DOMO is a BI platform that runs in the cloud. It comes with thousands of pre-built visualisations, such as over 1,500 list kinds and over 7,000 maps. Automated data detection is made possible by machine learning, which uses natural language alerts and queries to do this. Even after data has been created, the DOMO tool may still access, filter, sort, and organise it. By using your own colours, photos, and text, you may personalise your layout with this tool (Domo, 2022). One of the features of the DOMO tool is the ability to combine separate views. For instance, you may put all of your chosen key performance indicators—sales, ROI, performance measurement, and more—into one interface. You may separate the various table visualisations using the pop-up menus. The application allows users to customise the visual presentation by choosing from several list kinds, data series, and filters, allowing for interactive enhancement of the visualisation.

f. Utilising Power BI

Through the use of Power BI's integrated software services, apps, and linkages, disparate data sources may be transformed into cohesive, visually appealing, and interactive insights. The data might come from a variety of sources, including hybrid systems, Excel, or a database stored in the cloud. Power BI simplifies the process of connecting to existing data sources, visualising the findings, and sharing them in the cloud or with team members. The following are the main parts of Power BI and how they interact with one another:

Using a Windows programme or Power BI for Desktop,

- Power BI or any online SaaS solution,
- Windows, iOS, and Android version of Power BI for mobile apps.

One of the best things about Power BI is how affordable and readily available it is. It's a great tool for data visualisation. You may get Power BI Desktop for free. Downloading, installing, and using it is a breeze. Power BI facilitates interactive visualisations with simple customisation in reports and spreadsheets. Maps, charts, graphics, dashboards, R image scripts, and key performance indicator visualisation are just a few of the numerous features. The ability to connect data to XML and JSON formats and import data from several sources is a major benefit of using Power BI as a tool for data analysis. Power BI has several benefits, but among them is the ability to have immediate access to resources for large data. Also, it's worth mentioning that Excel connection brings the opportunity to load Excel data into Power BI. By importing raw data into Excel, you may make it accessible for processing, extract data from Power BI, and then effortlessly move it back to Excel. You may add many visualisations to the report and even set them up to interact with each other using Power BI (Collie, 2015).

g. Extra Resources

Data visualisation tools that have received accolades from Gartner include: TIOCO SpotFire, a platform that facilitates software integration and visual analysis for businesses. Data integration and analysis, quick idea discovery, and improved decision-making are all possible with this programme. Some large data surveys use TIBCO Spotfire, a platform for software that only "animates" data (Sistembul, 2022).

Access large data, manage data, analyse it, and display the results with the help of SAS VDA, a statistical analysis software programme from SAS (Statistical Analysis System). There is a wide variety of data analysis, data cleaning, and data analysis operation-related items offered by this company. Big data processing and visualisation are SAS's primary uses (Global Tech Magazine, 2022).

If you have data that you would want to turn into an info report or spreadsheet, you can do it for free using Google Data Studio. For the express aim of making a spreadsheet, Google Data Studio integrates many data sources and Google's marketing tools into a single interface. It features a straightforward UI and is easy to use (Newgen Apps, 2019).

One data discovery and visualisation tool that may help you make better choices is Qlik Sense. It lets you construct visualisations that are both versatile and dynamic. After an inspection or visualisation, issues may arise; the tool's licencing addresses these concerns. Qlik Sense's relational approach provides ongoing insights by answering inquiries continuously (Vizlib, 2022).

One such licenced tool is Amazon QuickSight. Organisations may use Amazon QuickSight to make data understandable for all employees by using automated machine learning, interactive spreadsheets, or natural language queries. A customer's decision-making process is the exclusive focus of QuickSight, which constantly supports millions of spreadsheet views for customers (AWS, 2022).

Table 1. Data visualization tools

Tool	Application	Advantage	Limitations
TABLEAU PUBLIC	Big data and machine learning	• Hadoop, SAP, and Teradata are just a few of the sophisticated database technologies that can be integrated with Salesforce. • Graphics that work can be made	• You can't set it to automatically renew reports. • SQL expertise is required, and the solution is not all-inclusive.
YELLOWFIN BI	**Spread sheets**	• Capacity to use up-to-date visualisations to track vital indicators, allowing for analysis of operational and strategic planning of the organisation. • Use the JavaScript API to add codeless functionality, action keys, and widgets to spreadsheets. Use JavaScript, CSS, and HTML to create filter controls and floating panels.	• No ability to modify OLAP-inherited data types or hierarchies. • Isn't useful for analysing profits and budgeting
SAP ANALYTICS CLOUD	**Cloud**	• The Smart Predict, Smart Insights, and Smart Discovery modules provide a data source that enables thorough analysis. • Remove the need to plan ahead while making decisions. • Automatically generate pertinent insights and descriptions; save time by selecting data to locate information.	• It doesn't always validate AI-based features using credible data. • There is insufficient pliability in data modelling.

continued on following page

Table 1. Continued

Tool	Application	Advantage	Limitations
ORACLE ANALYTICS CLOUD	**Process data in Natural Language**	• The capacity to detect insights using machine learning techniques and automatically generate underwater visualisations. • It offers the same data analysis in several visualisations via its user-friendly interface. • Through customised searches, gives precise solutions to certain business problems. • Research and analysis are made possible by it.	• The number of visuals is insufficient. • Regarding reinforcement and recovery, it is not obvious. • Visualization is not a part of it, unlike its rivals.
DOMO	**Cloud based business intelligence**	• The capacity to relax the requirements for in-depth analysis; the ability to ask and answer questions derived from ordinary life. • Clients and team members work together on visualisation, which cuts down on meeting time. • Capacity to document certain data points, add remarks, and make observations in a way that other customers can follow	• Scheduled CSV reports cannot include more than 5 MB of extra data for export. • Data cannot be easily removed from the platform. • The user interface is not intuitive enough.
POWER BI	**Spreadsheet and cloud**	• Data that is imported is cleaned and transformed based on what the user requires. • The server platform is secured by a firewall. • Anyone with an internet connection, a tablet, a laptop, a phone, etc., may access and share spreadsheets and reports.	• AutoML cannot be executed on a Power BI Desktop. • Automation after data model creation is likewise not an option. • An advanced position requires no intellect. • Graphical analysis is not available. • While DAX and the data model pose a threat comparable to Power BI, PowerQuery & m are the most potent Power BI tools.

Things to think about while choosing data analytics software

- The capacity to adapt to changing company needs and scale to meet those needs as they arise.
- Connecting preexisting company apps and third-party technologies to the analytics platform.
- Data and reporting capabilities that contribute to achieving company goals.
- Analytics solution costs, including as subscriptions, growth, and hidden expenses.
- As an added bonus, the platform offers customisation options, collaborative features, and built-in security.
- A straightforward interface and visualisation that are simple enough for anyone without technical training to utilise.
- Capacity to analyse structured, semi-structured, and unstructured data, as well as integrate data from various sources.

Important factors to consider while choosing data visualisation tools

- The most effective data visualisation tools make use of industry-standard visualisation techniques, drawing attention to key data trends.
- Single sign-on authentication mechanisms, role-based data access, and network security are all part of the robust built-in corporate security.
- Quickly build charts and graphs even if you don't have any technical knowledge thanks to the easy-to-use drag-and-drop components.
- Tools for training and assistance, with an emphasis on creating complicated visualisations.
- The ability to integrate and combine information gathered from a wide variety of internal and external sources.
- Visualisations, annotations, comments, and data-driven tales can all be easily shared and worked on with the help of the robust collaboration capabilities.
- Device portability to accommodate the increasing mobility of businesses.

Below table summarize the usage of tool by the peoples like Data Scientist, Business Analysts and Non-Technical users

Table 2. Usage of data visualization tools

Tool	Data Scientists	Business Analysts	Non-Technical Users
Tableau	**Interactive dashboards for analytics**	**Popular for business use**	**Drag-and-drop interface**
Matplotlib/Seaborn	**Detailed, customizable plots**	**Limited usage**	**Requires coding knowledge**
ggplot2	Statistical visualizations in R	Rarely used	Not user-friendly for beginners
D3.js	Dynamic, web-based visualizations	Too technical for analysts	Requires coding expertise
Plotly	Interactive plots across platforms	Sometimes used for analysis	Basic knowledge needed
Power BI	Advanced analytics features	Widely used in enterprises	Simple for beginners
Jupyter Notebooks	Supports multiple visualization libraries	Not common	Requires technical setup
Apache Superset	Open-source analytics	Used for big data exploration	Requires setup and technical skills
Qlik Sense	Sometimes for big data analysis	Preferred for self-service analytics	Intuitive design for users
SAP Analytics Cloud	Rarely used	Enterprise-level visualizations	Designed for end-users
Google Data Studio	Quick reports and dashboards	Free and lightweight for analysts	Ideal for non-technical users

Below table explains the practical outcome of Data visualization tools

Table 3. Practical outcome of data visualization tools

Tool	Practical Outcome
Tableau	**Interactive dashboards, visual storytelling, trend analysis.**
Matplotlib/Seaborn	**Customized, publication-quality graphs; deep data analysis; exploratory data analysis (EDA).**
ggplot2	Professional statistical graphics; efficient pattern analysis; research-oriented visualizations.
D3.js	Dynamic, web-based graphics; real-time visualizations; custom and complex charts.
Plotly	Interactive 3D plots and maps; integrated dashboards; data storytelling for technical users.
Power BI	Integration with Excel; real-time reporting and dashboards; quick business insights.
Jupyter Notebooks	Combines code and visuals; multi-library support; iterative analysis and technical presentations.
Apache Superset	Large-scale data exploration; custom SQL visualizations; real-time data analysis.

continued on following page

Table 3. Continued

Tool	Practical Outcome
Tableau	**Interactive dashboards, visual storytelling, trend analysis.**
Matplotlib/Seaborn	**Customized, publication-quality graphs; deep data analysis; exploratory data analysis (EDA).**
Qlik Sense	Self-service analytics; data discovery with an associative engine; real-time collaboration.
SAP Analytics Cloud	Predictive analytics; tailored enterprise dashboards; integrated financial and operational analytics.
Google Data Studio	Simple dashboards; free and lightweight reporting; collaborative sharing and editing.

IV. CONCLUSION

We conclude that the aforementioned technologies are appropriate for use in organisations after analysing them for visual data analysis and large data visualisation. In order to address ever-changing issues like illiquidity or loss creation, these technologies have been specifically designed. With the help of visualisation technologies, modern organisations may confidently and successfully advance their production and services. All users, buyers, producers, and supervisors benefit substantially from big data processing and visualising it. The use of visual information in decision-making and investment is gaining increasing attention. In today's fast-paced world, it's impossible to avoid using visual aids like tables and graphs. Especially in the realm of big data, the number of data visualisation tools is expanding at a fast pace, and these tools are continuously becoming better and have more analytical skills. Given that 90% of the information processed by the brain occurs visually—that is, in the form of pictures, graphs, and patterns—it's easy to see why data visualisation is the gold standard for businesses and any other field that requires visual analysis of data. So, visualisation tools are growing more and more popular, and their usage is outpacing what is really required.

Consequently, this section reviewed studies that have examined the application of big data visualisation for a variety of tools, such as analysis of tools, video data, and interactivity. Analysing large data using visualisation tools and looking at its key performance metrics is the main emphasis of the research. In conclusion, it is true that Big Data, Visualisation, Machine Learning, and Artificial Intelligence provide a formidable obstacle for analysts, managers, and professionals; yet, these technologies are quickly becoming an absolute need for all individuals. An essential component of any successful endeavour is access to relevant and insightful information, and the analysis that follows from the potential for engagement in processing and visualising large data provides a firm foundation for just that.

REFERENCES

Alharthi, A., Krotov, V., & Bowman, M. (2017). Addressing barriers to big data. https://www.researchgate.net/publication/317279522

Aybeyan, S. (2021). Systematic Review Of Big Data, Digital Transformation Areas And Industry 4.0 Trends In 2021. *International Scientific Journal Vision*, 6(2), 27–41.

Der, G., & Everitt, B. S. (2006). Statistical Analysis of Medical Data Using SAS. http://ftp.sas.com/samples/A60928

Jagadish, J., Gehrke, J., Labrinidis, A., Papakonstantinou, Y., Patel, J. M., Ramakrishnan, R., & Shahabi, C. (2014). Big Data and Its Technical Challenges. *Communications of the ACM*, 57(7), 86–94. DOI: 10.1145/2611567

Kennedy, H. (2016). Engaging with data visualization. https://journals.uic.edu/ojs/index.php/fm/rt/printerFriendly/6389/5652

Murali Mani, S. F. (2017). Effective Big Data Visualization. *Proceedings of IDEAS '17*.

Ohmann, A., & Floyd, M. (2015). *Creating Data Stories with Tableau Public*. Packt Publishing.

Rob Collie, A. S. (2015). *Power Pivot and Power BI. In Power Pivot and Power BI, Yayınevi: Holy Macro!* Books.

Roxane. (2020). Power BI in Clinical Data exploration. PHUSE Virtual EU Connect 2020.

Rushton. (2003). Public health, GİS and spatial analytic tools. Annu. Rev. Pub. Health.

Venkatraman. (2012). Cloud Computing A Research Roadmap In Coalesence With Software Engineering. *International Journal (Toronto, Ont.)*, 2(2).

Vinicius, Franco, Rampasso, & Anholon. (2022). Operationalizing Business Model Innovation through Big Data Analytics for Sustainable Organizations. Business model Innovation Research – Sustainability, 12(1).

Chapter 10
A Sentimental Analysis of Legal Documents Using Mask Attention BERT Networks

D. Thamarai Selvi
Department of Computer Science and Engineering, National Engineering College, India

S. Kalaiselvi
https://orcid.org/0000-0003-1923-3827
Department of Computer Science and Engineering, National Engineering College, India

V. Anitha
Department of Information Technology, National Engineering College, India

S. Santhi
Department of Information Technology, National Engineering College, India

V. Gomathi
Department of Computer Science and Engineering, National Engineering College, India

Sathish Kumar Sekar
East China University of Technology, China

ABSTRACT

Legal systems can function more efficiently by processing cases faster and having a higher case clearance rate when complex legal texts are automatically analysed for logical patterns. The most crucial task in doing this is classifying sentences in legal documents automatically based on their content. This chapter suggests a deep learning model for sentiment analysis-based legal text analysis and judgment generation. The transformer model is an innovative encoder-decoder that uses self-awareness to analyse speech patterns which runs noticeably quicker and allows for parallel processing. In this work, the glove embedding and the BERT algorithm—

DOI: 10.4018/979-8-3693-7868-7.ch010

bidirectional encoder representation for transformer model—are utilised to construct sentiment analysis for text categorization. Prior to extracting valuable data from textual input, a preprocessor is used to enhance the quality of the data. Next, pre-trained glove word embedding methods and term frequency-inverse document frequency (TF-IDF) feature weighting are used.

1. INTRODUCTION

Deep learning is an approach that uses Artificial Intelligence (AI) that makes computers capable of processing and comprehending data by simulating how the human brain functions. Deep learning models are able to generate precise insights and predictions since they are able to identify intricate patterns in text, audio, photos, and other forms of data. Natural Language Processing (NLP) powered by Artificial Intelligence entails teaching computer programs to understand data via human languages. Sentiment Analysis (SA), often known as sentiment mining, is a linguistic processing method for determining a document's expressive tenor. This technique is often used by organizations to determine and classify viewpoints about a certain good, service, or idea.

These days, individuals voice their thoughts and take part in conversations on social media sites like Facebook, Instagram, Twitter, and Amazon. Researchers have been inspired by data from various mediums to investigate opinion mining and public perceptions. Owing to social media's abundance of user-generated information, SA has become an essential part of NLP. Applications for SA are numerous and include web evaluation, techniques for storing and retrieving information, and much more. To keep in mind the final objective of studying it and unexpectedly extracting information, text processing is important. Even with the exponential growth of social media data repositories, conventional algorithms frequently have difficulties in precisely identifying the emotions ingrained in such vast amounts of data. Due to the widespread use of social networking sites, a number of professions have emerged that concentrate on analyzing social networks and their contents to obtain important information. SA aims to infer the feelings that the subject matter of a text conveys. The analysis of sentiment has been an important field under the field of NLP, with much early research investigating it, given the historical significance of the general public for making choices (Koroteev, 2021). By training complex bidirectional depictions from unlabeled texts and retraining on both right and left contexts concurrently in all layers, the BERT (Bidirectional Encoder Representations from Transformers) integrating layer improves this procedure (BERT 5). With the use of Global Vectors (GloVe) embedding and the stochastic gradient optimizer, this chapter describes the attention mask-based BERT algorithm. As a sort of word embedding known as GloVe Embeddings, two words' co-occurrence probabilities are represented as vector differences. To extract critical characteristics for SA, a novel textual representation technique that combines pre-trained GloVe word embeddings with TF-IDF weighting for features has been presented.

2. RELATED WORKS

Sentiment classification is a critical step in determining how people feel about a certain good, service, or idea. Several models for NLP proposed to address the issue of sentiment classification (Koroteev, 2021). In e-commerce, question-answering is significant because it enables prospective customers to proactively look for information that they need to make a purchase choice. In order to address consumer concerns, this research investigates the possibility of using customer evaluations as a useful source of information. The current popularity of Machine Reading Comprehension (MRC) on official sources (Xu, Liu, Shu, & Yu, 2019) has sparked passion for this method. Because of the rise in the volume of opportunistic text from Internet users, SA has gained enormous popularity in both study and industry. Conventional SA concentrates on categorizing a text's general sentiment but ignores crucial information like the particular object, subject, or element that the sentiment is directed towards (Hoang, Bihorac, & Rouces, 2019). One cannot emphasize how important information about context is to the majority of NLP applications. Several NLP tasks, such as emotion recognition from texts, significantly improve with the extraction of context. For NLP problems, the study discusses transformer-based models (Acheampong, Nunoo-Mensah, & Chen, 2021). Sentiment categorization is essential to comprehending people's perceptions of a given good, service, or idea. To address the issues of sentiment categorization, a number of NLP models have been presented (Munikar, Shakya, & Shrestha, 2019). This work presents a unique ACL-SA framework to solve problems including overfitting, excessive the number of dimensions, and inadequate semantic data.

This model combines TF-IDF grading and pre-trained GloVe embedded words with a CNN-bidirectional-LSTM architecture. Three layers of CNN is used to obtain contextual characteristics, using Max-pooling at the CNN layer's output, in order to reduce dimensionality problems in the feature space (Kamyab, Liu, & Adjeisah, 2021). By utilizing data from similar but different source domains, transfer learning seeks to improve target learners' performance on specific fields. When creating target learners, this method may lessen the requirement for substantial targeted-domain data. Transfer learning has become a well-known and exciting area of machine learning because of its many potential applications (Zhuang, Qi, Duan, Xi, Zhu, & Zhu, 2020). Transfer learning refers to methods for improving the accuracy of models through the use of information from several tasks or contexts in order to strengthen generalization skills. In NLP within the last two years, a number of transfer learning techniques and frameworks have surfaced, greatly outperforming the latest advances on a variety of NLP tasks (Ruder, Peters, Swayamdipta, & Wolf, 2019). An empirical approach is provided that estimates alternatives for various research subjects, data characteristics, and computational resources to enable well-informed approach choice according to implementation scenario. More than 12 million sentiment-labelled text samples from 272 datasets were used in a meta-analysis, which shows that while freshly developed transfer learning models frequently perform better, they can also surpass conventional scoreboard standards (Hartmann, Heitmann, Siebert, & Schamp, 2022). Transfer learning is a brand-new machine learning approach that employs prior knowledge to address various domain-specific challenges and yields cutting-edge prediction outcomes. Many academics in the field of SA use transfer learning (Liu, Shi, Ji, & Jia, 2019). SA extracts individual data from text by utilizing NLP and text mining. SA is a method of compiling and examining the views, ideas, and perceptions of individuals with reference to a variety of issues, goods, and services (Wankhade, Rao, & Kulkarni, 2022)

SA is a useful tool that organizations, policymakers, and academics may use to understand public opinion and attitude, which can improve making choices and yield beneficial company insights (Birjali, Kasri, & Beni-Hssane, 2021). An extensive overview of well-liked deep neural network models for analyzing sentiment is given in this study. With an emphasis on deep learning approaches and significant contributions from several experts, the study presents a framework for sentiment evaluation and explores how different architectures for deep learning affect it (Yadav & Vishwakarma, 2020). It also examined current work that uses deep learning to address issues with SA, including sentiment neutrality. It also examined term Frequency-Inverse Document Frequency (TF-IDF) models applied to different datasets as well as word embeddings (Dang, Moreno-García, & De la Prieta, 2020). The classic TF-IDF technique is enhanced in this research to produce weighted word vectors while including sentimental data into the process of word representation. Weighted word vectors are fed through a bidirectional Long Short-Term Memory (BiLSTM) system, that improves the appearance of comment vectors, in order to precisely capture contextual information. Then, a network of feedforward neural networks classifies the responses based on their emotional patterns (Xu, Meng, Qiu, Yu, & Wu, 2019). Nowadays, with so much unorganized information being created digitally every second, text communication on the internet may be quite confusing. This data has to be studied as soon as it is produced in order to fully understand human behavior. This procedure is aided by SA, which determines the opposing views of texts by indicating whether the author is favorable, unfavorable, or neutral toward a certain thing, group of people, location, or thing. (Nandwani

& Verma, 2021). The findings of a supplementary investigation were reported aiming at evaluating the current status of investigation in this subject by merging data from previous research, including systematic reviews of the literature and quantitative mapping research on sentiment evaluation. This tertiary research only includes secondary studies and adheres to the standards of systematic literature reviews (SLR). The findings of this post-secondary research offer an extensive overview of significant subjects and diverse techniques for managing diverse SA assignments (Ligthart, Catal, & Tekinerdogan, 2021). A performance study of many neural network models on a particular dataset is also included in the publication, with an evaluation of each model's efficacy at the conclusion of each analysis of sentiment assignment. The assessment concludes by highlighting existing problems and potential fixes for consideration in further work. On the basis of the knowledge gathered from past research, the future work section also offers concepts that may be encompassed into fresh models for deep learning to deliver improved outcomes. A few recommendations are generative adversarial networks, basic knowledge, cognition-based attention designs, sentiment-specific word embedding examples, BERT, and reinforcement learning techniques (Habimana, Li, Li, Gu, & Yu, 2020).

3. METHODOLOGY

Sentiment-based deep learning model is used to explore the responsiveness or non-responsiveness of legal papers in real court cases. This item includes the tests that employ a straightforward Sentiment model, to put it mildly. In spite of optimization, the results demonstrate improved performance on larger datasets, more consistent development patterns, and a growing number of training samples as compared to the traditional technique.

Long short-term connections are superior to Bag-of-Words (BoW) techniques for text classification because they can learn texts sequentially and extract features from data more efficiently. It might be challenging to quote the appropriate text in court papers because typically only a few words or short paragraphs are chosen to be relevant material. It can be challenging to feed large texts to the training without first eliminating the relevant passages because the sequence technique places restrictions on the length of the sequences. The trials have shown that BERT model training is time-consuming. With analytical tools based on conventional techniques, users can rapidly build a model by choosing a training set.

When incorporating deep learning into the present tool, adding GPU to the configuration as an additional modeling option for the users was taken into consideration. This is because it would need GPUs to speed up the training and forecasting processes in order to enhance the deep learning technique. A case statement's main text was made up of the verdict, summary, referral text, reference antecedent, major text, and connected papers. Only nouns and verbs remained in the text after stopwords and numerals were eliminated, making this the final data set. As particles can alter the meaning of the nouns that come before them in a sentence, the findings show that particles are a part of the noun tokens.

In many cases, the legal document is longer and more intricately organized than the data sets that are used. Accuracy was used to calculate the classification performance of the three methods. It suggests that employing BERT to simulate the sequential characteristics of words in legal language can enhance classification performance. Input vectors of a certain length that can be utilized to classify legal documents using predictive coding and a deep neural network model must be created using a predetermined collection of resources, such as books, films, and testing. Since two cases from separate courts could have information that is based on the same occurrence and is somewhat comparable, classifying legal documents shows how they differ in how they generate input data and presents difficulties when compiling two papers.

3.1. Bidirectional Encoder Representations From Transformers

BERT is built upon the Transformers deep learning model, which connects all output and input elements and computes weights between them dynamically based on their relationship. BERT is an open-source, a free framework for machine learning created to handle NLP. BERT provides context through surrounding content to assist computers in deciphering unclear words in text. Question and answer datasets can be used to modify the BERT framework once it has been pre-trained on text.

Language models could only read text sequentially that is, from left to right or from right to left rather than reading it continuously. BERT is unique in that it can concurrently read in both directions. Bidirectionality is the ability that is made possible by the creation of Transformers. BERT is pre-trained on Next Sentence Prediction and Mask Language Modelling, two discrete but related NLP tasks using this bidirectional capacity. A word is hidden within a sentence during Masked Language Model training, and the computer is trained to infer the concealed word (masked word) from the context of the hidden word. The Next Sentence Prediction training's objective would be to enable the computer to figure out whether there is a relationship between two given sentences.

Language models used to analyze text sequentially, either from left to right or left to right. BERT, however, introduces bidirectionality, enabling simultaneous reading in both directions. This bidirectional approach, made possible by the Transformer architecture, allows BERT to grasp context more effectively and resolve ambiguities that arise from word meanings changing based on their surroundings.

BERT's pre-training involves two key tasks: Masked Language Modeling (MLM) and Next Sentence Prediction (NSP). In MLM, words are arbitrarily hidden within sentences, and the model's job is to guess these hidden words by analyzing their context. Finding out if a given pair of sentences logically follows one another or if their relationship is arbitrary is the goal of NSP.

In essence, BERT is a transformer design with an encoder stack. A Transformer architecture is an encoder-decoder 30 network that uses attention on the decoder end and self-attention on the encoder end. While BERTLARGE's encoder stack has 24 layers, BERTBASE's only has 12. They are better than the Transformer design that uses six encoder layers. Moreover, the LARGE and BASE BERT designs include larger feedforward networks (768 and 1024 hidden units) and more attention heads (12 and 16 respectively) than the Transformer architecture proposed in the original study. It has eight attention heads and 512 hidden units. 340M parameters are present in BERT LARGE, while only 110M are present in BEST BASE.

BERT is structured around a Transformer encoder stack, differing from the original Transformer design, which includes both encoder and decoder components. The BERTBASE model consists of 12 encoder layers, while BERTLARGE features 24 layers. Additionally, BERTLARGE and BERTBASE have more attention heads (16 and 12, respectively) and larger feedforward networks (1024 and 768 hidden units) compared to the original Transformer architecture, which uses 8 attention heads and 512 hidden units. The parameter counts reflect this: BERTLARGE has approximately 340 million parameters, while BERTBASE has 110 million.

BERT is likely to have a big impact on voice and text-based search, which have historically been inaccurate because of Google's NLP techniques. BERT's contextual understanding is predicted to significantly enhance international SEO as it allows it to interpret common patterns across languages without requiring a full understanding of each one. BERT could greatly progress the field of artificial intelligence systems in general.

Effective NLP requires careful preprocessing of text data. Key preprocessing steps include:

1. **Raw Text Preparation**: Convert text to lowercase, remove punctuation, and structure it into manageable components.
2. **Text Normalization**: Standardize text to a consistent format, eliminating variations and irrelevant details to improve processing efficiency.
3. **Text Stemming**: Reduce words to their root forms, addressing potential issues such as over-stemming and under-stemming to enhance semantic understanding.
4. **Tokenization**: Divide text into tokens (words and sentences) to facilitate context analysis and model development.

5. **Removal of Special Characters**: Eliminate non-alphanumeric characters that do not contribute to text analysis.
6. **BoW**: Use a statistical model to assess text based on word frequency, ignoring word order.
7. **Stopword Removal**: Filter out frequently used words that carry minimal semantic value to focus on meaningful content.
8. **GloVe Embeddings**: Employ unsupervised learning to create word embeddings that capture word meanings based on co-occurrence statistics.

BERT is open source software that can be used by anybody. A state-of-the-art Q&A system may be trained in a matter of hours on a GPU and in 30 minutes on a cloud tensor processing unit (TPU), according to Google. Several other businesses, academic institutions, and Google divisions are continuously improving the BERT model architecture through supervised training. This is done to either make the model more effective (by changing the learning rate, for example) or to tailor it to specific tasks by pre-training it with contextual representations.

3.2. Working Process

Understanding spoken human language in its natural environment is the goal of the current NLP technique. For BERT model, selecting a word from a blank is frequently required. To do this, models are typically required to be trained utilizing a substantial set of specific, labelled training data. This requires linguists to manually label data in large batches. However, BERT was only trained on an unlabeled plain text corpus for pre-use. It continues to learn independently from the unlabeled text while it is being used in real-world applications. Its pre-training provides a "knowledge" foundation upon which additional knowledge can be placed. BERT can then be tailored based on the user's selections and the continuously expanding corpus of searchable content. This mechanism is known as transfer learning. For pre-use training, BERT was trained just on plain text corpora without labels. It continuously adapts and learns unsupervised abilities from the unlabeled text in real-world applications. This is in contrast to previous methods like GloVe and Word2vec, which would only translate a small portion of a word's meaning in one dimension to a vector. Word embedding is the name given to this kind of language processing. Because BERT is based entirely on self-attention processes, it is the first NLP technique. This is because its foundation are bidirectional Transformers. This is important because a word's meaning frequently changes as a phrase progresses. Each extra word adds to the overall meaning of the term the NLP algorithm is working on. In a sentence or phrase, the more words used generally, the more ambiguous the word in focus becomes.

Unlike text processing, NLP describes a computer's ability to understand human language. Text analysis, text production, and text manipulation are the only aspects of text processing. The legal document is used as a guide for examining other documents to see if they would have a favourable or unfavourable effect. The text file is loaded and after that, all punctuation is deleted and the text is converted to lowercase. There's one big string made up of all the strings. It is then required to separate and keep individual reviews in distinct list of elements.

3.3. Text Normalization

Text normalization is the process of giving a text that may not have had one canonical form previously. To improve the text's quality and get it ready for machine processing, pre-processing is done using text normalization. Normalization can help reduce the number of unique tokens in a text and eliminate variances from it and also revising the text by eliminating any unnecessary data. The goal of text normalization is to make the text better by removing unwanted and unimportant sections. Separating concerns is made feasible by normalizing text before storing or processing it, as this ensures consistency of input before actions are performed on it. Normalization is the process of making text less unpredictable and more akin to a predefined "standard." By doing this, the range of data that the computer has to analyse can be reduced, leading to an increase in efficiency.

3.4. Text Stemming

Stemming involves eliminating a word from its suffixes, prefixes, and other word elements until it reaches its root, or lemma. The process of stemming involves removing affixes from words to expose their core structure. NLP and Natural Language Understanding (NLU) both benefit from stemming. This happens when two over-stemmed words with the same root but separate stems are combined. False-positive results can also arise from over-stemming. False-negative outcomes when two words with the same root but different stems are stemmed can be explained by under-stemming.

3.5. Tokenization

The act of replacing sensitive information, such a credit card number, with a token i.e., a stand-in value is known as tokenization. Sensitive information still often has to be securely stored in one location with strict security measures for future reference. Tokenization involves breaking down the unprocessed text into comprehensible portions. Tokenization separates the source text into individual words and sentences called tokens. These tokens help with NLP model building or context understanding. By examining the word order in the text, tokenization aids in understanding its meaning.

3.6. Removal of Special Characters

Special characters are those that are neither numeric nor alphabetic. Punctuation marks and other symbols are few examples of it. Unlike alphanumeric characters, special characters can be employed in a variety of situations and in general, those characters never enhance the text in any form. Examples of its uses include parsing text upon the appearance of a particular special character or notifying when word expansions are required. They can be deleted from the text after being used to process the text in order to rid the NLP algorithms from any unnecessary information.

3.7. Bag of Words (BoW)

Text and documents are evaluated based on word count using a statistical language model known as BoW. This method does not take word order inside a document. BoW can be implemented using a Python dictionary, where each key denotes a word and each value denotes how frequently that word occurs in a document. Feature extractors that can be utilized in modeling, such as with machine learning approaches, can be made with this method. There are numerous methods to extract information from documents using this flexible and straightforward technique.

3.8. Removal of Stopwords

When a query is processed, stop words are not removed if they are the only words in the query. If every search phrase is removed during stop word processing, the result set is empty. Even in cases where all query phrases are stop words, search results will still be returned if stop word removal is deactivated. A class of frequently used terms in a language is called stop words. In English, “a,” “the,” “is,” “are,” and other words are stop words. Stop words are frequently used in text mining and NLP to remove overused and only partially meaningful terms. In order to take away the stop words, divide the text into tokens (words) and see if each token matches a word on the list of stop words. If the token matches a stop word, it is ignored. If not, add the token to the list of terms that are appropriate. The number of stop words in any human language is huge. The low-level information may get eliminated and increase the focus of the text on the important information by getting rid of these words.

3.9. GloVe

GloVe, an unsupervised learning technique, is trained on a vast amount of data to generate word embeddings that represent the semantics of the words. Then, these word embeddings can be used in other ML tasks with other small datasets. The trained token embeddings can be obtained using GloVe Embeddings. Although creating and training the own embeddings might not be feasible with small datasets, but doing so saves time. The underlying principle of GloVe word embeddings is to use statistics to infer word relationships. The co-occurrence matrix, in contrast to the occurrence matrix, indicates the frequency with which a given word pair appears together. A pair of words that commonly occur together is represented by each value in the co-occurrence matrix. It uses unsupervised learning to teach word embeddings for different word vector forms. The 50-dimensional GloVe vectors will be utilized in this function. When creating the embeddings for a GloVe model, the co-occurrence matrix created by the Corpus object is utilized. The dimensions of the GloVe: no_of_components is the dimension of the output vector produced by the GloVe algorithm, and learning_rate calculates how fast the algorithm reaches the minima. In the end, GloVe embedding was optimized using the stochastic gradient optimizer.

Optimisation is a mathematical technique where x is changed to minimize or maximize a function f(x). Realistic conditions will be minimized on a regular basis. Consequently, maximizing f(x) can only be accomplished by minimizing -f(x). The objective function is a kind of function f(x) that must be minimized or maximized. To get around the challenges with Gradient Descent, a minibatch uniformly selected from the training set can be sampled for each step of the algorithm. Choosing the model parameters that produce the most accurate results when compared to the expected ones can be done with ease using the straightforward yet effective stochastic gradient descent technique. Fitting linear classifiers and regressors under convex loss functions, such as (linear) Support Vector Machines and Logistic Regression, is made easy but incredibly effective with the use of Stochastic Gradient Descent (SGD).

When compared with Gradient Descent, Stochastic Gradient Descent is significantly faster and more appropriate for large datasets. The updates have a higher variance, since the gradient is only computed for one random point in every iteration rather than the entire dataset. SGD is more locally unstable than ADAM and reaches minima more frequently in flat or asymmetric basins or valleys, where it performs better in terms of generalization than other types of minima. The results consequently give reasons for the better generalization performance of SGD over ADAM. Since the gradient is a “stochastic approximation” of the “true” cost gradient, it is based on a single training sample. Because an update is made after each data instance has been examined, stochastic gradient descent may lead to substantially faster learning.

Figure 1. Process flow of the proposed work

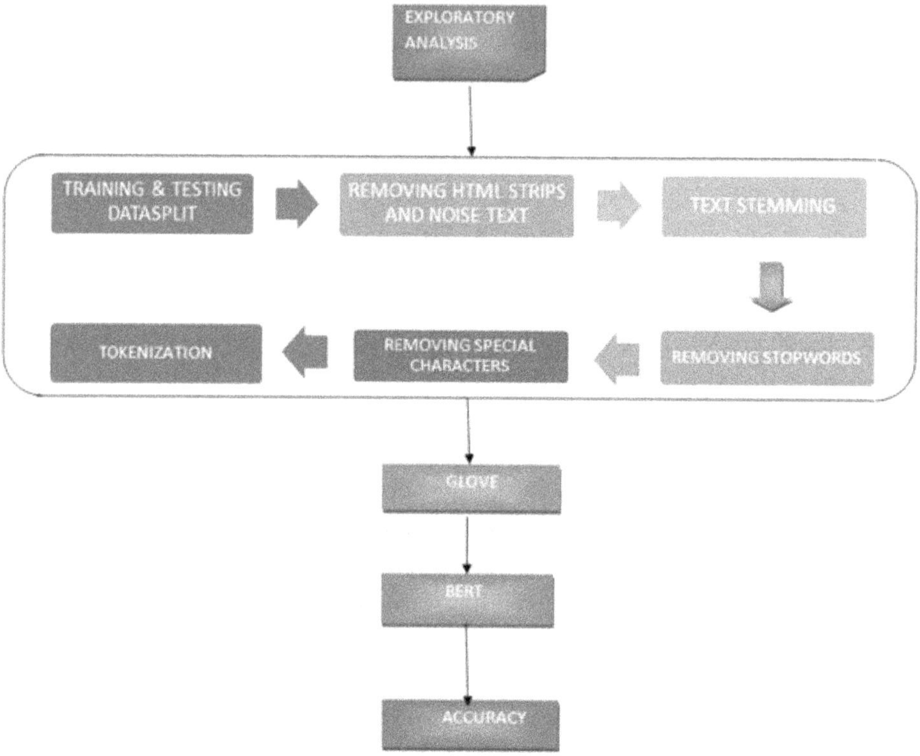

The figure 1 exhibits the process flow of proposed work by using different algorithms. Recurrent Neural Networks that learn to forecast the future from sequences of varying lengths employ BERT cells. Recurrent Neural Networks, can process any type of sequential data, including whole data streams (like audio or video) as well as single data points (like photographs). Normalization is incorporated into the process in certain ways.

Text rewriting and HTML stripping are removed, along with stop words. Also, the BoW model eliminates any special characters. For bidirectional encoder representation from transformer, these preprocesses are standard.

Figure 2. Sentiment analysis of mask attention BERT models

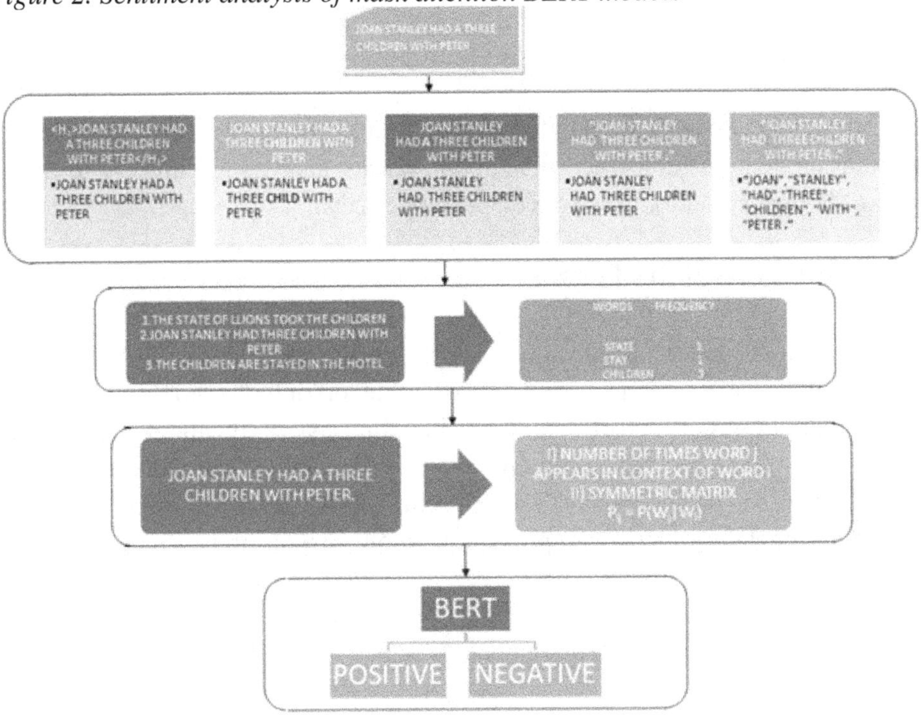

The figure 2 shows the internal sentimental analysis of mask attention BERT models and the derivation of the positive or negative outcome are shown in the figure. In real-world instances, this study investigates a deep learning model's capacity to binary classify data as either responsive or unresponsive using a BERT architecture. Even after optimization, the findings demonstrate a more stable development pattern, growing use of training samples, and a more significant performance on the larger dataset when compared to the traditional technique.

This paper looks into BERT's efficacy in document analysis utilising SA principles. Numerous mathematical and statistical tools were used to conduct the experiment. The Pandas library was utilised to manage and work with the corpus. Numerous characteristics of pandas can improve and as needed for a project, analyse data.

Keras contributed to the development of the BERT model. Additionally, Keras played a key role in integrating BERT with artificial neural networks. the process by which words are formed. Furthermore, embeddeds processed natural text using an open-source program that integrates cutting-edge statistical machine learning approaches. Colab, an incredible application for charting data which simplifies the process of creating graphs, charts and then presenting the analysis's findings is used.

4. EXPERIMENTAL RESULTS

4.1 Dataset

The "Public Support for High-Rise Buildings" dataset captures stakeholder opinions on high-rise construction in public spaces, analyzing sentiment to gauge support or opposition for urban development projects.

4.1.1. Structure of the Dataset

The dataset includes legal documents such as planning proposals, public consultations, zoning meeting minutes, and petitions, categorizing stakeholder opinions on the appropriateness of high-rise buildings in public spaces. It captures formal and semi-formal views from various groups, helping assess public support or opposition to high-rise urban developments. The dataset is categorized by different groups of individuals or stakeholders, who provide input on whether high-rise buildings are appropriate for specific public spaces.

Stakeholders are divided into several key categories based on their perceived interest or role in the urban development process:

1. **Local Residents:** Concerned about aesthetics, housing prices, traffic, and community impact from high-rise buildings.
2. **Urban Planners and Architects:** Support for high-rises as efficient urban growth, architecture, and land use solutions.
3. **Environmentalists:** Oppose high-rises due to concerns about ecological impact, green space loss, and sustainability.
4. **Government Officials and Policymakers:** Balance economic benefits with social equity and environmental concerns in development decisions.
5. **Developers and Investors:** Favour high-rise construction for financial returns, market demand, and long-term property value growth.
6. **General Public:** Opinions vary, from support for economic growth to scepticism about social and environmental consequences.

4.1.2. Sentiment Analysis of Legal Documents

The dataset uses sentiment analysis to classify viewpoints on high-rise buildings as positive, negative, or neutral, revealing public opinion patterns, stakeholder concerns, and the intensity of support or opposition.

4.2 Implementation

Thirty percent of the training data is utilized to evaluate the accuracy of the models, while the remaining seventy percent of the dataset is split into subsets for testing and training. For BERT, accuracy testing and training are carried out. BERT is used after the process to ascertain the accuracy and loss of the model. This method uses a stochastic gradient descent optimizer in conjunction with the GloVe for their embedding to increase precision.

Figure 3. Implementation of GloVe with the stochastic gradient descent optimizer

```
Epoch 1/10
200/200 - 48s - loss: 0.6728 - accuracy: 0.5932 - val_loss: 0.6559 - val_accuracy: 0.6950 - 48s/epoch - 242ms/step
Epoch 2/10
200/200 - 40s - loss: 0.6597 - accuracy: 0.6383 - val_loss: 0.6434 - val_accuracy: 0.6900 - 40s/epoch - 199ms/step
Epoch 3/10
200/200 - 39s - loss: 0.6493 - accuracy: 0.6583 - val_loss: 0.6363 - val_accuracy: 0.6950 - 39s/epoch - 197ms/step
Epoch 4/10
200/200 - 41s - loss: 0.6510 - accuracy: 0.6533 - val_loss: 0.6320 - val_accuracy: 0.6950 - 41s/epoch - 205ms/step
Epoch 5/10
200/200 - 39s - loss: 0.6480 - accuracy: 0.6583 - val_loss: 0.6293 - val_accuracy: 0.6950 - 39s/epoch - 193ms/step
Epoch 6/10
200/200 - 40s - loss: 0.6451 - accuracy: 0.6571 - val_loss: 0.6277 - val_accuracy: 0.6950 - 40s/epoch - 198ms/step
Epoch 7/10
200/200 - 38s - loss: 0.6460 - accuracy: 0.6596 - val_loss: 0.6265 - val_accuracy: 0.6950 - 38s/epoch - 192ms/step
Epoch 8/10
200/200 - 39s - loss: 0.6447 - accuracy: 0.6583 - val_loss: 0.6260 - val_accuracy: 0.6950 - 39s/epoch - 193ms/step
Epoch 9/10
200/200 - 41s - loss: 0.6429 - accuracy: 0.6583 - val_loss: 0.6255 - val_accuracy: 0.6950 - 41s/epoch - 207ms/step
Epoch 10/10
200/200 - 37s - loss: 0.6450 - accuracy: 0.6646 - val_loss: 0.6251 - val_accuracy: 0.6950 - 37s/epoch - 186ms/step
```

Figure 4. Explains the implementation of BERT along with their layers and the parameter ranges

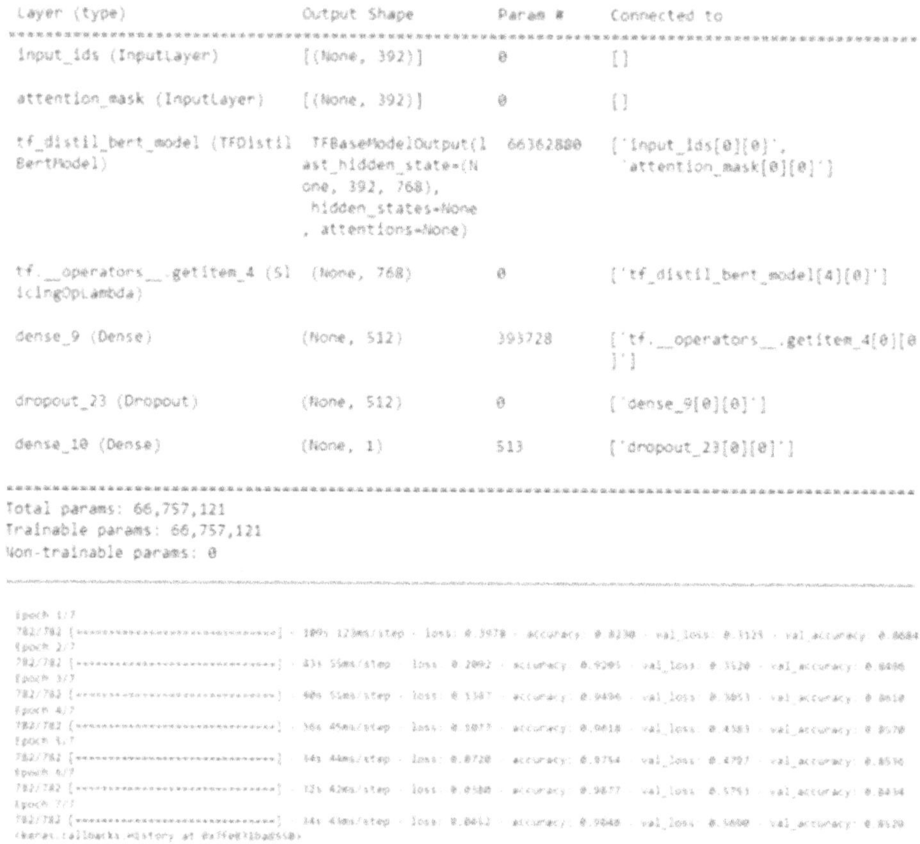

4.3 Implementation of Bert

To assess the models, the test dataset is used. The process is gone through again till a satisfied result is attained after manually selecting the hyper-parameter. Accuracy and loss are the assessment criteria that are considered for every model. Accuracy and loss for BERT is also shown in order to distinguish the impacts of the models. Lastly, the metrics such as Precision and defeat is utilized to compile the algorithm's output. The graphs shown in Figure 4 shows BERT accuracy in this instance. The figure explains the accuracy and loss percentage and their graph flow and also it gives the better accuracy and low level of loss.

With excellent precision and little loss, BERT received the highest ranking.

Accuracy is a measure employed to evaluate the overall efficiency of a model. When each lesson is equally important, it helps. It helps when every class has the same significance. It is determined by dividing the total number of projections by the sum of precise predictions.

A loss function evaluates the neural network's ability to accurately simulate the training data through a comparison of the expected and intended output values. The disparity in output during training between the objective and the anticipated is reduced.

Figure 5. Graph for accuracy and loss

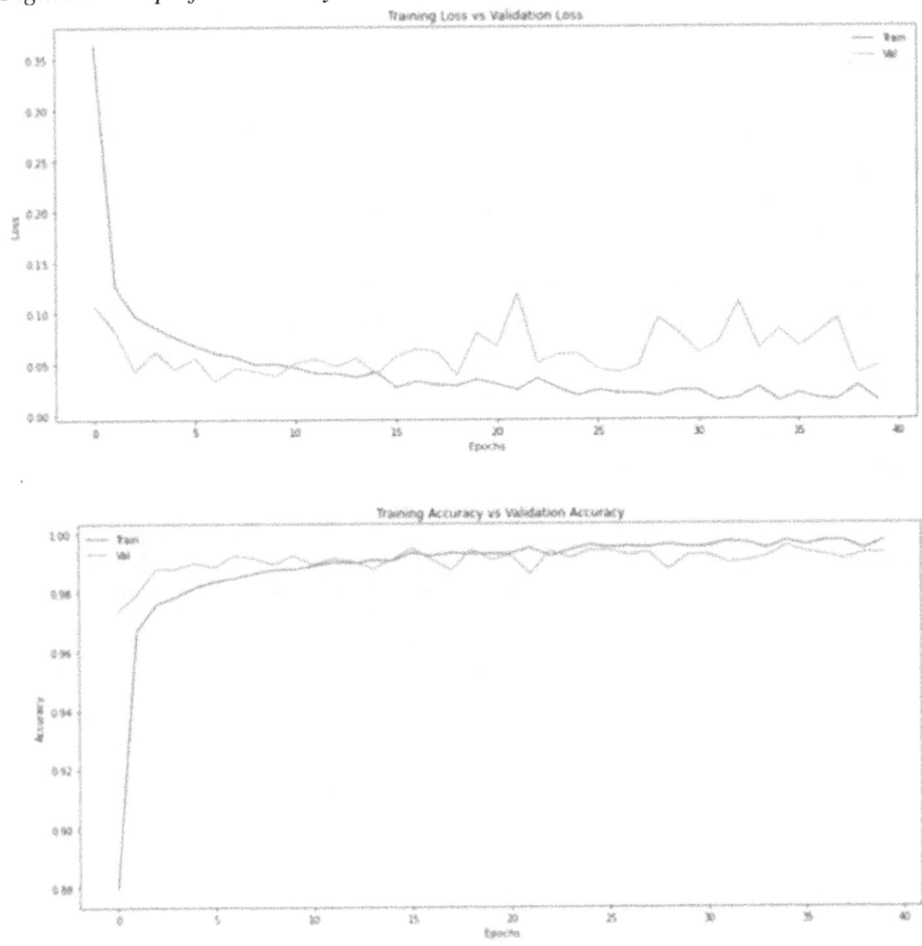

i) Comparative Analysis of GloVe and Word2vec

The implementation of global word-to-word co-occurrence counts throughout the whole corpus forms the basis of the GloVe model. However, Word2vec uses co-occurrence within the context of the native language. (Neighbouring words).

Table 1. Comparison of GloVe and word2vec

Algorithm	Accuracy	Loss	Val. Acc	Val. Loss
GLOVE	89.5	10.5	79.8	15.2
WORD2VEC	78.2	15.9	68.5	20.3

ii) Comparative Analysis of algorithms

According to the statistics, models generally perform better than LSTM, GRU, Bi-LSTM, and BERT. By combining data from many entries, BERT is more effective in capturing the underlying context. For particular types of data, such as word prediction in the input phrase and text parsing, BERT would outperform traditional LSTM and GRU, BiLSTM. In comparison to these models, BERT produces the best outcome. These are the comparative graphs for the gated recurrent unit, bidirectional encoder representation from transformers, bidirectional long short-term memory, and long short-term memory. Here, the figures display the accuracy and loss of the model. Compared to the BERT, the LSTM, Bi-LSTM, and GRU have reduced accuracy requirements.

Table 2. Comparison of existing algorithms

Algorithm	Accuracy	Loss
LSTM	93.75	24.76
GRU	92.86	38.3
Bi-LSTM	96.97	19.47
BERT	98.48	4.52

4.4 Performance Metrics

The performance metrics employed in this work include accuracy, loss, validation accuracy, and validation loss.

In this work, performance measurements such as accuracy, loss, validation accuracy, and validation loss are employed.

Accuracy: The accuracy of the model serves as a measure for its effectiveness in each class.

Accuracy = *Number of correct Predictions / Total number of Predictions*

Loss: A loss function compares the desired outcome with anticipated outcomes to determine the rate at which the neural network mimics the training set. During the training phase, the goal is to reduce the variation between expected and observed outputs.

Validation Accuracy: A performance indicator used to assess the efficacy of different models is validation accuracy. The k-fold cross-validation method frequently produces fewer biased models since all of the data points from the original dataset will appear in both the training and testing sets.

Validation Loss: The information provided by the training and validation loss values is crucial because it helps us identify any learning issues that may result in an underfit or an overfit model by illuminating how the learning performance varies over the course of an epoch.

5. CONCLUSION

Sentiment Analysis using deep learning models and related techniques applied to legal texts was covered in this paper. To evaluate BERT models, experiments are conducted on datasets with a variety of themes, including court cases and legal papers. This data, when paired with research's conclusions, allows us to fully comprehend how deep learning models are used to SA and how they work in tandem with text preparation strategies. This work investigates a deep learning model based on BERT's ability.

Even after optimisation, the results show a more constant growth pattern, increasing numbers of training samples needed, and a more meaningful performance on the bigger dataset when compared to the standard technique. Since legal papers are usually constituted of a few words or a small paragraph that are often chosen as pertinent content, the problem is citation of the suitable language or terms. Even still, systems that use a BoW without a sequence to better extract characteristics from data so that sentences or phrases may be understood are more effective than text categorization using three separate categories, which learn texts in sequences. This directly affects the study of explicable predictions. Exploring the similarities and differences between that methodology and the deep learning approach is covered in this chapter.

In particular, a significant portion of the work's labelled text contains annotations in the form of sentences. Consequently, using full-text texts to train these phrases may provide some insight on the appropriate adjustments. This work can be extended its focus to include non-textual data such as charts, legal diagrams or multimedia evidences. Such sophisticated multimodal fusion approaches and their application impacts in real-world contexts can be further explored in future studies.

REFERENCES

Acheampong, Nunoo-Mensah, & Chen. (2021). Transformer models for text-based emotion detection: a review of BERT-based approaches. .DOI: 10.1007/s10462-021-09958-2

Birjali, M., Kasri, M., & Beni-Hssane, A. (2021). A comprehensive survey on sentiment analysis: Approaches, challenges and trends. https://www.sciencedirect.com/science/article/abs/pii/S095070512100397X

Dang, N. C., Moreno-García, M. N., & De la Prieta, F. (2020). Sentiment Analysis Based on Deep Learning: A Comparative Study. https://www.mdpi.com/2079-9292/9/3/483

Habimana, Li, Li, Gu, & Yu. (2020). Sentiment analysis using deep learning approaches: an overview. .DOI: 10.1007/s11432-018-9941-6

Hoang, M., Bihorac, O. A., & Rouces, J. (2019). Aspect-Based Sentiment Analysis using BERT. https://aclanthology.org/W19-6120

Jochen, H. M. H., Siebert, C., & Schamp, C. (2022). More than a Feeling: Accuracy and Application of Sentiment Analysis. https://www.sciencedirect.com/science/article/pii/S0167811622000477

Kamyab, M., Liu, G., & Adjeisah, M. (2021). Attention-Based CNN and Bi-LSTM Model Based on TF-IDF and GloVe Word Embedding for Sentiment Analysis. https://www.mdpi.com/2076-3417/11/23/11255

Koroteev, M. V. (2021), BERT: A Review of Applications in Natural Language Processing and Understanding. https://arxiv.org/abs/2103.11943

Ligthart, A., Catal, C., & Tekinerdogan, B. (2021). Systematic reviews in sentiment analysis: A tertiary study. *Artificial Intelligence Review*, 54(7), 4997–5053. Advance online publication. DOI: 10.1007/s10462-021-09973-3

Liu, Shi, Ji, & Jia. (2019). A Survey of Sentiment Analysis Based on Transfer Learning. .DOI: 10.1109/ACCESS.2019.2925059

Munikar, M., Shakya, S., & Shrestha, A. (2019). Fine-grained Sentiment Classification using BERT. DOI: 10.1109/AITB48515.2019.8947435

Nandwani, P., & Verma, R. (2021). A review on sentiment analysis and emotion detection from text. https://link.springer.com/article/10.1007/s13278-021-00776-6

Ruder, S., Peters, M. E., Swayamdipta, S., & Wolf, T. (2019). Transfer Learning in Natural Language Processing. https://aclanthology.org/N19-5004/

Wankhade, M., Annavarapu, C. S. R., & Kulkarni, C. (2022). A survey on sentiment analysis methods, applications and challenges. https://link.springer.com/article/10.1007/s10462-022-10144-1

Xu, Meng, Qiu, Yu, & Wu. (2019). Sentiment Analysis of Comment Texts Based on BiLSTM. .DOI: 10.1109/ACCESS.2019.2909919

Xu, H., Liu, B., Shu, L., & Philip, S. Yu. (2019), BERT Post-Training for Review Reading Comprehension and Aspect-based Sentiment Analysis, /arXiv.1904.02232DOI: 10.48550

Yadav, A., & Vishwakarma, D. K. (2020). Sentiment analysis using deep learning architectures: A review. *Artificial Intelligence Review*, 53(6), 4335–4385. Advance online publication. DOI: 10.1007/s10462-019-09794-5

Zhuang, Qi, Duan, Xi, Zhu, & Zhu. (2020). A Comprehensive Survey on Transfer Learning. DOI: 10.1109/JPROC.2020.3004555

Chapter 11
AI Implementation for Smart Wearable

P. Mohammed Shameem
University of West London, UK

A. Sampath Dakshina Murthy
https://orcid.org/0000-0002-9960-6373
Vignan's Institute of Information Technology, India

Judy Flavia B.
SRM Institute of Science and Technology, India

Nidhya M. S.
https://orcid.org/0000-0002-1290-4520
Dayananda Sagar University, India

Mohit Tiwari
https://orcid.org/0000-0003-1836-3451
Bharati Vidyapeeth's College of Engineering, India

Balajee Maram
https://orcid.org/0000-0001-5635-5642
SR University, India

ABSTRACT

Evolution of AI in the medical field is the biggest challenge. Research organisations are committed to continuing the in-depth quest for intelligence because of specific long-term demands and challenges in medicine. Because of developments in areas like the internet of things, cloud computing, and 5G mobile networks, artificial intelligence (AI) technology is being used in healthcare. Additionally, improved public services are made possible by the extensive integration of IoT technology and artificial intelligence, which gradually enhances diagnostic and therapeutic capabilities. The authors join the thoughts behind unambiguous calculations like to portray situation-based applications like distant conclusion and clinical coordination, pediatric escalated care units, cardiovascular concentrated care units, trauma centers, venous thromboembolism, patient consideration, and imaging utilizing the web of things (IoT), the cloud, huge information examination, and AI in medical services.

DOI: 10.4018/979-8-3693-7868-7.ch011

1. INTRODUCTION

The healthcare system is struggling to keep up with the demands of a growing population. In the healthcare literature study, numerous issues were identified, including inadequate communication techniques, prolonged hospital stays, inefficient patient flow, and limited staffing. This chapter will attempt to achieve just that by addressing these issues. The availability of resources, data security, and communication infrastructure are the top concerns of IoT developers. When integrated with other possible critical obstacles, it causes a plethora of issues (Patel & Shah, 2021). As their populations grow, smart cities produce and implement innovative solutions to provide a more hospitable setting for their residents. We need a robust healthcare system so that workers may focus on their duties without undue distraction (Alizadeh, 2017). A patient record system that is supported by Internet of Things (IoT) devices and machine learning (ML) protocols and is linked with different healthcare apps was proposed by the author as part of a smart city paradigm. A patient record framework that functions admirably with the right detecting components and assemblies organized and unstructured information for ML examination is at the core of RHM's innovation and architecture (Chong et al., 2018). Communication protocols have emerged as a necessity in order to transfer information and signs between IoT gadgets, frameworks, and models (Alizadeh, 2017).

Figure 1. Basic elements for IoT-enabled health care system

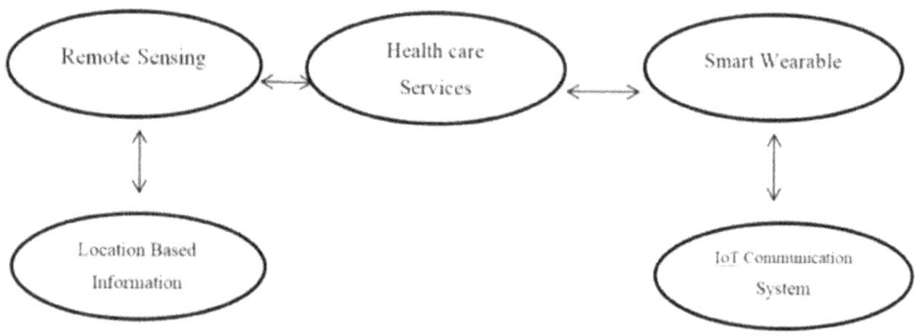

The relationship of various frameworks, models, and structures that are utilized to set in motion the central parts of an IoT-empowered medical care framework is displayed in Figure Administrations in these many structures have been depicted in detail (Mora, Deakin, & Reid, 2018). A brilliant city gives an unrivalled personal satisfaction that is both more helpful and more sumptuous. Residents are additionally getting the opportunity to partake in cultural exercises that straightforwardly add to addressing their necessities. To cooperate with and exploit these contributions, residents utilize different brilliant gadgets. The term "smart service" refers to a certain, high-tech network arrangement in which a large volume of citizen-provided data is sent across the Internet.

1.2 Services, Applications, and Remote Sensing in Healthcare

There have been several studies and uses of the notion of remote sensing in the field of healthcare monitoring services (Veenis & Brugts, 2020). In order to gather, maintain, and store patients' electronic health data (EHRs), a patient record management centre (PRMC) is essential to the smart city healthcare system (Deshmukh, 2017). The patient's vital signs are measured and recorded, including an electrocardiogram (ECG), blood pressure, and pulse. When a patient has a medical sensor attached to them, data about the outside environment, such as humidity and temperature, may be sent to a healthcare provider for analysis (Livingston et al., 2017).

1.3. Engineering and Design Principles RHM

The clinical sensors worn by the patient and the guardian's shrewd gadget both give information into the wellbeing checking framework. The wellbeing observing server (HMS) goes about as the framework's cerebrum, dissecting the patient's current condition and past clinical information to create an individualized medical care plan (IHP) in genuine time (Alghanim, Rahman, & Hossain, 2017). It likewise produces signal cautions, alerts, and exemptions during serious climate. A clinic administration for getting a wellbeing concern's determination, a wellbeing observing help for evaluation and management, and a fast reaction are the smartservice's center parts. The PRMC additionally manages information examination and capacity. The IHP gets consistent data from the prosperity noticing structure. From the composed report given by HMS and the patient's verifiable clinical information recovered from the PRMC, where all private records are safeguarded, the medical clinic framework empowers specialists to extrapolate data about a patient's wellbeing.

Data and information pertaining to a patient's health can be found in the PRMC, which houses electronic health records (Alghanim, Rahman, & Hossain, 2017). In addition, it sends out the constraint and protocol headers that are required by the linked systems. The health-tracking system stores data locally as well. As the essential for a smoothed out innovative design for brilliant medical care administration, this store houses the patient's clinical history and wellbeing data. The patient's verifiable wellbeing information and explicit data like their name, address, telephone number, and so on. are put away in an adaptable way in the patient's focal electronic wellbeing record (PC-EHR).

1.4 Sensing, Watching, and Managing

Smarter healthcare delivery requires sensors, monitoring, and control systems. These sensors' numbers automate healthcare professionals' monitoring and control. The information revealed by these sensors permit medical services specialists to computerize different observing and control techniques. The Internet of Things (IoT), wireless sensor networks, deep learning, and different innovations can be generally used to accomplish these objectives actually (Singh et al., 2021). Sensors might be either precisely embedded or worn remotely, for example, in smartwatches.

Information transmission happens through passages and remote organizations to arrive at medical services suppliers (Movassaghi, Abolhasan, & L-C, 2014). Electro-chemicalglucose sensors and other implanted sensors aid in diabetes monitoring and management (Lucisano, Routh, & Lin, 2016). Patients also use AI tools for diabetes self-management and customization. Patients with diabetes may employ systems that include sensors that communicate data to smartphones in order to monitor their blood sugar levels (Chaki, Ganesh, Cidham, & Theertan, 2020).

In the treatment of sleep apnea, rheumatoid arthritis, intracranial pressure, and cardiac arrhythmias, a number of additional high-tech sensors are utilized (Cook, Duncan, Sprint, & Fritz, 2018). The administration and operation of these devices are the primary obstacles. It's conceivable that those in control miss the mark on proper preparation or simply disregard to keep the hardware charged. In this way, it is pivotal to execute zero-impacts advancements (ZETs) to free the client from obligation regarding working and dealing with the sensors (Sharma, 2019). Sicknesses like cardiovascular infection and dementia are just two of numerous that might be followed the utilization of remote detecting. There must always be some kind of behavioral monitoring method included in the treatment for these kinds of diseases. According to one estimate, 47 million people worldwide will have dementia in 2017, an unprecedented number. By 2050, this figure is supposed to ascend to 132 million (Lucisano, Routh, & Lin, 2016). The Internet of Things and artificial intelligence, in conjunction with cutting-edge remote sensing technologies, would make the checking and control important for actually treating these infections less difficult.

1.5 Data Based on a Specific Location

Smart city data analyticssystems and implementations are ideal for location-based services. The user's location is determined by combining demographic and global positioning system data. The smart city integrates and analyses the gathered data to help healthcare professionals deliver high-quality treatment at convenient times and locations. Information is gathered through high-tech gadgets like cellphones and wristwatches. A location-based information system that makes use of GPS coordinates may determine a user's longitude and latitude.

1.6 Networks for the Internet of Things

Due to the exhaustion of IPv4 resources, IPv6 is playing a crucial role in the IoT transition (Kumar, Tiwari, & Zymbler, 2019). It's a tactic for packet-switched networks that allows for the transmission of datagrams from beginning to finish, as well as the provision of telecommunications and Internet convergence services and protocols for advanced networks (TISPAN) and 3GPP. It's an access point for other networks and the roaming service.Two potent technologies that help the IoT work are RFID and NFC (Catarinucci, Donno, & Mainetti, 2015).

RFID, or radio frequency identification, is a kind of short-range communication that automatically reads and tracks tags attached to items via the use of an electromagnetic field. RFID and coordinating sensor advances improve figuring, detecting, and systems administration limits in other latent frameworks, while likewise advancing various novel open doors inside the IoT worldview. IEEE 802.15.1, all the more regularly alluded to as Bluetooth, works in the 2.4 GHz global ISM (modern, logical, and clinical) band for short-range IoT applications. The Bluetooth particular vested party (SIG) pushed for Bluetooth low energy (BLE) to be remembered for the determinations for Bluetooth 4.0 and Bluetooth 5.

Media access control (Macintosh) and actual layer (PHY) necessities for remote LANs, frequently known as remote loyalty (Wi-Fi), are the primary focal point of IEEE 802.11. The biggest problem with this technology, in comparison to Zigbee and Bluetooth, is that it uses a lot of power. Alterations are expected to further develop versatility, wandering, and QoS executions all at the same time. IEEE 802.11ah low power Wi-Fi, for instance, functions admirably with an assortment of Web of Things use cases. They may provide quality of service, increased efficiency and productivity, scalability to many devices, and inexpensive solutions (Adame et al., 2014; Kiryanov et al., 2019; Maier & Ebrahimzadeh, 2018).

2. MODELS AND CONCEPTS FOR HEALTHCARE MONITORING FROM A DISTANCE

High humidity may damage some sensors, and certain temperatures can pose danger to certain types of energy sources (Ermes, Pärkkä, & Mäntyjärvi, 2008). A basic plan for a distant medical care framework shows how the fashioner functions inside these constraints to give new arrangements or refine existing ones. A few of the technologies and methods that are taken into consideration include the constrained application protocol (CoAP), support vector machine (SVM), k-means, clinical correlation analysis (CCA), Bluetooth, Wi-Fi, and RFID. The goal of Internet of Things-based healthcare systems is to enhance patient health and the quality of life in smart cities (Peña-Ayala, 2014).

2.1 Mobile Health-Centric Layout

Integration of the Internet of Things in healthcare systems necessitates an end-to-end architecture for linking IoT-based sensing devices to clinical caresystems (Almotiri, Khan, & Alghamdi, 2016). One such IoT-based paradigm that has been developed and incorporated into the healthcare system is mHealth.There are three distinct components to mHealth's structure. In the information-gathering layer, IoT-based technologies are used to specifically detect and collect health-related characteristics (Veenis & Brugts, 2020). Sensors that measure things like blood sugar or heart rate may be used to keep tabs on a person's fitness status (think Fitbit). The data storage layer incorporates both massive data storage and quick retrieval of medical records.The analysis of this sensor data occurs at the information processing layer, where several approaches are used, among them AI-based and non-AI-based algorithms (Dziak, Jachimczyk, & Kulesza, 2017). The detected data must be sent from the sensing devices to the storage layer and the processing layer.mHealth is straightforward and simple to use; it is compatible with Bluetooth Low Energy (BLE), ANT, Zigbee, Near Field Communication (NFC), and Wi-Fi.

2.2. A Design Based on 6LoWPAN

Internet Protocol (IP) based network systems are pervasive. Therefore, it is more tempting to use IP network systems to guarantee the transfer of IoT-based medical care information. However, the IPV6 system needs a lot of energy to handle all that data and bandwidth. For IoT-based systems, the idea that processing power would be available 24/7 adds a layer of complexity. In addition, 6LoWPAN (Tanaka, Minet, & Watteyne, 2019) has been recommended as the best paradigm for IoT-based network infrastructure.

2.3 CoAP-Based Design

In (Garcia-Carrillo, Marin-Lopez, Kandasamy, & Pelov, 2017), we see a description of the simulated CoAP at work in healthcare delivery systems. CoAP is a multi-tiered application protocol designed specifically for low-power sensors.

CoAP application systems provide both best-effort and reliable interactions via the use of constraint (CON) and acknowledgment (ACK) data, respectively. The CoAP protocol would allow healthcare networks to transmit sensed data over any available channel. Similar to HTTP, the CoAP application system includes four methods for exchanging sensed data: post, delete, get, and put.

2.4 Modelling From Health Care Standards

Chronic heart failure patients who participate in RHM have been shown to have better health (Veenis & Brugts, 2020), leading to fewer hospitalisations and better clinical results overall. Data collection for patient specialists (PAs) from on-board sensors, data transmission to a server, participation, and data sharing from various devices, and analysis to hand-off information back to the patient are just a piece of the ordinary features of the splendid contraptions that are becoming regular practice in RHM as vaults of information exchange. The effect of brilliant gadgets' battery strength on consistence with far off medical services observing frameworks is tried utilizing streamlining approaches used to a battery-based system (Sharma, 2019). System compliance might be improved by reducing the number of times a patient recharges their smartphone. The method for optimising battery life was field- and lab-tested.

The purpose of the experiment was to establish criteria for determining the efficacy of technologies in lowering the danger of cardiovascular disease (CVD). Utilizing creative nanosystems, bio-dynamic synthetics, PC investigation, and equipment combination, scientists had the option to achieve the direct activity and execution assessment vital for quick remedial decisions (Jain et al., 2021). Carbon nanotube (CNT) models and prototypes have been created using conformal patch antenna arrays in another endeavor (Patel & Shah, 2021). In their research, arrays of patch antennas were constructed using carbon nanotubes, which can be printed onto fabric using an ink jet printer. Radio recurrence (RF) transmitter framework schematics and reproduction in Agilent Progressed Plan Framework (Promotions) were used in the gearbox plan. The study recommended the precision of random designs and provided simulation methodologies to test their viability as well as diagnostic tools (Khan & Zubair, 2020). Thanks to a study of carbon nanotube (CNT) patch antennas, the design described in the paper improved antenna metrics like VSWR, return loss, gain, radiation pattern, and efficient energy harvesting (Patel & Shah, 2021). Due to its unusual electrical properties, CNT has been shown to have the potential for a polymer-CNT nanocomposite antenna that is less conformable. To further improve patients' RHM, RFtransmitters may be interleaved with cosy antennas for smooth ECG signal transmission.

3. REMOTE SENSING, MONITORING, AND CONTROLLING USING ARTIFICIAL INTELLIGENCE (AI), DEEP LEARNING (DL), MACHINE LEARNING (ML), AND BIG DATA

Prescient examination completed utilizing ML-based far off medical care observing administrations might help emergency clinics in quickly releasing patients. In order to better manage a group of patients with many risk factors, predictive analysis facilitates the creation of a risk stratification model. These models use patient-specific dynamic data to make predictions about future outcomes and formulate preventative measures. Insights that help profound advancing as a critical piece of ML (Rahman et al., 2020) corroborate the effectiveness of ML-based applications. Clinical factors and physiological indicators have been shown to be useful in predicting hospital readmissions (Chaki, Ganesh, Cidham, & Theertan, 2020). Here, a substantial amount of support for the patient health system may be incorporated. To facilitate data collecting and sharing in advanced information systems (Chaki, Ganesh, Cidham, & Theertan, 2020) contemporary institutions have begun to use mobile data gathering and inspection tools. However, it is important to account for data that is noisy, has been lost in transmission, or is incomplete.

3.1 Algorithms for Machine Learning

For tiny data analysis, it is important to identify the desired outcome. A challenging aspect of any IoT-powered smart world is choosing or synthesising the best data mining method. An algorithm's primary goals should be to provide valuable analytics, make accurate predictions of the future, and exert efficient management over the network and its resources (Sunhare, Chowdhary, & Chattopadhyay, 2020). Clustering methods and data may be used to uncover the structure of unlabeled data. The most widely used and well-described clustering method is K-means, which is explained in (Mahdavinejad, Rezvan, & Burcins, 2018). It's suitable for big data sets and a variety of data formats. The K-means algorithm was proposed for use in the administration of data from smart homes and smart cities in a research by (Gil et al., 2019). D-B scan, another clustering approach for organising unlabeled data, is presented in (Mahdavinejad, Rezvan, & Burcins, 2018). It's also used to group together little citizens in (Khan & Zubair, 2020).

Smart data anomalies and discrepancies may be discovered using two crucial techniques. The first is the precise tracking of anomalies and noisy data using the oneclass SVM and PCA-based anomaly detection algorithms described in (Mahdavinejad, Rezvan, & Burcins, 2018). One research looked for and identified activity outliers using one-class support vector machines (OCSVMs). Most often used algorithms (Grzelak & Podlaski, 2019) for value forecasting and sequence data grouping are those based on linear regression and support vector regression (SVR), both of which are detailed in (Mahdavinejad, Rezvan, & Burcins, 2018). These algorithms employ the selected models for processing and training data with fast-paced features. For instance, to classify the actions of intelligent citizens (Du et al., 2020), utilized a linear regression technique in real time (Ma et al., 2013). Neural networks are superior to other learning models for function approximation problems when it comes to classifying data. Furthermore, as precision in data is required, a multi-class neutral network, with its lengthy training period, should provide the optimum option. Khanet al. (n.d.) and Liu et al. (2019) both used SVM to categorise traffic data. According to Mahdavinejad, Rezvan, & Burcins (2018), two of the most used techniques for extracting data features are principal component analysis (PCA) and canonical correlation analysis (CCA). In addition, CCA may illustrate the connection between the two sets of information. Both PCA and CCA include variants that may be used to spot outliers.

3.2 Home Healthcare Remote Monitoring

Devices belonging to the Internet of Things include wireless sensors, microcontrollers, and radio transceivers. It takes into account the importance of healthcare for people in effectively monitoring, managing, detecting, and responding to data received from the system (Surantha et al., 2021). The United States and other forward-thinking nations have been early adopters of telehealth remote monitoring. The rising confidence in the adequacy of far off medical care in further developing patient wellbeing is generally liable for this shift (Avila et al., 2017). The outcomes showed that patients' assumptions for progress while involving IoT for eHealth were insignificant, which ought to empower item architects, medical care suppliers, and advertisers to pursue better association among gadgets and patients. Using R. J. Rosati's methods (Rosati, 2009), more than 100 remote screens were painstakingly introduced in the homes of patients with huge mental disabilities. Additionally, information regarding the patient's health, medications, and social network was gathered. This study endeavored to decide whether the beneficial outcomes of remote observing medical care on persistent improvement were essentially unique in relation to those displayed in hospitalized patients by utilizing a benchmark group that was generally indistinguishable from the dynamic gathering with the exception of the shortfall of remote checking. A significant decrease in hospitalisations was seen (proof of the value of remote monitoring in lieu of hospitalisation).Patients in the remote healthcare monitoring group showed a lower hospitalisation rate (35.6%) across all diagnoses than those in the control group (45.5%). Patients who were being monitored remotely had significantly fewer nurse visits per week than the control group. Remote patient checking (RPM) can give excellent consideration to the old and the basically wiped out in the solace of their own homes, as per research by T. Bratan and M. Clarke. This discredits that overseeing extreme clinical circumstances through far off medical care observing is unimaginable or unreasonable (Bratan, Ondokuz, & Clarke, 2006). Recent studies have presented a number of indicators of comprehensive detection and monitoring by using a totally automated AD monitoring report. Furthermore, the system separates among great and undesirable people (Khan & Zubair, 2020). The infrastructure of healthcare systems cannot function without the use of remote healthcare monitoring. Researchers in the UK found that RPM was used in 13 different healthcare initiatives and services. The study singled out eight initiatives for further scrutiny:

Conditions requiring close observing incorporate one with constant obstructive pneumonic infection (COPD), one with persistent cardiovascular breakdown (CHF), one with diabetes, and one with an unsound condition including the heart, circulatory strain, or heartbeat. Despite the fact that an association with essential consideration was remembered for the frameworks' models and operational framework before to the drive, they were not gathering their common wellbeing administrations goals. In the wake of evaluating the framework's defects, they fostered an essential consideration based, clinically-coordinated checking framework.

3.3 Medical Internet of Things Use Cases

One more element of IoT administrations is the nearby observing of IoT applications (Islam et al., 2015). A medical care framework structure with many scientific information applications for dealing with information sources like electronic wellbeing records and clinical pictures has been the subject of late exploration (Palanisamy & Thirunavukarasu, 2019). Although app usage by people with illnesses and others is inevitable, it is clear that app creation is driven by demand for certain services (Lucisano, Routh, & Lin, 2016). One might infer that administrations are fixated on what the maker brings to the table, while applications are custom fitted to the end clients. A couple of late applications that have used different ML calculations likewise incorporate effective evaluating of drunkards, feeling recognition in utilitarian advances, and mishap power expectation for extreme wounds (Jayadev & Bellary, 2021). Impressive innovative work (Research and development) consideration has been paid to IoT-driven medical services frameworks and advancements, including how the IoT could support pediatric and geriatric consideration, persistent illness observing, individual health, and movement the executives. Many types of modern technology, including gadgets, wearables, and medical instruments, were described in (Islam et al., 2015). conveyance of different operations should be visible in these original medical care items and gadgets. The following is a discussion of several single- and clustered-condition applications for the Internet of Things in healthcare.

Table 1 provides a review of the many uses, scenarios, and implementations of IoT-based sensors in the healthcare industry.

3.4 Applications for Smart Devices in Healthcare Implementations

Electronic contraptions that are constrained by sensors in savvy gadgets have seen an ascent being developed as of late. This shift demonstrates how smart gadgets have emerged as primary motivators for Internet of Things innovation. If you want to provide flawless, reliable, and mobile services across a wide range of devices, you'll need to integrate IoT with those fields [30]. For brilliant gadgets to be a useful instrument in the conveyance of clinical consideration, different programming applications and equipment things have been worked to guarantee their interoperability with savvy gadgets (Islam et al., 2015). A top to bottom examination of wellbeing applications' highlights and the way that they associate with those of brilliant gadgets was spread out in purposeful detail (Jayadev & Bellary, 2021). Patient applications and health apps in general were covered in the article. Auxiliary applications, which include those that may assist educate, train, and enlighten people about healthcare, were also considered.

The accompanying clinical issues may be advantageously checked and analyzed utilizing the capacities currently accessible on shrewd gadgets. Moreover, progress is useful in the clinical sciences for making exact judgments and giving help. Differentiating between chronic care for complex diseases and emergency care like trips to the emergency department may be aided by this. Multiple symptoms manifest in patients with advanced cases of diabetes. Asthma assaults, extreme respiratory plot hindrances, hypersensitive rhinitis, and other nasal-related respiratory, cardiovascular, vascular, metabolic, cutaneous, and irresistible symptoms (Chong et al., 2018). In Table 1, we have a brief overview of the available commercial medical goods that might be considered cornerstone products for IoT-based network health gadgets.

Table 1. Wearable Internet of Things devices for medical use

Smart wearable	Use cases	Technology applied	Description
Glucose Level Sensing	Checking sugar levels regularly. Share physiological data between patients and doctors in real time.	IoT, IPv6	a device that is safe to use and can measure glucose levels in the blood. It has a glucose screen, some sort of foundation handling, and either a call or PC interface.
Electrocardiogram Monitoring	Detecting electromagnetic signals using an algorithm for ECG monitoring	Electrocardiogram, IoT frameworks, anomaly detection	Network for ECG monitoring in the Internet of Things that relies on wireless data capture and transmission
Blood Pressure Monitoring	Use with an Internet of Things device, such as an Apple Smart Device, to record blood pressure readings. The taking of blood pressure was also computerised using an Internet of Things terminal.	IoT frameworks, Pressure Sensor	An IoT-based BP monitor is created by splicing together a KIT metre for blood pressure and an NFCcellularphone. The integrated methods are superior for measuring blood pressure.
Body Temperature Monitor	Used for taking readings and sending them in real time, temperature monitors	Thermometer Sensors, IoT System	A thermometer and an Internet of Things channel are needed for this. Body temperature is measured and sent over the Internet of Things' RFIDnode.
Oxygen Saturation Monitoring	Gadgets that screen patients' oxygen levels continuously and ready clinical staff to any progressions in their condition are turning out to be more normal.	Oximeter, IoT system	To facilitate real-time data transfer between the patient (who may be at a distant location) and the healthcare provider, the oximeter is connected to an IoT channel, like Bluetooth or the Web.
Rehabilitation System	Helps hemiplegic patients recover more quickly by giving them access to self-care tools inside their rehabilitation platform.	IoT Frameworks, Machine Learning	With the intention of providing real-time data on the mental state of rehabilitation patients, a smart rehabilitation network that is based on the Internet of Things (IoT) is suggested.
Wheelchair Management	Develop a high-tech wheelchair with health monitoring capabilities.	IoT Frameworks, Machine Learning	A possible future wheelchair design might have a WBANintegration that would beam in sensors steered by the IoT network, resulting in a completely automatedwheelchairs app.
Imminent Healthcare	Management of private health and fitness, monitoring of chronic diseases, care for children and the elderly, and more	IoThNet framework, Intelligent Security Model	The Internet of Things (IoT) has the potential to mobilise services, infrastructures, and applications to improve medical reception throughout the world and security.

To aid in collecting useful information from data, it's important to investigate the use of DL in an SDN in depth. M-IoT optimises spectrum and network channel resources while reducing bandwidth output and increasing efficiency of compression algorithms. Pressure models and their utilization in the transmission of information through remote channels are the subject of much review (Misra et al., 2008).Genetic calculation (GA), firefly calculation (FF), particles warm optimization (PSO), rider enhancement calculation (ROA), and whale improvement calculation (WOA) are only a couple of instances of the numerous ML calculations proposed for use in assault recognition and counteraction (Reddy and Shyam, 2020). Pressure strategies and models for encoding information content passed on through the M-IoT structure, nonetheless, are deficient in existing concrete works. There has to be much research into this field, particularly with regards to encoding techniques for M-IoT data services and the network's resource limitations.

CONCLUSION

In the medical field, IoT solutions have progressed from a basic layout to very sophisticated computing architectures. Where artificial intelligence and the internet of things have played crucial roles in healthcare, their implementation has been just as crucial. The significant objective of this study was to distinguish which applications truly worked. We perceived that few models, including mHealth, 6LoWPAN, CoAP, and IEEE 11073, may be used to move information dependably and to work on present methodology by examining models and plans for distant medical care checking. In addition, methods that impacted access to healthcare were emphasised here. To identify whether resources and technologies were feasible, a literature review was conducted. Through this systematic literature analysis and comparison, we also found that smart healthcare design and model evolution has produced several difficulties. Despite the difficulties, there is always room for progress and refining. One issue brought to light is the absence of a single standard across medical institutions across organisations and areas, highlighting the need for change to maintain data integrity. Since a lot of information must be collected, the system is certain to become intricate, which might cause problems with coordination and storage. Another problem revealed by the study is the identification and analysis of data across disparate linked platforms and devices. One alternative is to design a patient- and physician-friendly open mHealth paradigm. Doctors will be able to keep better tabs on their patients' health thanks to a centralised hub for telemedicine services and guidance. mHealth and other mobile architectures have the potential to lessen the frequency and severity of medical mistakes and simplify the delivery of care.

REFERENCES

Adame, T., Bel, A., Bellalta, B., Barcelo, J., & Oliver, M. (2014). *IEEE 802.11ah: The Wi-Fi approach for M2M communications*. IEEE Xplore. DOI: 10.1109/wfi-cloud.2016.24

Alghanim, A. A., Rahman, S. M. M., & Hossain, M. A. (2017). Privacy analysis of smart city healthcare services. In Proceedings - 2017 IEEE International Symposium on Multimedia, ISM 2017 (pp. 394–398). Institute of Electrical and Electronics Engineers Inc. DOI: 10.1109/ISM.2017.79

Alizadeh, T. (2017). An investigation of IBM's smarter cities challenge: What do participating cities want? *Cities (London, England)*, 63, 70–80. DOI: 10.1016/j.cities.2016.12.009

Almotiri, S., Khan, M., & Alghamdi, M. (2016). Mobile health (m-Health) system in the context of IoT. In 2016 IEEE 4th International Conference on Future Internet of Things and Cloud Workshops (FiCloudW). DOI: 10.1109/wficloud.2016.24

Avila, K., Sanmartin, P., Jabba, D., & Jimeno, M. (2017). Applications based on service-oriented architecture (SOA) in the field of home healthcare. *Sensors (Basel)*, 17(8), 1703. DOI: 10.3390/s17081703 PMID: 28757557

Ben Arfi, W., Ben Nasr, I., Kondrateva, G., & Hikkerova, L. (2021). The role of trust in intention to use the IoT in eHealth: Application of the modified UTAUT in a consumer context. *Technological Forecasting and Social Change*, 167, 120688. DOI: 10.1016/j.techfore.2021.120688

Bratan, T., Ondokuz, M. C., & Clarke, M. (2006). *Optimum design of remote patient monitoring systems*. IEEE Engineering in Medicine and Biology Society. DOI: 10.1109/IEMBS.2006.260729

Catarinucci, L., De Donno, D., Mainetti, L., Palano, L., Patrono, L., Stefanizzi, M. L., & Tarricone, L. (2015). An IoT-aware architecture for smart healthcare systems. *IEEE Internet of Things Journal*, 2(6), 515–526. Advance online publication. DOI: 10.1109/JIOT.2015.2417684

Chaki, J., Thillai Ganesh, S., Cidham, S. K., & Ananda Theertan, S. (2020). Machine learning and artificial intelligence based diabetes mellitus detection and self-management: A systematic review. *Journal of King Saud University. Computer and Information Sciences*. Advance online publication. DOI: 10.1016/j.jksuci.2020.06.013

Chong, J., Cho, C., & Tabei, F. (2018). *Motion and noise artifact-resilient atrial fibrillation detection using a smartphone.* IEEE Xplore. DOI: 10.1109/JETCAS.2018.2818185

Cook, D. J., Duncan, G., Sprint, G., & Fritz, R. L. (2018). Using smart city technology to make healthcare smarter. *Proceedings of the IEEE*, 106(4), 708–722. DOI: 10.1109/JPROC.2017.2787688 PMID: 29628528

Deshmukh, P. (2017). Design of cloud security in the EHR for Indian healthcare services. *Journal of King Saud University. Computer and Information Sciences*, 29(3), 281–287. DOI: 10.1016/j.jksuci.2016.01.002

Du, S., Li, T., Gong, X., & Horng, S.-J. (2020). A hybrid method for traffic flow forecasting using multimodal deep learning. *International Journal of Computational Intelligence Systems*, 13(1), 85. DOI: 10.2991/ijcis.d.200120.001

Dziak, D., Jachimczyk, B., & Kulesza, W. J. (2017). IoT-based information system for healthcare application: Design methodology approach. *Applied Sciences (Basel, Switzerland)*, 7(6), 596. DOI: 10.3390/app7060596

Ermes, M., Pärkkä, J., & Mäntyjärvi, J. (2008). *Detection of daily activities and sports with wearable sensors in controlled and uncontrolled conditions*. IEEE Xplore. DOI: 10.1109/TITB.2007.899496

Garcia-Carrillo, D., Marin-Lopez, R., Kandasamy, A., & Pelov, A. (2017). A CoAP-based network access authentication service for low-power wide area networks: LO-CoAP-EAP. *Sensors (Basel)*, 17(11), 2646. DOI: 10.3390/s17112646 PMID: 29149040

Gil, D., Johnsson, M., Mora, H., & Szymański, J. (2019). Review of the complexity of managing big data of the Internet of Things. *Complexity*, 2019(1), 1–12. DOI: 10.1155/2019/4592902

Grzelak, D., & Podlaski, K. (2019). *Analyze the effectiveness of an algorithm for identifying Polish characters in handwriting based on neural machine learning technologies*. Elsevier.

Islam, S. M. R., Kwak, D., Kabir, M. H., Hossain, M., & Kwak, K. S. (2015). The Internet of Things for healthcare: A comprehensive survey. *IEEE Access : Practical Innovations, Open Solutions*, 3, 678–708. DOI: 10.1109/ACCESS.2015.2437951

Jain, S., Nehra, M., Kumar, R., Dilbaghi, N., Hu, T. Y., Kumar, S., Kaushik, A., & Li, C. (2021). Internet of medical things (IoMT)-integrated biosensors for point-of-care testing of infectious diseases. *Biosensors & Bioelectronics*, 179, 113074. DOI: 10.1016/j.bios.2021.113074 PMID: 33596516

Jayadev, P. G., & Bellary, S. (2021). A hybrid approach for classification and identification of iris damaged levels of alcohol drinkers. *Journal of King Saud University. Computer and Information Sciences*. Advance online publication. DOI: 10.1016/j.jksuci.2021.01.004

Khan, A., & Zubair, S. (2020). An improved multi-modal based machine learning approach for the prognosis of Alzheimer's disease. *Journal of King Saud University. Computer and Information Sciences*. Advance online publication. DOI: 10.1016/j.jksuci.2020.04.004

Kiryanov, A. G., Krotov, A. V., Lyakhov, A. I., & Khorov, E. M. (2019). Algorithm for dynamic power control and scheduling in IEEE 802.11ax infrastructure networks. *Journal of Communications Technology and Electronics*, 64(8), 900–909. DOI: 10.1134/S1064226919080230

Kumar, S., Tiwari, P., & Zymbler, M. (2019). Internet of things is a revolutionary approach for future technology enhancement: A review. *Journal of Big Data*, 6(1), 111. Advance online publication. DOI: 10.1186/s40537-019-0268-2

Liu, M., Wang, Y., Yao, C., Zou, J., Luo, Y., Li, T., & Bai, G. (2019). A class-incremental learning method based on one class support vector machine. *Journal of Physics: Conference Series*, 1267(1), 12007. DOI: 10.1088/1742-6596/1267/1/012007

Livingston, G., Sommerlad, A., Orgeta, V., Costafreda, S. G., Huntley, J., Ames, D., Ballard, C., Banerjee, S., Burns, A., Cohen-Mansfield, J., Cooper, C., Fox, N., Gitlin, L. N., Howard, R., Kales, H. C., Larson, E. B., Ritchie, K., Rockwood, K., Sampson, E. L., & Mukadam, N. (2017). Dementia prevention, intervention, and care. *Lancet*, 390(10113), 2673–2734. Advance online publication. DOI: 10.1016/S0140-6736(17)31363-6 PMID: 28735855

Lucisano, J., Routh, T., & Lin, J. (2016). *Glucose monitoring in individuals with diabetes using a long-term implanted sensor/telemetry system and model*. IEEE Xplore.

Mahdavinejad, M., Rezvan, M., & Burcins, M. (2018). *Machine learning for Internet of Things data analysis: A survey*. Elsevier. DOI: 10.1016/j.dcan.2017.10.002

Maier, M., & Ebrahimzadeh, A. (2018). *The tactile internet: Automation or augmentation of the human?* IEEE Xplore.

Misra, S., Reisslein, M., & Xue, G. (2008). A survey of multimedia streaming in wireless sensor networks. *IEEE Communications Surveys and Tutorials*, 10(4), 18–39. Advance online publication. DOI: 10.1109/SURV.2008.080404

Mora, L., Deakin, M., & Reid, A. (2018). Strategic principles for smart city development: A multiple case study analysis of European best practices. *Technological Forecasting and Social Change*, 142, 70–97. DOI: 10.1016/j.techfore.2018.07.035

Movassaghi, S., Abolhasan, M., & J. L-C. (2014). Wireless body area networks: A survey. IEEE Xplore.

Palanisamy, V., & Thirunavukarasu, R. (2019). Implications of big data analytics in developing healthcare frameworks – a review. *Journal of King Saud University. Computer and Information Sciences*, 31(4), 415–425. Advance online publication. DOI: 10.1016/j.jksuci.2017.12.007

Patel, B., & Shah, P. (2021). Operating system support, protocol stack with key concerns and testbed facilities for IoT: A case study perspective. *Journal of King Saud University. Computer and Information Sciences*. Advance online publication. DOI: 10.1016/j.jksuci.2021.01.002

Peña-Ayala, A. (2014). Ontology agents and their applications in the web-based education systems: Towards an adaptive and intelligent service artificial intelligence on education view project. Springer. DOI: 10.1007/978-3-540-88071-4_11

Chapter 12
Analysis on Implantable IoT Sensors

C. H. Gangadhar
Prasad V. Potluri Siddhartha Institute of Technology, India

Ramakrishna Kolikipogu
https://orcid.org/0000-0002-3253-8476
Chaitanya Bharathi Institute of Technology, India

K. Santarao
GMR Institute of Technology, India

Benita Christopher
Westford University, UAE

Nidhya M. S.
https://orcid.org/0000-0002-1290-4520
Dayananda Sagar University, India

ABSTRACT

Miniaturization has allowed for greater efficiency and increased power in implantable electronic devices. Glucose levels, blood pressure, and cerebral activity are just few of the many physiological characteristics that may be tracked with the use of biomedical sensors. A body area network, also known as a wireless sensor network, is primarily comprised of a set of sensors operating in tandem inside a human body. The present status of the workmanship in remote biomedical sensor correspondence and controlling frameworks are talked about in this chapter, alongside their expected applications. Additionally, up-to-date integration techniques are outlined for making the sensors smaller and well suited for implantation. For a collection of sensors to function as a BAN, they must first join forces to establish a network. At long last,

DOI: 10.4018/979-8-3693-7868-7.ch012

versatility approaches for embedded sensors are provided, along with details on the challenges that must be overcome throughout the development of such networks.

1. INTRODUCTION

Due to their decreasing size and increasing efficiency, implantable electronic devices are becoming more applicable in a wide range of new contexts. Chemical sensors, glucose monitors, oxygen sensors, brain implants, and cochlear implants are all examples of implanted medical technology (Frost & Meyerhoff, 2002), (McKean & Gough, 1988), (Wise et al., 2004), (Olsson & Wise, 2005). Their ongoing improvement is clearing the path for widespread intra-human deployment. The concept of a body area network (BAN) arises naturally from the idea of a collection of sensors monitoring various parts of a human being. When used in, on, or around a human being, the devices that make up a BAN form a wireless sensor network (WSN) ((IEEE Standards Association, 2012). Biomedical sensors and wireless connectivity are built into a limited number of devices that make up this system (Honeine et al., 2011).

Many of the difficulties encountered by BANs and WSNs are also encountered by WSNs, but BANs present their own unique set of issues. The implant must be small enough to fit in the body, but not too small, and the implant's environment must not degrade the implant's electromagnetic signals or the quality of the communication connection. The issue of biocompatibility. Due to the constraints of battery life and other power sources, high power efficiency is essential (Hannan et al., 2014). Data safety must be ensured throughout communication since private and sensitive medical information will be communicated, and interchanges should be dependable as they might be conveying earnest data about the singular's perilous sicknesses. This chapter will examine implanted sensors and sensor networks, first looking at biological applications and then at the most cutting-edge sensors available today. Because

sensors must provide data to an external reader for access by the individual or medical staff, we will go through and explain the methods that make this possible. It will be discussed how to power the gadget without using batteries, allowing for a more compact design. Thanks to developments in both material science and manufacturing methods, another age of devices is arising that is more fit than any time in recent memory for implantation. This chapter will describe these integrating efforts. Since wireless sensor networks are the focus here, challenges associated with these types of in-body sensors in the networking realm will be discussed. There have been reports of self-impelled gadgets, and the authors were motivated to discuss some of these propulsion systems by the prospect of mobile sensors that may be deployed in a variety of locations throughout the human body.

2. APPLICATIONS

In order to better diagnose, manage, and treat patients, medical professionals may take use of a wide assortment of devices created in the biomedical region. In this article, we will discuss sensors, the devices used to detect and report on biological signals to medical professionals. Since wireless sensor networks are the focus of this book, only wireless sensors will be discussed and presented. Sensors will be shown in their medical use, and gadgets will be discussed.

2.1 Intraocular Pressure

Keeping track of a patient's intraocular pressure (IOP) is crucial for medical professionals diagnosing and managing glaucoma. This condition is the subsequent driving reason for visual deficiency, and it is normal to affect very nearly 80 million individuals overall by 2020 ((Quigley, 1996). Contact lenses (Chiou et al., 2016), (Leonardi et al., 2009) and other non-invasive technologies may indirectly detect IOP by seeing the cornea's curvature change as a result of the increased pressure, while implanted sensors (Ghaed et al., 2013), (Chitnis et al., 2013), (Kouhani, Weber, & Li, 2017), (Donida et al., 2015), (Shih, Shen, & Otis, 2011) can take a direct reading of the IOP from inside the eye. According to this chapter's writers, the most advanced IOP device currently available is described in Ref. (Ghaed et al., 2013). The 1.5 mm2 sensor uses wireless communication and requires just 7 W of power, which may be provided by solar energy harvesting.

Figure 1. Intraocular pressure

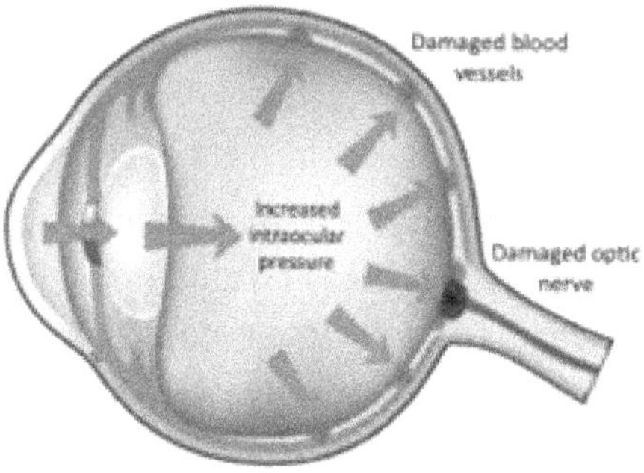

2.2 Neural Activity

Several applications may benefit from the information gleaned by monitoring neural activity. It has several applications, including the study of behavior (Fan et al., 2011), the control of prosthetic limbs through a brain-machine interface (Seo et al., 2016), and the diagnosis of neurological dysfunctions such epilepsy (Chen et al., 2014). The action potentials of neurons may be monitored either from deep brain regions using implanted needles (Rhew et al., 2014) or from the

surface of the cortex (Chen et al., 2014), (Muller et al., 2015), (Mestais et al., 2015), (Gao et al., 2012), the latter of which has the advantage of minimizing cortical scarring and facilitating long-term, stable measurements. Even devices that can capture the electrical movement of neurons in the fringe of the sensory system have been developed (Seo et al., 2016). The device described in Ref. (Muller et al., 2015) is now regarded as the pinnacle of implanted brain sensors. It is a 64-channel, 42.25 mm2 RF-powered sensor that transmits data at 1 Mbps while using just 225 W. Although Ref. (Seo et al., 2016) provides a smaller device with a 120 W power consumption, its single-channel design limits its usefulness.

2.3 Bladder Pressure

In order to properly diagnose bladder dysfunctions, measuring bladder pressure is crucial. It is not possible to record certain symptoms in an acute measurement at the hospital since they can only be caused in regular everyday activities like walking. Permanent monitoring through implant is required, ideally with little or no patient pain. You may see some examples of such tools in Refs. (Majerus et al.,

2012), (Majerus et al., 2015), (Lee et al., 2014), (Kim, Powell, & Ziaie, 2014). In Ref. (Kim, Powell, & Ziaie, 2014), a 40 mm2 sensor is shown that uses just 16 W, has the ability to transmit power through sound waves, and uses LC resonance for its communications.

2.4 Glucose

Traditional glucose monitoring has included the patient themselves taking a blood sample via a finger prick. This technique has the drawback of being uncomfortable for the patient and being limited to taking readings at certain times. Alternatives that can be implanted are now being studied and have been described (Vaddiraju et al., 2015), (Dehennis et al., 2013). The patient's quality of life is enhanced by the ability to monitor glucose levels in real time, which may then be utilized to set off alerts or even to regulate implanted insulin pumps autonomously. In Ref. (Vaddiraju et al., 2015), a wireless, needle-implantable, 0.5 0.5 5 mm3 sensor is reported that is powered and communicates by light.

2.5 Blood Pressure

Overall, high blood pressure accounts for 30 percent of all deaths and hospitalizations (Aldaoud et al., 2015). Causes an increase in the probability of developing cardiovascular disease, heart issues, strokes, and aneurysms. Being such a crucial essential parameter, regular monitoring might be useful to the medical personnel in making diagnoses. Multiple proposals for wireless, implantable blood pressure monitors may be found in Refs. (Aldaoud et al., 2015), (Cong et al., 2009), (Park et al., 2016), (Murphy et al., 2013). Furthermore, Ref. (Cheong et al., 2012) presents a sensor that can detect blood pressure in order to manage vascular graft deterioration through blood flow. The vascular unite pulse sensor portrayed in Ref. (Cheong et al., 2012) is now regarded as the gold standard. This sensor is 2.67 mm2 in size and is held in place by two coils inside a vascular graft. The gadget has a sensitivity of 0.176 mmHg, consumes just 21.6 W, and does digital backscattering of pressure.

2.6 pH

Several physiological characteristics and functions are affected by the pH of an answer as a result of the job it plays in the synthetic reactions the solution undergoes. Tumor pH may be utilized to detect microbial presence and as a wound healing indicator (Gou et al., 2014). In Refs. (Cao et al., 2013), (Ativanichayaphong et al., 2010), an oesophageal pH sensor is used to watch gastroesophageal reflux illness (GERD). In order to regulate the etiology of dental caries, Ref. (Farella et al., 2016) uses pH measurements in the mouth. When it comes to implanted pH sensors, the device described in Ref. (Gou et al., 2014) is currently the gold standard. It consolidates carbon nanotube- based sensors (which needn't bother with a reference cathode) with a RFID label that regulates information onto a carrier supplied from outside. It has a detection range of 2-12, and it works for 120 days.

2.7 Intracranial Pressure

When it comes to treating TBIs, intracranial pressure is a crucial biological metric. Catheters placed into the cranial cavity are necessary for current procedures, but they are painful, may induce infection, and can even cause a patient to bleed to death.

(Fan et al., 2011), (Chen et al., 2014). In Refs. (Chen et al., 2014), (Behfar et al., 2015), (Kang et al., 2016), (Meng et al., 2012), we see minimally invasive approaches using wireless sensors. In Ref. (Chen et al., 2014), Chen et al. reported passive sensors with sizes as small as 1 1 0.5 mm3. Wireless and battery-free functioning enabled pressure readings to be taken from 0 to 100 mmHg.

2.8 Electromyography

Electromyography (EMG) is a noninvasive technique used to monitor electrical potentials in muscles; this information has applications in areas as varied as disease and injury diagnosis, functional electrical stimulation, and prosthetic limb control. In Refs. (Kneisz et al., 2015), (Zhang et al., 2013), we see examples of wireless electromyography (EMG) sensors. In Ref. (Zhang et al., 2013), a sensor for monitoring EMG and ECG is shown; it has four simple channels, a chip that utilizes 19 W (while examining from one channel), and imparts at 200 kbps while using 160 W of power. The device's adaptability stems from its ability to be powered by either radio frequency (RF) power transmission or thermoelectric energy collection.

Figure 2. Electromyography

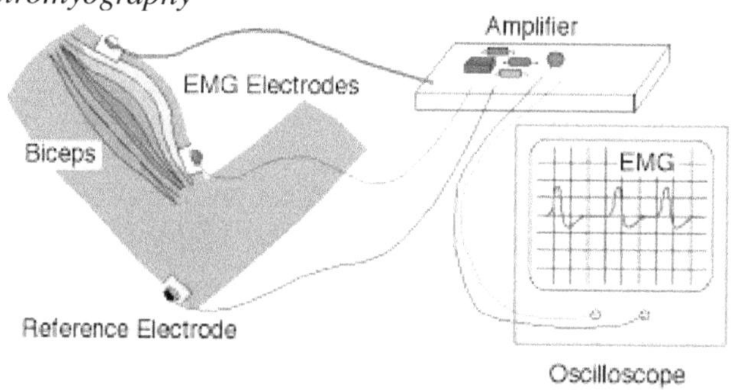

2.9 Electrocardiogram

Electrocardiogram (ECG) readings provide doctors with a detailed picture of a patient's heart and may be used to diagnose a variety of cardiac conditions, including arrhythmias and heart attacks (myocardial infarctions). There have been suggestions made in Refs. (Zhang et al., 2013), (Jeon et al., 2014) for wireless ECG monitoring. The gadget described in Ref. (Jeon et al., 2014) pushes the envelope in terms of power budgets due to its unprecedentedly low consumption of 64 nW. However, it does not provide real-time observation; instead, it just records anomalous occurrences for later wireless broadcast. Ref. (Zhang et al., 2013) discusses a device that is now state-of-the-art for continuous monitoring, which we have already addressed.

Figure 3. Electrocardiogram

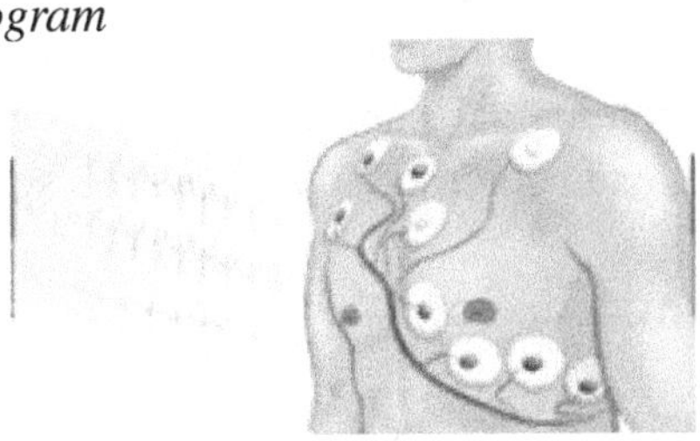

3 COMMUNICATIONS

Intra-body communication (IBC) (Hayami et al., 2016), (Anderson & Sodini, 2013) and ultrasound (US) (Santagati & Melodia, 2017) are two examples of the successful and promising methods of communication that have been documented. The first involves passing data through electrical impulses via the host's biological tissue. The second uses ultrasounds, a mechanical wave with frequencies exceeding 20 kHz that is poorly absorbed by tissue due to its high frequency. Since radio frequency (RF) is the most extensively used means of communication, this section will concentrate on sensors that can communicate through RF. Both latent and dynamic RF correspondence methods will be talked about, alongside specific gadgets that utilization them in practice.

3.3 Passive RF Communication (PRFC)

A wireless implant and an external device both have linked coils, and their resonance frequency is used for communication. The implant's coil is connected to the sensor, and the impedance of the coil changes as the parameter for which the sensor is sensitive changes. As a result, a change in the parameter of interest, such as IOP, will cause a corresponding change in the resonance frequency of the connected coils. This method typically does not need any power from the embed (Chitnis et al., 2013), (Kouhani, Weber, & Li, 2017), (Park et al., 2016), (Murphy et al., 2013), (Chen et al., 2014), (Behfar et al., 2015), since it is the obligation of the outside peruser to recognize the impedance change in the embed's loop and, from this, register the worth of the detected boundary. Because of the decreased need for power and the absence of processing circuitry, smaller implants are now feasible. From a BAN point of view, this kind of communication may be used whenever an on-body reader is a viable option (for instance, during intraocular pressure observing, where the outside peruser can be housed in the patient's spectacles).

3.4 Active RF Communication (ARFC)

Here we discuss implantable sensors that use an internal antenna and radio frequency (RF) signal to connect with the outside environment. In Ref. (Aldaoud et al., 2015), instead of the more typical inductive coupling, the authors resorted to capacitive coupling. Biological tissue on the host is used as a dielectric between metallic plates on the sensor and the per user, the two of which might be worn on the body or implanted. Due to the increased conductive ness of the tissue at higher frequencies, it is essential that these operations be performed at the lowest feasible frequencies. Correspondence by inductive coupling, completed between two loops, has the advantage of being more effective than far-field correspondence. However, in order to achieve optimal performance, exact alignment between coils is required. Further, in contrast to far field, which may be employed at great distances, the space between coils must be maintained as narrow as possible. The accessible area, the power budget, and the radiation safety regulations all factor into the decision between these two powering options. The supplied examples do not show any correlation between the sensor's intended use and the selection of inductive coupling or far-field transmission. Choosing between passive and active communication methods is a crucial step in the process of creating an implanted sensor. Since the transfers can uphold the cumbersome batteries or remote power move (WPT) parts, and the embedded sensor can utilize an oscillator to balance the information into the hand-off's RF signal and backscatter it,passive communication is a viable option when it comes to BANs, even if the implanted sensors have severe volume.

Inductive linkages may be used in situations when there is sufficient processing power on the sensor. When this is in place, the sensor is capable of handling more information, such as from numerous channels. Whenever a long range is needed yet on-body or implantable relays aren't an option, far-field communication is the way to go.

Table 1. Application of implantable devices and communication

Applications	Communications
Intraocular Pressure	**Passive Rf Communication (Prfc)**
Bladder Pressure	
Pressure Blood	
Intracranial Pressure	
Neural Activity	**Active Rf Communication (Arfc)**
Glucose	

In the above table it is depicted that the implantable devices which are applied to find pressure EEG, ECG, various pressure, these can be measured and communicated by passive and active communication.

4. POWERING

To achieve the goal of miniaturizing sensors, a trade-off should be made between the size of the battery, and subsequently the size of the actual gadget, and its independence; this is especially important given that replacing the battery may necessitate an invasive surgical procedure with potential health consequences (Rasouli & Phee, 2010), (Gould, 2006). Interest in this topic is shown by the abundance of articles produced over the last several years, many of which seek to find novel and dependable fueling answers for embedded gadgets with an end goal to expand their valuable life and therapist their physical footprint. You can see a visual illustration of the many powering options for electronic devices in Figure 1.

4.1 Energy Harvesting

Techniques for extracting usable quantities of energy from the general climate to drive a gadget or charge a battery are called energy gathering, and they may one day give capacity to biomedical hardware since they have the potential to generate infinite energy, greatly extending the devices' useful lifetime. However, it is not always easy to successfully harvest energy from the environment since the quantity of energy available is unpredictable and usually rather low, necessitating the employment of specialized power management circuitry (Rasouli & Phee, 2010), (Hudak & Amatucci, 2008). Research in the subject of energy gathering is of huge interest notwithstanding the aforementioned restrictions because of the ongoing trend toward lower power requirements in electronic circuits (Mitcheson et al., 2008). Among the many methods offered for energy harvesting, thermoelectric generators, biomechanical energy, sun oriented power, biofuel, and RF energy reapers stand out as particularly promising.

Thermoelectric Generators

Thermal energy from temperature differences may be converted into electricity using thermoelectric generators, which are solid-state electronics (Snyder, 2008). Because of their low size, lack of moving components, and great durability, these power sources are attractive for use in implanted devices (Leonov et al., 2007). These devices are based on the Seebeck phenomenon, which asserts that a temperature gradient will cause a metal or semiconductor to create an electrical voltage across itself. (Bell, 2008).

Biomechanical Energy Harvesters

The human body is a rich wellspring of biomechanical energy. Breathing, solid extending, body weight during movement, and heart beats all contribute to this phenomenon. Transduction mechanisms are used to convert energy kinds, with electromagnetic and piezoelectric processes being the most frequent. There are two main types of biomechanical energy harvesters, vibrational and force- driven. Force-driven harvesters depend on the utilization of mechanical power, though vibrational collectors utilize the inertial energy of a given mass (Rasouli & Phee, 2010).

The generator's potential for use in surgically implanted medical devices was also investigated. After 30 minutes of surgery, it had been put on the right ventricle mass of a canine's heart, at which point it had generated 80 mJ of energy. (Goto, 1998).

Solar Power

Scientists discovered that solar cells might provide enough energy to run medical implants. These cells may still collect energy when implanted under the skin since some light, especially near-infrared light, can pass through the skin (The International Commission on Non-Ionizing Radiation Protection, 2006). Approximately 10% of the approaching power per millimeter of skin is absorbed at 632.8 nm, and 11.5% is absorbed at 904 nm (Enwemeka, 2001). Even yet, these systems have a number of limitations, the most significant ones being their bulky dimensions, limited efficiency, and tissue heating (Ben Amar, Kouki, & Cao, 2015). As described in Refs. (Ghaed et al., 2013), (Haeberlin et al., 2014), sun based power gathering cells have been developed, with the possibility to create 1.1 W/mm2 in the eye and 34 W/mm2 under the skin.

Biofuel

By use of electrochemical processes, biofuel cells convert the energy stored in biological reactions into electricity. The anode and cathode of a biofuel cell undergo oxidation and reduction processes, respectively, to create an electric current that may be used to power an electronic device. Benefits of this technology include, for instance, the fuel cell's compatibility with the human body. Low collected power levels, as well as gradual anode and cathode deterioration, are, on the other hand, potential obstacles. There are several references detailing the many benefits of using biofuel cells that may be implanted into live animals. (Katz & MacVittie, 2013), (Katz, 2015).

RF Energy Harvesting

Radio frequency (RF) energy harvesting is the practice of converting ambient electromagnetic waves, such as those emitted by cell phone towers, into usable electricity. The energy from these waves might be used to power electronics. Whether or not this approach is enough for powering a particular application depends on the amount of accessible radiation, the proficiency of the power transformation component, and the actual furthest reaches of the gadget. There is some doubt regarding the viability of this device-powering technology, despite the fact that power levels under 1 W can be recuperated, because of the size restriction of embedded clinical gadgets and the normal surrounding RF power densities. (Hudak & Amatucci, 2008).

Wireless Power Transfer

Until far, the most implantable energy collecting methods have only produced negligible amounts of electricity. As a result, it's important to think about whether or not a specialized power emitter may be used to charge the gadgets. Relevant technologies arise, including the utilization of optical energy, ultrasounds, and radio frequency waves.

Optical Link

It has been proposed that optical waves be used to power medical implants because, unlike radio frequency (RF) waves, they do not disrupt surrounding communication networks. According to Ref. (Goto et al., 2001), transcutaneous power transmission was achieved by embedding a variety of silicondiodes with an area of 2.1 cm2 1-3 mm underneath the skin. It has been guaranteed that a lithium battery could be charged utilizing close infrared light at 810 nm with a power thickness of 22 mW/cm2 to the point that it could run a business pacemaker for 24 hours, however the expansion in skin temperature was simply 1.4°C.

Ultrasonic Link

Like optical waves, ultrasonic waves don't disrupt electromagnetic fields or surrounding communication equipment. To do this, they cause a vibration in the tissue, and then use a transducer, such a piezoelectric transducer, to change the dynamic energy into electrical energy (Rasouli & Phee, 2010). Due to its drawbacks, ultrasonic power transfer is currently only used in implanted medical devices. The contact between the transmitter and the tissue is crucial to the transmission's success, since an impedance mismatch or a lack of proper alignment between the transmitter and beneficiary may radically bring down the sign's solidarity (Arra et al., 2007).

Radio Frequency Link

One of the most miniaturization-promising forms of electromagnetic radiation is radio frequency (RF), which is sufficient for long-distance energy delivery (Katz, 2014). As long as the specific absorption rate (SAR) is not surpassed, its ingestion by organic tissues doesn't cause harm. Inductive coupling is often used to transmit electricity to medical equipment since it is less likely to be absorbed by natural tissue at lower frequencies. This procedure has been used to drive a few inserts in the past, including artificial hearts, brain prostheses, and cochlear implants (Kurs et al., 2007), (Kim et al., 2012), (Ho et al., 2014), (Ho, Kim, & Poon, 2013). This technique is widely used, although it has significant limitations, for example, loop decoupling inferable from misalignment, since it calls for precise placement of transmitter and reception coils (Flynn & Fotopoulou, 2011), (Flynn & Fotopoulou, 2013), (Aldhaher, Luk, & Whidborne, 2014). Also, for example, curl decoupling inferable from misalignment, since it calls because inductive coupling has a limited range that follows exponential decay (a near- field phenomena). In order to get around these restrictions, antennas in the middle or far field might be used. Less efficient than earlier inductive systems, this one takes into account longer distances between the power source and the objective. (Visser, 2013).

Integration

So far in this chapter we have seen how silicon microelectronics are used in several implanted electronic devices. Because to advances in manufacturing methods and microelectronics, the size of implanted electronics has decreased. These days, there's a push to make them even smaller, so they can be implanted with less effort and discomfort to the patient. Success stories will be used to illustrate the progress that has been achieved over the previous several years towards this objective.

A wireless pressure monitoring sensor measuring just 1 mm 1 mm 0.1 mm3 has been developed by Chen et al. (Chen et al., 2014). The design was verified in vivo using a 2.5 2.5 0.1 mm3 device. At its core, the sensor is a resounding circuit comprised of an inductive radio wire and a strain touchy capacitor. When pressure is applied, the LC circuit's resonant frequency shifts, and this change is picked up by an external reader, which is then used to calculate pressure values. Mostafalu et al. (Mostafalu et al., 2016) developed threads that can perform as sensors, microfluidics, and electronics due to their unique features. Threads embedded with materials like carbon nanotubes were utilized as cathodes for estimating pH, glucose, and other analytes, while hydrophobic threads served as microfluidic channels. Traditional electronics were situated on a separate layer, and they were responsible for establishing connections and processing the signal from the electrodes. pH and strain measuring devices made from fabric have been successfully tested in vivo. Smart sutures and bandages might be developed as a result of this study. The aforementioned gadgets are instances of how fabrication technology has allowed for miniaturization without sacrificing functionality.

Biodegradable and Stretchable Sensors

New materials, including stretchy and biodegradable ones, have been suggested, investigated, and verified in recent years for use in implanted sensors (Rogers, Someya, & Huang, 2010), (Yin, Cheng, Mao, Haasch, Liu, Xie, et al., 2014), (Yin,

Huang, Xu, Zhang, Lam, Cheng, et al., 2014), (Someya, Bao, & Malliaras, 2016), (Hwang et al., 2012). Temporary sensors made from biodegradable materials may, for instance, be implanted after surgery to track how well wounds are healing and how active germs are, and then gradually break down in the human body over time. The organism's natural elimination mechanisms would subsequently purge the waste products of this process. This would reduce the frequency of implant retrieval procedures and its associated drawbacks, such as patient pain, infection risk, and the need to schedule more time in the operating room. Polymer (PLGA) and magnesium or silicon foil were used to create the ICP sensor that Kang et al. (Kang et al., 2016) successfully tested in a rat. The sensor was able to detect ICP continuously for 3 days before its components were reabsorbed by the body. A pressure sensor was built by Luo et al. (Luo et al., 2014) using a variable capacitor and a loop. The authors of this study provided evidence of the device's biodegradation. The sensor's resonant frequency varied within the initial 21 hours of submersion in a saline arrangement, suggesting that it was adjusting to its new environment. For the next 86 hours, the resonance frequency remained unchanged, demonstrating the device's stability and marking the sensor's optimum operating time. After this point, the sensor's performance degrades to the point that it can no longer be used. In Ref. (Hwang et al., 2012), the authors suggest a temporary device that can control bacterial development in a specific area of the body, such as a surgical or implant site. An inductive coil made of magnesium, a silicon resistor, and silk were used to create this heater. The resistor would be heated by an external RF field by around 5 degrees Celsius, which would kill any bacteria in the area. How crystalline the silk is determines how long it will last. It is also possible to create batteries that decompose naturally (Ref. (Yin, Huang, Xu, Zhang, Lam, Cheng, et al., 2014)). These could run an LED and a wireless signal generator operating at 58 MHz.

Figure 4. Implantable biodegradable sensor

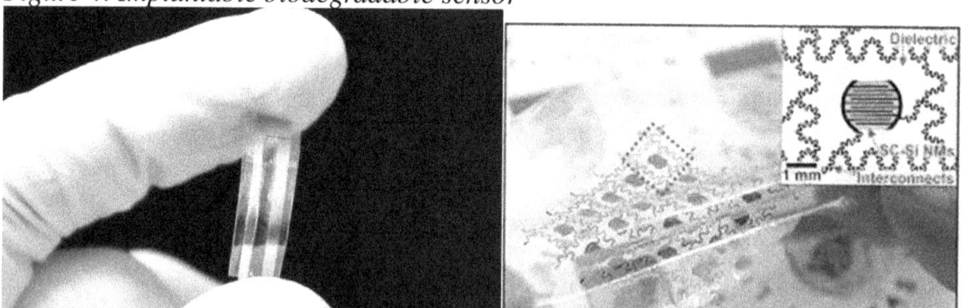

In addition, stretchy electronics are finally becoming a practical possibility (Someya, Bao, & Malliaras, 2016). Patient pain might be considerably decreased with the introduction of implanted devices if sensors could be bent and twisted without losing their qualities. Coplanar waveguides and electronic eyeball cameras are only two examples of devices that have been successfully demonstrated. There is a critical need for advancements in integration methods and material science in the field of medical sensors. Smaller gadgets with the same robust capabilities are in great demand because they open the door to new uses and enhance existing ones. Patient comfort and device dependability may both benefit from flexible and stretchy sensors, since they provoke less of a negative reaction from the human body. Last but not least, biodegradable sensors hold great promise since they may be implanted to screen a boundary for a specific measure of time and then consumed by the body without ill effect.

Figure 5. Flexible sensor

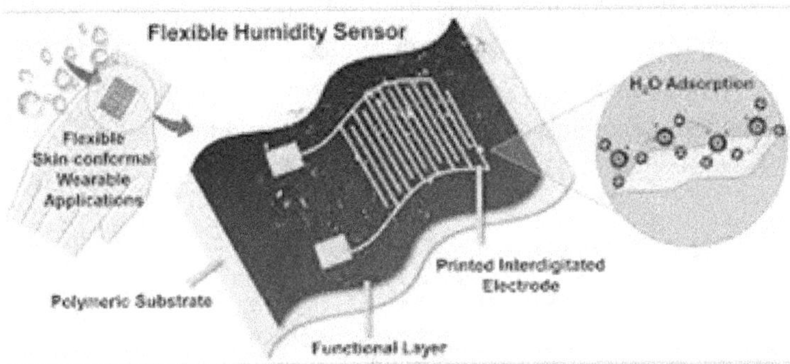

Node Mobility

Methods of propulsion for tiny implanted devices or robots have been suggested in recent years. Medical researchers are interested in sensors that can move through bodily fluids because it would enable a single device to do measurements and diagnostics across a larger region than has ever been possible previously.

Steerable devices might potentially be used for less invasive surgery and tailored medicine administration. The wireless implanted device shown in Ref. (Pivonka, Yakovlev, Poon, & Meng, 2012) has a 34 mm2 footprint. Magneto hydrodynamics (MHD) is the foundation of its propulsion system. This may be accomplished with a permanent magnet by creating a steady attractive field of around 0.1 T. Through the medium's conductive liquid, the gadget applies flows of the Mama significant degree, producing a power in the attractive field. The device is then impelled by an equivalent and restricting power. A 1.86 GHz WPT framework not only provides power, but also transmits motion directives in the form of modulation on the power carrier. In salt water, the gadget is capable of a manageable pace of 5.3 mm/sec. Using gas strain from electrolytic air pockets shaped on the encompassing liquid, Hsieh et al. (Hsieh et al., 2014) made a remote- controlled gadget with a drive system. It has a speed of 0.3 mm/s and a power requirement of around 200 W. There are electrodes for electrolysis located at strategic points throughout the apparatus, allowing for precise control over the location of electrolysis. A 10 MHz inductive coupling connection not only provides electricity, but also transmits orders to regulate the robot's speed and direction of travel. The overall size of the locomotive chip is 21.2 mm2, and this includes the receiving coil and electrodes. Although this device is slower than the one disclosed in Ref. (Pivonka, Yakovlev, Poon, & Meng, 2012), it does not call for any extra parts like permanent magnets. Systems for moving remote gadgets through a fluid medium were considered. These devices' stated WPT, communication, and steering skills are a crucial first step toward completely independent or remote-controlled sensors and actuators integrating a Boycott that are fit for crossing, for example, through the course, the stomach related framework, or the bladder. They would be able to do microsurgery or medicine administration at specific sites while also taking measurements and sending the results outside the body.

CONCLUSION

Implantable sensor BANs are getting very close to being a standard tool in the medical industry. This would represent a huge step forward for patient care, since constant, unrestricted monitoring of crucial indicators would be possible. A variety of developing power sources make it feasible for these gadgets to be as compact as possible while yet functioning endlessly. The same holds true for modes of communication, which often use less power; in fact, entirely passive modes of communication that may be employed with very tiny devices have been recorded. Continued discussion of communications has brought up concerns about security and networking challenges, and solutions to these problems have been offered. As of late, there has been a lot of interest in the utilization of biodegradable and flexible materials for sensor manufacturing, and this interest has led to the description of integration methods that make this possible. At long last, we have evidence of the mobility processes that make possible the deployment of exploratory sensors; they pave the way for widespread monitoring with a single device. In conclusion, advances in biomedical sensors are paving the way for fully operational, patient-specific BANs that will soon prove to be indispensable tools for health monitoring in both the hospital context and the patients' day-to-day life.

REFERENCES

Agrawal, D. R., Tanabe, Y., Weng, D., Ma, A., Hsu, S., Liao, S.-Y., Zhen, Z., Zhu, Z.-Y., Sun, C., Dong, Z., Yang, F., Tse, H. F., Poon, A. S. Y., & Ho, J. S. (2017). Conformal phased surfaces for wireless powering of bioelectronic microdevices. *Nature Biomedical Engineering*, 1(3), 43. DOI: 10.1038/s41551-017-0043 PMID: 29226018

Aldaoud, A., Laurenson, C., Rivet, F., Yuce, M. R., & Redouté, J. (2015). Design of an inductively powered implantable wireless blood pressure sensing interface using capacitive coupling. *IEEE/ASME Transactions on Mechatronics*, 20(1), 487–491. DOI: 10.1109/TMECH.2014.2322614

Aldhaher, S., Luk, P. C. K., & Whidborne, J. F. (2014). Electronic tuning of misaligned coils in wireless power transfer systems. *IEEE Transactions on Power Electronics*, 29(11), 5975–5982. DOI: 10.1109/TPEL.2014.2297993

Anderson, G. S., & Sodini, C. G. (2013). Body coupled communication: The channel and implantable sensors. *2013 IEEE International Conference on Body Sensor Networks (BSN)*, 3–7. DOI: 10.1109/BSN.2013.6575490

Arra, S., Leskinen, J., Heikkila, J., & Vanhala, J. (2007). Ultrasonic power and data link for wireless implantable applications. In *2007 2nd International Symposium on Wireless Pervasive Computing* (pp. 567–571). IEEE. DOI: 10.1109/ISWPC.2007.342668

Ativanichayaphong, T., Tang, S. J., Hsu, L. C., Huang, W. D., Seo, Y. S., & Tibbals, H. F.. (2010). An implantable batteryless wireless impedance sensor for gastroesophageal reflux diagnosis. *IEEE MTT-S International Microwave Symposium Digest*, 608–611. DOI: 10.1109/MWSYM.2010.5516775

Bazaka, K., & Jacob, M. (2012). Implantable devices: Issues and challenges. *Electronics (Basel)*, 2(1), 1–34. DOI: 10.3390/electronics2010001

Behfar, M. H., Björninen, T., Moradi, E., Sydänheimo, L., & Ukkonen, L. (2015). Biotelemetric wireless intracranial pressure monitoring: An in vitro study. *International Journal of Antennas and Propagation*, 2015, 1–10. DOI: 10.1155/2015/918698

Bell, L. E. (2008). Cooling, heating, generating power, and recovering waste heat with thermoelectric systems. *Science*, 321(5895), 1457–1461. DOI: 10.1126/science.1158899 PMID: 18787160

Ben Amar, A., Kouki, A. B., & Cao, H. (2015). Power approaches for implantable medical devices. *Sensors (Basel)*, 15(11), 28889–28914. DOI: 10.3390/s151128889 PMID: 26580626

Cao, H., Rao, S., Tang, S., Tibbals, H. F., Spechler, S., & Chiao, J.-C. (2013). Batteryless implantable dual-sensor capsule for esophageal reflux monitoring. *Gastrointestinal Endoscopy*, 77(4), 649–653. DOI: 10.1016/j.gie.2012.10.029 PMID: 23290721

Chavez-Santiago, R., Garcia-Pardo, C., Fornes-Leal, A., Valles-Lluch, A., Vermeeren, G., Joseph, W., Balasingham, I., & Cardona, N. (2015). Experimental path loss models for in-body communications within 2.36–2.5 GHz. *IEEE Journal of Biomedical and Health Informatics*, 19(3), 1–1. DOI: 10.1109/JBHI.2015.2418757 PMID: 25838532

Chavez-Santiago, R., Sayrafian-Pour, K., Khaleghi, A., Takizawa, K., Wang, J., Balasingham, I., & Li, H.-B. (2013). Propagation models for IEEE 802.15.6 standardization of implant communication in body area networks. *IEEE Communications Magazine*, 51(8), 80–87. DOI: 10.1109/MCOM.2013.6576343

Cheffena, M. (2015). Performance evaluation of wireless body sensors in the presence of slow and fast fading effects. *IEEE Sensors Journal*, 15(10), 5518–5526. DOI: 10.1109/JSEN.2015.2443251

Chen, L. Y.. (2014). Continuous wireless pressure monitoring and mapping with ultrasmall passive sensors for health monitoring and critical care. *Nature Communications*, 5, 5028. DOI: 10.1038/ncomms6028 PMID: 25284074

Chen, W.. (2014). A fully integrated 8-channel closed-loop epileptic seizure control. *IEEE Journal of Solid-State Circuits*, 49(1), 232–247. DOI: 10.1109/JSSC.2013.2284346

Cheong, J. H., Ng, S. S. Y., Liu, X., Xue, R.-F., Lim, H. J., Khannur, P. B., Chan, K. L., Lee, A. A., Kang, K., Lim, L. S., He, C., Singh, P., Park, W.-T., & Je, M. (2012). An inductively powered implantable blood flow sensor microsystem for vascular grafts. *IEEE Transactions on Biomedical Engineering*, 59(9), 2466–2475. DOI: 10.1109/TBME.2012.2203131 PMID: 22692871

Chiou, J. C., Hsu, S.-H., Liao, Y.-T., Huang, Y.-C., Yeh, G.-T., Kuei, C.-K., & Dai, K.-S. (2016). Toward a wirelessly powered on-lens intraocular pressure monitoring system. *IEEE Journal of Biomedical and Health Informatics*, 20(5), 1216–1224. DOI: 10.1109/JBHI.2016.2594058 PMID: 27479980

Chitnis, G., Maleki, T., Samuels, B., Cantor, L. B., & Ziaie, B. (2013). A minimally invasive implantable wireless pressure sensor for continuous IOP monitoring. *IEEE Transactions on Biomedical Engineering*, 60(1), 250–256. DOI: 10.1109/TBME.2012.2205248 PMID: 22736631

Cong, P. (2009). A wireless and batteryless 130 milligram 300 μW 10-bit implantable blood pressure sensing microsystem for real-time genetically engineered mice monitoring. *IEEE International Solid-State Circuits Conference, 44*(12), 428–429.

Dehennis, A., Mailand, M., Grice, D., Getzlaff, S., & Colvin, A. (2013). A near-field-communication (NFC) enabled wireless fluorimeter for fully implantable biosensing applications. *IEEE International Solid-State Circuits Conference,* 298–299. DOI: 10.1109/ISSCC.2013.6487743

Donida, A. (2015). A 0.036 mbar circadian and cardiac intraocular pressure sensor for smart implantable lens. *Digest of Technical Papers - IEEE International Solid-State Circuits Conference*, 58, 392–393.

Enwemeka, C. S. (2001). Attenuation and penetration of visible 632.8 nm and invisible infra-red 904 nm light in soft tissues. *Official Journal of World Association for Laser Therapy*, 13, 95–101.

Fan, D., Rich, D., Holtzman, T., Ruther, P., Dalley, J. W., Lopez, A., Rossi, M. A., Barter, J. W., Salas-Meza, D., Herwik, S., Holzhammer, T., Morizio, J., & Yin, H. H. (2011). A wireless multi-channel recording system for freely behaving mice and rats. *PLoS One*, 6(7), 1–9. DOI: 10.1371/journal.pone.0022033 PMID: 21765934

Farella, M., Loke, C., Sander, S., Songini, A., Allen, M., Mei, L., & Cannon, R. D. (2016). Simultaneous wireless assessment of intra-oral pH and temperature. *Journal of Dentistry*, 51, 49–55. DOI: 10.1016/j.jdent.2016.05.012 PMID: 27263031

Flynn, B. W., & Fotopoulou, K. (2011). Wireless power transfer in loosely coupled links. *Power*, 47(2), 416–430.

Flynn, B. W., & Fotopoulou, K. (2013). Rectifying loose coils: Wireless power transfer in loosely coupled inductive links with lateral and angular misalignment. *IEEE Microwave Magazine*, 14(2), 48–54. DOI: 10.1109/MMM.2012.2234634

Frost, M. C., & Meyerhoff, M. E. (2002). Implantable chemical sensors for real-time clinical monitoring: Progress and challenges. *Current Opinion in Chemical Biology*, 6(5), 633–641. DOI: 10.1016/S1367-5931(02)00371-X PMID: 12413548

Gao, H., Walker, R. M., Nuyujukian, P., Makinwa, K. A. A., Shenoy, K. V., Murmann, B., & Meng, T. H. (2012). HermesE: A 96-channel full data rate direct neural interface in 0.13 µm CMOS. *IEEE Journal of Solid-State Circuits*, 47(4), 1043–1055. DOI: 10.1109/JSSC.2012.2185338

Ghaed, M. H., Chen, G., Haque, R., Wieckowski, M., Kim, Y., Kim, G., Lee, Y., Lee, I., Fick, D., Kim, D., Seok, M., Wise, K. D., Blaauw, D., & Sylvester, D. (2013). Circuits for a cubic-millimeter energy-autonomous wireless intraocular pressure monitor. *IEEE Transactions on Circuits and Systems. I, Regular Papers*, 60(12), 3152–3162. DOI: 10.1109/TCSI.2013.2265973

Goto, H. (1998). Feasibility of using the automatic generating system for quartz watches as a leadless pacemaker power source: A preliminary report. *Medical & Biological Engineering & Computing*, 20(1), 9–11.

Goto, K., Nakagawa, T., Nakamura, O., & Kawata, S. (2001). An implantable power supply with an optically rechargeable lithium battery. *IEEE Transactions on Biomedical Engineering*, 48(7), 830–833. DOI: 10.1109/10.930908 PMID: 11442295

Gou, P., Kraut, N. D., Feigel, I. M., Bai, H., Morgan, G. J., Chen, Y., Tang, Y., Bocan, K., Stachel, J., Berger, L., Mickle, M., Sejdić, E., & Star, A. (2014). Carbon nanotube chemiresistor for wireless pH sensing. *Scientific Reports*, 4(1), 1–6. DOI: 10.1038/srep04468 PMID: 24667793

Gould, P. A. (2006). Complications associated with implantable cardioverter-defibrillator replacement in response to device advisories. *Journal of the American Medical Association*, 295(16), 1907–1913. DOI: 10.1001/jama.295.16.1907 PMID: 16639049

Haeberlin, A., Zurbuchen, A., Schaerer, J., Wagner, J., Walpen, S., Huber, C., Haeberlin, H., Fuhrer, J., & Vogel, R. (2014). Successful pacing using a batteryless sunlight-powered pacemaker. *Europace : European Pacing, Arrhythmias, and Cardiac Electrophysiology : Journal of the Working Groups on Cardiac Pacing, Arrhythmias, and Cardiac Cellular Electrophysiology of the European Society of Cardiology*, 16(10), 1534–1539. DOI: 10.1093/europace/euu127 PMID: 24916431

Hannan, M. A., Mutashar, S., Samad, S. A., & Hussain, A. (2014). Energy harvesting for implantable biomedical devices: Issues and challenges. *Biomedical Engineering Online*, 13(1), 79. DOI: 10.1186/1475-925X-13-79 PMID: 24950601

Hayami, H., Takehara, H., Nagata, K., Haruta, M., Noda, T., Sasagawa, K., Tokuda, T., & Ohta, J. (2016). Wireless image-data transmission from an implanted image sensor through a living mouse brain by intra-body communication. *Japanese Journal of Applied Physics*, 55(4), 04EM03-1–04EM03-5. DOI: 10.7567/JJAP.55.04EM03

Ho, J. S., Kim, S., & Poon, A. S. Y. (2013). Midfield wireless powering for implantable systems. *Proceedings of the IEEE*, 101(6), 1369–1378. DOI: 10.1109/JPROC.2013.2251851

Ho, J. S., Yeh, A. J., Neofytou, E., Kim, S., Tanabe, Y., Patlolla, B., Beygui, R. E., & Poon, A. S. Y. (2014). Wireless power transfer to deep-tissue microimplants. *Proceedings of the National Academy of Sciences of the United States of America*, 111(22), 7974–7979. DOI: 10.1073/pnas.1403002111 PMID: 24843161

Honeine, P. (2011). Wireless sensor networks in biomedical: Body area networks. *Systems, Signal Processing and Their Applications (WOSSPA),International Workshop, 1*, 388–391. DOI: 10.1109/WOSSPA.2011.5931518

Hsieh, J. Y., Kuo, P.-H., Huang, Y.-C., Huang, Y.-J., Tsai, R.-D., Wang, T., Chiu, H.-W., Wang, Y.-H., & Lu, S.-S. (2014). A remotely controlled locomotive IC driven by electrolytic bubbles and wireless powering. *IEEE Transactions on Biomedical Circuits and Systems*, 8(6), 787–798. DOI: 10.1109/TBCAS.2014.2382341 PMID: 25576574

Hudak, N. S., & Amatucci, G. G. (2008). Small-scale energy harvesting through thermoelectric, vibration, and radiofrequency power conversion. *Journal of Applied Physics*, 103(10), 101301-1, 101301–101324. DOI: 10.1063/1.2918987

Hwang, S.-W., Tao, H., Kim, D.-H., Cheng, H., Song, J.-K., Rill, E., Brenckle, M. A., Panilaitis, B., Won, S. M., Kim, Y.-S., Song, Y. M., Yu, K. J., Ameen, A., Li, R., Su, Y., Yang, M., Kaplan, D. L., Zakin, M. R., Slepian, M. J., & Rogers, J. A. (2012). A physically transient form of silicon electronics. *Science*, 337(6102), 1640–1644. DOI: 10.1126/science.1226325 PMID: 23019646

IEEE Standards Association. (2012). IEEE Standard for Local and Metropolitan Area Networks—Part 15.6: Wireless Body Area Networks. *IEEE Std.*, 271. Advance online publication. DOI: 10.1109/IEEESTD.2012.6161600

Jeon, D., Chen, Y.-P., Lee, Y., Kim, Y., Foo, Z., Kruger, G., Oral, H., Berenfeld, O., Zhang, Z., Blaauw, D., & Sylvester, D. (2014). An implantable 64nW ECG-monitoring mixed-signal SoC for arrhythmia diagnosis. *Digest of Technical Papers - IEEE International Solid-State Circuits Conference*, 57, 416–417. DOI: 10.1109/ISSCC.2014.6757494

Kang, S., Murphy, R. K. J., Hwang, S.-W., Lee, S. M., Harburg, D. V., Krueger, N. A., Shin, J., Gamble, P., Cheng, H., Yu, S., Liu, Z., McCall, J. G., Stephen, M., Ying, H., Kim, J., Park, G., Webb, R. C., Lee, C. H., Chung, S., & Rogers, J. A. (2016). Bioresorbable silicon electronic sensors for the brain. *Nature*, 530(7588), 71–76. DOI: 10.1038/nature16492 PMID: 26779949

Katz, E. (2014). *Implantable Bioelectronics*. DOI: 10.1002/9783527673148

Katz, E. (2015). Implantable biofuel cells operating in vivo: Providing sustainable power for bioelectronic devices. In *2015 6th International Workshop on Advances in Sensors and Interfaces (IWASI)* (pp. 2–13). IEEE. DOI: 10.1109/IWASI.2015.7184958

Katz, E., & MacVittie, K. (2013). Implanted biofuel cells operating in vivo – Methods, applications, and perspectives. *Energy & Environmental Science*, 6(10), 2791. DOI: 10.1039/c3ee42126k

Kim, A., Powell, C. R., & Ziaie, B. (2014). An implantable pressure sensing system with electromechanical interrogation scheme. *IEEE Transactions on Biomedical Engineering*, 61(7), 2209–2217. DOI: 10.1109/TBME.2014.2318023 PMID: 24800754

Kim, S., Ho, J. S., Chen, L. Y., & Poon, A. S. Y. (2012). Wireless power transfer to a cardiac implant. *Applied Physics Letters*, 101(7), 1–5. DOI: 10.1063/1.4745600

Kneisz, L., Unger, E., Lanmuller, H., & Mayr, W. (2015). In vitro testing of an implantable wireless telemetry system for long-term electromyography recordings in large animals. *Artificial Organs*, 39(10), 897–902. DOI: 10.1111/aor.12626 PMID: 26471141

Kouhani, M. H. M., Weber, A., & Li, W. (2017). Wireless intraocular pressure sensor using stretchable variable inductor. *Proceedings of IEEE International Conference on Micro Electro Mechanical Systems*, 557–560. DOI: 10.1109/MEMSYS.2017.7863467

Kurs, A., Karalis, A., Moffatt, R., Joannopoulos, J. D., Fisher, P., & Soljačić, M. (2007). Wireless power transfer via strongly coupled magnetic resonances. *Science*, 317(5834), 83–86. DOI: 10.1126/science.1143254 PMID: 17556549

Lee, W. S., Kim, A., Ziaie, B., Raghunathan, V., & Powell, C. R. (2014). UPlink: An ultra-low-power implantable wireless system for long-term ambulatory urodynamics. *2014 IEEE Biomedical Circuits and Systems Conference (BioCAS) –. Proceedings*, 384–387, 384–387. Advance online publication. DOI: 10.1109/BioCAS.2014.6981743

Leonardi, M., Pitchon, E. M., Bertsch, A., Renaud, P., & Mermoud, A. (2009). Wireless contact lens sensor for intraocular pressure monitoring: Assessment on enucleated pig eyes. *Acta Ophthalmologica*, 87(4), 433–437. DOI: 10.1111/j.1755-3768.2008.01404.x PMID: 19016660

Leonov, V., Torfs, T., Fiorini, P., & Van Hoof, C. (2007). Thermoelectric converters of human warmth for self-powered wireless sensor nodes. *IEEE Sensors Journal*, 7(5), 650–656. DOI: 10.1109/JSEN.2007.894917

Luo, M., Martinez, A. W., Song, C., Herrault, F., & Allen, M. G. (2014). A microfabricated wireless RF pressure sensor made completely of biodegradable materials. *Journal of Microelectromechanical Systems*, 23(1), 4–13. DOI: 10.1109/JMEMS.2013.2290111

Majerus, S. (2015). Wireless implantable pressure monitor for conditional bladder neuromodulation. *IEEE Biomedical Circuits and Systems Conference (BioCAS) – Proceedings*, 2–5. DOI: 10.1109/BioCAS.2015.7348337

Majerus, S. J. A., Garverick, S. L., Suster, M. A., Fletter, P. C., & Damaser, M. S. (2012). Wireless, ultra-low-power implantable sensor for chronic bladder pressure monitoring. *ACM Journal on Emerging Technologies in Computing Systems*, 8(2), 1–13. DOI: 10.1145/2180878.2180883 PMID: 26778926

McKean, B. D., & Gough, D. A. (1988). A telemetry-instrumentation system for chronically implanted glucose and oxygen sensors. *IEEE Transactions on Biomedical Engineering*, 35(7), 526–532. DOI: 10.1109/10.4581 PMID: 3209214

Meng, X., Browne, K., Huang, S. M., Cullen, D. K., Tofighi, M. R., & Rosen, A. (2012). Dynamic study of wireless intracranial pressure monitoring of rotational head injury in swine model. *Electronics Letters*, 48(7), 363–364. DOI: 10.1049/el.2012.0281

Mestais, C. S., Charvet, G., Sauter-Starace, F., Foerster, M., Ratel, D., & Benabid, A. L. (2015). WIMAGINE: Wireless 64-channel ECoG recording implant for long-term clinical applications. *IEEE Transactions on Neural Systems and Rehabilitation Engineering*, 23(1), 10–21. DOI: 10.1109/TNSRE.2014.2333541 PMID: 25014960

Mitcheson, P. D., Yeatman, E. M., Rao, G. K., Holmes, A. S., & Green, T. C. (2008). Energy harvesting from human and machine motion for wireless electronic devices. *Proceedings of the IEEE*, 96(9), 1457–1486. DOI: 10.1109/JPROC.2008.927494

Mostafalu, P., Akbari, M., Alberti, K. A., Xu, Q., Khademhosseini, A., & Sonkusale, S. R. (2016). A toolkit of thread-based microfluidics, sensors, and electronics for 3D tissue embedding for medical diagnostics. *Microsystems & Nanoengineering*, 2(April), 16039. DOI: 10.1038/micronano.2016.39 PMID: 31057832

Muller, R., Le, H.-P., Li, W., Ledochowitsch, P., Gambini, S., Bjorninen, T., Koralek, A., Carmena, J. M., Maharbiz, M. M., Alon, E., & Rabaey, J. M. (2015). A minimally invasive 64-channel wireless μECoG implant. *IEEE Journal of Solid-State Circuits*, 50(1), 344–359. DOI: 10.1109/JSSC.2014.2364824

Murphy, O. H., Bahmanyar, M. R., Borghi, A., McLeod, C. N., Navaratnarajah, M., Yacoub, M. H., & Toumazou, C. (2013). Continuous in vivo blood pressure measurements using a fully implantable wireless SAW sensor. *Biomedical Microdevices*, 15(5), 737–749. DOI: 10.1007/s10544-013-9759-7 PMID: 23559403

Ntouni, G. D., Lioumpas, A. S., & Nikita, K. S. (2014). Reliable and energy-efficient communications for wireless biomedical implant systems. *IEEE Journal of Biomedical and Health Informatics*, 18(6), 1848–1856. DOI: 10.1109/JBHI.2014.2300151 PMID: 25375682

Olsson, R., & Wise, K. (2005). A three-dimensional neural recording microsystem with implantable data compression circuitry. *IEEE International Solid-State Circuits Conference,* 558–559. DOI: 10.1109/ISSCC.2005.1494117

Park, J., Kim, J.-K., Patil, S., Park, J.-K., Park, S. A., & Lee, D.-W. (2016). A wireless pressure sensor integrated with a biodegradable polymer stent for biomedical applications. *Sensors (Basel),* 16(6), 1–10. DOI: 10.3390/s16060809 PMID: 27271619

Pivonka, D., Yakovlev, A., Poon, A. S. Y., & Meng, T. (2012). A mm-sized wirelessly powered and remotely controlled locomotive implant. *IEEE Transactions on Biomedical Circuits and Systems*, 6(6), 523–532. DOI: 10.1109/TBCAS.2012.2232665 PMID: 23853253

Quigley, H. A. (1996). Number of people with glaucoma worldwide. *The British Journal of Ophthalmology*, 80(5), 389–393. DOI: 10.1136/bjo.80.5.389 PMID: 8695555

Ramachandran, V. R. K., Havinga, P. J. M., & Meratnia, N. (2016). HACMAC: A reliable human activity-based medium access control for implantable body sensor networks. In *BSN 2016 – 13th Annual International Body Sensor Networks Conference* (pp. 383–389). IEEE. DOI: 10.1109/BSN.2016.7516292

Rasouli, M., & Phee, L. S. J. (2010). Energy sources and their development for application in medical devices. *Expert Review of Medical Devices*, 7(5), 693–709. DOI: 10.1586/erd.10.20 PMID: 20822391

Rhew, H. G., Jeong, J., Fredenburg, J. A., Dodani, S., Patil, P. G., & Flynn, M. P. (2014). A fully self-contained logarithmic closed-loop deep brain stimulation SoC with wireless telemetry and wireless power management. *IEEE Journal of Solid-State Circuits*, 49(10), 2213–2227. DOI: 10.1109/JSSC.2014.2346779

Rogers, J. A., Someya, T., & Huang, Y. (2010). Materials and mechanics for stretchable electronics. *Science*, 327(5973), 1603–1607. DOI: 10.1126/science.1182383 PMID: 20339064

Santagati, E. G., & Melodia, T. (2017). Experimental evaluation of impulsive ultrasonic intrabody communications for implantable biomedical devices. *IEEE Transactions on Mobile Computing*, 16(2), 367–380. DOI: 10.1109/TMC.2016.2561277

Santagati, G. E., Melodia, T., Galluccio, L., & Palazzo, S. (2015). Medium access control and rate adaptation for ultrasonic intrabody sensor networks. *IEEE/ACM Transactions on Networking*, 23(4), 1121–1134. DOI: 10.1109/TNET.2014.2316675

Seo, D., Neely, R. M., Shen, K., Singhal, U., Alon, E., Rabaey, J. M., Carmena, J. M., & Maharbiz, M. M. (2016). Wireless recording in the peripheral nervous system with ultrasonic neural dust. *Neuron*, 91(3), 529–539. DOI: 10.1016/j.neuron.2016.06.034 PMID: 27497221

Shih, Y., Shen, T., & Otis, B. (2011). A 2.3 μW wireless intraocular pressure/temperature monitor. *IEEE Journal of Solid-State Circuits*, 46(11), 2592–2601. DOI: 10.1109/JSSC.2011.2164134

Snyder, J. (2008). Small thermoelectric generators. *The Electrochemical Society Interface*, 17(3), 54–56. DOI: 10.1149/2.F06083IF

Someya, T., Bao, Z., & Malliaras, G. G. (2016). The rise of plastic bioelectronics. *Nature*, 540(7633), 379–385. DOI: 10.1038/nature21004 PMID: 27974769

The International Commission on Non-Ionizing Radiation Protection. (2006). ICNIRP statement on far infrared radiation exposure. *Health Physics*, 91(6), 630–645. DOI: 10.1097/01.HP.0000240533.50224.65 PMID: 17099407

Vaddiraju, S. (2015). Needle-implantable, wireless biosensor for continuous glucose monitoring. *2015 IEEE 12th International Conference on Wearable and Implantable Body Sensor Networks (BSN),* 2–6. DOI: 10.1109/BSN.2015.7299421

Visser, H. (2013). Far-field RF energy transport. In *IEEE Radio and Wireless Symposium* (pp. 34–36). IEEE. DOI: 10.1109/RWS.2013.6486632

Wise, K. D., Anderson, D. J., Hetke, J. F., Kipke, D. R., & Najafi, K. (2004). Wireless implantable microsystems: High-density electronic interfaces to the nervous system. *Proceedings of the IEEE*, 92(1), 76–97. DOI: 10.1109/JPROC.2003.820544

Yin, L., Cheng, H., Mao, S., Haasch, R., Liu, Y., Xie, X., Hwang, S.-W., Jain, H., Kang, S.-K., Su, Y., Li, R., Huang, Y., & Rogers, J. A. (2014). Dissolvable metals for transient electronics. *Advanced Functional Materials*, 24(5), 645–658. DOI: 10.1002/adfm.201301847

Yin, L., Huang, X., Xu, H., Zhang, Y., Lam, J., Cheng, J., & Rogers, J. A. (2014). Materials, designs, and operational characteristics for fully biodegradable primary batteries. *Advanced Materials*, 26(23), 3879–3884. DOI: 10.1002/adma.201306304 PMID: 24652717

Zhang, Y., Zhang, F., Shakhsheer, Y., Silver, J. D., Klinefelter, A., Nagaraju, M., Boley, J., Pandey, J., Shrivastava, A., Carlson, E. J., Wood, A., Calhoun, B. H., & Otis, B. P. (2013). A batteryless 19 μW MICS/ISM-band energy harvesting body sensor node SoC for ExG applications. *IEEE Journal of Solid-State Circuits*, 48(1), 199–213. DOI: 10.1109/JSSC.2012.2221217

Zheng, G., Fang, G., Orgun, M. A., Shankaran, R., & Dutkiewicz, E. (2014). Securing wireless medical implants using an ECG-based secret data sharing scheme. In *2014 14th International Symposium on Information and Communication Technology (ISC)* (pp. 373–377). IEEE. DOI: 10.1109/ISCIT.2014.7011935

Zheng, G., Fang, G., Shankaran, R., Orgun, M. A., & Dutkiewicz, E. (2017). Multiple ECG fiducial points-based random binary sequence generation for securing. *IEEE Journal of Biomedical and Health Informatics*, 21(3), 655–663. DOI: 10.1109/JBHI.2016.2546300 PMID: 27046882

Chapter 13
Attacks in IoT Healthcare Wearable Sensors

A. Sampath Dakshina Murthy
https://orcid.org/0000-0002-9960-6373
Vignan's Institute of Information Technology, India

Nidhya M. S.
https://orcid.org/0000-0002-1290-4520
Dayananda Sagar University, India

E. Gurumoorthi
CMR College of Engineering and Technology, India

Mohit Tiwari
https://orcid.org/0000-0003-1836-3451
Bharati Vidyapeeth's College of Engineering, India

ABSTRACT

The internet of things (IoT) concept has recently received a lot of attention in the IT industry. It makes it easier to share data and connect to the internet. Smart surveillance, environmental monitoring, smartphones, and body sensors all make use of the internet of things (IoT). However, serious new threats to consumers' safety and privacy have emerged as a result of the internet of things' rapid growth. Due to the millions of IoT devices that are at risk, an attacker could quickly hack into an application, render it unreliable, and steal valuable user data and information. Both the architecture of the internet of things and the many forms of cyberattacks on these devices are examined in this chapter. It aims to advance IoT research by shedding light on the numerous security issues IoT is currently facing and the available security solutions we can use to make IoT devices safer. To uncover appropriate security solutions for securing IoT devices, the authors analyse them in this

DOI: 10.4018/979-8-3693-7868-7.ch013

research across three categories: secure authentication, secure communications, and application security.

1. INTRODUCTION

As more and more aspects of society, industry, and commerce get digitised, the significance of information technology and cyber security grows. We rely heavily on reliable information technology and safe information infrastructures since the Internet is used in so many governmental, corporate, and private sector procedures and duties. Protecting vital information networks and ensuring Web security are now fundamental concerns that need serious effort on everyone's part. Because of the interconnected nature of today's networks, even assaults on networks in other nations may compromise our own.

The proliferation of wireless and cloud computing technologies in recent years because the spreading of remote monitoring applications for wide area management systems that make use of cloud services. Advantech offers remote I/O and sensor modules that use remote correspondence innovation like Wi-Fi, 4G, LoRaWAN, NB-IoT/LTE-M, and restrictive LPWAN (Sub-G) through IoT conventions to diminish the time it takes for information to venture out from the field to the cloud.

1.1 Threats to Embedded Systems

Understanding where security flaws, particularly in embedded systems, originate is a prerequisite to developing effective countermeasures. There are typically three types of flaws in embedded devices:

- Weaknesses in the implementation
- Weaknesses in the design
- Weaknesses in deployment

Vulnerabilities in deployment stem ("Apple Developer Documentation," 2015) from mistakes made by the user during setup or operation. Some examples of this include employing simple passwords or no passwords at all, or failing to turn on necessary security settings. Important initial steps have been taken to address this particular problem, with laws having been implemented in California and other jurisdictions mandating IoT devices to use unique passwords.

Errors in the code create implementation vulnerabilities, which may be used by hackers during an attack. The prototypical implementation vulnerability is the buffer overflow attack. Incorrectly seeding random number generators is another typical mistake that leads to easily-guessable security keys. Implementation flaws may be fixed by following a standard software development lifecycle and testing it thoroughly, such as Microsoft's Security Development Lifecycle or the OWASP Secure Software Development Lifecycle.

Vulnerabilities in the design of a device occur when appropriate safety precautions were not included during its creation. An illustration of a design flaw is the utilization of control interfaces without user authentication, as well as the utilization of communication protocols that transmit passwords and other sensitive information in plaintext. Gadgets that need secure boot and grant unapproved far off firmware overhauls or "secondary passages" intended to give remote admittance to troubleshooting and support are two additional less intolerable occasions.

2. PROTECTION FOR IOT DEVICES

With IoT, the physical and virtual worlds become one seamless whole. Since there is less and less of a solid barrier between them, cyber-attacks may have tangible impacts on one's personal or professional life. Cyberphysical systems ("Sensor Overview," 2017) on the Internet of Things or in sensor networks have such little resources that traditional security procedures and approaches like firewalls, intrusion detection systems, and anti-virus software cannot be utilised to protect them.

2.1 Security Protocols for Wireless Equipment

Because of how they work—especially when they link to other computers or the Internet—wireless devices are vulnerable to cyber and hacker assaults. The IT security of these systems is sometimes negatively affected by the constraints imposed by restricted resources. The assurance of the protection aims requires adaptation to the particular conditions, which means that tried and proven and somewhat standardised methods and processes are frequently inapplicable ("Who Leads OS Share in Internet of Things Era," 2017).

Mirai

The Mirai virus looks for ARC-processor-based IoT devices online. This computer's CPU is loaded with a stripped-down version of Linux. If the factory-default credentials for a device are still in use, Mirai will infect it.

Stuxnet

Stuxnet is a computer worm created specifically to identify certain types of nuclear equipment. Stuxnet is designed to harm software rather than infiltrate networks. In 2010, five Iranian enterprises engaged in industrial automation fell prey to Stuxnet, marking its official discovery. Stuxnet is thought to have been developed by Israel and the United States to disrupt Iran's nuclear program.

Attack on a Casino in Tasmania

Casino owner based in Tasmania In 2021, a cyberattack on Federal Group caused problems with the company's hotel booking systems and pokies/slot machines. The ransomware assault compromised the data of millions of consumers, and it is yet unknown whether or not the organisation paid the attackers' demanded ransom.

Assault by Jeep

Two security researchers, Chris Valasek and Charlie Miller, broke into a Jeep while it was moving at 70 miles per hour on a highway. They cracked its powerplant, multimedia system, and braking system. What's worse is that they did it from the safety of their own house, hacking into the Jeep's control panel.

2.2 Attacks on a Medical Device

Medtronic disclosed a critical vulnerability in several of their implanted devices in March 2019 ("Sensor Stack," 2017). One of the company's cardiac gadgets was found to have a "major cybersecurity hole" by DHS. St. Jude Medical was another medical provider targeted in an assault, leading to the FDA recalling 465,000 implanted pacemakers. Instead of removing the implants, patients got an update to the software.

Password Security Flaws

Embedded or hard-coded credentials are a security issue for both IT and IoT infrastructures. Hackers may compromise the device directly if the credentials are easy to guess or are hard-coded. The intruder may not even need to guess the password if it is the system default. A recent example of such an assault on the IoT is the Mirai virus.

Mirai attacked routers, cameras, and DVRs in the Internet of Things using a list of 61 commonly used hard-coded default usernames and passwords. Because of the virus, a huge botnet was created. 400,000 linked devices were "enslaved" by it.

Infected devices (or "zombies") spread the Mirai malware and were used to perform the first ever 1Tbps Distributed Denial-of-Service (DDoS) assault against critical infrastructure in September 2016. It stopped everything running on Amazon Web Services, including GitHub, Netflix, Twitter, and Airbnb.

Criminals utilize hash key decryption programmes that store databases of commonly used hash keys and passwords. Logins from multiple IP addresses should be prevented. This greatly limits the ability to travel between borders.

There aren't any regular updates or bug patches, and the update system is broken.

The connection and ease of use of IoT goods are crucial in their development. Although they may seem safe when first purchased, hackers may later find ways to exploit weaknesses.

Without frequent upgrades, Internet of Things devices gradually grow more susceptible to cyberattacks. **Satori** is malicious software that acts and spreads much as Mirai did. Satori may transfer a worm from one device to another without any assistance from a person. First, it's not distributed merely through password guessing; researchers have also found that it specifically targets weaknesses in certain bands of Wi-Fi routers. Second, unlike IoT malware like SuperH and ARC, Satori has been discovered attacking intelligent processor designs.

Insecure Interfaces are a Problem

All IoT devices process data and share it with one another. Many security flaws in IoT devices are caused by unsecured interfaces, and these apps, services, and protocols are essential for communication ("Sensors," 2017). The web, application programming interfaces, the cloud, and mobile interfaces are all linked to vulnerabilities that might be exploited to steal information or corrupt a device. Weak or nonexistent encryption, together with a lack of device authentication and authorization, are frequent occurrences.

Identification of Equipment. In this way, only authorized users and programmes that can prove they know the secret may access the linked device and the data it creates.

Digital certificates, please. They make it possible for a digital object (a computer, an IoT device, etc.) to safely send information to the intended recipients. A reliable Certificate Authority will most often issue certificates in the X509 format. They make it possible for us to verify the authenticity of any individual IoT device.

To lessen the likelihood of a breach, businesses should develop stringent device authentication and authorization protocols that can protect mobile and cloud interfaces. Every Internet of Things (IoT) device on a company's network should have a certificate issued in accordance with the X.509 standard. The OT manager may use this to recognize, authenticate, and provide permissions to any Internet of Things device on the network. If anything seems off, we may simply disconnect the gadget from the internet. IoT security concerns are therefore greatly mitigated. Effective identification technology may help filter out the bad actors and identify the good ones.

Weak protection of transmitted and stored information

- The most typical reasons for data security issues in IoT applications are insecure connectivity and data storage. Compromises in device security pose a significant threat to the confidentiality of data stored in the IoT.
- Researchers from Darktrace said in 2017 that they had uncovered a sophisticated assault on a casino that remained nameless.

When dealing with sensitive data, cryptography is an effective tool. Companies should utilize robust data encryption to protect customer information. In the event of a data leak or cyberattack, this may be quite helpful. Federated machine learning (which is still under development) must be included. Edge computing is used for machine learning in FML, so the data stays put. The cloud is only used for analytics. Many of the security issues plaguing the IoT might be mitigated in this way.

Poor oversight of Internet of Things gadgets

- An exploration delivered in July 2020 took a gander at in excess of 5 million Internet of Things (IoT), IoMT (Internet of Medical Things), and unmanaged connected gadgets in medical services, retail, producing, and the existence sciences. It indicates an alarmingly high number of security flaws and threats across a wide range of IoT devices.

Shadow IoT (equipment used without IT's knowledge), noncompliance, and faulty and potentially dangerous medical devices recalled by the FDA are all examples. Unsettling patterns and data are presented in the study. About 15% of the gadgets were unidentified or unauthorised. Between 5% and 19% were using an unmaintained, older OS. Almost half of IT departments altered their preexisting Internet of Things security solutions or made educated guesses in order to increase visibility.

More than half of respondents (51%) were unaware of the types of smart items present on their network. Seventy-five percent of deployments had VLAN breaches. Eighty-six percent of healthcare installations utilized more than 10 devices subject to FDA recall. 95% of healthcare networks have Alexa or Echo devices integrated, but wait, there's more. MRI and CT scanners were found to be in operation on several social media sites.

Data Tampering is Altering health data to produce false alarms or suppress critical warnings (Arora, Agarwal, & Gupta, 2021) showed how tampered glucose-monitoring data could result in inappropriate insulin administration. Re-sending previously captured data to the system, simulating false readings. (Chen, Zhang, & Liu, 2019) discussed how replay attacks could disrupt continuous monitoring systems. Overloading the network or device, making it unresponsive (Xu, Zhang, & Luo, 2020) examined how DoS attacks on wearable sensors could delay critical medical alerts. Repeatedly triggering device operations to drain the battery. Lounis and Peralta (2021) addressed how attackers could exploit wearable sensor vulnerabilities to deplete device resources. Blocking communication channels to disrupt data transmission (Liu, Zhou, & Jiang, 2021). demonstrated how jamming attacks could impede emergency response systems relying on wearable devices. Faking a device's identity to mislead the healthcare system (Patel, Desai, & Singh, 2020). discussed how spoofing attacks could inject malicious data into healthcare databases. Using stolen health data to deduce sensitive information (Wang, Li, & Zhao, 2019). analyzed privacy risks in wearable devices, particularly in the context of health insurance fraud.

Insecurity in the Internet of Things

In one hospital, even a Tesla was connected to the network. Businesses are put in jeopardy by these potentially harmful ties. In the United States, the healthcare sector is the primary target of ransomware groups. It has become the leading cause of healthcare data breaches nationwide.

This is what has happened as a consequence of recent ransomware attacks:

- Interruptions to operations,
- Customer information and security were at risk,
- The potential for monetary and data loss
- Reputational Damage
- The good news is that.
- These holes and IoT security concerns may be mitigated to a great extent by the use of IoT security systems.

In order to effectively manage their networks, businesses need to employ a full-time Operation Technology (OT) Manager. In order to improve network security, outdated devices must either be withdrawn from service or updated to use the latest firmware. Companies should control the network by dividing it up into smaller, more manageable pieces. Security checks on vulnerabilities, firmware upgrades, alerting, and reporting should be performed frequently and continuously on all IoT devices and networks.

Lack of Experience with IoT Devices

It is necessary to institute training and skill improvement programmes. It can make a huge impact if teams are given more opportunities to learn via interactive seminars, newsletters, and bulletins, and "Hacker Fridays," when team members are given the opportunity to try their hand at hacking a designated smart device. The strength of IoT will be proportional to the level of expertise and preparation of team members.

The pressure on a business to evolve to meet customers' demands is immense. Careful planning is needed for business updation. Retraining and Up skilling - Companies with deep pockets may pay for their workers to be retrained and upskilled in cutting-edge technology. A company must provide funds for this as part of its overall IT budget. Reports indicate that this method increased employee loyalty and retention at large IT companies. To prepare for an uncertain future, firms should priorities recruitment rather than trying to fulfil current demands.

Creating a pipeline for the future requires anticipating the requirements of the business and its consumers. It is crucial to train and employ cybersecurity experts who are up for the difficulties posed by the Internet of Things (IoT) and, more critically, who can bring about necessary organizational changes in how the business handles its IoT connection.

Secure Internet of Things Devices

1. The Mainspring of M2MLabs

Machine-to-machine (M2M) application development is made easier using M2MLabs Mainspring, an open-source application framework. Fleet management, smart grid, and other remote IoT security monitoring applications are among them. Data validation and normalization, long-term storage, and retrieval capabilities are included, as are adaptable device modelling, setup, communication between devices and applications, and storage.

2. Flutter

Flutter is an open-source programmable processor center for use in gadgets projects by beginners, understudies, and experts the same. The impressive variety of Flutter is its key selling factor. The wireless range of this Arduino-based board is more than 0.5 miles. In addition, a router is not necessary for inter-flutter board communication. It is easy to use and secure (256-bit AES encryption) as well.

3. The Eclipse Internet of Things Initiative

Lua is a programming language that we have undoubtedly heard about. Many Internet of Things projects are available in Eclipse. These could be anything from Lua-based application frameworks and services to open-source IoT protocol and utility implementations.

4. Kinoma

Kinoma is an open-source hardware prototyping platform developed by Marvell Semiconductor. DIY electrical device prototyping is now possible with Kimona Create. Kimona Studio is a real, usable IDE.

5. Node-RED

Using Node-Red, we can visually link physical devices, application programming interfaces (APIs), and web-based services. Node-RED is a browser-based flow editor that helps developers connect devices, services, and APIs. It is built on Node.js and advertises itself as “a visual tool for wiring the Internet of Things.” It is compatible with the Raspberry Pi and has a module ecosystem of more than 60,000 add-ons.

1. Security in Internet-of-Things Networks

Security in an IoT network is more challenging than in a conventional network because of the greater variety of communication protocols, IoT security standards, and device capabilities. Connecting the IoT devices to the Internet's backend systems requires a secure network connection.

2. IoT Device Detection

It empowers clients to confirm IoT gadgets in various ways, from involving a static secret phrase for every client to further developed processes like two-factor verification, computerized endorsements, and biometrics (“Core Motion,” 2017). Many IoT authentication scenarios are M2M-based and do not involve human interaction, in contrast to traditional business networks, where a person enters a credential. Here are some examples of suppliers: Baimos Innovations, Covisint, Endow Datacard, and Gemalto.

3. Security for Internet of Things Gadgets

Protecting the data integrity, encrypting it while it is in transit between IoT edge devices and back-end systems, and preventing hackers from sniffing the data ("SmartThings Developer Documentation," 2017). Numerous gadgets and profiles in the Web of Things forestall the utilization of standard encryption procedures and conventions.

4. IoT Security Analytics

Technology like this can gather, aggregate, monitor, and normalize data from IoT devices and then warn users to suspect or policy-breaking behavior.

5. Internet of Things API Safety

Data exchange between Internet of Things (IoT) devices, back-end systems, and apps may be authenticated and authorised using REST-based APIs with accompanying documentation (Shen, Pei, Yang, & Guan, 2015). An essential component of API security is ensuring the integrity of data in transit between edge devices and back-end systems, as well as identifying threats and attacks against APIs. There are numerous types of vendors, including the following: Akana, Apigee/Google, Axway, CA Technologies, Mashery/TIBCO, and MuleSoft are just a few examples.

Most Frequent IoT Vertical Markets

Agriculture, farming, energy, business, finance, healthcare, industrial, retail, transportation, and the Internet of Things are some of the most prominent applications (Owusu, Han, Das, Perrig, & Zhang, 2012). Numerous sensors generate a wealth of new data about the location, status, behavior, use, configuration, and performance of connected devices in these areas. Following this new knowledge, the chapter presents a new business model. In particular, it shows how much more satisfied customers may be for businesses who produce, support, and service IoT goods. After outlining a concrete application, we discuss the primary needs for providing "Anything as a Service" in the IoT.

Cybersecurity for the Internet of Things

- There is no doubt that IoT security is intricate, but specialists are well-versed in the most effective methods of risk evaluation and prevention.
- Working together with professionals facilitates IoT rollouts.
- There is no denying that this approach strengthens safety.

1. IoT security must be built from the bottom up.

The importance of cybersecurity in the Internet of Things is emphasised by Juniper Research Principal Analyst Steffen Sorrell. Businesses should start by laying a solid foundation for security and concentrating on the basics ("Waca: Wearable-Assisted Continuous Authentication Framework with Motion Sensors," 2017). This requires figuring out what dangers the gadgets and networks face. To analyse risk and deliver the best solution, it is advisable for smaller firms or those inexperienced with security best practises to bring in outside experts.

2. Addressing security challenges with the Internet of Things

The aims of the three security pillars must be achieved, and this is a subject of good security by design.

These are the three pillars of security:

- Guaranteed Privacy
- Honesty
- Easily Accessible

Implementing security measures like encryption as soon as possible with the help of professional expertise may help businesses avoid unauthorised access to data, devices, and software. As a consequence, data integrity and service availability have been improved thanks to these safeguards.

Internet of Things (IoT) Sensor Security

All Internet of Things devices, including sensor devices, must have strong security measures in place. The data collected by sensors is the lifeblood of any Internet of Things system. Protecting the privacy and security of IoT data is essential (Diao, Liu, Zhou, & Zhang, 2014). Adding protection to sensors is a difficult problem. When developing a sensor device, it's important to keep the price down, but doing so typically means sacrificing some of the built-in security protections present in more expensive platforms. Despite the limited resources of these gadgets, essential security features may still be implemented, although with some compromises. Encryption may be supported by sensors, but they may be restricted to using shorter key lengths than more powerful systems. The resultant encryption is weaker, but the data may not be vital enough to warrant a full-scale assault anyhow. The reason for this is that the IoT system will have already made use of the data by the time it is encrypted.

Safe Startup

Secure boot ensures that the device will only run code that was developed by the original equipment manufacturer (OEM) or another authorized source by employing cryptographic code signing methods. Prior to stacking the firmware picture, a gadget with secure boot capacities works out a cryptographically protected hash of the picture. To confirm the authenticity of the image, this hash esteem is contrasted with a formerly recorded hash esteem. Using a public key to sign the hash value ensures that only authorised software from the original equipment manufacturer (OEM) may run.

Safe Software Upgrade

Secure firmware updates ensure that a device's firmware can be updated, but only with firmware from the device's OEM or another reputable source. Cryptographically secure hash approval, as secure boot, is utilized to check the firmware before it is introduced on the gadget. Before downloading the updated firmware image, the Internet of Things device may use machine-to-machine authentication protocols to confirm the legitimacy of the upgrade server (Tippenhauer, Pöpper, Rasmussen, & Capkun, 2011).

Confidential Conversations

The very definition of an IoT device requires it to be able to communicate wirelessly with others in the network. Different devices will use different methods of communication, despite the presence of ZigBee, Bluetooth Low Energy (BLE), Wi-Fi, cellular data, and Ethernet, are all possibilities. It is crucial to maintain the safety of all communications, regardless of the medium used for transmission or the protocol used for talking. The usage of TLS or DTLS is recommended. Remote advancements like ZigBee and BLE have encryption coordinated into the convention, however they additionally have known shortcomings, consequently application information encryption is something to ponder for them.

Security for Data

While data is being communicated via a network, it is protected by security protocols, this protection does not extend to the data's storage on the device itself. There have been major data breaches caused by information taken from or retrieved from abandoned devices. If there is important information on the gadget, engineers should think about encrypting it.

Safe Internet of Things edge devices and gateways

The security of the network as a whole must be considered, in addition to the security features built into individual sensor devices. In the Internet of Things, sensors often relay information to a gateway or edge device for further processing. Both the gateway or edge device and the sensors it communicates with need to be protected by rigorous security measures.

CONCLUSION

Cyber security for the Internet of Things (IoT) is a significant barrier for businesses using this technology and should be given top priority. When an organization's IoT security measures are in place, they can return their attention to IoT's key aims, which include process optimisation, service quality enhancement, cost reduction, and customer experience enhancement.

IoT and ICS/OT devices will continue to permeate our daily lives for the foreseeable future. Professionals in the field of cybersecurity are responsible for preventing these gadgets from becoming a hindrance rather than a help in our daily lives.

REFERENCES

Android. (2017, March 10). *Introduction to the sensor and location platform in Windows*. https://msdn.microsoft.com/en-us/library/windows/desktop/dd318936(v=vs.85).aspx

Android. (2017, March 10). *Sensor stack*. https://source.android.com/devices/sensors/sensor-stack.html

Android. (2017, October 23). *Sensor overview*. https://developer.android.com/guide/topics/sensors/sensors_overview.html

Apple. (2015, December 1). *Apple developer documentation*. https://developer.apple.com/documentation

Apple. (2017, October 23). *Core motion*. https://developer.apple.com/documentation/coremotion

Arora, S., Agarwal, P., & Gupta, R. (2021). Tampering vulnerabilities in IoT-enabled glucose monitors. *Health Informatics Journal*, 27(4), 1–12. DOI: 10.1177/14604582211058512

Bari, N., Mani, G., & Berkovich, S. (2013). Internet of things as a methodological concept. In *Fourth International Conference on Computing for Geospatial Research and Application (COM. Geo)* (pp. 48–55). IEEE. DOI: 10.1109/COMGEO.2013.8

Blackberry. (2017, March 10). *Sensors*. https://developer.blackberry.com/native/documentation/device_comm/sensors/

Chen, W., Zhang, H., & Liu, X. (2019). Addressing replay attacks in healthcare monitoring systems. *Journal of Cybersecurity*, 15(2), 203–212.

Diao, W., Liu, X., Zhou, Z., & Zhang, K. (2014). Your voice assistant is mine: How to abuse speakers to steal information and control your phone. In *Proceedings of the 4th ACM Workshop on Security and Privacy in Smartphones & Mobile Devices* (pp. 63–74). ACM. DOI: 10.1145/2666620.2666623

Liu, Q., Zhou, Z., & Jiang, W. (2021). Jamming attacks on wireless medical devices: Mitigation and detection. *Wireless Networks*, 27(8), 456–470.

Lounis, A., & Peralta, R. (2021). IoT healthcare sensors and battery depletion threats. *ACM Transactions on Cyber-Physical Systems*, 5(3), 45–61.

Owusu, E., Han, J., Das, S., Perrig, A., & Zhang, J. (2012). Accessory: Password inference using accelerometers on smartphones. In *Proceedings of the Twelfth Workshop on Mobile Computing Systems & Applications* (p. 9). ACM. DOI: 10.1145/2162081.2162095

Patel, M., Desai, A., & Singh, R. (2020). Location tracking and user profiling in IoT healthcare. *International Journal of Security*, 15(4), 202–216.

Shen, C., Pei, S., Yang, Z., & Guan, X. (2015). Input extraction via motion sensor behavior analysis on smartphones. *Computers & Security*, 53, 143–155. DOI: 10.1016/j.cose.2015.06.013

SmartThings. (2017, July 7). *SmartThings developer documentation*. http://docs.smartthings.com/en/latest/architecture/index.html

Spectrum Matters Indeed. (2017, April). *Who leads OS share in the Internet of Things era?*https://spectrummattersindeed.blogspot.com/2017/04/who-leads-os-share-in-internet-of.html

Tippenhauer, N. O., Pöpper, C., Rasmussen, K. B., & Capkun, S. (2011). On the requirements for successful GPS spoofing attacks. In *Proceedings of the 18th ACM Conference on Computer and Communications Security* (pp. 75–86). ACM. DOI: 10.1145/2046707.2046719

Waca. (2017, October 23). *Waca: Wearable-assisted continuous authentication framework with motion sensors*. https://web.eng.fiu.edu/selcuk/pubs.html

Wang, J., Li, C., & Zhao, H. (2019). Privacy risks in IoT healthcare: A study on wearable devices. *Health Policy and Technology*, 8(2), 132–142. DOI: 10.1016/j.hlpt.2019.05.003

Xu, J., Zhang, Y., & Luo, P. (2020). Denial-of-service vulnerabilities in wearable IoT healthcare systems. *Journal of Systems and Software*, 165, 110573. DOI: 10.1016/j.jss.2020.110573

Chapter 14
IoT Technologies 5G and 6G

Charanjeet Singh
Deenbandhu Chhotu Ram University of Science and Technology, India

M. Prasad
Vellore Institute of Technology, Chennai, India

B. Aarthi
https://orcid.org/0000-0001-6485-8848
SRM Institute of Science and Technology, India

Ranjeet Yadav
https://orcid.org/0000-0003-0891-8556
Government Polytechnic Daman, India

Nidhya M. S.
https://orcid.org/0000-0002-1290-4520
Dayananda Sagar University, India

Balajee Maram
https://orcid.org/0000-0001-5635-5642
SR University, India

ABSTRACT

Optical wireless technologies have garnered significant attention in recent years due to their potential to address the growing demands of 5G and 6G networks. These technologies promise to revolutionize physical-world applications by providing enhanced energy efficiency, higher speeds, and cost-effective solutions. However, their implementation faces numerous challenges, particularly in the context of sensors deployed in the internet of things (IoT). This chapter examines critical issues such as the limitations of wireless optical communication, frequent handovers, inter-cell interference losses caused by atmospheric variations, and the need to mitigate flickering effects. By analyzing these challenges, the authors aim to contribute to the development of robust and sustainable optical wireless communication systems, paving the way for their seamless integration into next-generation IoT ecosystems.

DOI: 10.4018/979-8-3693-7868-7.ch014

INTRODUCTION

Wireless optical communication (WOC) is a promising method for establishing high-speed and high- capacity communication networks because it makes use of an optical carrier in the near-infrared (IR) and visible bands. Radio Frequency (RF)-based technologies have become the standard in wireless communication. As Internet data traffic continues to increase, current technologies are being pushed to their limits in order to maintain acceptable levels of speed, security, and affordability. Wireless communication encompasses not just the RF domain of the electromagnetic spectrum but also the IR regime. These networks are often referred to as "wireless optical communication" (WOC) networks.

As the market for wireless optical devices has exploded in recent years, we have seen a correspondingly large increase in the sophistication and use of WOC technology. It's exciting to see this technology emerge as a potential solution to the issue of high bandwidth demands and "last mile bottleneck." Ground-to-LEO, LEO-to-GEO/LEO-to-ground, GEO-to-ground, LEO/GEO-to-aircraft, deep-space probes, ground stations, unmanned aerial vehicles (UAVs), high-altitude platforms (HAPs), etc. are only a few of the numerous commercial uses of WOC technology (Lucy & Lang, 1968; Lipsett, McIntyre, & Liu, 1969; Arruego et al., 2009; Kazemlou, Hranilovic, & Kumar, 2011). It is also used in radio astronomy, space radio communication, the military, and remote sensing, among other fields. FSO interconnects (FSOI) refer to the usage of WOC technology in connectors between chips or boards across very small

distances. The increasing interest in FSOI may be attributed to the fact that it has the capacity to meet the demanding communication needs of modern optoelectronic devices. In comparison to electronic very large-scale integration (VLSI) technology, this method may allow for the development of connectivity networks that are faster, use less power, and come in smaller containers. However, FSOI is expensive due to the high price of optoelectronic components, integration, and overall packaging. With 1000 channels per PCB and a 1mm optical beam array at 1 Gbps per channel, (Hirabayashi, Yamamoto, & Hino, 2004) experimentally achieved a throughput of up to 1 Tbps per PCB.

In heavily populated metropolitan areas, where road construction is expensive and time-consuming, FSO connectivity provides a practical alternative. Both short- and long-distance communications over tens of kilometers are possible over terrestrial FSO lines. By linking LAN nodes located in various buildings on the same campus or in the same building as the business, short-range networks provide rapid data transfer to remote users. Connecting new networks or extending long-distance FSO communications up to existing fibre rings in major cities is possible. These connections aren't meant for the general public, but they do provide essential services to underlying networks.

LITERATURE SURVEY

Massive Machine-Type Communications (mMTC) supports large-scale IoT devices. Ultra-Reliable Low-Latency Communications (URLLC) are essential for mission-critical applications such as autonomous vehicles and healthcare (Chen, Li, & Zhao, 2019). Enhanced Mobile Broadband (eMBB) enables high-speed IoT applications, including smart cities and immersive augmented reality (Li, Zhao, & Sun, 2021). Healthcare IoT is a Remote patient monitoring, telemedicine, and emergency response (Shafiq, Guo, & Nazir, 2020). Industrial IoT (IIoT) is a Real-time monitoring and predictive maintenance in factories (Lu, Li, & Zhang, 2021). Smart Cities are Integration of 5G with IoT devices for traffic management, energy optimization, and surveillance (Yang, Zhou, & Wang, 2020). Terahertz Communication enables ultra-high data rates for IoT applications (Dang, Amin, Shihada, & Alouini, 2020). AI Integration is a AI-driven network optimization, enabling autonomous decision-making in IoT systems (Saad, Bennis, & Chen, 2021). Haptic Communications supports real-time tactile experiences, beneficial for remote surgeries and virtual reality (Latva-aho & Leppänen, 2021). Smart Agriculture is a precision farming using AI and edge computing for soil monitoring and resource optimization. Space IoT is a Integration of satellite networks with terrestrial IoT devices for global connectivity (Giordani, Polese, & Mezzavilla, 2020). Digital Twins is a Real-time virtual replicas of physical systems for predictive maintenance in industries (Mumtaz, Adeel, & Al-Dulaimi, 2021).

WOC May Be Broken Down into Five Different Types Based On Its Effective Range:

(i) Ultra short-range WOC – application in a completely optical lab-on-a-chip setup or for inter-chip communication.
(ii) Short-range WOC – utilized in WBANs or WPANs (wireless LANs) that connect people's bodies.
(iii) Medium-range WOC – utilized for infrared (IR) or visible light (VLC) communication inside for WLANs, car-to-car, and car-to-grid applications.
(iv) Long-range WOC – used for landline telephone connections between buildings or metro areas.
(v) Ultra-long-range WOC – used in far space missions, interstellar connections, and ground-based satellite communications.

There are two main types of WOC: outdoor WOC, which is also known as free-space optical (FSO) communication, and indoor WOC. The angle between the transmitter and receiver divides the indoor WOC system into segments.

Figure 1. Wireless Optical Communication system categorization (Source: https:// arxiv.org)

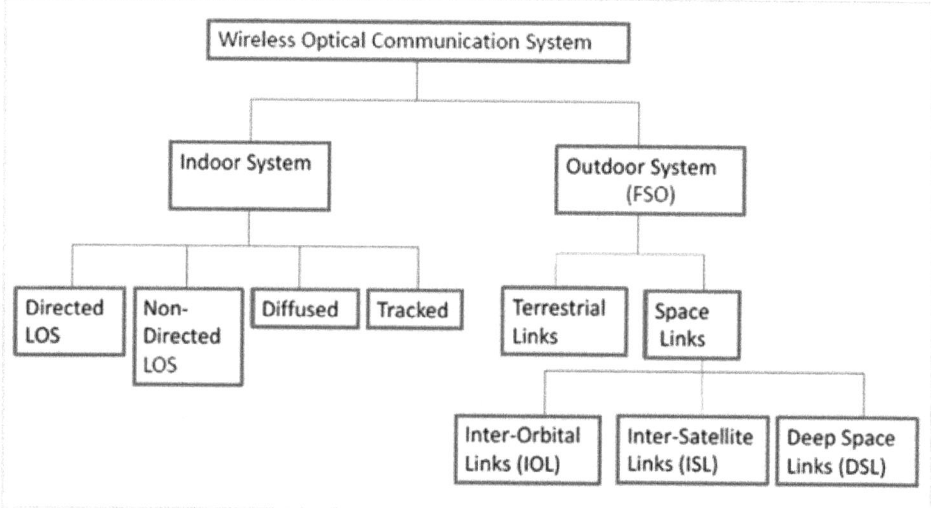

Optical Wireless Indoor Networking

Wherever a hardwired connection would be inconvenient to install, such as inside a building, wireless optical communication lines provide a flexible alternative. Transmitters are light sources like lasers or LEDs, while receivers are photodetectors. When compared to radio frequency equipment or the current copper wires, these devices and their driving circuits are very cost effective. In addition, optical signals do not penetrate walls, making indoor WOC a highly secure technology that prevents eavesdropping. This is in contrast to electromagnetic waves, which may create interference. Both the visible light spectrum and the infrared light spectrum contain these optical waves, are capable of providing very high frequency ranges (THz). Due to their low power consumption, these gadgets may also be used in portable terminals. There are several benefits to using an indoor optical wireless system, however the system's performance may be hindered by a number of drawbacks. These deficiencies are caused by a number of factors, including (i) Optoelectronic devices' slow speed, significant path loss, indoor noise from incandescent, fluorescent, or solar lighting, multipath dispersion, and interference from artificial noise sources are all problems. The system's reach is limited because eye safety regulations restrict the average transmission wattage .

LEDs and LDs are the most prevalent types of optical sources utilised in IR transmitters for indoor WOC. LEDs are favoured over LDs because they are more practical in many ways, including cost, modulation bandwidth, operating region linearity, and operating region features. LEDs are not extremely powerful since they are non-directional optical sources. In light of this, it is possible to employ a series of LEDs to make up for the reduced power output. LEDs, however, have a hard time functioning at speeds beyond 100 Mbps. Laser diodes may be utilised for data speeds in the gigabit per second range. As they are very coordinated and could cause optical harm, laser diodes can't be used straightforwardly for indoor WOC due to eye safety requirements.

Link Configuration Types

The degree of directionality of the transmitter and the width of the field of view (FOV) of the receiver detector are the two most important criteria for determining the kind of indoor optical connection that will be used. From this, we may identify four primary classes of link topology: direct LOS, non-direct LOS, diffuse, and multi-beam quasi-diffuse.

i. Directed LOS System

Both the transmitter's beam angle and the receiver's field of vision in such a WOC system are very restricted, limiting the system to point-to-point or LOS communication only. Receiver and transmitter alignment is critical for maximizing service quality. Communication cannot proceed if the LOS route is blocked

Figure 2. Directed LOS link

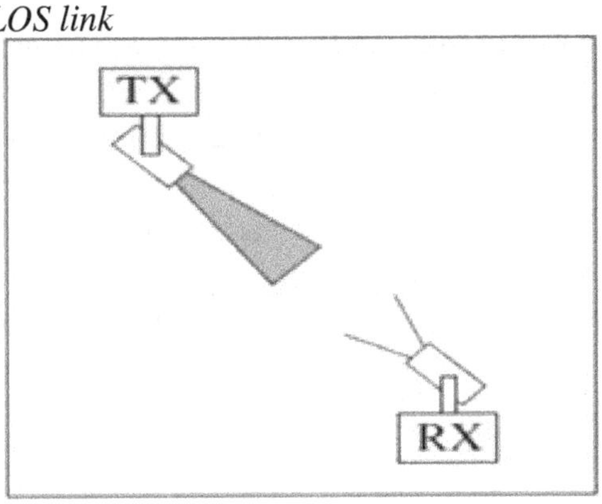

The figure provides a visual depiction of the connection. For many years, this setup has been standard for low-data-rate remote-control applications (Savage, 2002; Forrester, 2013; Andy96877, n.d.; Laser Communications, n.d.) on consumer electronics like TVs and stereos. TX- transmitter, RX- receiver. Portable devices like computers, mobile equipment, personal digital assistants, etc. may communicate with one another using this method. Hybrid LOS links are another kind of LOS connection that may be established depending on the degree of directionality. Both the sender and the receiver will be looking directly at each other, but the sender's divergence angle will be substantially greater than the recipient's field of view. Although this setup offers more coverage than directed LOS, it does so at the expense of power economy and is plagued by blocking issues.

Advantages:

- Greater efficiency with less wasted energy due to route loss
- Multipath distortion has been reduced.
- Greater suppression of outside light
- Increased linkage spending

Disadvantages:

- Mobility in a normal interior setting is impossible with links because they are so vulnerable to blockage (or shadowing).
- It is less adaptable since it does not allow for broadcast connections between several nodes.
- Inconvenient for certain uses is the need for precise alignment between the transmitter and receiver.

ii. System With No Directional LOS (Non-Directed LOS)

Point-to-multipoint communication is a good fit for an interior system like this. There is no need for precise alignment since both the transmitter's bar point and the beneficiary's field of vision are sufficiently large. The user's range of motion is limited by this mechanism. The transmitter and detector field of view (FOV) of this sort of connection are both sufficiently large to encompass an entire building. When opposed to directed LOS, such connections don't need precise pointing and alignment. For a given connection distance and transmission power, however, the received irradiance is reduced in this instance. It gives you the freedom of movement you need. For bigger rooms, optical cells may be created and managed independently of one another using transmitters with precisely calibrated beam divergence.

Figure 3. Non-directed LOS link

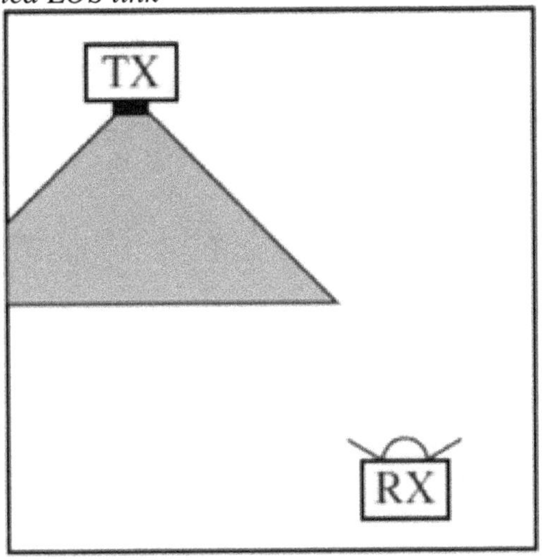

Users within the cell's range can access a data rate of up to 10 Mbps over this connection, which can reach distances of tens of metres.

Advantages:

- Boost portability for the end-user
- Greater resistance to shadowing
- Remove the necessity for finger pointing
- Compatible with point-to-multipoint broadcasting

Disadvantages:

- Due to wider beam divergence, the received signal is distorted by multipath as it is reflected off of walls and other objects in the room.
- Power efficiency is lower.

iii. Dispersed Network (Diffused)

The antenna of the transmitter in such a setup points upward. Multiple bounces off the ceiling and walls ensure that the light reaches the wide-angle receiver. This system does not experience LOS path blocking because of the system's redundancy in transmission paths.

Figure 4. Diffused link

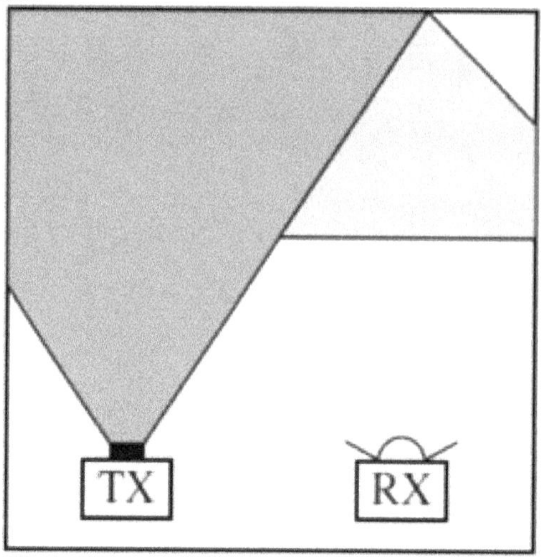

Advantages:

- The optical sign is communicated around the room utilizing the reflected characteristics of the walls and roof, accordingly exact arrangement between the transmitter and recipient is pointless.
- This connection is more durable and versatile since it is less prone to blocking and shadowing.

Disadvantages:

- Severe multipath distortion
- Extremely low link range (5 m), with optical way deficiency of 50-70 dB. The IEEE 802.11 infrared actual layer standard favors the diffuse link configuration. Data speeds of up to 50 Mbps are supported, and its typical form is shown in Fig.

iv. Tracked System

The receiver and the transmitter in a tracked system are able to follow each other. Effective tracking necessitates the use of either mechanical or electronic control.

Optical Transmission in Open Spaces / Outdoors

Transmission of information via free-space optical correspondence requires an immediate view between the source and the objective. Here, the source data signal is adjusted on the optical transporter and afterward permitted to travel unguided through the environment or free space to the objective recipient. Proliferation of optical pillar through environment and free space is expected for both ground-to-satellite (optical uplink) and satellite-to-ground (optical downlink). Consequently, these associations are a half breed of earthly and space-based technologies.

Figure 5. Uses for FSO link communications

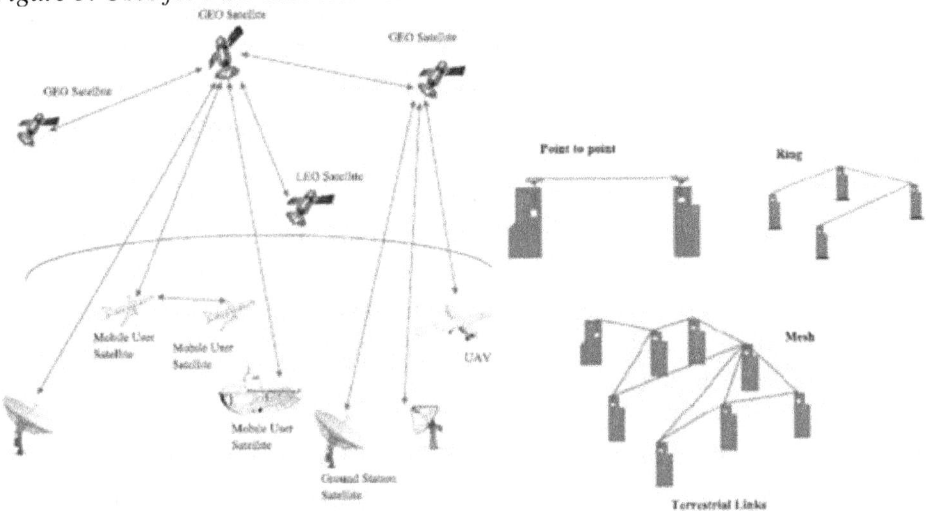

Figure 6. FSO block diagram

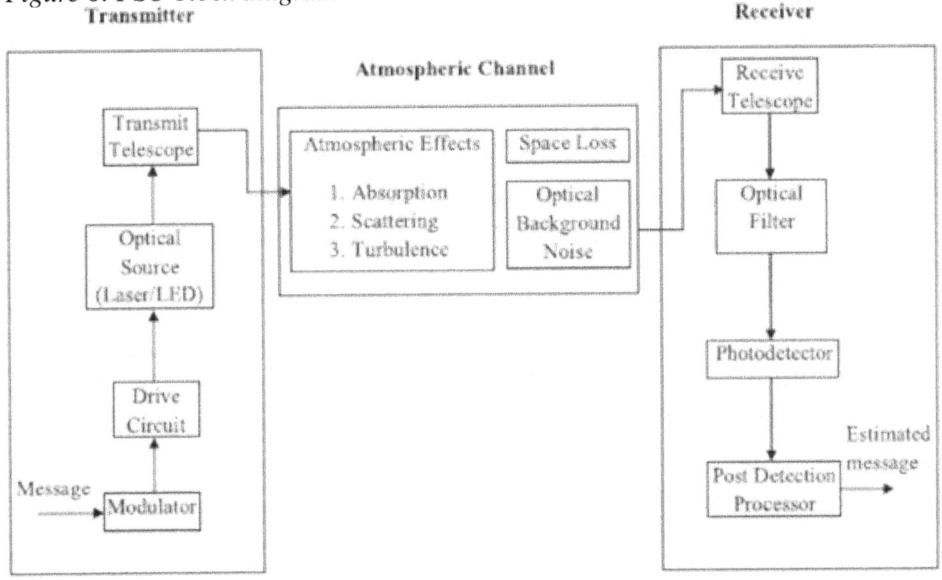

The FSO communication connection, like other communication technologies, is made up of the transmitter, the channel, and the receiver.

(i) Transmitter: Tweaking the message signal onto the optical transporter for climatic engendering to the recipient is its significant job. The modulator (a), the driver circuit for the optical source (b) to settle the optical radiations against temperature variances, and (c) the collimator or telescope (which gathers, collimates, and coordinates the optical radiations towards the recipient) are the three most significant pieces of the transmitter. Force adjustment (IM), in which the source information is balanced on the irradiance/power of the optical transporter, is by far the most used kind of modulation. This may be accomplished either by directly correlating the message signal to be broadcast with the driving current of the optical source or by utilizing an outer modulator.
(ii) Route: Due to its dependence on the atmosphere as a propagation medium, the FSO communication route is vulnerable to weather conditions beyond human control. These variables attenuate and degrade the received signal but have no consistent characteristics. When it comes to FSO system performance, the channel is often a limiting factor.
(iii) The Recipient(s): Its main job is to get back the data that was sent out from the optical radiation that came in. A receiver telescope, filter, photodetector, and demodulator are its constituent parts. The optical radiation is gotten by the getting telescope and centered onto the photodetector .The incident optical signal is focused on the photodetector, which turns it into an electrical signal, by use of the optical filter, which also serves to attenuate ambient radiation.

i. Terrestrial Links

The terrestrial FSO technology is used for metro area expansion or interbuilding connectivity. This is mainly a line-of-sight conversation. It can be used for x-haul of 3G/4G/5G mobile communications and in case of a natural disaster.

ii. Space Link

A connection between two satellites in low Earth orbit (LEO) is known as an inter-satellite link. Satellites in low Earth orbit (LEO) may communicate with those in geostationary Earth orbit (GEO) through an inter-orbital connection. Tight arrangement and following, low power utilization, and being lightweight are fundamental measures for space applications

The Design of the WOC Infrastructure

A WOC framework comprises of three significant subsystems: Transmitter, channel, and beneficiary. Figure 3 shows a block schematic of a typical FSO communication system. In RF communication, the antenna plays a function similar to that of the transmit optics and receive optics.

Figure 7. FSO communication system

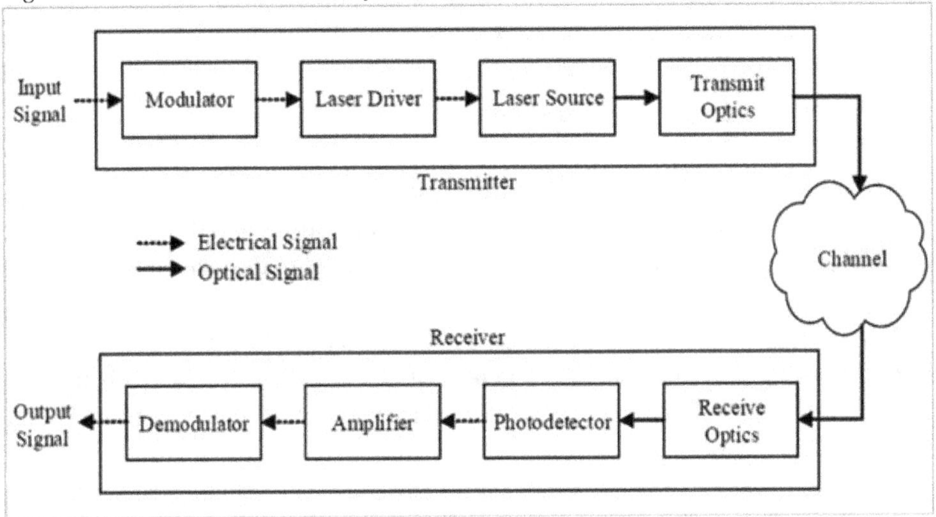

i. Transmitter

The job of the transmitter is to take the data and transform it into a signal format that can be sent over the chosen channel. The modulator controls the laser driver by altering the information signal. In order to transfer data from the electrical domain to the optical domain, the laser diode is used as the optical source. In order to send the laser's signal to the receiver, the system relies on transmit optics.

ii. Channel

The WOC system supports a variety of channels, including air and water. In the event of the barometrical channel, the sign experiences capricious lessening attributable to factors like mist, murkiness, cloud, and downpour. Temperature fluctuations in the atmosphere cause a medium's refractive index to fluctuate, leading to turbulence. An FSO communication link's performance is primarily constrained by atmospheric turbulence.

iii. Receiver

The episode optical sign is gathered by the get optics in the collector and focused on the photodetector. The photodetector is responsible for transforming the optical sign into an electrical one. Then the enhancer supports the sign and furthermore raises the sign to-clamor proportion (SNR).Last but not least, the demodulator provides an approximation of the input signal.

The Waves of the WOC System

Atmospheric influences, attenuation, eye safety standards, component availability, pricing, and background noise level all play a role in determining the optimal wavelength. The overall spectrum of wavelengths is identical to that which is employed in optical fibre transmission.

Most of FSO correspondence frameworks are intended to work in the windows of 780-850nm and 1520- 1600nm. The benefit of utilizing these groups is that the parts are broadly available since they are used in fiber optic organizations and other modern and purchaser applications.

The gain of an antenna decreases with increasing wavelength. Therefore, it is preferable to operate at shorter wavelengths. However, regulations regarding the protection of the eyes permit the transmission of significantly more power in the higher wavelengths.

i. Benefits of WOC

Due to its shorter wavelength of operation, the WOC system offers various benefits over RF communication systems.

Increased bandwidth

The capacity of a communication system to convey information grows in proportion to the square of the carrier frequency. The available bandwidth in optical communication is roughly 105 times that of the RF communication system.

Free space electromagnetic radiation

The establishment of an FSO communication link does not necessitate any prior licencing at this time. It simplifies creating and launching an FSO communication system.

Enhanced safety

The bar disparity is relative to the frequency. Similar to WOC communication, RF communication's operating wavelength and beam divergence are significantly larger than those of WOC communication. Since the beam is focused in a small area, it increases safety and conserves energy.

Lighter and weaker

The intensity of the got power is more noteworthy for a given sent power due to small beam divergence. It paves the way for less complicated and lighter-weight radio equipment. The antenna gain decreases as the square of the frequency of activity increments. A small recieving wire in the WOC framework might deliver better addition.The Downside of the WOC System Need for LOS Because of the narrow beam divergence, LOS is essential for reliable transmission. Must have the ability to point and track. Again, building vibrations represent a difficult issue to the improvement of a solid correspondence connection because of narrow beam divergence. Reliable functioning necessitates the use of precise pointing and tracking technologies.

Atmospheric effects

Haze and fog have a significant influence on WOC transmission owing to the significant attenuation of optical signals. Daytime temperature fluctuations inherently cause random changes in the air's refractive index. This random variation in receiver intensity is caused by atmospheric turbulence.

Background noise power

The sun's area corresponding to the transmitter and collector is a significant variable. Sun is a possible source of background noise. A WOC connection can be severely degraded by environmental noise in some cases.

Applications

WOC communication can be used in a wide variety of contexts. Principal domains of use are:

- Inter-structure dialogue
- Recovery-oriented software
- Connections to outer space and satellites
- To supplement a primary optical fibre connection
- X-haul to a mobile communication system that supports 3G, 4G, and 5G

The FSO innovation is acquiring expanding prevalence for Gbps capacity correspondence network. To reduce the impact of the weather and improve throughput in all types of weather, researchers have been focusing on WOC systems. The utilization of refined forward mistake remedy methods and opening averaging are a portion of the empowering influences for a hearty correspondence connect.

CONCLUSION

Due to efficiency of Optical Wireless technologies s has attracted a lot of attention. It might pave the path for several implementations of 5G and 6G in the physical world. Challenges with energy, speed, and cost are discussed in this chapter as they pertain to sensors in the Internet of Things. We analyzed challenges of IoT technologies like wireless optical communication, frequent handover, inter cell interference loss due to atmospheric changes and flickering avoidance. WOC has a number of advantages compared to other technologies.

REFERENCES

Andy. (n.d.). Visible light communication—VLC & Pure VLCTM. Retrieved from http://andy96877.blogspot.com/p/visiblelight-communication-vlc-is-data.html

Arruego, I., Guerrero, H., Rodriguez, S., Martinez-Oter, J., Jimenez, J., Dominguez, J., Martin-Ortega, A., de Mingo, J., Rivas, J., Apestigue, V., Sanchez, J., Iglesias, J., Alvarez, M., Gallego, P., Azcue, J., Ruiz de Galarreta, C., Martin, B., Alvarez-Herrero, A., Diaz-Michelena, M., & Torres, J. (2009). OWLS: A ten-year history in optical wireless links for intra-satellite communications. *IEEE Journal on Selected Areas in Communications*, 27(9), 1599–1611. DOI: 10.1109/JSAC.2009.091210

Chen, S., Li, Q., & Zhao, Y. (2019). 5G-enabled IoT for mission-critical applications. *IEEE Internet of Things Journal*, 6(3), 4730–4740. DOI: 10.1109/JIOT.2019.2899012

Dang, S., Amin, O., Shihada, B., & Alouini, M. (2020). What should 6G be? *Nature Electronics*, 3(1), 20–29. DOI: 10.1038/s41928-019-0355-6

Forrester, G. (2013, July). Free space optics, in Digital Air Wireless. Retrieved from https://www.digitalairwireless.com/wireless-blog/2013-07/free-space-optics.html

Giordani, M., Polese, M., & Mezzavilla, M. (2020). Integrating satellite and terrestrial IoT in 6G networks. *IEEE Communications Magazine*, 58(1), 67–73. DOI: 10.1109/MCOM.2020.190052

Hirabayashi, K., Yamamoto, T., & Hino, S. (2004). Optical backplane with free-space optical interconnections using tunable beam deflectors and a mirror for bookshelf-assembled terabit per second class asynchronous transfer mode switch. *Optical Engineering (Redondo Beach, Calif.)*, 37, 1332–1342.

Kazemlou, S., Hranilovic, S., & Kumar, S. (2011). All-optical multihop free-space optical communication systems. *Journal of Lightwave Technology*, 29(18), 2663–2669. DOI: 10.1109/JLT.2011.2160615

Laser Communications. (n.d.). Laser communications. Retrieved from https://lasercommunications.weebly.com/

Latva-aho, M., & Leppänen, K. (2021). *Key drivers and research challenges for 6G ubiquitous wireless intelligence. 6G Flagship*. University of Oulu.

Li, X., Zhao, Z., & Sun, J. (2021). Enhanced mobile broadband for IoT in 5G networks. *IEEE Access : Practical Innovations, Open Solutions*, 9, 234–247. DOI: 10.1109/ACCESS.2021.3045645

Lipsett, M. S., McIntyre, C., & Liu, R. (1969). Space instrumentation for laser communications. *IEEE Journal of Quantum Electronics*, 5(6), 348–349. DOI: 10.1109/JQE.1969.1081959

Lu, Y., Li, Q., & Zhang, X. (2021). Industrial IoT applications with 5G technologies. *Journal of Industrial Information Integration*, 25, 100265. DOI: 10.1016/j.jii.2021.100265

Lucy, R. F., & Lang, K. (1968). Optical communications experiments at 6328 Å and 10:6. *Applied Optics*, 7(10), 1965–1970. DOI: 10.1364/AO.7.001965 PMID: 20068920

Mumtaz, S., Adeel, A., & Al-Dulaimi, A. (2021). Digital twins in 6G-enabled IoT systems. *IEEE Wireless Communications*, 28(6), 134–141. DOI: 10.1109/MWC.2021.9620107

Saad, W., Bennis, M., & Chen, M. (2021). A vision of 6G wireless systems: Applications, trends, technologies, and open research problems. *IEEE Network*, 34(3), 134–142. DOI: 10.1109/MNET.001.1900287

Savage, N. (2002). Linking with light. IEEE Spectrum. Retrieved from https://spectrum.ieee.org/semiconductors/optoelectronics/linking-with-light

Shafiq, M., Guo, S., & Nazir, A. (2020). 5G and IoT in healthcare: Applications and challenges. *Computers in Biology and Medicine*, 122, 103810. DOI: 10.1016/j.compbiomed.2020.103810

Yang, F., Zhou, X., & Wang, H. (2020). Smart cities powered by 5G and IoT: A case study. *IEEE Communications Magazine*, 58(1), 23–29. DOI: 10.1109/MCOM.2020.190029

Compilation of References

Abadi, M., Chu, A., & Goodfellow, I.Deep learning with differential privacy. *Proceedings of the 2016 ACM SIGSAC Conference on Computer and Communications Security*, 308–18. DOI: 10.1145/2976749.2978318

Abdel-Hamid, O., Mohamed, A.-R., Jiang, H., Deng, L., Penn, G., & Yu, D. (2014). Convolutional neural networks for speech recognition. *IEEE/ACM Transactions on Audio, Speech, and Language Processing*, 22(10), 1533–1545. DOI: 10.1109/TASLP.2014.2339736

Abdulla, A., Naim, A., Muniasamy, A., Mohammed, A. B., Bilfaqih, S. M., & Sabahath, A. (2024). Optimizing business insights data visualization applications in sales forecasting, marketing analytics, and financial reporting. *Advances in Business Information Systems and Analytics*, 103–124. DOI: 10.4018/979-8-3693-6537-3.ch006

Acheampong, Nunoo-Mensah, & Chen. (2021). Transformer models for text-based emotion detection: a review of BERT-based approaches. .DOI: 10.1007/s10462-021-09958-2

Adame, T., Bel, A., Bellalta, B., Barcelo, J., & Oliver, M. (2014). *IEEE 802.11ah: The Wi-Fi approach for M2M communications*. IEEE Xplore. DOI: 10.1109/wfi-cloud.2016.24

Aggarwal, C. C. (2015). *Data Mining: The Textbook*. Springer. DOI: 10.1007/978-3-319-14142-8

Aggrawal, R., & Pal, S. (2020). Sequential feature selection and machine learning algorithm-based patient's death events prediction and diagnosis in heart disease. *SN Computer Science*, 1(6), 1–8. DOI: 10.1007/s42979-020-00370-1

Agrawal, D. R., Tanabe, Y., Weng, D., Ma, A., Hsu, S., Liao, S.-Y., Zhen, Z., Zhu, Z.-Y., Sun, C., Dong, Z., Yang, F., Tse, H. F., Poon, A. S. Y., & Ho, J. S. (2017). Conformal phased surfaces for wireless powering of bioelectronic microdevices. *Nature Biomedical Engineering*, 1(3), 43. DOI: 10.1038/s41551-017-0043 PMID: 29226018

Ahmed, I., Jeon, G., & Piccialli, F. (2021). A deep-learning-based smart healthcare system for patient's discomfort detection at the edge of Internet of things. IEEE Internet of Things Journal, 8(13).

Ahmed, M., Khan, M., & Anwar, A. (2021). Analyzing the Impact of API on Data Collection in Cloud-Based Applications. *Journal of Cloud Computing (Heidelberg, Germany)*, 10(1), 15–24.

Ahuja, L. (2019). *Crime against women: Analysis and prediction using data mining techniques.* Big Data, Cloud and Parallel Computing.

Ajibade, S. S., & Adediran, A. (2016). An overview of big data visualization techniques in data mining. *International Journal of Computer Science and Information Technology Research*, 4(3), 105–113.

Akila, D. (2019). *Crime against women (CAW) analysis and prediction in Tamilnadu police using data mining techniques. International Journal of Recent Technology and Engineering.*

Aldaoud, A., Laurenson, C., Rivet, F., Yuce, M. R., & Redouté, J. (2015). Design of an inductively powered implantable wireless blood pressure sensing interface using capacitive coupling. *IEEE/ASME Transactions on Mechatronics*, 20(1), 487–491. DOI: 10.1109/TMECH.2014.2322614

Aldhaher, S., Luk, P. C. K., & Whidborne, J. F. (2014). Electronic tuning of misaligned coils in wireless power transfer systems. *IEEE Transactions on Power Electronics*, 29(11), 5975–5982. DOI: 10.1109/TPEL.2014.2297993

Al-Garadi, M. A., Mohamed, A., Al-Ali, A. K., Du, X., Ali, I., & Guizani, M. (2020). A survey of machine and deep learning methods for Internet of things (IoT) security. IEEE Communications Surveys & Tutorials, 22(3), 1646–1685. DOI: 10.1109/COMST.2020.2988293

Alghanim, A. A., Rahman, S. M. M., & Hossain, M. A. (2017). Privacy analysis of smart city healthcare services. In Proceedings - 2017 IEEE International Symposium on Multimedia, ISM 2017 (pp. 394–398). Institute of Electrical and Electronics Engineers Inc. DOI: 10.1109/ISM.2017.79

Alharthi, A., Krotov, V., & Bowman, M. (2017). Addressing barriers to big data. https://www.researchgate.net/publication/317279522

Alizadeh, T. (2017). An investigation of IBM's smarter cities challenge: What do participating cities want? *Cities (London, England)*, 63, 70–80. DOI: 10.1016/j.cities.2016.12.009

Almalki, M. (2022). Statistical Techniques in Data Exploration: A Comprehensive Review. *International Journal of Data Science and Analytics*, 15(2), 102–118.

Anderson, G. S., & Sodini, C. G. (2013). Body coupled communication: The channel and implantable sensors. *2013 IEEE International Conference on Body Sensor Networks (BSN),* 3–7. DOI: 10.1109/BSN.2013.6575490

Android. (2017, March 10). *Introduction to the sensor and location platform in Windows*. https://msdn.microsoft.com/en-us/library/windows/desktop/dd318936(v=vs.85).aspx

Android. (2017, March 10). *Sensor stack.* https://source.android.com/devices/sensors/sensor-stack.html

Android. (2017, October 23). *Sensor overview*. https://developer.android.com/guide/topics/sensors/sensors_overview.html

Andy. (n.d.). Visible light communication—VLC & Pure VLCTM. Retrieved from http://andy96877.blogspot.com/p/visiblelight-communication-vlc-is-data.html

Apple. (2015, December 1). *Apple developer documentation*. https://developer.apple.com/documentation

Apple. (2017, October 23). *Core motion*. https://developer.apple.com/documentation/coremotion

Arora, S., Agarwal, P., & Gupta, R. (2021). Tampering vulnerabilities in IoT-enabled glucose monitors. *Health Informatics Journal*, 27(4), 1–12. DOI: 10.1177/14604582211058512

Arra, S., Leskinen, J., Heikkila, J., & Vanhala, J. (2007). Ultrasonic power and data link for wireless implantable applications. In *2007 2nd International Symposium on Wireless Pervasive Computing* (pp. 567–571). IEEE. DOI: 10.1109/ISWPC.2007.342668

Arruego, I., Guerrero, H., Rodriguez, S., Martinez-Oter, J., Jimenez, J., Dominguez, J., Martin-Ortega, A., de Mingo, J., Rivas, J., Apestigue, V., Sanchez, J., Iglesias, J., Alvarez, M., Gallego, P., Azcue, J., Ruiz de Galarreta, C., Martin, B., Alvarez-Herrero, A., Diaz-Michelena, M., & Torres, J. (2009). OWLS: A ten-year history in optical wireless links for intra-satellite communications. *IEEE Journal on Selected Areas in Communications*, 27(9), 1599–1611. DOI: 10.1109/JSAC.2009.091210

Aryal, S., Alimadadi, A., Manandhar, I., Joe, B., & Cheng, X. (2020). Machine learning strategy for gut microbiome-based diagnostic screening of cardiovascular disease. *Hypertension*, 76(5), 1555–1562. DOI: 10.1161/HYPERTENSIONA-HA.120.15885 PMID: 32909848

Asamoah, D. (2022). Improving data visualization skills: A curriculum design. *International Journal of Education and Development Using Information and Communication Technology*, 18(1), 213–235.

Ativanichayaphong, T., Tang, S. J., Hsu, L. C., Huang, W. D., Seo, Y. S., & Tibbals, H. F.. (2010). An implantable batteryless wireless impedance sensor for gastroesophageal reflux diagnosis. *IEEE MTT-S International Microwave Symposium Digest,* 608–611. DOI: 10.1109/MWSYM.2010.5516775

Avila, K., Sanmartin, P., Jabba, D., & Jimeno, M. (2017). Applications based on service-oriented architecture (SOA) in the field of home healthcare. *Sensors (Basel)*, 17(8), 1703. DOI: 10.3390/s17081703 PMID: 28757557

Aybeyan, S. (2021). Systematic Review Of Big Data, Digital Transformation Areas And Industry 4.0 Trends In 2021. *International Scientific Journal Vision*, 6(2), 27–41.

Bahuguna, P. C., Srivastava, R., & Tiwari, S. (2023). Two-decade journey of green human resource management research: A bibliometric analysis. *Benchmarking*, 30(2), 585–602. DOI: 10.1108/BIJ-10-2021-0619

Bandi, A., & Fellah, A. (2017). Crafting a data visualization course for the tech industry. *Journal of Computing Sciences in Colleges*, 33(2), 46–56.

Bari, N., Mani, G., & Berkovich, S. (2013). Internet of things as a methodological concept. In *Fourth International Conference on Computing for Geospatial Research and Application (COM. Geo)* (pp. 48–55). IEEE. DOI: 10.1109/COMGEO.2013.8

Barraclough, S., Piggott, D., Till, K., Kerr, A., & Emmonds, S. (2023). Creating a shared mental model of performance: Coaches' perspectives of key position-specific soccer actions. *International Journal of Sports Science & Coaching*.

Bating, C., & Scannapieco, M. (2009). Data Quality. In Data Management and Data Quality.

Bazaka, K., & Jacob, M. (2012). Implantable devices: Issues and challenges. *Electronics (Basel)*, 2(1), 1–34. DOI: 10.3390/electronics2010001

Behfar, M. H., Björninen, T., Moradi, E., Sydänheimo, L., & Ukkonen, L. (2015). Biotelemetric wireless intracranial pressure monitoring: An in vitro study. *International Journal of Antennas and Propagation*, 2015, 1–10. DOI: 10.1155/2015/918698

Behrens, J. T. (1997). Principles and procedures of exploratory data analysis. *Psychological Methods*, 2(2), 141–149. DOI: 10.1037/1082-989X.2.2.131

Bell, L. E. (2008). Cooling, heating, generating power, and recovering waste heat with thermoelectric systems. *Science*, 321(5895), 1457–1461. DOI: 10.1126/science.1158899 PMID: 18787160

Ben Amar, A., Kouki, A. B., & Cao, H. (2015). Power approaches for implantable medical devices. *Sensors (Basel)*, 15(11), 28889–28914. DOI: 10.3390/s151128889 PMID: 26580626

Ben Arfi, W., Ben Nasr, I., Kondrateva, G., & Hikkerova, L. (2021). The role of trust in intention to use the IoT in eHealth: Application of the modified UTAUT in a consumer context. *Technological Forecasting and Social Change*, 167, 120688. DOI: 10.1016/j.techfore.2021.120688

Berrar, D., Lopes, P., & Dubitzky, W. (2019). Incorporating domain knowledge in machine learning for soccer outcome prediction. *Machine Learning*, 108(1), 97–126. DOI: 10.1007/s10994-018-5747-8

Berson, I. R., & Berso, M. J. (2009). Making sense of social studies with visualization tools. *Social Education*, 73(3), 124–126.

Bertels, S. (2021). Data Quality Frameworks: A Review and Future Directions. *Journal of Database Management*, 13(3), 45–58.

Bhauvaneswari, N. S. (2019). *Data mining techniques to analyze and predict crimes*. IJRTE.

Bhola, J., Shabaz, M., Dhiman, G., Vimal, S., Subbulakshmi, P., & Soni, S. K. (2021). Performance evaluation of multilayer clustering network using distributed energy efficient clustering with enhanced threshold protocol. *Wireless Personal Communications*. Advance online publication. DOI: 10.1007/s11277-021-08780-x PMID: 34456513

Bhola, J., Soni, S., & Cheema, G. K. (2020). Genetic algorithm based optimized leach protocol for energy efficient wireless sensor networks. *Journal of Ambient Intelligence and Humanized Computing*, 11(3), 1281–1288. DOI: 10.1007/s12652-019-01382-3

Bhowmick, S. (2019). *Analysis of crimes against women in India using regression.* IJEAT.

Birjali, M., Kasri, M., & Beni-Hssane, A. (2021). A comprehensive survey on sentiment analysis: Approaches, challenges and trends. https://www.sciencedirect.com/science/article/abs/pii/S095070512100397X

Blackberry. (2017, March 10). *Sensors.* https://developer.blackberry.com/native/documentation/device_comm/sensors/

Bollen, J., Mao, H., & Zeng, X. (2011). Twitter Mood Predicts the Stock Market. *Journal of Computational Science*, 2(1), 1–8. DOI: 10.1016/j.jocs.2010.12.007

Brandão, B., De Lima, T. W., Soares, A., Melo, L., & Maximo, M. R. (2022). Multiagent reinforcement learning for strategic decision making and control in robotic soccer through self-play. *IEEE Access : Practical Innovations, Open Solutions*, 10, 72628–72642. DOI: 10.1109/ACCESS.2022.3189021

Bratan, T., Ondokuz, M. C., & Clarke, M. (2006). *Optimum design of remote patient monitoring systems.* IEEE Engineering in Medicine and Biology Society. DOI: 10.1109/IEMBS.2006.260729

Breiman, L. (1996). Bagging Predictors. *Machine Learning*, 24(2), 123–140. DOI: 10.1007/BF00058655

Brosch, T., & Tam, R. (2023). Manifold learning of brain MRIs by deep learning. Med Image Comput Comput Assist Interv, 16, 633–40. DOI: 10.1007/978-3-642-40763-5_78

Buscema, M., Breda, M., & Lodwick, W. (2013). Training with Input Selection and Testing (TWIST) Algorithm: A significant advance in pattern recognition performance of machine learning. *Journal of Intelligent Learning Systems and Applications*, 5(1), 29–38. DOI: 10.4236/jilsa.2013.51004

Cairo, A. (2013). *The Functional Art: An Introduction to Information Graphics and Visualization.* New Riders.

Cao, H., Rao, S., Tang, S., Tibbals, H. F., Spechler, S., & Chiao, J.-C. (2013). Batteryless implantable dual-sensor capsule for esophageal reflux monitoring. *Gastrointestinal Endoscopy*, 77(4), 649–653. DOI: 10.1016/j.gie.2012.10.029 PMID: 23290721

Cao, N., & Cui, W. (2016). Overview of text visualization techniques. In *Introduction to text visualization* (pp. 11–40). Springer. DOI: 10.2991/978-94-6239-186-4_2

Catarinucci, L., De Donno, D., Mainetti, L., Palano, L., Patrono, L., Stefanizzi, M. L., & Tarricone, L. (2015). An IoT-aware architecture for smart healthcare systems. *IEEE Internet of Things Journal*, 2(6), 515–526. Advance online publication. DOI: 10.1109/JIOT.2015.2417684

Chaki, J., Thillai Ganesh, S., Cidham, S. K., & Ananda Theertan, S. (2020). Machine learning and artificial intelligence based diabetes mellitus detection and self-management: A systematic review. *Journal of King Saud University. Computer and Information Sciences*. Advance online publication. DOI: 10.1016/j.jksuci.2020.06.013

Chaudhuri, K., Monteleoni, C., & Sarwate, A. (2011). Differentially private empirical risk minimization. *Journal of Machine Learning Research*, 12, 1069–1109. PMID: 21892342

Chaudhuri, S., Dayal, U., & Narasayya, V. (2011). Data Warehousing and Business Intelligence: A Survey. *ACM Computing Surveys*, 45(4), 1–43.

Chavez-Santiago, R., Garcia-Pardo, C., Fornes-Leal, A., Valles-Lluch, A., Vermeeren, G., Joseph, W., Balasingham, I., & Cardona, N. (2015). Experimental path loss models for in-body communications within 2.36–2.5 GHz. *IEEE Journal of Biomedical and Health Informatics*, 19(3), 1–1. DOI: 10.1109/JBHI.2015.2418757 PMID: 25838532

Chavez-Santiago, R., Sayrafian-Pour, K., Khaleghi, A., Takizawa, K., Wang, J., Balasingham, I., & Li, H.-B. (2013). Propagation models for IEEE 802.15.6 standardization of implant communication in body area networks. *IEEE Communications Magazine*, 51(8), 80–87. DOI: 10.1109/MCOM.2013.6576343

Cheffena, M. (2015). Performance evaluation of wireless body sensors in the presence of slow and fast fading effects. *IEEE Sensors Journal*, 15(10), 5518–5526. DOI: 10.1109/JSEN.2015.2443251

Cheng, C., & Chiu, H. (2017). An artificial neural network model for the evaluation of carotid artery stenting prognosis using a National-Wide Database. *Proceedings of the 39th Annual International Conference of the IEEE Engineering in Medicine and Biology Society (EMBC),* 2566–2569. DOI: 10.1109/EMBC.2017.8037381

Cheng, J.-Z., Ni, D., Chou, Y.-H., Qin, J., Tiu, C.-M., Chang, Y.-C., Huang, C.-S., Shen, D., & Chen, C.-M. (2016). Computer-aided diagnosis with deep learning architecture: Applications to breast lesions in US images and pulmonary nodules in CT scans. *Scientific Reports*, 6(1), 24454. DOI: 10.1038/srep24454 PMID: 27079888

Chen, L. Y.. (2014). Continuous wireless pressure monitoring and mapping with ultrasmall passive sensors for health monitoring and critical care. *Nature Communications*, 5, 5028. DOI: 10.1038/ncomms6028 PMID: 25284074

Chen, S., Li, Q., & Zhao, Y. (2019). 5G-enabled IoT for mission-critical applications. *IEEE Internet of Things Journal*, 6(3), 4730–4740. DOI: 10.1109/JIOT.2019.2899012

Chen, W.. (2014). A fully integrated 8-channel closed-loop epileptic seizure control. *IEEE Journal of Solid-State Circuits*, 49(1), 232–247. DOI: 10.1109/JSSC.2013.2284346

Chen, W., Zhang, H., & Liu, X. (2019). Addressing replay attacks in healthcare monitoring systems. *Journal of Cybersecurity*, 15(2), 203–212.

Chen, Z. (2023). Artificial intelligence-virtual trainer: Innovative didactics aimed at personalized training needs. *Journal of the Knowledge Economy*, 14(2), 2007–2025. DOI: 10.1007/s13132-022-00985-0

Cheong, J. H., Ng, S. S. Y., Liu, X., Xue, R.-F., Lim, H. J., Khannur, P. B., Chan, K. L., Lee, A. A., Kang, K., Lim, L. S., He, C., Singh, P., Park, W.-T., & Je, M. (2012). An inductively powered implantable blood flow sensor microsystem for vascular grafts. *IEEE Transactions on Biomedical Engineering*, 59(9), 2466–2475. DOI: 10.1109/TBME.2012.2203131 PMID: 22692871

Chhabra, G., Kumar, S., Gupta, S., & Nagpal, P. (2023). Machine Learning for Individual Performance Analysis and Sports Analytics. In *Artificial Intelligence to Analyze Psychophysical and Human Lifestyle* (pp. 113–127). Springer Nature Singapore. DOI: 10.1007/978-981-99-3039-5_10

Chiou, J. C., Hsu, S.-H., Liao, Y.-T., Huang, Y.-C., Yeh, G.-T., Kuei, C.-K., & Dai, K.-S. (2016). Toward a wirelessly powered on-lens intraocular pressure monitoring system. *IEEE Journal of Biomedical and Health Informatics*, 20(5), 1216–1224. DOI: 10.1109/JBHI.2016.2594058 PMID: 27479980

Chitnis, G., Maleki, T., Samuels, B., Cantor, L. B., & Ziaie, B. (2013). A minimally invasive implantable wireless pressure sensor for continuous IOP monitoring. *IEEE Transactions on Biomedical Engineering*, 60(1), 250–256. DOI: 10.1109/TBME.2012.2205248 PMID: 22736631

Chong, A. Y. L. (2017). Predicting online shopping behaviour using data mining techniques. *International Journal of Retail & Distribution Management*, 45(4), 382–402.

Chong, J., Cho, C., & Tabei, F. (2018). *Motion and noise artifact-resilient atrial fibrillation detection using a smartphone*. IEEE Xplore. DOI: 10.1109/JETCAS.2018.2818185

Choudhury, A. (2022). Data Science Applications in Retail: A Systematic Review. *Journal of Retailing and Consumer Services*, 66, 102923.

Chung, H. (2004). *Crime data mining: A general framework and some examples*. ACM SIGPLAN.

Chy, M. K. H., & Buadi, O. N. (2023). Role of data visualization in finance. *American Journal of Industrial and Business Management*, 13(08), 841–856. DOI: 10.4236/ajibm.2023.138047

Cong, P. (2009). A wireless and batteryless 130 milligram 300 μW 10-bit implantable blood pressure sensing microsystem for real-time genetically engineered mice monitoring. *IEEE International Solid-State Circuits Conference, 44*(12), 428–429.

Constantinou, A. C. (2019). Dolores: A model that predicts football match outcomes from all over the world. *Machine Learning*, 108(1), 49–75. DOI: 10.1007/s10994-018-5703-7

Cook, D. J., Duncan, G., Sprint, G., & Fritz, R. L. (2018). Using smart city technology to make healthcare smarter. *Proceedings of the IEEE*, 106(4), 708–722. DOI: 10.1109/JPROC.2017.2787688 PMID: 29628528

Correia, R. B., Li, L., & Rocha, L. M. (2016). Monitoring potential drug interactions and reactions via network analysis of instagram user timelines. *Pacific Symposium on Biocomputing*, 21, 492–503. DOI: 10.1142/9789814749411_0045 PMID: 26776212

Cossich, V. R., Carlgren, D., Holash, R. J., & Katz, L. (2023). Technological Breakthroughs in Sport: Current Practice and Future Potential of Artificial Intelligence, Virtual Reality, Augmented Reality, and Modern Data Visualization in Performance Analysis. *Applied Sciences (Basel, Switzerland)*, 13(23), 12965. DOI: 10.3390/app132312965

Cram, D. (2021). *Data Communication: A Pragmatic Approach*. Routledge.

Dang, N. C., Moreno-García, M. N., & De la Prieta, F. (2020). Sentiment Analysis Based on Deep Learning: A Comparative Study. https://www.mdpi.com/2079-9292/9/3/483

Dang, S., Amin, O., Shihada, B., & Alouini, M. (2020). What should 6G be? *Nature Electronics*, 3(1), 20–29. DOI: 10.1038/s41928-019-0355-6

Davenport, T. H., & Prusak, L. (1998). *Working Knowledge: How Organizations Manage What They Know*. Harvard Business Press.

Dehennis, A., Mailand, M., Grice, D., Getzlaff, S., & Colvin, A. (2013). A near-field-communication (NFC) enabled wireless fluorimeter for fully implantable biosensing applications. *IEEE International Solid-State Circuits Conference,* 298–299. DOI: 10.1109/ISSCC.2013.6487743

Der, G., & Everitt, B. S. (2006). Statistical Analysis of Medical Data Using SAS. http://ftp.sas.com/samples/A60928

Deshmukh, P. (2017). Design of cloud security in the EHR for Indian healthcare services. *Journal of King Saud University. Computer and Information Sciences*, 29(3), 281–287. DOI: 10.1016/j.jksuci.2016.01.002

Deuker, A., Wittkugel, J., Dublin, Y., Klatt, S., Körner, S., Vogt, T., . . . Klemp, M. (2023). Analyzing the effect of reduced field sizes on tactical behaviour in 11 versus 11 football practice. In World Congress on Science and Football 2023: Enhance Performance Engage Society (p. 240).

Dhar, V. (2013). Data Science and Prediction. *Communications of the ACM*, 56(12), 64–73. DOI: 10.1145/2500499

Diamond, M., & Mattia, A. (2017). Data visualization: An exploratory study into the software tools used by businesses. *Journal of Instructional Pedagogies*, 18, 1–13.

Diao, W., Liu, X., Zhou, Z., & Zhang, K. (2014). Your voice assistant is mine: How to abuse speakers to steal information and control your phone. In *Proceedings of the 4th ACM Workshop on Security and Privacy in Smartphones & Mobile Devices* (pp. 63–74). ACM. DOI: 10.1145/2666620.2666623

Donida, A. (2015). A 0.036 mbar circadian and cardiac intraocular pressure sensor for smart implantable lens. *Digest of Technical Papers - IEEE International Solid-State Circuits Conference*, 58, 392–393.

Dovgan, N. (2023). The Pivotal Role of Technology in Enhancing Athletic Performance: Insights and Future Directions. DOI: 10.2139/ssrn.4602857

Du, S., Li, T., Gong, X., & Horng, S.-J. (2020). A hybrid method for traffic flow forecasting using multimodal deep learning. *International Journal of Computational Intelligence Systems*, 13(1), 85. DOI: 10.2991/ijcis.d.200120.001

Dwork, C. (2011). Differential privacy. In *Encyclopedia of Cryptography and Security* (pp. 338–340). Springer. DOI: 10.1007/978-1-4419-5906-5_752

Dziak, D., Jachimczyk, B., & Kulesza, W. J. (2017). IoT-based information system for healthcare application: Design methodology approach. *Applied Sciences (Basel, Switzerland)*, 7(6), 596. DOI: 10.3390/app7060596

Elmqvist, N. (2018). The Role of Interactive Visualization in Data Science. *Information Visualization*, 17(3), 201–207.

Elsisi, M., Tran, M.-Q., Mahmoud, K., Mansour, D.-E. A., Lehtonen, M., & Darwish, M. M. F. (2021). Towards secured online monitoring for digitalized GIS against cyber-attacks based on IoT and machine learning. *IEEE Access : Practical Innovations, Open Solutions*, 9, 78415–78427. DOI: 10.1109/ACCESS.2021.3083499

Enwemeka, C. S. (2001). Attenuation and penetration of visible 632.8 nm and invisible infra-red 904 nm light in soft tissues. *Official Journal of World Association for Laser Therapy*, 13, 95–101.

Ermes, M., Pärkkä, J., & Mäntyjärvi, J. (2008). *Detection of daily activities and sports with wearable sensors in controlled and uncontrolled conditions*. IEEE Xplore. DOI: 10.1109/TITB.2007.899496

Esteva, A. (2021). A guide to deep learning in healthcare. *Nature Medicine*, 27(1), 15–25. PMID: 30617335

Esteva, A., Kuprel, B., Novoa, R. A., Ko, J., Swetter, S. M., Blau, H. M., & Thrun, S. (2017). Dermatologist-level classification of skin cancer with deep neural networks. *Nature*, 542(7639), 115–118. DOI: 10.1038/nature21056 PMID: 28117445

Fan, D., Rich, D., Holtzman, T., Ruther, P., Dalley, J. W., Lopez, A., Rossi, M. A., Barter, J. W., Salas-Meza, D., Herwik, S., Holzhammer, T., Morizio, J., & Yin, H. H. (2011). A wireless multi-channel recording system for freely behaving mice and rats. *PLoS One*, 6(7), 1–9. DOI: 10.1371/journal.pone.0022033 PMID: 21765934

Farella, M., Loke, C., Sander, S., Songini, A., Allen, M., Mei, L., & Cannon, R. D. (2016). Simultaneous wireless assessment of intra-oral pH and temperature. *Journal of Dentistry*, 51, 49–55. DOI: 10.1016/j.jdent.2016.05.012 PMID: 27263031

Few, S. (2009). *Now You See It: Simple Visualization Techniques for Quantitative Analysis*. Analytics Press.

Few, S. (2020). *Storytelling with Data: A Data Visualization Guide for Business Professionals*. Wiley.

Fiaz, A. S.. (2016). Data visualization: Enhancing big data more adaptable and valuable. *International Journal of Applied Engineering Research: IJAER*, 11(4), 2801–2804.

Flynn, B. W., & Fotopoulou, K. (2011). Wireless power transfer in loosely coupled links. *Power*, 47(2), 416–430.

Flynn, B. W., & Fotopoulou, K. (2013). Rectifying loose coils: Wireless power transfer in loosely coupled inductive links with lateral and angular misalignment. *IEEE Microwave Magazine*, 14(2), 48–54. DOI: 10.1109/MMM.2012.2234634

Forrester, G. (2013, July). Free space optics, in Digital Air Wireless. Retrieved from https://www.digitalairwireless.com/wireless-blog/2013-07/free-space-optics.html

Friedman, J. H. (2001). Greedy Function Approximation: A Gradient Boosting Machine. *Annals of Statistics*, 29(5), 1189–1232. DOI: 10.1214/aos/1013203451

Frost, M. C., & Meyerhoff, M. E. (2002). Implantable chemical sensors for real-time clinical monitoring: Progress and challenges. *Current Opinion in Chemical Biology*, 6(5), 633–641. DOI: 10.1016/S1367-5931(02)00371-X PMID: 12413548

Furmanova, K., Gratzl, S., Stitz, H., Zichner, T., Jaresova, M., Lex, A., & Streit, M. (2020). Taggle: Combining overview and details in tabular data visualizations. *Information Visualization*, 19(2), 114–136. DOI: 10.1177/1473871619878085

Gandomi, A., & Haider, M. (2015). Beyond the Hype: Big Data Concepts, Methods, and Analytics. *International Journal of Information Management*, 35(2), 137–144. DOI: 10.1016/j.ijinfomgt.2014.10.007

Gao, H., Walker, R. M., Nuyujukian, P., Makinwa, K. A. A., Shenoy, K. V., Murmann, B., & Meng, T. H. (2012). HermesE: A 96-channel full data rate direct neural interface in 0.13 μm CMOS. *IEEE Journal of Solid-State Circuits*, 47(4), 1043–1055. DOI: 10.1109/JSSC.2012.2185338

Garcia-Carrillo, D., Marin-Lopez, R., Kandasamy, A., & Pelov, A. (2017). A CoAP-based network access authentication service for low-power wide area networks: LO-CoAP-EAP. *Sensors (Basel)*, 17(11), 2646. DOI: 10.3390/s17112646 PMID: 29149040

Ghaed, M. H., Chen, G., Haque, R., Wieckowski, M., Kim, Y., Kim, G., Lee, Y., Lee, I., Fick, D., Kim, D., Seok, M., Wise, K. D., Blaauw, D., & Sylvester, D. (2013). Circuits for a cubic-millimeter energy-autonomous wireless intraocular pressure monitor. *IEEE Transactions on Circuits and Systems. I, Regular Papers*, 60(12), 3152–3162. DOI: 10.1109/TCSI.2013.2265973

Gilad-Bachrach, R., Dowlin, N., & Laine, K.CryptoNets: applying neural networks to encrypted data with high throughput and accuracy. *International Conference on Machine Learning*, 201–10.

Gil, D., Johnsson, M., Mora, H., & Szymański, J. (2019). Review of the complexity of managing big data of the Internet of Things. *Complexity*, 2019(1), 1–12. DOI: 10.1155/2019/4592902

Giordani, M., Polese, M., & Mezzavilla, M. (2020). Integrating satellite and terrestrial IoT in 6G networks. *IEEE Communications Magazine*, 58(1), 67–73. DOI: 10.1109/MCOM.2020.190052

Goodfellow, I., Bengio, Y., & Courville, A. (2016). *Deep Learning*. MIT Press.

Goto, H. (1998). Feasibility of using the automatic generating system for quartz watches as a leadless pacemaker power source: A preliminary report. *Medical & Biological Engineering & Computing*, 20(1), 9–11.

Goto, K., Nakagawa, T., Nakamura, O., & Kawata, S. (2001). An implantable power supply with an optically rechargeable lithium battery. *IEEE Transactions on Biomedical Engineering*, 48(7), 830–833. DOI: 10.1109/10.930908 PMID: 11442295

Gould, P. A. (2006). Complications associated with implantable cardioverter-defibrillator replacement in response to device advisories. *Journal of the American Medical Association*, 295(16), 1907–1913. DOI: 10.1001/jama.295.16.1907 PMID: 16639049

Gou, P., Kraut, N. D., Feigel, I. M., Bai, H., Morgan, G. J., Chen, Y., Tang, Y., Bocan, K., Stachel, J., Berger, L., Mickle, M., Sejdić, E., & Star, A. (2014). Carbon nanotube chemiresistor for wireless pH sensing. *Scientific Reports*, 4(1), 1–6. DOI: 10.1038/srep04468 PMID: 24667793

Gröger, G., & Plümer, L. (2012). CityGML – Interoperable semantic 3D city models. [ISPRS]. *ISPRS Journal of Photogrammetry and Remote Sensing*, 71, 12–33. DOI: 10.1016/j.isprsjprs.2012.04.004

Grover, V., Chiang, R. H., Liang, T. P., & Zhang, D. (2018). Creating strategic business value from big data analytics: A research framework. *Journal of Management Information Systems*, 35(2), 388–423. DOI: 10.1080/07421222.2018.1451951

Grzelak, D., & Podlaski, K. (2019). *Analyze the effectiveness of an algorithm for identifying Polish characters in handwriting based on neural machine learning technologies*. Elsevier.

Gulshan, V., Peng, L., Coram, M., Stumpe, M. C., Wu, D., Narayanaswamy, A., Venugopalan, S., Widner, K., Madams, T., Cuadros, J., Kim, R., Raman, R., Nelson, P. C., Mega, J. L., & Webster, D. R. (2016). Development and validation of a deep learning algorithm for the detection of diabetic retinopathy in retinal fundus photographs. *Journal of the American Medical Association*, 316(22), 2402–2410. DOI: 10.1001/jama.2016.17216 PMID: 27898976

Gurram, R. T. (2024). The evolution of data visualization tools and their impact on business decision-making : A historical analysis. *International Journal of Scientific Research in Computer Science. Engineering and Information Technology*, 10(6), 467–473. DOI: 10.32628/CSEIT24106192

H2O.ai. (2023). Automated Machine Learning: Best Practices and Implementation. H2O.ai Whitepaper.

Habimana, Li, Li, Gu, & Yu. (2020). Sentiment analysis using deep learning approaches: an overview. .DOI: 10.1007/s11432-018-9941-6

Haeberlin, A., Zurbuchen, A., Schaerer, J., Wagner, J., Walpen, S., Huber, C., Haeberlin, H., Fuhrer, J., & Vogel, R. (2014). Successful pacing using a batteryless sunlight-powered pacemaker. *Europace : European Pacing, Arrhythmias, and Cardiac Electrophysiology : Journal of the Working Groups on Cardiac Pacing, Arrhythmias, and Cardiac Cellular Electrophysiology of the European Society of Cardiology*, 16(10), 1534–1539. DOI: 10.1093/europace/euu127 PMID: 24916431

Han, J., Pei, J., & Kamber, M. (2011). Data Mining: Concepts and Techniques. Elsevier.

Han, J., Pei, J., & Kamber, M. (2011). *Data Mining: Concepts and Techniques.* Morgan Kaufmann.

Hannan, M. A., Mutashar, S., Samad, S. A., & Hussain, A. (2014). Energy harvesting for implantable biomedical devices: Issues and challenges. *Biomedical Engineering Online*, 13(1), 79. DOI: 10.1186/1475-925X-13-79 PMID: 24950601

Hastie, T., Tibshirani, R., & Friedman, J. (2009). *The Elements of Statistical Learning: Data Mining, Inference, and Prediction.* Springer. DOI: 10.1007/978-0-387-84858-7

Hayami, H., Takehara, H., Nagata, K., Haruta, M., Noda, T., Sasagawa, K., Tokuda, T., & Ohta, J. (2016). Wireless image-data transmission from an implanted image sensor through a living mouse brain by intra-body communication. *Japanese Journal of Applied Physics*, 55(4), 04EM03-1–04EM03-5. DOI: 10.7567/JJAP.55.04EM03

He, K., Zhang, X., Ren, S., & Sun, J. (2016). *Deep residual learning for image recognition.2016 IEEE Conference on Computer Vision and Pattern Recognition (CVPR)*. IEEE. DOI: 10.1109/CVPR.2016.90

Hermann, K. M., Kocisky, T., & Grefenstette, E. (2015). Teaching machines to read and comprehend. *Adv Neural Inf Process Syst*, 201, 1693–701.

Herold, M., Goes, F., Nopp, S., Bauer, P., Thompson, C., & Meyer, T. (2019). Machine learning in men's professional football: Current applications and future directions for improving attacking play. *International Journal of Sports Science & Coaching*, 14(6), 798–817. DOI: 10.1177/1747954119879350

Hirabayashi, K., Yamamoto, T., & Hino, S. (2004). Optical backplane with free-space optical interconnections using tunable beam deflectors and a mirror for bookshelf-assembled terabit per second class asynchronous transfer mode switch. *Optical Engineering (Redondo Beach, Calif.)*, 37, 1332–1342.

Hoang, M., Bihorac, O. A., & Rouces, J. (2019). Aspect-Based Sentiment Analysis using BERT. https://aclanthology.org/W19-6120

Hochreiter, S., & Schmidhuber, J. (1997). Long Short-Term Memory. *Neural Computation*, 9(8), 1735–1780. DOI: 10.1162/neco.1997.9.8.1735 PMID: 9377276

Hohman, F., Wongsuphasawat, K., Kery, M. B., & Patel, K. (2020, April). Understanding and visualizing data iteration in machine learning. In *Proceedings of the 2020 CHI Conference on Human Factors in Computing Systems* (pp. 1–13). ACM. DOI: 10.1145/3313831.3376177

Ho, J. S., Kim, S., & Poon, A. S. Y. (2013). Midfield wireless powering for implantable systems. *Proceedings of the IEEE*, 101(6), 1369–1378. DOI: 10.1109/JPROC.2013.2251851

Ho, J. S., Yeh, A. J., Neofytou, E., Kim, S., Tanabe, Y., Patlolla, B., Beygui, R. E., & Poon, A. S. Y. (2014). Wireless power transfer to deep-tissue microimplants. *Proceedings of the National Academy of Sciences of the United States of America*, 111(22), 7974–7979. DOI: 10.1073/pnas.1403002111 PMID: 24843161

Honeine, P. (2011). Wireless sensor networks in biomedical: Body area networks. *Systems, Signal Processing and Their Applications (WOSSPA),International Workshop, 1*, 388–391. DOI: 10.1109/WOSSPA.2011.5931518

Hsieh, J. Y., Kuo, P.-H., Huang, Y.-C., Huang, Y.-J., Tsai, R.-D., Wang, T., Chiu, H.-W., Wang, Y.-H., & Lu, S.-S. (2014). A remotely controlled locomotive IC driven by electrolytic bubbles and wireless powering. *IEEE Transactions on Biomedical Circuits and Systems*, 8(6), 787–798. DOI: 10.1109/TBCAS.2014.2382341 PMID: 25576574

Huang, X., Jagota, V., Espinoza-Muñoz, E., & Flores-Albornoz, J. (2021). Tourist hot spots prediction model based on optimized neural network algorithm. *International Journal of System Assurance Engineering and Management*. Advance online publication. DOI: 10.1007/s13198-021-01226-4

Hubáček, O., Šourek, G., & Železný, F. (2019). Learning to predict soccer results from relational data with gradient boosted trees. *Machine Learning*, 108(1), 29–47. DOI: 10.1007/s10994-018-5704-6

Hudak, N. S., & Amatucci, G. G. (2008). Small-scale energy harvesting through thermoelectric, vibration, and radiofrequency power conversion. *Journal of Applied Physics*, 103(10), 101301-1, 101301–101324. DOI: 10.1063/1.2918987

Hwang, S.-W., Tao, H., Kim, D.-H., Cheng, H., Song, J.-K., Rill, E., Brenckle, M. A., Panilaitis, B., Won, S. M., Kim, Y.-S., Song, Y. M., Yu, K. J., Ameen, A., Li, R., Su, Y., Yang, M., Kaplan, D. L., Zakin, M. R., Slepian, M. J., & Rogers, J. A. (2012). A physically transient form of silicon electronics. *Science*, 337(6102), 1640–1644. DOI: 10.1126/science.1226325 PMID: 23019646

Hyndman, R. J., & Athanasopoulos, G. (2018). *Forecasting: Principles and Practice*. OTexts.

IEEE Standards Association. (2012). IEEE Standard for Local and Metropolitan Area Networks—Part 15.6: Wireless Body Area Networks. *IEEE Std.*, 271. Advance online publication. DOI: 10.1109/IEEESTD.2012.6161600

Igarashi, A., & O'Connell, A. (2020). *Data Visualization: A Practical Introduction*. Princeton University Press.

Islam, S. M. R., Kwak, D., Kabir, M. H., Hossain, M., & Kwak, K. S. (2015). The Internet of Things for healthcare: A comprehensive survey. *IEEE Access : Practical Innovations, Open Solutions*, 3, 678–708. DOI: 10.1109/ACCESS.2015.2437951

Jagadish, J., Gehrke, J., Labrinidis, A., Papakonstantinou, Y., Patel, J. M., Ramakrishnan, R., & Shahabi, C. (2014). Big Data and Its Technical Challenges. *Communications of the ACM*, 57(7), 86–94. DOI: 10.1145/2611567

Jain, A. (2021). Machine Learning in Finance: Applications and Challenges. *Journal of Financial Services Research*, 59(2), 245–262.

Jain, S., Nehra, M., Kumar, R., Dilbaghi, N., Hu, T. Y., Kumar, S., Kaushik, A., & Li, C. (2021). Internet of medical things (IoMT)-integrated biosensors for point-of-care testing of infectious diseases. *Biosensors & Bioelectronics*, 179, 113074. DOI: 10.1016/j.bios.2021.113074 PMID: 33596516

James, G., Witten, D., Hastie, T., & Tibshirani, R. (2013). *An Introduction to Statistical Learning: With Applications in R*. Springer. DOI: 10.1007/978-1-4614-7138-7

Javideh, M. R. (2011). Detecting and investigating crime by means of data mining: A general crime matching framework. *Procedia Computer Science*.

Jayadev, P. G., & Bellary, S. (2021). A hybrid approach for classification and identification of iris damaged levels of alcohol drinkers. *Journal of King Saud University. Computer and Information Sciences*. Advance online publication. DOI: 10.1016/j.jksuci.2021.01.004

Jeon, D., Chen, Y.-P., Lee, Y., Kim, Y., Foo, Z., Kruger, G., Oral, H., Berenfeld, O., Zhang, Z., Blaauw, D., & Sylvester, D. (2014). An implantable 64nW ECG-monitoring mixed-signal SoC for arrhythmia diagnosis. *Digest of Technical Papers - IEEE International Solid-State Circuits Conference*, 57, 416–417. DOI: 10.1109/ISSCC.2014.6757494

Ji, B., Wang, Y., Song, K., Li, C., Wen, H., Menon, V. G., & Mumtaz, S. (2021). A survey of computational intelligence for 6G: Key technologies, applications and trends. *IEEE Transactions on Industrial Informatics*, 17(10), 7145–7154. DOI: 10.1109/TII.2021.3052531

Jin, J., Rong, D., Pang, Y., Ye, P., Ji, Q., Wang, X., Wang, G., & Wang, F. Y. (2022). An agent-based traffic recommendation system: Revisiting and revising urban traffic management strategies. *IEEE Transactions on Systems, Man, and Cybernetics. Systems*, 52(11), 7289–7301. DOI: 10.1109/TSMC.2022.3177027

Jochen, H. M. H., Siebert, C., & Schamp, C. (2022). More than a Feeling: Accuracy and Application of Sentiment Analysis. https://www.sciencedirect.com/science/article/pii/S0167811622000477

Jordan, M. I., & Mitchell, T. M. (2015). Machine learning: Trends, perspectives, and prospects. *Science*, 349(6245), 255–260. DOI: 10.1126/science.aaa8415 PMID: 26185243

Joshi, S. (2020). Crime analysis through machine learning. *ic-ETITE*.

Jurafsky, D., & Martin, J. H. (2021). *Speech and Language Processing: An Introduction to Natural Language Processing, Computational Linguistics, and Speech Recognition* (3rd ed.). Pearson.

Kamyab, M., Liu, G., & Adjeisah, M. (2021). Attention-Based CNN and Bi-LSTM Model Based on TF-IDF and GloVe Word Embedding for Sentiment Analysis. https://www.mdpi.com/2076-3417/11/23/11255

Kang, S., Murphy, R. K. J., Hwang, S.-W., Lee, S. M., Harburg, D. V., Krueger, N. A., Shin, J., Gamble, P., Cheng, H., Yu, S., Liu, Z., McCall, J. G., Stephen, M., Ying, H., Kim, J., Park, G., Webb, R. C., Lee, C. H., Chung, S., & Rogers, J. A. (2016). Bioresorbable silicon electronic sensors for the brain. *Nature*, 530(7588), 71–76. DOI: 10.1038/nature16492 PMID: 26779949

Karakaya, A., Ulu, A., & Akleylek, S. (2022). GOALALERT: A novel real-time technical team alert approach using machine learning on an IoT-based system in sports. *Microprocessors and Microsystems*, 93, 104606. DOI: 10.1016/j.micpro.2022.104606

Katz, E. (2014). *Implantable Bioelectronics*. DOI: 10.1002/9783527673148

Katz, E. (2015). Implantable biofuel cells operating in vivo: Providing sustainable power for bioelectronic devices. In *2015 6th International Workshop on Advances in Sensors and Interfaces (IWASI)* (pp. 2–13). IEEE. DOI: 10.1109/IWASI.2015.7184958

Katz, E., & MacVittie, K. (2013). Implanted biofuel cells operating in vivo – Methods, applications, and perspectives. *Energy & Environmental Science*, 6(10), 2791. DOI: 10.1039/c3ee42126k

Kazemlou, S., Hranilovic, S., & Kumar, S. (2011). All-optical multihop free-space optical communication systems. *Journal of Lightwave Technology*, 29(18), 2663–2669. DOI: 10.1109/JLT.2011.2160615

Kedir, N. S., Somi, S., Fayek, A. R., & Nguyen, P. H. (2022). Hybridization of reinforcement learning and agent-based modeling to optimize construction planning and scheduling. *Automation in Construction*, 142, 104498. DOI: 10.1016/j.autcon.2022.104498

Kelly, J. P. (2017). Televizual: Data visualization in industry and academia. DOI: 10.59350/hz092-wt871

Kennedy, H. (2016). Engaging with data visualization. https://journals.uic.edu/ojs/index.php/fm/rt/printerFriendly/6389/5652

Kenwright, B. (2023). Data collection during active gameplay: Unveiling a multifaceted portrait of the individual. In *Games as Stealth Assessments* (pp. 192–219). IGI Global. DOI: 10.4018/979-8-3693-0568-3.ch008

Khalaf, O. A. (2019). Automating Data Cleaning: An Overview of Methods and Challenges. *Data Science and Engineering*, 4(4), 295–307.

Khan, A. (2023). Data Science in Transportation: Opportunities and Applications. *Transportation Research Part C, Emerging Technologies*, 138, 103584.

Khan, A., & Zubair, S. (2020). An improved multi-modal based machine learning approach for the prognosis of Alzheimer's disease. *Journal of King Saud University. Computer and Information Sciences*. Advance online publication. DOI: 10.1016/j.jksuci.2020.04.004

Kim, A., Powell, C. R., & Ziaie, B. (2014). An implantable pressure sensing system with electromechanical interrogation scheme. *IEEE Transactions on Biomedical Engineering*, 61(7), 2209–2217. DOI: 10.1109/TBME.2014.2318023 PMID: 24800754

Kim, S., Ho, J. S., Chen, L. Y., & Poon, A. S. Y. (2012). Wireless power transfer to a cardiac implant. *Applied Physics Letters*, 101(7), 1–5. DOI: 10.1063/1.4745600

Kirk, A. (2019). *Data Visualisation: A Handbook for Data Driven Design*. SAGE Publications.

Kiryanov, A. G., Krotov, A. V., Lyakhov, A. I., & Khorov, E. M. (2019). Algorithm for dynamic power control and scheduling in IEEE 802.11ax infrastructure networks. *Journal of Communications Technology and Electronics*, 64(8), 900–909. DOI: 10.1134/S1064226919080230

Kneisz, L., Unger, E., Lanmuller, H., & Mayr, W. (2015). In vitro testing of an implantable wireless telemetry system for long-term electromyography recordings in large animals. *Artificial Organs*, 39(10), 897–902. DOI: 10.1111/aor.12626 PMID: 26471141

Kodati, S. (2018). Analysis of heart disease using data mining tools Orange and Weka. *Global Journal of Computer Science and Technology*, 18(1), 1–9. DOI: 10.17487/GJCSCT/18.1.1

Koroteev, M. V. (2021), BERT: A Review of Applications in Natural Language Processing and Understanding. https://arxiv.org/abs/2103.11943

Kotsiantis, S. B. (2006). Data Preprocessing for Supervised Learning. *International Journal of Computational Science*, 1(2), 111–117.

Kouhani, M. H. M., Weber, A., & Li, W. (2017). Wireless intraocular pressure sensor using stretchable variable inductor. *Proceedings of IEEE International Conference on Micro Electro Mechanical Systems*, 557–560. DOI: 10.1109/MEMSYS.2017.7863467

Kreps, J., Narkhede, N., & Rao, J. (2011). Kafka: A Distributed Messaging System for Log Processing. *Proceedings of the NetDB*.

Kumar, A., & Ravi, V. (2016). A survey of data mining techniques for fraud detection. *Journal of Network and Computer Applications*, 75, 120–134.

Kumar, M. N., Jagota, V., & Shabaz, M. (2021). Retrospection of the optimization model for designing the power train of a formula student race car. *Scientific Programming*, 2021, 9. DOI: 10.1155/2021/9465702

Kumar, S. M., & Belwal, M. (2017). Performance dashboard: Cutting-edge business intelligence and data visualization. In *2017 International Conference on Smart Technologies for Smart Nation (SmartRechCon)* (pp. 1–6). IEEE. DOI: 10.1109/SmartTechCon.2017.8358558

Kumar, S., Tiwari, P., & Zymbler, M. (2019). Internet of things is a revolutionary approach for future technology enhancement: A review. *Journal of Big Data*, 6(1), 111. Advance online publication. DOI: 10.1186/s40537-019-0268-2

Kurs, A., Karalis, A., Moffatt, R., Joannopoulos, J. D., Fisher, P., & Soljačić, M. (2007). Wireless power transfer via strongly coupled magnetic resonances. *Science*, 317(5834), 83–86. DOI: 10.1126/science.1143254 PMID: 17556549

Lal, R., Deb, N., & Gogoi, D. M. (2024). Assessing the role of digital data visualization tools in the advertising industry for informed business decision-making. In *Advances in Business Information Systems and Analytics* (pp. 189–208). DOI: 10.4018/979-8-3693-6537-3.ch009

Lan, Z., Chen, M., Goodman, S., Gimpel, K., Sharma, P., & Soricut, R. (2020). *ALBERT: A lite bert for self-supervised learning of language representations.In ICLR 2020? Eighth International Conference on Learning Representations.* La Jolla: ICLR.

Lan, D., & Shin, I. (2023). Boosting in-transit entertainment: Deep reinforcement learning for intelligent multimedia caching in bus networks. *Soft Computing*, 27(24), 1–17. DOI: 10.1007/s00500-023-09354-8

Lande, O. B. S., Johnson, E., Adeleke, G. S., Amajuoyi, C. P., & Simpson, B. D. (2024). The role of data visualization in strategic decision making: Case studies from the tech industry. *Computer Science & IT Research Journal, 5*(6), 1374–1390. DOI: 10.51594/csitrj.v5i6.1223

Laser Communications. (n.d.). Laser communications. Retrieved from https://lasercommunications.weebly.com/

Latha, C. B. C., & Jeeva, S. C. (2019). Improving the accuracy of prediction of heart disease risk based on ensemble classification techniques. *Informatics in Medicine Unlocked*, 16, 100203. Advance online publication. DOI: 10.1016/j.imu.2019.100203

Latva-aho, M., & Leppänen, K. (2021). *Key drivers and research challenges for 6G ubiquitous wireless intelligence. 6G Flagship*. University of Oulu.

Lawrence. (2015). Using machine learning algorithms to analyze crime data. *MLAIJ*.

LeCun, Y., Bengio, Y., & Haffner, P. (2015). Gradient-based learning applied to document recognition. *Proceedings of the IEEE*, 86(11), 2278–2324. DOI: 10.1109/5.726791

Lee, J., Kao, H. A., & Yang, S. (2014). Service Innovation and Smart Analytics for Industry 4.0 and Big Data Environment. *Procedia CIRP*, 16, 3–8. DOI: 10.1016/j.procir.2014.02.001

Lee, W. S., Kim, A., Ziaie, B., Raghunathan, V., & Powell, C. R. (2014). UP-link: An ultra-low-power implantable wireless system for long-term ambulatory urodynamics. *2014 IEEE Biomedical Circuits and Systems Conference (BioCAS) –. Proceedings*, 384–387, 384–387. Advance online publication. DOI: 10.1109/BioCAS.2014.6981743

Lei, T., Barzilay, R., & Jaakkola, T. (2016). Rationalizing neural predictions. DOI: 10.18653/v1/D16-1011

Leonardi, M., Pitchon, E. M., Bertsch, A., Renaud, P., & Mermoud, A. (2009). Wireless contact lens sensor for intraocular pressure monitoring: Assessment on enucleated pig eyes. *Acta Ophthalmologica*, 87(4), 433–437. DOI: 10.1111/j.1755-3768.2008.01404.x PMID: 19016660

Leoni, D. (2012). Non-interactive differential privacy: a survey. *Proceedings of the First International Workshop on Open Data*, 40–52. DOI: 10.1145/2422604.2422611

Leonov, V., Torfs, T., Fiorini, P., & Van Hoof, C. (2007). Thermoelectric converters of human warmth for self-powered wireless sensor nodes. *IEEE Sensors Journal*, 7(5), 650–656. DOI: 10.1109/JSEN.2007.894917

Ligthart, A., Catal, C., & Tekinerdogan, B. (2021). Systematic reviews in sentiment analysis: A tertiary study. *Artificial Intelligence Review*, 54(7), 4997–5053. Advance online publication. DOI: 10.1007/s10462-021-09973-3

Lipsett, M. S., McIntyre, C., & Liu, R. (1969). Space instrumentation for laser communications. *IEEE Journal of Quantum Electronics*, 5(6), 348–349. DOI: 10.1109/JQE.1969.1081959

Liu, Shi, Ji, & Jia. (2019). A Survey of Sentiment Analysis Based on Transfer Learning. .DOI: 10.1109/ACCESS.2019.2925059

Liu, D. (2013). Burglary crime analysis using logistic regression. *International Conference on Human Interface and the Management of Information (HIMI).*

Liu, M., Wang, Y., Yao, C., Zou, J., Luo, Y., Li, T., & Bai, G. (2019). A class-incremental learning method based on one class support vector machine. *Journal of Physics: Conference Series*, 1267(1), 12007. DOI: 10.1088/1742-6596/1267/1/012007

Liu, Q., Zhou, Z., & Jiang, W. (2021). Jamming attacks on wireless medical devices: Mitigation and detection. *Wireless Networks*, 27(8), 456–470.

Liu, S., Liu, S., & Cai, W.Early diagnosis of Alzheimer's disease with deep learning. *International Symposium on Biomedical Imaging*, 1015–18. DOI: 10.1109/ISBI.2014.6868045

Livingston, G., Sommerlad, A., Orgeta, V., Costafreda, S. G., Huntley, J., Ames, D., Ballard, C., Banerjee, S., Burns, A., Cohen-Mansfield, J., Cooper, C., Fox, N., Gitlin, L. N., Howard, R., Kales, H. C., Larson, E. B., Ritchie, K., Rockwood, K., Sampson, E. L., & Mukadam, N. (2017). Dementia prevention, intervention, and care. *Lancet*, 390(10113), 2673–2734. Advance online publication. DOI: 10.1016/S0140-6736(17)31363-6 PMID: 28735855

Li, X., Zhao, Z., & Sun, J. (2021). Enhanced mobile broadband for IoT in 5G networks. *IEEE Access : Practical Innovations, Open Solutions*, 9, 234–247. DOI: 10.1109/ACCESS.2021.3045645

Lounis, A., & Peralta, R. (2021). IoT healthcare sensors and battery depletion threats. *ACM Transactions on Cyber-Physical Systems*, 5(3), 45–61.

Lucisano, J., Routh, T., & Lin, J. (2016). *Glucose monitoring in individuals with diabetes using a long-term implanted sensor/telemetry system and model.* IEEE Xplore.

Lucy, R. F., & Lang, K. (1968). Optical communications experiments at 6328 Å and 10:6. *Applied Optics*, 7(10), 1965–1970. DOI: 10.1364/AO.7.001965 PMID: 20068920

Luo, M., Martinez, A. W., Song, C., Herrault, F., & Allen, M. G. (2014). A microfabricated wireless RF pressure sensor made completely of biodegradable materials. *Journal of Microelectromechanical Systems*, 23(1), 4–13. DOI: 10.1109/JMEMS.2013.2290111

Lu, Y., Li, Q., & Zhang, X. (2021). Industrial IoT applications with 5G technologies. *Journal of Industrial Information Integration*, 25, 100265. DOI: 10.1016/j.jii.2021.100265

Magesh, G., & Swarnalatha, P. (2021). Optimal feature selection through a cluster-based DT learning (CDTL) in heart disease prediction. *Evolutionary Intelligence*, 14(2), 583–593. DOI: 10.1007/s12065-019-00336-0

Mahdavinejad, M., Rezvan, M., & Burcins, M. (2018). *Machine learning for Internet of Things data analysis: A survey*. Elsevier. DOI: 10.1016/j.dcan.2017.10.002

Maier, M., & Ebrahimzadeh, A. (2018). *The tactile internet: Automation or augmentation of the human?* IEEE Xplore.

Majerus, S. (2015). Wireless implantable pressure monitor for conditional bladder neuromodulation. *IEEE Biomedical Circuits and Systems Conference (BioCAS) – Proceedings,* 2–5. DOI: 10.1109/BioCAS.2015.7348337

Majerus, S. J. A., Garverick, S. L., Suster, M. A., Fletter, P. C., & Damaser, M. S. (2012). Wireless, ultra-low-power implantable sensor for chronic bladder pressure monitoring. *ACM Journal on Emerging Technologies in Computing Systems*, 8(2), 1–13. DOI: 10.1145/2180878.2180883 PMID: 26778926

Marr, B. (2017). *Data Strategy: How to Profit from a World of Big Data, Analytics and the Internet of Things*. Kogan Page.

Mayer-Schönberger, V., & Cukier, K. (2013). *Big Data: A Revolution That Will Transform How We Live, Work, and Think.* Houghton Mifflin Harcourt.

McClendon, L. (2015). *Using machine learning algorithms to analyze crime data.* MLAIJ. DOI: 10.5121/mlaij.2015.2101

McKean, B. D., & Gough, D. A. (1988). A telemetry-instrumentation system for chronically implanted glucose and oxygen sensors. *IEEE Transactions on Biomedical Engineering*, 35(7), 526–532. DOI: 10.1109/10.4581 PMID: 3209214

McSherry, F., & Talwar, K. (2007). Mechanism design via differential privacy. *48th Annual IEEE Symposium on Foundations of Computer Science,* 94–103.

Mendes-Neves, T., Mendes-Moreira, J., & Rossetti, R. J. (2021, September). A data-driven simulator for assessing decision-making in soccer. In *EPIA Conference on Artificial Intelligence* (pp. 687-698). Cham: Springer International Publishing. DOI: 10.1007/978-3-030-86230-5_54

Meng, X., Browne, K., Huang, S. M., Cullen, D. K., Tofighi, M. R., & Rosen, A. (2012). Dynamic study of wireless intracranial pressure monitoring of rotational head injury in swine model. *Electronics Letters*, 48(7), 363–364. DOI: 10.1049/el.2012.0281

Mestais, C. S., Charvet, G., Sauter-Starace, F., Foerster, M., Ratel, D., & Benabid, A. L. (2015). WIMAGINE: Wireless 64-channel ECoG recording implant for long-term clinical applications. *IEEE Transactions on Neural Systems and Rehabilitation Engineering*, 23(1), 10–21. DOI: 10.1109/TNSRE.2014.2333541 PMID: 25014960

Meyer, P. J. (2020). Data Normalization Techniques for Improved Model Performance. *Data Science Journal*, 19(1), 10.

Millett, G. A., Jones, A. T., Benkeser, D., Baral, S., Mercer, L., Beyrer, C., Honermann, B., Lankiewicz, E., Mena, L., Crowley, J. S., Sherwood, J., & Sullivan, P. S. (2020). Assessing differential impacts of COVID-19 on black communities. *Annals of Epidemiology*, 47, 37–44. DOI: 10.1016/j.annepidem.2020.05.003 PMID: 32419766

Miotto, R., Li, L., Kidd, B. A., & Dudley, J. T. (2016). Deep patient: An unsupervised representation to predict the future of patients from the electronic health records. *Scientific Reports*, 6(1), 26094–26094. DOI: 10.1038/srep26094 PMID: 27185194

Mishra, T., Wang, M., Metwally, A. A., Bogu, G. K., Brooks, A. W., Bahmani, A., Alavi, A., Celli, A., Higgs, E., Dagan-Rosenfeld, O., Fay, B., Kirkpatrick, S., Kellogg, R., Gibson, M., Wang, T., Hunting, E. M., Mamic, P., Ganz, A. B., Rolnik, B., & Snyder, M. P. (2020). Pre-symptomatic detection of COVID-19 from smartwatch data. *Nature Biomedical Engineering*, 4(12), 1208–1220. DOI: 10.1038/s41551-020-00640-6 PMID: 33208926

Misra, S., Reisslein, M., & Xue, G. (2008). A survey of multimedia streaming in wireless sensor networks. *IEEE Communications Surveys and Tutorials*, 10(4), 18–39. Advance online publication. DOI: 10.1109/SURV.2008.080404

Mitchell, T. M. (1997). *Machine Learning*. McGraw-Hill.

Mitcheson, P. D., Yeatman, E. M., Rao, G. K., Holmes, A. S., & Green, T. C. (2008). Energy harvesting from human and machine motion for wireless electronic devices. *Proceedings of the IEEE*, 96(9), 1457–1486. DOI: 10.1109/JPROC.2008.927494

Mitra, S. (2018). Survey of analysis of crime detection techniques using data mining and machine learning. *Journal of Physics:IOP Conf Series*.

Mo, X., Hu, B., Xu, C., & Yang, Y. (2022, December). Research on virtual human swarm football collaboration technology based on reinforcement learning. In *2022 IEEE 21st International Conference on Ubiquitous Computing and Communications (IUCC/CIT/DSCI/SmartCNS)* (pp. 357-364). IEEE. DOI: 10.1109/IUCC-CIT-DSCI-SmartCNS57392.2022.00062

Mohan, S., Irumalai, C., & Srivastava, G. (2019). Effective heart disease prediction using hybrid machine learning techniques. *IEEE Access : Practical Innovations, Open Solutions*, 7, 81542–81554. DOI: 10.1109/ACCESS.2019.2923707

Monaghesh, E., & Hajizadeh, A. (2020). The role of telehealth during COVID-19 outbreak: A systematic review based on current evidence. *BMC Public Health*, 20(1), 1193. DOI: 10.1186/s12889-020-09301-4 PMID: 32738884

Mora, L., Deakin, M., & Reid, A. (2018). Strategic principles for smart city development: A multiple case study analysis of European best practices. *Technological Forecasting and Social Change*, 142, 70–97. DOI: 10.1016/j.techfore.2018.07.035

Mostafalu, P., Akbari, M., Alberti, K. A., Xu, Q., Khademhosseini, A., & Sonkusale, S. R. (2016). A toolkit of thread-based microfluidics, sensors, and electronics for 3D tissue embedding for medical diagnostics. *Microsystems & Nanoengineering*, 2(April), 16039. DOI: 10.1038/micronano.2016.39 PMID: 31057832

Mourtzis, D., Zogopoulos, V., Katagis, I., & Lagios, P. (2018). Augmented Reality based Visualization of CAM Instructions towards Industry 4.0 paradigm: A CNC Bending Machine case study. *Procedia CIRP*, 70, 368–373. DOI: 10.1016/j.procir.2018.02.045

Movassaghi, S., Abolhasan, M., & J. L-C. (2014). Wireless body area networks: A survey. IEEE Xplore.

Mozgovoy, M., Preuss, M., & Bidarra, R. (2021). Team sports for Game AI benchmarking revisited. *International Journal of Computer Games Technology*, 2021, 1–9. DOI: 10.1155/2021/5521877

Muller, R., Le, H.-P., Li, W., Ledochowitsch, P., Gambini, S., Bjorninen, T., Koralek, A., Carmena, J. M., Maharbiz, M. M., Alon, E., & Rabaey, J. M. (2015). A minimally invasive 64-channel wireless μECoG implant. *IEEE Journal of Solid-State Circuits*, 50(1), 344–359. DOI: 10.1109/JSSC.2014.2364824

Mumtaz, S., Adeel, A., & Al-Dulaimi, A. (2021). Digital twins in 6G-enabled IoT systems. *IEEE Wireless Communications*, 28(6), 134–141. DOI: 10.1109/MWC.2021.9620107

Munikar, M., Shakya, S., & Shrestha, A. (2019). Fine-grained Sentiment Classification using BERT. DOI: 10.1109/AITB48515.2019.8947435

Murali Mani, S. F. (2017). Effective Big Data Visualization. *Proceedings of IDEAS '17*.

Murphy, O. H., Bahmanyar, M. R., Borghi, A., McLeod, C. N., Navaratnarajah, M., Yacoub, M. H., & Toumazou, C. (2013). Continuous in vivo blood pressure measurements using a fully implantable wireless SAW sensor. *Biomedical Microdevices*, 15(5), 737–749. DOI: 10.1007/s10544-013-9759-7 PMID: 23559403

Nalbandian, A., Sehgal, K., Gupta, A., Madhavan, M. V., McGroder, C., Stevens, J. S., Cook, J. R., Nordvig, A. S., Shalev, D., Sehrawat, T. S., Ahluwalia, N., Bikdeli, B., Dietz, D., Der-Nigoghossian, C., Liyanage-Don, N., Rosner, G. F., Bernstein, E. J., Mohan, S., Beckley, A. A., & Wan, E. Y. (2021). Post-acute COVID-19 syndrome. *Nature Medicine*, 27(4), 601–615. DOI: 10.1038/s41591-021-01283-z PMID: 33753937

Nandwani, P., & Verma, R. (2021). A review on sentiment analysis and emotion detection from text. https://link.springer.com/article/10.1007/s13278-021-00776-6

Nasarian, E., Abdar, M., Fahami, M. A., Alizadehsani, R., Hussain, S., Basiri, M. E., Zomorodi-Moghadam, M., Zhou, X., Pławiak, P., Acharya, U. R., Tan, R. S., & Sarrafzadegan, N. (2020). Association between work-related features and coronary artery disease: A heterogeneous hybrid feature selection integrated with balancing approach. *Pattern Recognition Letters*, 133, 33–40. DOI: 10.1016/j.patrec.2020.02.010

Ngai, E. W., Hu, Y., Wong, Y. H., Chen, Y., & Sun, X. (2011). The Application of Data Mining Techniques in Financial Fraud Detection: A Classification Framework and an Academic Review of Literature. *Decision Support Systems*, 50(3), 559–569. DOI: 10.1016/j.dss.2010.08.006

Nikfarjam, A., Sarker, A., O'Connor, K., Ginn, R., & Gonzalez, G. (2015). Pharmacovigilance from social media: Mining adverse drug reaction mentions using sequence labeling with word embedding cluster features. *Journal of the American Medical Informatics Association : JAMIA*, 22(3), 671–681. DOI: 10.1093/jamia/ocu041 PMID: 25755127

Ntiloudi, D., Giannakoulas, G., Parcharidou, D., Panagiotidis, T., Gatzoulis, M. A., & Karvounis, H. (2016). Adult congenital heart disease: A paradigm of epidemiological change. *International Journal of Cardiology*, 218, 269–274. DOI: 10.1016/j.ijcard.2016.05.046 PMID: 27240150

Ntouni, G. D., Lioumpas, A. S., & Nikita, K. S. (2014). Reliable and energy-efficient communications for wireless biomedical implant systems. *IEEE Journal of Biomedical and Health Informatics*, 18(6), 1848–1856. DOI: 10.1109/JBHI.2014.2300151 PMID: 25375682

O'Brien, K. A., & O'Keeffe, M. (2022). Reimagining the role of technology in sport officiating: How artificial intelligence (AI) supports the design and delivery of ecologically dynamic development processes. *Managing Sport and Leisure*, 1–13. DOI: 10.1080/23750472.2022.2126996

O'Neil, C. (2016). *Weapons of Math Destruction: How Big Data Increases Inequality and Threatens Democracy*. Crown Publishing Group.

Ohmann, A., & Floyd, M. (2015). *Creating Data Stories with Tableau Public*. Packt Publishing.

Olsson, R., & Wise, K. (2005). A three-dimensional neural recording microsystem with implantable data compression circuitry. *IEEE International Solid-State Circuits Conference,* 558–559. DOI: 10.1109/ISSCC.2005.1494117

Owusu, E., Han, J., Das, S., Perrig, A., & Zhang, J. (2012). Accessory: Password inference using accelerometers on smartphones. In *Proceedings of the Twelfth Workshop on Mobile Computing Systems & Applications* (p. 9). ACM. DOI: 10.1145/2162081.2162095

Palanisamy, V., & Thirunavukarasu, R. (2019). Implications of big data analytics in developing healthcare frameworks – a review. *Journal of King Saud University. Computer and Information Sciences*, 31(4), 415–425. Advance online publication. DOI: 10.1016/j.jksuci.2017.12.007

Panghal, R. (2024). The role of data visualization in decision making – case of D-mart. *International Journal For Multidisciplinary Research*, 6(3), 19630. Advance online publication. DOI: 10.36948/ijfmr.2024.v06i03.19630

Parbat, B., Dwivedi, A. K., & Vyas, O. P. (2010). Data visualization tools for WSNs: A glimpse. *International Journal of Computer Applications*, 2(1), 14–20. DOI: 10.5120/617-868

Park, J., Kim, J.-K., Patil, S., Park, J.-K., Park, S. A., & Lee, D.-W. (2016). A wireless pressure sensor integrated with a biodegradable polymer stent for biomedical applications. *Sensors (Basel)*, 16(6), 1–10. DOI: 10.3390/s16060809 PMID: 27271619

Patel, B., & Shah, P. (2021). Operating system support, protocol stack with key concerns and testbed facilities for IoT: A case study perspective. *Journal of King Saud University. Computer and Information Sciences*. Advance online publication. DOI: 10.1016/j.jksuci.2021.01.002

Patel, M., Desai, A., & Singh, R. (2020). Location tracking and user profiling in IoT healthcare. *International Journal of Security*, 15(4), 202–216.

Pathak, A. K., & Valan, J. A. (2020). A predictive model for heart disease diagnosis using fuzzy logic and decision tree. In *Smart Computing Paradigms: New Progresses and Challenges* (pp. 131–140). Springer. DOI: 10.1007/978-981-13-9680-9_10

Pavlopoulos, G. A., Wegener, A. L., & Schneider, R. (2008). A survey of visualization tools for biological network analysis. *BioData Mining*, 1(1), 1–11. DOI: 10.1186/1756-0381-1-12 PMID: 19040716

Peña-Ayala, A. (2014). Ontology agents and their applications in the web-based education systems: Towards an adaptive and intelligent service artificial intelligence on education view project. Springer. DOI: 10.1007/978-3-540-88071-4_11

Pfefferbaum, B., & North, C. S. (2020). Mental health and the COVID-19 pandemic. *The New England Journal of Medicine*, 383(6), 510–512. DOI: 10.1056/NEJMp2008017 PMID: 32283003

Phan, N., Wang, Y., & Wu, X. Differential privacy preservation for deep auto-encoders: an application of human behavior prediction. *Proceedings of the Thirtieth AAAI Conference on Artificial Intelligence,* 1309–16. DOI: 10.1609/aaai.v30i1.10165

Pivonka, D., Yakovlev, A., Poon, A. S. Y., & Meng, T. (2012). A mm-sized wirelessly powered and remotely controlled locomotive implant. *IEEE Transactions on Biomedical Circuits and Systems*, 6(6), 523–532. DOI: 10.1109/TBCAS.2012.2232665 PMID: 23853253

Prasoon, A., Petersen, K., & Igel, C. (2013). Deep feature learning for knee cartilage segmentation using a tri-planar convolutional neural network. *Medical Image Computing and Computer-Assisted Intervention : MICCAI.*, 16, 246–253. PMID: 24579147

Protevi, J. (2023). Esprit de Corps and thinking on (and with) your feet: Standard, enactive, and poststructuralist aspects of relational autonomy and collective intentionality in team sports. *The Southern Journal of Philosophy*, 61(S1), 24–38. DOI: 10.1111/sjp.12525

Provost, F., & Fawcett, T. (2013). *Data Science for Business: What You Need to Know about Data Mining and Data-Analytic Thinking*. O'Reilly Media.

Quigley, H. A. (1996). Number of people with glaucoma worldwide. *The British Journal of Ophthalmology*, 80(5), 389–393. DOI: 10.1136/bjo.80.5.389 PMID: 8695555

Raffel, C. (2020). Exploring the Limits of Transfer Learning with a Unified Text-to-Text Transformer. *Journal of Machine Learning Research*, 21(140), 1–67.

Raghupathi, W., & Raghupathi, V. (2014). Big Data Analytics in Healthcare: Promise and Potential. *Health Information Science and Systems*, 2(1), 1–10. DOI: 10.1186/2047-2501-2-3 PMID: 25825667

Rahimian, P., Oroojlooy, A., & Toka, L. (2021, October). Towards optimized actions in critical situations of soccer games with deep reinforcement learning. In 2021 IEEE 8th International Conference on Data Science and Advanced Analytics (DSAA) (pp. 1-12). IEEE. DOI: 10.1109/DSAA53316.2021.9564207

Rahimian, P., Van Haaren, J., Abzhanova, T., & Toka, L. (2022). Beyond action valuation: A deep reinforcement learning framework for optimizing player decisions in soccer. In 16th Annual MIT Sloan Sports Analytics Conference. MIT.

Rahimian, P., & Toka, L. (2023). A data-driven approach to assist offensive and defensive players in optimal decision making. *International Journal of Sports Science & Coaching.*

Ramachandran, V. R. K., Havinga, P. J. M., & Meratnia, N. (2016). HACMAC: A reliable human activity-based medium access control for implantable body sensor networks. In *BSN 2016 – 13th Annual International Body Sensor Networks Conference* (pp. 383–389). IEEE. DOI: 10.1109/BSN.2016.7516292

Rasouli, M., & Phee, L. S. J. (2010). Energy sources and their development for application in medical devices. *Expert Review of Medical Devices*, 7(5), 693–709. DOI: 10.1586/erd.10.20 PMID: 20822391

Rein, R., & Memmert, D. (2016). Big data and tactical analysis in elite soccer: Future challenges and opportunities for sports science. *SpringerPlus*, 5(1), 1–13. DOI: 10.1186/s40064-016-3108-2 PMID: 27610328

Rhew, H. G., Jeong, J., Fredenburg, J. A., Dodani, S., Patil, P. G., & Flynn, M. P. (2014). A fully self-contained logarithmic closed-loop deep brain stimulation SoC with wireless telemetry and wireless power management. *IEEE Journal of Solid-State Circuits*, 49(10), 2213–2227. DOI: 10.1109/JSSC.2014.2346779

Ribeiro, M. T., Singh, S., & Guestrin, C. (2016). Why should I trust you? Explaining the predictions of any classifier. *ACM Conferences on Knowledge Discovery and Data Mining*, 1135–44. DOI: 10.18653/v1/N16-3020

Rishabh, S. (2021). *K-means clustering analysis of crimes on Indian women*. ASPG.

Rob Collie, A. S. (2015). *Power Pivot and Power BI. In Power Pivot and Power BI, Yayınevi: Holy Macro!* Books.

Rogers, J. A., Someya, T., & Huang, Y. (2010). Materials and mechanics for stretchable electronics. *Science*, 327(5973), 1603–1607. DOI: 10.1126/science.1182383 PMID: 20339064

Rønningen, M. H. (2021). The genesis of data-driven decision-making in the world of soccer tactics: deciphering the potential of big data (Master's thesis, University of Agder).

Roxane. (2020). Power BI in Clinical Data exploration. PHUSE Virtual EU Connect 2020.

Rubini, P. E., & Subasini, C. A. (2021). A cardiovascular disease prediction using machine learning algorithms. *Annals of R.S.C.B.*, 25(2), 904–912. https://www.researchgate.net/publication/350312435

Ruder, S., Peters, M. E., Swayamdipta, S., & Wolf, T. (2019). Transfer Learning in Natural Language Processing. https://aclanthology.org/N19-5004/

Rushton. (2003). Public health, GİS and spatial analytic tools. Annu. Rev. Pub. Health.

Rustemi, E., & Tahiri, M. (2022). *The role of visualization in understanding data.* 28-31. DOI: 10.5281/ZENODO.7125689

Saad, W., Bennis, M., & Chen, M. (2021). A vision of 6G wireless systems: Applications, trends, technologies, and open research problems. *IEEE Network*, 34(3), 134–142. DOI: 10.1109/MNET.001.1900287

Sadiku, M. N. O. (2016). Data visualization. *International Journal of Engineering Research and Advanced Technology*, 2(12), 11–16.

Saklani, A. (2023). Integrating technology into physical education: Exploring the dynamics of AI, virtual reality, apps, and wearables for an enhanced educational odyssey.

Saltos, G., & Cocea, M. (2017). An exploration of crime prediction using data mining on open data. *International Journal of Information Technology & Decision Making*, 16(5), 1155–1181. DOI: 10.1142/S0219622017500250

Sankaran, A. (2020). The Role of IoT in Data Collection and Analysis: Opportunities and Challenges. *Journal of Internet of Things*, 1, 45–56.

Santagati, E. G., & Melodia, T. (2017). Experimental evaluation of impulsive ultrasonic intrabody communications for implantable biomedical devices. *IEEE Transactions on Mobile Computing*, 16(2), 367–380. DOI: 10.1109/TMC.2016.2561277

Santagati, G. E., Melodia, T., Galluccio, L., & Palazzo, S. (2015). Medium access control and rate adaptation for ultrasonic intrabody sensor networks. *IEEE/ACM Transactions on Networking*, 23(4), 1121–1134. DOI: 10.1109/TNET.2014.2316675

Sathyadevan, M. S. (2014). *Crime analysis and prediction using data mining*. ICN-SC. DOI: 10.1109/CNSC.2014.6906719

Savage, N. (2002). Linking with light. IEEE Spectrum. Retrieved from https://spectrum.ieee.org/semiconductors/optoelectronics/linking-with-light

Schutt, R., & O'Neil, C. (2013). *Doing Data Science: Straight Talk from the Frontline*. O'Reilly Media.

Sehgal, S. (2017). A review: Crime analysis using data mining techniques and algorithms. *International Conference on Computing Communication and Automation.*

Seo, D., Neely, R. M., Shen, K., Singhal, U., Alon, E., Rabaey, J. M., Carmena, J. M., & Maharbiz, M. M. (2016). Wireless recording in the peripheral nervous system with ultrasonic neural dust. *Neuron*, 91(3), 529–539. DOI: 10.1016/j.neuron.2016.06.034 PMID: 27497221

Shafiq, M., Guo, S., & Nazir, A. (2020). 5G and IoT in healthcare: Applications and challenges. *Computers in Biology and Medicine*, 122, 103810. DOI: 10.1016/j.compbiomed.2020.103810

Shah, D., Patel, S., & Bharti, S. K. (2020). Heart disease prediction using machine learning techniques. *SN Computer Science*, 1(6), 1–6. DOI: 10.1007/s42979-020-00365-y

Sharma, M. (2023). Data Science Applications in Healthcare: A Review of Recent Trends. *Health Informatics Journal*, 29(1), 22–34.

Shen, C., Pei, S., Yang, Z., & Guan, X. (2015). Input extraction via motion sensor behavior analysis on smartphones. *Computers & Security*, 53, 143–155. DOI: 10.1016/j.cose.2015.06.013

Shih, Y., Shen, T., & Otis, B. (2011). A 2.3 μW wireless intraocular pressure/temperature monitor. *IEEE Journal of Solid-State Circuits*, 46(11), 2592–2601. DOI: 10.1109/JSSC.2011.2164134

Shneiderman, B., Plaisant, C., & Hesse, B. W. (2013). Improving healthcare with interactive visualization. *Computer*, 46(5), 58–66. DOI: 10.1109/MC.2013.38

Shokri, R., & Shmatikov, V. (2015). Privacy-preserving deep learning. *Proceedings of the 22nd ACM SIGSAC Conference on Computer and Communications Security*, 1310–21.

SmartThings. (2017, July 7). *SmartThings developer documentation.* http://docs.smartthings.com/en/latest/architecture/index.html

Snyder, J. (2008). Small thermoelectric generators. *The Electrochemical Society Interface*, 17(3), 54–56. DOI: 10.1149/2.F06083IF

Solove, D. J. (2020). *Understanding Privacy*. Harvard University Press.

Someya, T., Bao, Z., & Malliaras, G. G. (2016). The rise of plastic bioelectronics. *Nature*, 540(7633), 379–385. DOI: 10.1038/nature21004 PMID: 27974769

Spectrum Matters Indeed. (2017, April). *Who leads OS share in the Internet of Things era?*https://spectrummattersindeed.blogspot.com/2017/04/who-leads-os-share-in-internet-of.html

Spencer, R., Abtah, F., & Abdelhamid, N. (2020). Exploring feature selection and classification methods for predicting heart disease. *Digital Health*, 6, 1–10. DOI: 10.1177/2055207620914777 PMID: 32284873

Srivastava, D. (n.d.). An introduction to data visualization tools and techniques in various domains. Unpublished manuscript.

Strauch, C. (2011). *NoSQL Databases. Lecture Notes*. Stuttgart Media University.

Takci, H. (2018). Improvement of heart attack prediction by the feature selection methods. *Turkish Journal of Electrical Engineering and Computer Sciences*, 26, 1–10. DOI: 10.3906/elk-1611-235

The International Commission on Non-Ionizing Radiation Protection. (2006). ICNIRP statement on far infrared radiation exposure. *Health Physics*, 91(6), 630–645. DOI: 10.1097/01.HP.0000240533.50224.65 PMID: 17099407

The Michael J. Fox Foundation for Parkinson's Research. (2016). Subtyping Parkinson's disease with deep learning models. https://www.michaeljfox.org/foundation/grant-detail.php?grant_id=1518

Tippenhauer, N. O., Pöpper, C., Rasmussen, K. B., & Capkun, S. (2011). On the requirements for successful GPS spoofing attacks. In *Proceedings of the 18th ACM Conference on Computer and Communications Security* (pp. 75–86). ACM. DOI: 10.1145/2046707.2046719

Tomar, D., & Agarwal, S. (2014). Feature selection based Least Square Twin Support Vector Machine for diagnosis of heart disease. *International Journal of Bio-Science and Bio-Technology*, 6(2), 69–82. DOI: 10.14257/ijbsbt.2014.6.2.07

Tramèr, F., Zhang, F., & Juels, A.Stealing machine learning models via prediction apis. *USENIX Security Symposium*.

Troiano, G., & Nardi, A. (2021). Vaccine hesitancy in the era of COVID-19. *Public Health*, 194, 245–251. DOI: 10.1016/j.puhe.2021.02.025 PMID: 33965796

Tsokos, A., Narayanan, S., Kosmidis, I., Baio, G., Cucuringu, M., Whitaker, G., & Király, F. (2019). Modeling outcomes of soccer matches. *Machine Learning*, 108(1), 77–95. DOI: 10.1007/s10994-018-5741-1

Tukey, J. W. (1977). *Exploratory Data Analysis*. Addison-Wesley.

Vaddiraju, S. (2015). Needle-implantable, wireless biosensor for continuous glucose monitoring. *2015 IEEE 12th International Conference on Wearable and Implantable Body Sensor Networks (BSN),* 2–6. DOI: 10.1109/BSN.2015.7299421

Venkatraman. (2012). Cloud Computing A Research Roadmap In Coalesence With Software Engineering. *International Journal (Toronto, Ont.)*, 2(2).

Vijay Fidelis, J., & Karthikeyan, E. (2022). Optimization of Artificial Neural Network Parameters in Selection of Players for Soccer Match. In *Sustainable Advanced Computing: Select Proceedings of ICSAC 2021* (pp. 275-288). Singapore: Springer Singapore. DOI: 10.1007/978-981-16-9012-9_23

Vinicius, Franco, Rampasso, & Anholon. (2022). Operationalizing Business Model Innovation through Big Data Analytics for Sustainable Organizations. Business model Innovation Research – Sustainability, 12(1).

Visser, H. (2013). Far-field RF energy transport. In *IEEE Radio and Wireless Symposium* (pp. 34–36). IEEE. DOI: 10.1109/RWS.2013.6486632

Voigt, L., Friedrich, J., Grove, P., Heinrich, N., Ittlinger, S., Iskra, M., Koop, L., Michirev, A., Sparascio, S., & Raab, M. (2023). Advancing judgment and decision-making research in sport psychology by using the body as an informant in embodied choices. *Asian Journal of Sport and Exercise Psychology*, 3(1), 47–56. DOI: 10.1016/j.ajsep.2022.09.006

Vyas, S., & Bhargava, D. (2021). Smart Health Systems. Singapore: Springer. DOI: 10.1007/978-981-16-4201-2

Waca. (2017, October 23). *Waca: Wearable-assisted continuous authentication framework with motion sensors*. https://web.eng.fiu.edu/selcuk/pubs.html

Wang, J., & Chen, J. (2022). Design and Research of Dynamic Evolution System in Football Tactics Under Computational Intelligence. *Mathematical Problems in Engineering*, 2022, 2022. DOI: 10.1155/2022/3772236

Wang, J., Li, C., & Zhao, H. (2019). Privacy risks in IoT healthcare: A study on wearable devices. *Health Policy and Technology*, 8(2), 132–142. DOI: 10.1016/j.hlpt.2019.05.003

Wang, Y. (2023). Advanced Web Scraping Techniques for Big Data Collection. *Journal of Web Engineering*, 22(1), 12–30.

Wang, Z. (2020). Cheat sheets for data visualization techniques. In *Proceedings of the 2020 CHI Conference on Human Factors in Computing Systems* (pp. 1–13). ACM. DOI: 10.1145/3313831.3376658

Wankhade, M., Annavarapu, C. S. R., & Kulkarni, C. (2022). A survey on sentiment analysis methods, applications and challenges. https://link.springer.com/article/10.1007/s10462-022-10144-1

Ward, M. O., Grinstein, G., & Keim, D. (2015). *Interactive data visualization: Foundations, techniques, and applications.* CRC Press. DOI: 10.1201/b18379

Wedel, M., & Kannan, P. K. (2016). Marketing Analytics for Data-Rich Environments. *Journal of Marketing*, 80(6), 97–121. DOI: 10.1509/jm.15.0413

Wise, K. D., Anderson, D. J., Hetke, J. F., Kipke, D. R., & Najafi, K. (2004). Wireless implantable microsystems: High-density electronic interfaces to the nervous system. *Proceedings of the IEEE*, 92(1), 76–97. DOI: 10.1109/JPROC.2003.820544

Witten, I. H., Frank, E., Hall, M. A., & Pal, C. J. (2016). *Data Mining: Practical Machine Learning Tools and Techniques.* Morgan Kaufmann.

Wolpert, D. H. (1992). Stacked Generalization. *Neural Networks*, 5(2), 241–259. DOI: 10.1016/S0893-6080(05)80023-1 PMID: 18276425

Womack, R. (2014). Data visualization and information literacy. *IASSIST Quarterly*, 38(1), 12–17. DOI: 10.29173/iq619

Xu, H., Liu, B., Shu, L., & Philip, S. Yu. (2019), BERT Post-Training for Review Reading Comprehension and Aspect-based Sentiment Analysis, /arXiv.1904.02232DOI: 10.48550

Xu, Meng, Qiu, Yu, & Wu. (2019). Sentiment Analysis of Comment Texts Based on BiLSTM. .DOI: 10.1109/ACCESS.2019.2909919

Xu, J., Zhang, Y., & Luo, P. (2020). Denial-of-service vulnerabilities in wearable IoT healthcare systems. *Journal of Systems and Software*, 165, 110573. DOI: 10.1016/j.jss.2020.110573

Yadav, A., & Vishwakarma, D. K. (2020). Sentiment analysis using deep learning architectures: A review. *Artificial Intelligence Review*, 53(6), 4335–4385. Advance online publication. DOI: 10.1007/s10462-019-09794-5

Yang, F., Zhou, X., & Wang, H. (2020). Smart cities powered by 5G and IoT: A case study. *IEEE Communications Magazine*, 58(1), 23–29. DOI: 10.1109/MCOM.2020.190029

Yao, A. C. (1982). Protocols for secure computations. *23rd Annual Symposium on Foundations of Computer Science (SFCS 1982)*, 160–4. DOI: 10.1109/SFCS.1982.38

Yeung, C. C., & Fujii, K. (2023). A Strategic Framework for Optimal Decisions in Football 1-vs-1 Shot-Taking Situations: An Integrated Approach of Machine Learning, Theory-Based Modeling, and Game Theory. arXiv preprint arXiv:2307.14732.

Yin, L., Cheng, H., Mao, S., Haasch, R., Liu, Y., Xie, X., Hwang, S.-W., Jain, H., Kang, S.-K., Su, Y., Li, R., Huang, Y., & Rogers, J. A. (2014). Dissolvable metals for transient electronics. *Advanced Functional Materials*, 24(5), 645–658. DOI: 10.1002/adfm.201301847

Yin, L., Huang, X., Xu, H., Zhang, Y., Lam, J., Cheng, J., & Rogers, J. A. (2014). Materials, designs, and operational characteristics for fully biodegradable primary batteries. *Advanced Materials*, 26(23), 3879–3884. DOI: 10.1002/adma.201306304 PMID: 24652717

Yoo, Y., Brosch, T., & Traboulsee, A.Deep learning of image features from unlabeled data for multiple sclerosis lesion segmentation. *International Workshop on Machine Learning in Medical Imaging*, 117–24. DOI: 10.1007/978-3-319-10581-9_15

Zaharia, M., Chowdhury, M., Franklin, M. J., Shenker, S., & Stoica, I. (2010). Spark: Cluster Computing with Working Sets. *Proceedings of the 2nd USENIX conference on Hot topics in cloud computing*.

Zhang, Y., Zhang, F., Shakhsheer, Y., Silver, J. D., Klinefelter, A., Nagaraju, M., Boley, J., Pandey, J., Shrivastava, A., Carlson, E. J., Wood, A., Calhoun, B. H., & Otis, B. P. (2013). A batteryless 19 μW MICS/ISM-band energy harvesting body sensor node SoC for ExG applications. *IEEE Journal of Solid-State Circuits*, 48(1), 199–213. DOI: 10.1109/JSSC.2012.2221217

Zhao, X. (2017). Exploring transfer learning for crime prediction. *ICDMW*.

Zhao, Y., & Dyer, E. B. (2024, June 10). Data visualization renarrated: Probing the role of renarrating in data visualization reimagining. *Proceedings of the 18th International Conference of the Learning Sciences - ICLS 2024*. DOI: 10.22318/icls2024.847189

Zheng, G., Fang, G., Orgun, M. A., Shankaran, R., & Dutkiewicz, E. (2014). Securing wireless medical implants using an ECG-based secret data sharing scheme. In *2014 14th International Symposium on Information and Communication Technology (ISC)* (pp. 373–377). IEEE. DOI: 10.1109/ISCIT.2014.7011935

Zheng, G., Fang, G., Shankaran, R., Orgun, M. A., & Dutkiewicz, E. (2017). Multiple ECG fiducial points-based random binary sequence generation for securing. *IEEE Journal of Biomedical and Health Informatics*, 21(3), 655–663. DOI: 10.1109/JBHI.2016.2546300 PMID: 27046882

Zhuang, Qi, Duan, Xi, Zhu, & Zhu. (2020). A Comprehensive Survey on Transfer Learning. DOI: 10.1109/JPROC.2020.3004555

About the Contributors

Paul Devasahayam Manuel is a Professor at Kuwait University, Kuwait. He holds a Ph.D. obtained from the University of Newcastle, Australia, a Master of Science from the University of Saskatchewan, Canada, and another Ph.D. from the Indian Institute of Technology, India. His research interests lie in the areas of Information Systems, Algorithms, and Cheminformatics. He possesses administrative skills in the ABET Accreditation Process and software expertise in Enterprise Resource Planning (ODOO) and Machine Learning using Python. Throughout his career, Paul has received several accolades, including the Best Teacher Award (2010 – 2011) and Distinguished Lecturer Award (2008 – 2009) from Kuwait University, as well as the Industry Relationship Award (2002 – 2003) from KFUPM, Saudi Arabia. A significant project he contributed to is the UNESCO-HP Brain Gain Initiative, which was recognized by UNESCO, with an honor received in the presence of Former US President Bill Clinton in Berlin. Additionally, Paul Manuel is listed in the 'World's Top 2% Scientist 2022' by Stanford University and Elsevier Foundation. Furthermore, he played a crucial role in the development and preparation of the ISC Department's Self-Study Report, which was rated among the top 50 worldwide by ABET in 2017.

Kalim Uddin Qureshi is an Associate Professor in the Information Science Department at Kuwait University, Kuwait. He holds a Doctor Engineer degree obtained from the Department of Computer Science and Systems Engineering at Muroran Institute of Technology, Japan, awarded by the Japanese Government. Prior to this, he earned a Master of Science in Engineering from the same institution and worked as a Research Student there. Dr. Qureshi's research interests encompass a wide range of areas including Distributed Computing, Grid Computing, Medical Imaging, Information Systems Development, System Performance Measurement, Information Security, and Computer Forensics. With over 8 years of industry-based research and microprocessor-based product development experience, coupled with 24 years of academic teaching and research experience, he brings a wealth of knowledge and expertise to his field. He has extensive experience serving on academic committees, including ABET Accreditation (16 years), Curriculum Committee (24 years), Labs, Library, Computing Facilities planning committee (24 years), and Graduate Program Committee (24 years). Dr. Qureshi has published 58 journal papers, showcasing his contributions to the academic and research community. His dedication to advancing knowledge in his field and his commitment to education make him a valuable asset to Kuwait University and the wider academic community.

V.Thamilarasi received the Ph.D. degree in computer science, with specialization of Digital Image Processing from Periyar University, Salem, Tamilnadu, India, in 2022. She has more than 9 years of working experience as Lecturer, Assistant Professor. She is currently an Assistant Professor in the Department of Computer Science, Sri Sarada College for Women(Autonomous), Salem, Tamilnadu, India. She has published several research papers in prestigious international journals, 2 book chapters and one of her paper received Best Paper Award in 2021. She also got Young Researcher Award in 2023, International Excellence Award in 2023 and A P J Abdul Kalam Award in 2024 . She has been serving as the Reviewer for Elsevier, Springer and Scopus journals. Her area of research interest include Medical Image Processing, Artificial Intelligence, Machine Learning, Computer Vision and Deep Learning.

* * *

Sampath Dakshina Murthy Achanta graduated with a B.Tech in Electronics and Communication Engineering in 2013 and an M.Tech in Digital Electronics and Communication Engineering in 2015. He is an Assistant Professor at Vignan's Institute of Information Technology's Department of Electronics and Communication Engineering (A). In Guntur, Andhra Pradesh, Ph.D.from Electronics and Communication Engineering at Koneru Lakshmaiah Education Foundation Deemed University. Gait analysis in Pattern Recognition, Image & Video Processing, Fuzzy Logic, and Neural Networks are among his major interests. He has 60 articles published in international journals. He has four patents, has 2 books published, and has won 5 international and 5 national awards. He is a Life Member of the I.S.R.S., the IEI, the C.S.I., and the MIET. He is on the editorial boards of Scopus and SCI journals and serves as a reviewer for them. He has a combined teaching and research experience of 5 years.

Harishchander Anandaram completed a PhD in bioengineering, an M.Tech., and a B.Tech. in bioinformatics from the Sathyabama Institute of Science and

Technology, Chennai, in 2020, 2011, and 2009. In his bachelor's and master's theses, he worked on analyzing resistance in HIV protease inhibitors based on molecular mechanics and machine learning studies, a collaborative project with IIT Madras. In his PhD thesis, he worked on pharmacogenomics and miRNA-regulated networks in psoriasis, a collaborative project with Georgetown University, USA, JIPMER, India, CIBA, India, and ILS, India. His thesis illustrated a multi-disciplinary approach by combining computational biophysics and molecular biology machine learning. While doing a PhD, He had the opportunity to collaborate with international researchers and have publications in reputed international journals in bioinformatics and systems biology. He has received the prestigious "Young Scientist Award" from "The Melinda Gates Foundation" for his research abstract on "The Implications of miRNA Dynamics in Infectious Diseases". To date, he has reviewed more than 200 manuscripts in systems biology.

Gourav Arora currently serves as an Assistant Professor in the Department of Computer Science and Engineering at PCTE Institute of Engineering & Technology, Ludhiana. He earned his M.Tech in Computer Science & Engineering from CT University, Ludhiana. With over 2.5 years of experience Er. Gourav has dedicated over a decade to teaching various Computer Science subjects to undergraduate and postgraduate students. His academic journey includes publishing papers in prestigious national and international journals and conferences. His primary areas of interest encompass Machine Learning, Data Science, Artificial Intelligence and UX/UI, reflecting his deep commitment to advancing these fields through research and education.

Aarthi B. is currently working as an Assistant Professor in the Department of CSE at SRMIST, Ramapuram campus, Chennai. She completed her Master's degree in Computer Science and Engineering (M.E., CSE) from Anna University in 2013. She has completed her doctorate degree in the field of sentiment analysis at SRM Institute of Science and Technology, Kattankulathur, from September 2024. She has 8 years of teaching experience and possesses strong programming skills. She has published more than 10 research articles in National and International Journals and Conferences. Her research interests are Natural Language Processing, Deep learning, IoT and GenAI.

Anup Bhange is working as Head of Department of Computer Application at K.D.K. College of Engineering Nagpur Estb: 1984. He has around 14 + years of teaching experience. His interested research area is Network Security, Cloud Computing, and DBMS etc. (50b932de-80fd-4cb1-8ee3d-2ddd2514b51e)

Kumuthini C. is working as a Professor in Dr. N.G.P arts and Science College,She has published more than 10 articles in indexed journals and also participated in various national and international conferences.

Shairy Kalra currently serves as an Assistant Professor in the Department of Computer Science and Engineering at PCTE College of Engineering & Technology, Ludhiana. He earned his M.Tech in Information Technology from Guru Nanak Dev Engineering College, Ludhiana. With over 13 years of experience Er. Shairy has dedicated over a decade to teaching various Computer Science subjects to undergraduate and postgraduate students. His academic journey includes publishing more than 9 research papers in prestigious national and international journals and conferences. His primary areas of interest encompass Database Management and Full Stack Web Development, reflecting his deep commitment to advancing these fields through research and education.

Gurpreet Kaur previously served as an Assistant Professor and Deputy Dean in the Department of Computer Science and Engineering at PCTE College of Engineering & Technology, Ludhiana. She earned her M.Tech in Information Technology from Guru Nanak Dev Engineering College, Ludhiana. With over 13 years of teaching experience, she specialized in Java, Web Development, and Full Stack Development, imparting knowledge to undergraduate and postgraduate students. During her tenure, she published research papers in prestigious national and international journals and conferences. Her primary areas of interest include Web Development, and Full Stack Development. She has now moved to Australia, where she aims to continue her journey of academic and professional excellence in Computer Science and Engineering.

Kriushanth M. is an Assistant Professor of Data Science at St. Joseph's College (Autonomous), Tiruchirappalli. His areas of interest include Cloud Computing, IoT, Data Science, Data Analytics, AI, and ML. He is a member of various academic bodies, including Data Science Central, the Salesforce Trailblazer Data Science Community, the National Institute for Technical Training & Skill Development, the International Association of Engineers, and the Board of Studies for BCA and MCA at Sacred Heart College. He has published numerous research articles in international journals and conferences and has filed three Indian patents. Dr. Kriushanth has also served as a resource person for faculty development programs (FDPs), professional development programs (PDPs), webinars, seminars, workshops, and invited talks at various colleges. Additionally, he has organized several conferences, workshops, training programs, seminars, and webinars.

Prasad M. received the B.Tech, M.Tech and Phd Degree in Information Technology, Information Security and Mobile Communication from Pondicherry University, Pondicherry in 2008, 2010 and 2017 respectively. He is currently working in VIT Chennai campus School of Computing Science and Engineering. He is having various professional memberships like IEEE senior membership, ACM, ACM, ISTE and CSI. Having 10 Indian Patents, 2 Australian Patents and 1 German Patent. Area of Interest Cyber Security, IoT, Drone with AI and ML. As Editor and Reviewer in various journals.

Balajee Maram earned his doctorate from Bharathiar University, Coimbatore, Master Degree in Computer Science and Engineering from Anna University, Chennai, Master of Business Administration from Alagappa University, Karaikudi, MA (Master of Communication and Journalism) form Alagappa University, Karaikudi. He is currently working as an Professor in the Department of Computer Science and Artificial Intelligence, SR University, Warangal. I have more than 19 years of Teaching, 5 years of industry and 6 years of Research experience. I have 100 research publications in reputed journals where 32 papers are indexed by SCIE and 37 papers indexed by SCOPUS. I have guided 14 UG projects and 2 PG projects. I have filed 4 Indian patents and been granted 2 Australian patents. I have organized one National workshop and one National Conference. I have published 3 book chapters indexed by SCOPUS. I have authored for 8 books titled "Data Communication and Networking" and "XML & Web-Services". I have received "Best Researcher Award 2018" from DK International Research Foundation, "Best Researcher Award 2018" from 117th International Research Awards on Engineering, Science and Management.

Nidhya M. S. earned her doctorate from Bharathiar University, Coimbatore, Master degree in Computer science and Master of Philosophy in the same field from Bharathidasan University, Trichy. She is currently working as an Associate Professor in School of Computer Applications, Dayananda University, Innovation Campus, Bangaluru, Karnataka. She is having 19 years of teaching experience. She published various articles in reputed journals such as IEEE and Springer. She published various books and book chapters in CRC Press and IGI Global. She has also registered, published and receives Indian and International Patents grant. She received various Awards as Best Academician Award and Research Award in Global Education and Corporate Leadership Awards and Super Woman Award from FSIA. She is an editorial board member in International Journal of Sensors and Sensor Networks (IJSSN) Science Publishing Group 1 Rockefeller Plaza, New York, NY 10020, U.S.A. Her research interest includes Wireless Sensor Networks, Cloud Computing, IoT and Mobile Computing.

Sathees Kumar Nataraj holds a PhD, M.Sc., and B. E., in Mechatronics Engineering, specializing in robotics, digital signal processing, and artificial intelligence. He began his academic career as an Assistant Professor at Madanapalle Institute of Technology & Science (2016–2018) and has been with the University of Technology Bahrain (UTB) since January 2019, currently serving as the Program Head of the Mechatronics Engineering Department. Dr. Sathees has published in reputed journals and conference proceedings indexed in Scopus and Web of Science. He is a Chartered Engineer (C-Eng) with IET-INDIA and a member of IET, MIE, and IEEE.

Yusliza Off is an academic and researcher with a focus on computer science and education. She specializes in areas such as artificial intelligence, data science, image steganography and educational technology, with projects that emphasize innovative digital solutions in these fields. With working experience as an software engineer in Panasonic AVC Network Sdn Bhd, she is now actively involved in educational initiatives in Universiti Teknologi Malaysia (UTM) Johor Bahru, with extensive experience as a head of research group, UTM Big Data Center fellow, program coordinator and active roles in academic support. She continues to contribute to both research and the academic community.

P. Pushpa is currently working as a lecturer in The school of software engineering, East China University of technology, Nanchang, china. She is proficient in jave programming and has extensive participation in research publications in bigdata, IoT, machine learning concepts, and cloud security, and also patent in 5G Mobile technology.

Uma Rani R. is currently working as Principal in Sri Sarada College for Women (Autonomous), Salem-16. She finished her Master of Computer Applications from Regional Engineering College, Trichy, M.Phil. from Mother Teresa University, Kodaikanal and Ph.D. from Periyar university in 2006. Her area of interest includes data mining and image processing, network security, and mobile communications. She has published 145 research articles in international journals and authored 3 books. She has acted as resource person in national and international conferences and then chaired technical sessions too.

R. Roselin earned her Ph.D. in Computer Science, specialization in Digital Image Processing, from Periyar University, Salem, Tamil Nadu, India, in 2013. With over 15 years of academic experience, she currently serves as an Associate Professor in the Department of Computer Science at Sri Sarada College for Women (Autonomous), Salem, Tamil Nadu, India. She has authored numerous research papers in esteemed international journals and contributed three book chapters. Her research interests include Medical Image Processing, Artificial Intelligence, Machine Learning, Computer Vision, and Deep Learning.

Hemalatha S. is an accomplished academic and researcher in the field of Computer Science and Engineering. She holds a Postdoctoral position at Manipur International University, specializing in Mobile Ad hoc Networks (MANET) Security. She completed her Ph.D. in Computer Science and Engineering at Anna University, Tamil Nadu, India, in January 2016, with a focus on Mobile Security. Dr. Hemalatha earned her Master's degree in Computer Science and Engineering with First Class honors from Arulmigu Meenakshi Amman College of Engineering and her Bachelor's degree in the same discipline. She also holds a Diploma in Computer Technology with First Class with honors. In addition, she completed an MBA in Education Management from Alagappa University in 2008, further enhancing her expertise in the administrative and leadership aspects of education.Her extensive research contributions include over 200 journal publications, 8 patents, and 1 copyright.She is an active member of several professional organizations, including the Computer Society of India (CSI) and the Indian Society for Technical Education (ISTE). Dr. Hemalatha serves as a reviewer and editor for various prestigious journals, contributing her knowledge and experience to the advancement of research in her field. Her diverse academic background, leadership in education, and extensive research make her a prominent figure in Computer Science and Engineering.

Kalaiselvi S received her Ph.D degree from Faculty of Information and Communication Engineering from Anna University Chennai. She is Currently Working as an Associate Professor, Department of Computer Engineering at National Engineering College, kovilpatti. She has 15 years of experience. Her main research interests are Remote Sensing, Image processing and Data Analytics. She is a member of Professional bodies like IEEE and IEEE CS. She has published 20+ Research Papers in Scopus and SCI Journals. . She acted as a reviewer for Elsevier and Springer journals..

Lakshmi Devi S. is Assistant Professor, Department of Comptuter Science, Sri Krishna Adithya College of Arts & Science. 19 year of Teaching Experience of UG & PG, Research. Area of research is data mining, Machine Laering, Deep Learning, image processing.

Poorana Senthilkumar S. received his Bachelor of Science degree in Computer Science from Bharathiar University, Coimbatore, in 2004 and his Master of Computer Applications degree from Anna University, Chennai, in 2008. He successfully completed his Ph.D. from Bharathiar University and served as an Assistant Professor in the Department of Computer Applications at Dr. N.G.P.

Arts and Science College, Coimbatore, Tamil Nadu, India. A lifetime member of IAENG, he has authored over 10 research articles in esteemed National/International Journals. His extensive experience spans 14 years in teaching and 10 years in research, with a focus on Internet of Things, LLNs, VANET, Cloud Computing, Artificial Intelligence, Machine Learning, and WSN Networks.

K. Santa Rao is currently working as Assistant Professor in the department of Mechanical Engineering at GMR Institute of Technology, Rajam, India. He is a mechanical engineer with post graduation in CAD/CAM. He pursued his Ph.D. from Jawaharlal Nehru Technological University of Kakinada in India, in the field of manufacturing. He hold 13 years of teaching experience. He has his research papers published in several popular indexed journals.

Charanjeet Singh is Assistant Professor, Department of Electronics & Communication Engineering, Deenbandhu Chhotu Ram, University of Science and Technology, India.

T. Jayasudha is a Research Scholar in Computer Science at Sri Sarada College for Women (Autonomous), Salem-16. She has published her research in reputed journals, contributing significantly to her field. Her work emphasizes innovation and academic rigor, reflecting her commitment to advancing knowledge. She actively engages in scholarly activities to address emerging challenges in Computer Science.

Kirti Hemant Wanjale received her Ph.D degree from Faculty of Computer Engineering from SSSTUMS, Sehore MP. She is Currently Working as Professor, Department of Computer Engineering at Vishwakarma Institute of Technology Pune. She has 22 years of experience. Her main research interests are Wireless Sensor Networks, Internet of Things (IoT), Cyber physical systems, Machine Learning. She is a member of Professional bodies like IEEE,ISTE, CSI and IAENG. She has published 50+ Research Papers in National and International Journals & 20+ Conference papers. She is working on editorial board on various Journals. She also working as reviewer for IEEE access publications. She has 15 patent granted in her name. Also she has written 2 books published by CRC Press.

Ranjeet Yadav received his B.Tech in Electronics and Communication Engineering from JNTU Hyderabad, India in 2008 and received his M.Tech in 2011, from same University. He had completed PhD from Amity University Rajasthan, India. He has presented and participated in several conferences, seminar and published papers in International Journals. He has several years of teaching experience in Diploma and Engineering level. His area of interest is Mobile Communication and Wireless Communication.

Index

Symbols

5G 265, 325, 327, 334, 338, 339, 340
6G 149, 325, 338, 339, 340

A

AI-driven Health Monitoring 207
ANOVA 94, 107, 108, 112, 113
Artificial Intelligence 3, 5, 27, 47, 51, 95, 121, 124, 125, 127, 148, 149, 150, 154, 155, 156, 157, 173, 176, 177, 225, 239, 244, 249, 263, 264, 265, 268, 272, 277, 278, 281

B

Bar Charts 21, 58, 59, 65, 80, 213
Benefits 4, 24, 30, 32, 35, 46, 57, 62, 141, 228, 229, 232, 233, 256, 293, 328, 336
BERT 172, 243, 244, 247, 248, 249, 250, 254, 255, 257, 258, 260, 261, 263, 264
Big Data 1, 12, 27, 28, 33, 56, 57, 91, 116, 120, 125, 149, 150, 154, 156, 157, 165, 167, 179, 207, 209, 210, 213, 220, 221, 222, 223, 226, 227, 228, 229, 230, 232, 233, 235, 238, 239, 241, 272, 279, 280, 281
Big Data Analytics 149, 179, 207, 209, 222, 227, 228, 241, 281

C

Cardiovascular Disease 154, 175, 178, 181, 182, 184, 188, 193, 202, 204, 205, 206, 271, 287
Classification 18, 19, 20, 75, 98, 101, 102, 158, 172, 175, 183, 184, 193, 194, 195, 196, 197, 199, 202, 203, 204, 205, 206, 208, 211, 212, 213, 217, 222, 245, 247, 248, 263, 280
Cloud Computing 166, 169, 219, 223, 228, 241, 265, 310
Communication 10, 11, 34, 43, 45, 49, 50, 51, 57, 62, 91, 116, 164, 212, 213, 215, 217, 219, 226, 228, 246, 266, 269, 270, 284, 285, 289, 290, 291, 294, 298, 299, 300, 301, 302, 308, 311, 313, 315, 316, 317, 320, 325, 326, 327, 328, 329, 330, 334, 335, 336, 337, 338, 339
Crime Prediction 116, 117

D

Data Analysis 1, 8, 13, 19, 26, 27, 31, 39, 42, 48, 55, 57, 58, 62, 65, 66, 89, 93, 94, 115, 121, 124, 134, 181, 186, 210, 213, 214, 216, 219, 223, 225, 226, 227, 228, 229, 230, 232, 233, 236, 238, 239, 272, 280
Data Modeling 16, 41
Data Normalization 191, 211, 214, 221
Data Privacy 45, 63, 154, 168, 180, 207, 209, 213, 216, 217
Data Science 1, 2, 5, 6, 7, 8, 9, 11, 12, 23, 25, 26, 27, 28, 150, 175, 176, 177, 178, 179, 180, 182, 207, 208, 209, 210, 211, 212, 215, 216, 217, 218, 219, 220, 221, 223
Data Trends 237
Data Visualization 1, 7, 8, 13, 21, 23, 27, 29, 30, 31, 32, 33, 34, 35, 36, 37, 38, 39, 40, 41, 42, 43, 44, 45, 46, 47, 48, 49, 50, 51, 52, 53, 55, 56, 57, 58, 59, 60, 61, 62, 63, 64, 89, 90, 91, 92, 148, 210, 211, 212, 213, 220, 221, 235, 238, 241
Deep Learning 2, 27, 97, 123, 127, 153, 154, 155, 156, 157, 158, 163, 164, 165, 166, 167, 168, 169, 170, 171, 172, 173, 174, 176, 178, 179, 204, 207, 208, 209, 210, 211, 213, 215, 220, 243, 244, 246, 247, 248, 255, 261, 263, 264, 268, 272, 279
Deep Learning Algorithm 165, 172
Deep Reinforcement Learning 119, 120, 121, 122, 123, 124, 134, 146, 149, 150

F

Feature Extraction 119, 120, 122, 126, 129, 146, 157, 161
Feature Optimization 128, 131

H

Healthcare 6, 14, 25, 26, 29, 30, 37, 38, 39, 44, 47, 48, 50, 61, 63, 89, 92, 153, 154, 155, 156, 158, 164, 165, 167, 168, 170, 171, 175, 178, 179, 180, 181, 182, 207, 208, 209, 210, 211, 213, 214, 215, 216, 217, 218, 220, 222, 223, 229, 265, 266, 267, 268, 269, 270, 271, 273, 274, 275, 276, 277, 278, 279, 281, 309, 314, 315, 318, 322, 323, 327, 340
Heart Disease 63, 179, 181, 182, 183, 188, 189, 202, 203, 205, 206, 212
Hypothesis 11, 35, 94, 106, 109, 110, 113, 114, 210

I

Implantable Medical Devices 300
Internet of Things 28, 163, 171, 211, 222, 265, 266, 268, 269, 270, 273, 274, 275, 276, 277, 278, 279, 280, 309, 311, 313, 314, 315, 316, 317, 318, 319, 320, 321, 322, 323, 325, 338, 339
IoT 9, 33, 52, 149, 155, 164, 171, 214, 218, 222, 265, 266, 268, 269, 270, 272, 273, 274, 275, 276, 277, 278, 279, 281, 283, 309, 310, 311, 312, 313, 314, 315, 316, 317, 318, 319, 320, 321, 322, 323, 325, 327, 338, 339, 340

L

Legal Document 248, 251
Linear Regression 21, 94, 97, 102, 103, 110, 114, 115, 203, 273
LSTM 127, 245, 260, 263

M

Machine Learning 1, 2, 3, 4, 5, 8, 13, 27, 28, 33, 35, 47, 51, 52, 56, 91, 93, 94, 95, 96, 97, 99, 101, 102, 103, 110, 116, 120, 121, 124, 125, 126, 134, 148, 149, 151, 154, 155, 157, 158, 166, 167, 171, 172, 173, 174, 176, 177, 178, 179, 181, 182, 183, 185, 191, 194, 202, 204, 205, 206, 207, 208, 209, 210, 211, 212, 213, 214, 215, 216, 217, 218, 219, 220, 221, 222, 231, 232, 234, 235, 236, 239, 245, 246, 248, 252, 255, 266, 272, 276, 278, 279, 280, 314
Mask Attention 243, 255
Mobility 237, 297, 298, 330

O

Outcome Prediction 119, 120, 122, 126, 136, 137, 138, 140, 141, 142, 143, 144, 146, 148, 208

P

Patient Care Management 37, 39, 207
Powering 290, 291, 293, 299, 303

S

Scatter Plot 83
Security Solutions 309, 314
Sensors 12, 155, 210, 267, 268, 269, 270, 271, 273, 275, 276, 278, 279, 283, 284, 285, 286, 288, 289, 290, 291, 295, 296, 297, 298, 299, 300, 301, 303, 304, 305, 306, 309, 313, 315, 318, 319, 320, 321, 322, 323, 325, 338
Sentiment Analysis 243, 244, 256, 261, 263, 264
Soccer Game 120, 122, 123, 134, 137, 138, 139, 140, 141, 142, 143, 144, 146, 147

V

Visual Data Analysis 225, 226, 227, 228, 229, 230, 239
Visual Elements 49, 225, 226
Visual Representation 5, 48, 62, 66, 225, 226

W

WOC 326, 327, 328, 329, 335, 336, 337, 338